White Gloves of the Doorman

The Works of Leon Rooke

White Gloves of the Doorman

The Works of Leon Rooke

Edited by
BRANKO GORJUP

TORONTO

Exile Editions
2004

This edition is published by Exile Editions Limited,
20 Dale Avenue, Toronto, Ontario, Canada   M4W 1K4

Sales Distribution:
McArthur & Company c/o Harper Collins
1995 Markham Road, Toronto, ON M1B 5M8
toll free: 1 800 387 0117   (fax) 1 800 668 5788

Design & Composition by MICHAEL P. M. CALLAGHAN
Cover Photograph/Concept by FRANCESCO VALENTE GORJUP
Typeset at MOONS OF JUPITER, TORONTO, ONTARIO
Printed and Bound at GAUVIN IMPRIMERIE, HULL, QUEBEC

DVD Documentary "Tongue and Groove: A Portrait of Leon
Rooke" © Branko Gorjup and Paola Marino, 2004

The publisher wishes to acknowledge the assistance toward
publication of the Canada Council.

The Canada Council | Le Conseil des Arts
FOR THE ARTS | DU CANADA
SINCE 1957 | DEPUIS 1957

This book has been published with the financial assistance from
the Peter Paul Charitable Foundation, Toronto.

ISBN 1-55096-611-1

For Francesca and Francesco

CONTENTS

CHAPTER THREE: SHORT STORIES AND NOVELLAS

CHAPTER FOUR: NOVELS

INTRODUCTION

Leon Rooke's work — a very large body of work that includes six novels and seventeen story collections, as well as scores of published and staged plays — has been translated into several languages, is widely anthologized and has met with consistently high praise from Canadian, American and European reviewers. Yet his achievement has remained, paradoxically, largely unacknowledged by Canadian academics.

One of the principal aims of the present collection, therefore, is to correct this oversight. By initiating a more comprehensive discussion of Rooke's place in the context of Canadian and world writing, this book, assembled in part from the existing material and in part from material especially written for it, accomplishes some 'ground-breaking' critical work. Through describing, interpreting and evaluating Rooke's fiction, it should help us to modulate the way in which we see Rooke's *oeuvre*. But it will also, inevitably, search for possible answers as to why Rooke's entry into the Canadian literary canon — despite his having produced some of this country's most original and stylistically sophisticated and innovative fiction — has been so painfully slow.

Twenty-seven individuals generously and with sustained enthusiasm participated in this project; they come from several different countries, making the collection truly international in outlook. From the beginning, I consciously avoided the dominance of any particular 'school' of theoretical or ideological discourse, to allow for a greater diversity of points of view. What I set out to accomplish was to make available to the reader wide-ranging and generically diverse 'encounters' with Rooke's work. Thus, the reader will find a mixture of scholarly studies, ruminations, speculations, autobiographical vignettes, affectionate parodies, and conversations, all loosely organized into six chapters, each featuring one aspect of Rooke's literary personality.

Chapter One, "Portrait of the Artist," gathers six pieces that examine the phenomenon called Rooke. Some of these — especially Lawrence Naumoff's "Leon Rooke," M.A.C. Farrant's "Fat Leon," and Anne Michaels' "The Incomparable Experience of Hearing," — are tributes to an admired practitioner of the art of fiction and as, in the cases of Naumoff and Farrant, to a respected teacher. Naumoff's piece builds an impressionistic sketch of Rooke when he was still living in North Carolina, making a name for himself as a young writer of a "thoroughly bohemian" cast who was, of necessity, a "natural outsider," turning "the boondocks agape." The piece by Tom McHaney, "Ill-fitting Revolving Chair," is a documentary portrayal of the young Rooke, taking us back to a brief, little-known period in the early 1960s when Rooke worked as an "information officer" in the News Bureau of the University of North Carolina at Chapel Hill. Russell Brown's 1980 essay, "What the Rooke Said," employs a documentary angle of vision outlining, in a critical/autobiographical manner the young professor's fascination with Rooke's narrative voice. Brown investigates the evolution of Rooke's voice and seeks to answer the question: where is the voice in Rooke's fiction coming from? While searching for the voice's provenance, Brown traces and describes the initial stage of Rooke's emergence onto the Canadian literary scene. Barry Callaghan's playful 'story,' "On a Leap Year Night in Havana, A Man in a White Suit Who Said He Was Leon Rooke," is a *tour-de-force* rendition (in an unmistakably Rooke-like narrative voice) of a typically Rookean imaginative world, with Rooke-the-performer impersonating Rooke-the-creator. The piece called "Fat Leon," by one of Rooke's former students, M.A.C. Farrant, likewise 'appropriates' from the *maestro* his distinct storytelling form to create a profile of him as an archaeologist of the imagination, a flamboyant magician in love with words.

Chapter Two, entitled "Critical Context," presents three different but complementary discussions of the relationship between Rooke's work and the Canadian critical environment. Russell Brown's essay "Rooke's Move," published in 1984, is one of the earliest serious attempts by a Canadian scholar to take stock of Rooke's literary achievements up to that point in time. Written in the form of a chronicle, Brown's essay documents Rooke's ascendancy as a unique and a somewhat puzzling new presence in the Canadian literary *hortus conclusus*. Brown also monitors growing respect and admiration by a small group of writers, editors, and academics for Rooke's work, the group that fell, like Rooke himself, outside the conventional flock of practising realists. Brown's essay shows Rooke's masterful hand in transforming the old storytelling tradition by substituting open-endedness for closure and by rejecting the omniscient, objective, authoritative point of view.

Kent Thompson's review article "The Performing Artist," published a decade after Brown's piece, describes three salient aspects of Rooke's work, which in the 1980s were considered uncommon in the Canadian literary context. Thompson begins with Rooke's theatrical flamboyance, his powerful and highly dramatized approach to the oral delivery of his written work. This is followed by a discussion of Rooke's unique diction, his uncanny ability to reproduce the language of authentic human speech. Predominantly, according to Thompson, Rooke's fiction employs an "authentic American voice" from the southern United States — and this is a skill for which Rooke would not "receive much credit in Canada." Finally, for Thompson, the most important quality of Rooke's best work, and one that differentiates him from the vast majority of his contemporaries in Canada, is what he describes as Rooke's "theological, Christian thinking."

John Metcalf's piece, "This Here Jasper Is Gittin Ready to Talk," provides an overview of Rooke's writing career from the point of view of a fellow writer who has been one of Rooke's determined admirers and a promoter of his fiction from the beginning. Written specifically for this collection, Metcalf's essay is also an historical assessment, covering some three decades of Rooke's activity and the role he has played in the Canadian writing community. Metcalf argues that the "academic neglect of Rooke's work is easily understandable" because not many academics "actually read contemporary writing." And if they do, he suggests, they could not be fond of Rooke's playfulness, because playfulness is not considered of much value "in any of the arts in Canada." Consequently, Rooke's notion of story as performance, the very flamboyance of the delivery, also noted by Thompson, would be overlooked. But the main reason for Rooke's neglect by academics, Metcalf points out, echoing Brown's earlier comment, is that Rooke's writing progressively moved away from "normative realism into fable, fantasy, pastiche of genre," and into multiple "shapes of his own invention." Rooke's style, according to Metcalf, did not "endear" him to Canadian academics whose "hastily cobbled canon really had no room for his shenanigans; shenanigans, furthermore, which were suspiciously American." Leon Rooke's importance in the Canadian literary context is nevertheless clear to Metcalf, who says that "his work, his teaching, and his performances over the years have helped to give the short story in Canada a new and different emphasis," an emphasis that moved from the story of "content" to the story as "verbal and rhetorical *performance*." Metcalf describes Rooke as a pioneer "who effected the verbal and rhetorical revolution" in Canadian writing.

Chapter Three offers a series of close readings of several stories and a novella. It opens with a seminal essay by a senior European critic, Simone Vauthier, entitled "Dangerous Crossing: A Reading of Leon Rooke's 'The Birth Control King of the Upper Volta.'" Vauthier's piece effectively sets the critical direction for the other French contributors in this collection, and in particular that of Michèle Kaltemback; this direction is fundamentally a narratological approach to Rooke's fiction. Vauthier's study is a lengthy and in-depth examination of one of Rooke's most complex stories, "The Birth Control King of the Upper Volta," which she analyzes as a prime example of postmodernist, self-reflexive fiction. In discussing the text, she places particular emphasis on the fictionality of biographies and on the relationships among the narrator, the narratee, and the author. The dynamics of such a triangulated mechanism in the story, argues Vauthier, shift attention from the narrator to the reader in the production of textual meaning.

Kaltemback's essay, "In the Path of Leon Rooke's Sidestepping Narrator: Two Views," borrows from Vauthier the idea that every Rooke story is a "perilous adventure." Kaltemback discusses Rooke's narrative technique, emphasising the reader's compulsory participation in the process of decoding the story's meaning. The reader is 'dragged' into the narrative in order to close what Kaltemback calls the "gap between the referential and fictional worlds." Using the story "Art" as illustrative of these ideas, she shows how the narrator acts as "creator," then as "created object" when the reader discovers that he is a painted character inside a painting, and finally as an "absence" when he eventually fades out of his own artefact, taking his place beside the reader as an observer.

Published in 1987, Danièle Pitavy-Souques' study entitled "Fabric of Dreams / Fabrication of Dreams: *A Bolt of White Cloth*" initially picks up the idea of a symbiotic relationship between reader and storyteller that was postulated by the previous two contributors. She stresses the importance of the storyteller's need to feel "confident" that the reader will follow him into his invented world, because only when such confidence is actualized can an "interrogation" of the fictionalized reality be undertaken.

Pitavy-Souques' discussion includes a number of stories from the collection *A Bolt of White Cloth*. What these stories have in common is an active interaction between the imaginary and the mundane, which, she maintains, transforms the ordinary into a sign and gives the imaginary the status of the real. By combining "fable and delirium" with the "exploration of certain extreme limiting situations" of everyday life, Rooke's stories, argues Pitavy-Souques, raise profound questions about contemporary reality.

Janice Kulyk Keefer's essay describes "The Heart Must from Its Breaking" as one of Rooke's most powerful and innovative works of fiction, arguing that it skilfully incorporates (among other things) a "Gothic subject matter, multiple narrators and the 'witness statement' form." Kulyk Keefer also investigates this story's strong affinities with such "pre-postmodern texts as Henry James' *The Turn of the Screw* and other late Victorian 'Ghost Stories'" and examines the "intersection of contemporary and traditional literary forms and social and metaphysical assumptions" that lie beneath these forms. Her discussion reveals the complexity of Rooke's story in its emotional, visionary, and stylistic representation of reality.

Equally compelling is Nicole Côté's reading of one of Rooke's most focused and phenomenologically grounded stories, "The Only Daughter," which opens for discussion and revision one of the most frequently revisited themes in Western literature, the theme of transformation. Côté identifies and explicates the fairy tale structure that propels the heroine's tribulations and, ultimately, her self-authentication. The story's structure, she points out, is analogous to that of a classical quest. In a variation upon the traditional male story about the rites of passage, a "daughter" is ejected from the "(relative) innocence of living an undifferentiated life with her mother to the (relative) experience of becoming a woman and the daughter of her father."

With the last essay in this group, "How Much Do I Love Thee, Let Me Count the Ways: Postmodernity, Language and Love Games in Rooke's 'The Guacamole Game,'" contributed by Eva Darias-Beautell, we return, as the title signals, to a postmodernist reading of Rooke. Darias-Beautell provides a close examination of the novella's gender relations within its language games — both of which are, as she points out, at the heart of the Rookean fictional landscape. Since language has "come to replace reality," the game principle, in accordance with a postmodernist reading, "replaces the principle of truth." Thus, the characters in the novella play out their roles in the absence of reality, because the story had, in any case, already taken place at the outset of the narrative. As the characters, husband and wife, are engaged in playing the game, suggests Darias-Beautell, "they explore the possibility of relating to each other — talking about love — in this ever more complex world of simulacra."

Chapter Four is dedicated to the novel. It opens with Francesca Romana Paci's rigorous examination of *Fat Woman* in terms of the individual's revolt against determinism. Through the bittersweet life of the novel's extraordinary character, Ella Mae Hopkins, Rooke is able, says Paci, to examine the depths of human fate *in extremis*. She outlines a compelling philosophical correspondence between Rooke's *Fat Woman* and Malraux's *La condition humaine*, notwithstanding obvious differences between the two works. Both authors, writes Paci, share the notion of "pity for the human flesh . . . a knowledge of the impossibility of overcoming . . . destiny, but at the same time a compulsion to resist, to fight for sense and value, and ultimately rebirth."

The following two essays, by Anna Pia De Luca and Michael H. Keefer, discuss Rooke's *Shakespeare's Dog* in terms of its metafictional qualities. De Luca engages the novel from the point of view of historiographic parody, illustrating how Rooke rewrites and reinvents the official historical version of Shakespeare's formative years, which follow his marriage to Anne Hathaway and precede his departure for the London stage. Keefer, a Renaissance scholar, brings to his discussion of Rooke aspects of the Shakespearian critical apparatus, and suggests that with *Shakespeare's Dog*, Rooke anticipated "contemporary criticism's 'decentring' of Shakespeare." In fact, according to Keefer, Rooke's novel creates a "double decentring" by anchoring the narrative "in a canine rather than human consciousness," and by using it to create a Shakespeare "who is not yet 'Shakespeare.'"

The next section of Chapter Four is dedicated to Rooke's fourth novel, *A Good Baby*, and opens with two reviews. The first, by Joan Thomas, foregrounds the novel's central preoccupation, represented by a clash between the forces of good and evil, and played out in an "abysmal world" of poverty, isolation, and madness. When "hope and fortitude" triumph in such a world, as they eventually do in *A Good Baby*, writes Thomas, the "effect is dazzling" — and the novel is transformed into a symbol of affirmation. The second review, by Rosemary Sullivan, is fundamentally a tribute to Rooke's craft of creation, his ability to capture a landscape together with its characters that is in essence totally phenomenological. Some might call Rooke's novel "magic (or diabolic) realism," Sullivan says, when its greater and more "exquisite achievement is that it's slice-of-life reality." She commends Rooke for being a "good sneak thief" who "steals so beautifully from life."

In "Novels and Dreams: On Leon Rooke's *A Good Baby*," Douglas Glover takes off in an altogether different direction, bringing to the discussion of Rooke's novel the notion that novels, the best novels, are like dreams. Like dreams, they come out of silence and "use image patterning as a device for suggesting meaning," and like dreams they are "available for interpretations," possessing a "central luminous mystery at their core" that attracts readers and critics to decode, to penetrate beyond the surface of the words. *A Good Baby* is one such dream-novel with a luminous mystery at its core, the baby who illuminates the dark, misty, inscrutable landscape into which the reader is pulled by the narrative and by his or her desire to be illuminated.

Peter Cumming's "When Men Have Babies: The Good Father in *A Good Baby*" deals with the 'feminization' of men, a theme that is both current and controversial among feminists. Cumming finds in Rooke's novel a perfect model that embodies the polarized male in its archetypal manifestations of good and evil. On the one hand, this polarized male is, like Truman, a "diabolical incarnation of patriarchy's 'True Man'; and on the other, as represented by Toker, he is a potential "new man and a good father," a feminized, nurturing male.

Few critics or reviewers have paid significant attention to Rooke's use of satire, irony and humour. Even fewer have commented on his political satire. Mike Matthews' "Leon Rooke's Political Satires" closely examines this important aspect of Rooke's fiction, focusing on two works, the novel *Who Goes There* and the collection of stories "How I Saved the Province." His textual analysis is based on what he describes as "the violent conjunction" of two stylistic extremes, "the rhetorical and the poetical," both characteristic of all of Rooke's writing. The dislocations created by these stylistic modes, according to Matthews, are part of Rooke's "comedy of bad manners." Rooke's galaxy of the satirized may shock us, but we applaud "the sheer vitality of those who return from the grave, from limbo, or from the recesses and refuse bins of life to continue their journey."

The Fall of Gravity, Rooke's most recent novel, published in 2000, is here discussed by three contributors, in three different formats. Neil Besner's contribution is an essay focusing on the performative and restorative aspects of Rooke's diction. The performative strategies, Besner suggests, are evident in the "gathering of voices (in dialogue, in monologue, in direct address, in sidelong reflection) that perform writing as if it were speaking." The restorative aspect of diction for Besner is "the novel's key and governing impulse," which serves to heal "the broken sanctity of the family, and ultimately that of humanity as a whole." If Keath Fraser's piece on *The Fall of Gravity* is, as he asserted apologetically in a letter to me, a "mere sketch of an article," it is nonetheless a sketch that points us well beyond its own outline. "A Word in Appreciation of Leon Rooke's "Mustard-Cutting" in *The Fall of Gravity*," as Fraser's piece is aptly entitled, is a condensed and insightful meditation on the nature of Rooke's idiomatic language. Described by Fraser as the "mother of archetype," "Rooke's language begins incorrigibly in the commonplace" — as all idiomatic languages do — building on its "lowest common denominators, inevitably defying the fall of gravity in the manner of a Gothic cathedral." Rounding off the discussion on *The Fall of Gravity*, and closing Chapter Four, is Russell Banks' "Foreword" to the French translation of the novel. Like Besner and Fraser, Banks zooms in on the novel's language, more specifically on its voice and the narrator's wizardry in using it. Rooke's voices are 'talking' to us, says Banks. That is one of the things that Rooke, "here and in all his work, does best." And Rooke's writing talks in many voices because Rooke is "large enough, skilled and gifted enough, and has a sufficiently generous heart to embody all his characters, male and female, young and old, and even to embody his narrator."

Chapter Five, which features two interviews with Leon Rooke, concludes the present collection of essays and other texts, and allows the reader to spend some time in the company of Rooke, to directly experience his thoughts, his ideas about his art and about himself as an artist. In the early interview conducted by Karen Mulhallen, Rooke is led into an engaging conversation about the provenance of his marginalized characters — like Ella Mae Hopkins from *Fat Woman* — and about his wish to give these characters a dignified and meaningful existence. The second and more recent interview by Branko Gorjup brings into focus some of Rooke's ruminations on the art of writing and the role of fiction in society, on the immigrant experience, on the formation of national canons and on many other topics related to our contemporary world.

The final chapter contains a greatly enlarged, updated bibliography of works by and about Leon Rooke, with separate indexes by name and title. Finally, I am pleased to announce the insertion, at the back of the book, of an exciting new DVD entitled "Tongue and Groove: A Portrait of Leon Rooke." This one-hour documentary, directed by Paola Marino, is set largely in the author's home and features readings by Leon Rooke and friends. With its high-voltage excerpts from "Muffins," "Wy Wn Th Calld Yr Nam You Did Not Answr," "Moths," *Shakespeare's Dog*, and *Fat Woman*, this DVD demonstrates the incomparable energy of Leon Rooke in performance and explores through conversation and commentary the defining qualities of his work.

Branko Gorjup

ACKNOWLEDGEMENTS

Some of the contributions in this volume first appeared in the following books, journals and newspapers: "Rooke's Move," *Essays on Canadian Writing* 30 (Winter 1984-85); "The Performing Artist," *Essays on Canadian Writing* (Spring, 1995); "In the Path of Leon Rooke's Sidestepping Narrator: Two Views," a re-working of two essays into one: "A Man Locked up in a Freezer: A Reading of Leon Rooke's Story 'The Blue Baby,'" published in English in *Commonwealth* 12.1 (Autumn 1989), and "A Fading Painting, A Growing Story by Leon Rooke," which appeared in French in *Image et Recit*, Presses de la Sorbonne Nouvelle, 1993; "Leon Rooke's *Shakespeare's Dog*: A Postmodern Historiographic Parody," *Atti del Convegno dell' Associazione Italiana di Anglistica*, Parma: 1992; "Leon Rooke Works Wonders," *The Winnipeg Free Press*, 25 Nov. 1989; "A Good Baby," *Brick* 40 (1991); "A Reading of Leon Rooke's 'The Birth Control King of the Upper Volta,'" *Journal of the Short Story in English / Les Cashiers de la nouvelle*, no. 4, Presses de l'Université d'Angers, (Spring 85); "When Men Have Babies: The Good Father in Leon Rooke's *A Good Baby*," *Textual Studies in Canada* 8 (1996); "Foreword," *En chute libre (The Fall od Gravity)*, Paris: Edition Phebus, 2002; "Lingering on Posted Land: An Interview with Leon Rooke," *WLT Magazine (World Literature Today)* 3.1 (Apr-June 2003); all the other contributions were commissioned for this volume.

This book would not have been possible without the good will of the contributors, their critical judgement and investigative intelligence, and their ability to imagine the significance of such a collection.

Very special thanks go to Deborah Brent of The Peter Paul Charitable Foundation whose generous financial support has sustained this and many other projects in the past.

A number of people have worked on the production of the manuscript: Jenny Kitson who skilfully and expediently shepherded the manuscript through the initial stages of text-editing, Chris Doda who patiently marshalled disparate styles into a unified text, Nina Callaghan whose final and meticulous proofreading prepared the manuscript for type-setting and Michael Callaghan who spent countless hours and a huge amount of patience in putting it all together.

I am deeply grateful to Leon and Constance Rooke—to Leon for his encouragement and his open-armed readiness to help, particularly in the compilation of the bibliography, and to Constance for her understanding of the project and the sound advice with which she assisted the editor from the beginning.

I am especially indebted to Paola Marino, the gifted, enthusiastic and self-less director of the video-documentary on Leon Rooke, "Tongue and Groove," (enclosed in this volume), and to her assistant Kenneth Mohammed for his contribution in providing a helpful hand during the lengthy hours of filming.

To Juan Opitz, a wonderful musician and sound engineer, I am grateful for his generous help and encouragement in the production of the video-documentary.

My special thanks go to Dubravko Barać for his invaluable work on the Index and for his adaptation of the Bibliography to an electronic, interactive text, which is available on the Web: www.leonrooke.com.

In completing this book, I owe a unique debt to my wife Francesca Valente and to my son Francesco. To them this book is dedicated in admiration, gratitude and love.

CHAPTER ONE
PORTRAIT OF THE ARTIST

LEON ROOKE

LAWRENCE NAUMOFF

Leon was born at two o'clock in the morning and it is my guess that, unlike other babies, he enjoyed the experience and when slapped and therefore encouraged to begin crying his way into life, he laughed.

It's also likely that Leon chose to be born specifically when he was, and that he waited until it was two a.m. to enter, knowing, somehow, that he was destined to be the archetypal stray dog of a writer and that the time of day best suited to howling and wandering and reflection, was then.

Rooke emerged, and he liked what he saw. He decided to stay and see what would happen. Soon he discovered writing and women and the comforting warmth of fine Scotch whiskey. And that was all before he was five years old.

There is a statue and a plaque in the courthouse square honouring Leon, a famous man now, as the "Father of Roanoke Rapids." That marker had gone up much earlier, though, because by the time he was fourteen, the registrar in the birth certificate office had commissioned a rubber stamp embossed with the words *Leon Rooke* on it to keep from having to type in his name so often.

At the age of 18, at Mars Hill College, as a freshman, Leon discovered, in the basement of the department of veterinary science, a 500-year-old letter that had been written by Shakespeare's dog.

He graduated at the age of 19 with the degree of DCE, or, in Latin, *Dickum Cum Ezlee.*

He began collecting rare coins then, and moved to New Orleans under the mistaken impression that the old French quarter was a coin that was worth a lot of money. Unable to find it, he began writing stories with a unique and original vision and prose that strolled across the page like a Louisiana lady in a silk blouse on a hot day. You couldn't take your eyes off it and you wanted more.

• • •

I first met Leon in 1965 in Chapel Hill, North Carolina, at that time the intellectual and artistic centre of the state and region. He had been hired to teach writing by his old friend, Jessie Rehder, who ran the program at the University.

Jessie was a big sad old lady with red hair that looked like it had been cut with a lawn mower. She loved her students and she loved her writer friends and she loved someone else, as well, in a way that wasn't sanctioned at the time, and that made her sad. It was hard to tell whether she was crying or laughing most of the time — it looked the same on her — but the way she adored Leon was clearly in happiness.

I met Leon, then, at a late hour when he'd locked himself out of his office and I, a young writer, was roaming around the empty literary night on that beautiful campus. We knew each other as being part of the same crowd, but hadn't yet become friends.

Leon was the most thoroughly bohemian and natural outsider I knew. Being a bohemian writer at that time, in the South, was something like being a White Negro Jewish Communist Yankee Godless Revolutionary Artist of Immorality, Perversion and Sedition. It was confusing. The natives could see the man was White, which was good, but everything else was not only wrong, it was downright scary. *Bring the women and children inside, there's something out there in the street that looks like trouble!*

They were right.

He shook up the politicians. He even helped launch Senator Jesse Helms' political career when he wrote and published, in the university-sponsored *Carolina Quarterly*, his famous story, "The Ice House Gang," in 1966.

In that story, on a hot, humid summer day, the young couple pay a man to let them go inside the ice house. Inside, they 'fornicate,' as Senator Helms said, on a 'hundred pound block of ice.' For some reason, this shook up the Senator, who wasn't a senator then, but only a television commentator, and he railed about it and hoped to call down the wrath of decent Southern men upon Leon and the University.

Nothing happened, which shows that the power of literature in those times in the South was either strong enough to withstand the bad breath of bizarre politics, or inconsequential.

We don't know whether Leon had the good fortune, back then, to have known a woman as dazzling and adventuresome as the character Sydney in that story, but it was a true and undeniable fact that Leon had conjured up a memorably powerful gal.

Later, he did meet someone that impressive, Connie Raymond, and after a few years of rural courtship, he married her. Connie was a uniquely talented and intelligent woman, and well-bred (except in matters of Leon, leave out the 'r') and was a PhD candidate at the time.

Leon and Connie rented a single storey, depression era country house that had never been much even when it was new. It was east of Chapel Hill, where the land changes from rolling piedmont hills and shady hardwoods to flat, gray-white clay fields and turpentine-sap pine trees, sticky, where they bled, as thick, amber glue.

It was as if all the female characters from Leon's novels had joined together and sent Connie to meet him. They must have said to each other, "Let's see if this guy's got anything other than a way with words, and can live up to all this stuff he's been writing about us."

The house where they lived while Connie continued her academic studies, and Leon studied her, had been painted white at one time, but, as I recall, it was covered with German siding, which never held paint. Slick, hard yellow pine boards milled with a smooth scalloped channel along the bottom edge of the lap. German siding shed paint like a dog shedding fur on a hot summer day. It came out in clumps, dropped off the boards, peeled off sometimes as cleanly as peeling layers from an onion.

The metal roof on that little house was painted green, faded, but intact. Metal roofing, called 5-V, for its surface shape, covered many rural pitched roofs, all of them, it seemed, painted either red, green or black. The tin was attached to nailers, one-by-sixes or -eights, spaced about two feet apart, nailed to the rafters like wide ladder rungs. Below them was the attic space, and below it the ceilings, almost always uninsulated. Hard rain coming down on those tin roofs was so loud TVs couldn't be heard.

Leon and Connie had an old Crosley television set in that house. The set couldn't hold a picture any more firm and steady than a drunk trying to walk a straight line. The furniture was old, some of it reduced to nesting material. The companionship in that home was stellar, however, and being an artist, acclaimed and recognized, and having a good woman, a few good yard dogs outside, a cat or two inside or under the house in the cool of the crawlspace, friends over for an afternoon or evening, cheap wine, good food, and lots of laughter, was just about pure heaven at that time, in North Carolina, in the early years of Leon's career and life. It was enough. It was more than enough. It was a writer's life.

It was a hundred thousand words of wisdom, humour and heart that followed, as he left North Carolina, the adventures of this cross-country man who says:

> A man of my nature, he always on the move, on the go to the some-where he never been, headed for the somewhere he never get to in all the world. I think sometime the sun it will not shine on me another day, but there it come, over the hill, over the meadow dusk green in the dew . . . yes, there it come, one more time, pret-ty you pleased and pretending like the fool that it never shine the day before.[1]

---

[1] "Further Adventures of a Cross-Country Man," which was originally published in the Spring, 1967 *Carolina Quarterly*.

ILL-FITTING REVOLVING CHAIR

TOM MCHANEY

In the early 1960s, Leon Rooke worked as an "information officer" in the University of North Carolina at Chapel Hill's "News Bureau" — essentially the office that disseminated publicity and managed news, good and bad, to the state's weekly and daily newspapers. Mostly the staff wrote news stories, some of them as bland as reports of which students from whatever counties had received what honours. Often, however, there were opportunities for short human interest features tied to campus life and longer features about university research or special programs aimed to the front pages of special sections of Sunday papers in Charlotte, Greensboro, Durham, or Raleigh, North Carolina. At the time Leon looked a bit like the young Thomas Wolfe who had made his goat leaps around the Chapel Hill campus forty-five years earlier: tall, thin, with a raw-boned mountain man shamble and a wry drawl. He didn't seem to fit very well into his old wooden revolving work chair or into the knee hole of his desk. He did not, in other ways, fit into the rhythm and mood of the News Bureau. He had done his training as a writer with novelist John Ehle, who himself was a bit of an exile in the Film and Video program housed far from the university's English Department. Leon's ill-fitting chair and desk sat at one end of a long narrow office space and faced the desk of the Bureau's director, a cherubic retired newspaperman named Pete Ivey. Ivey actually had a high regard for creative writers as long as they didn't work for him and showed more or less perfect loyalty to the University of North Carolina. He regularly visited the dramatist Paul Green and became very excited when Walker Percy won the National Book Award for *The Moviegoer*. Leon was simply restive and soon he and the News Bureau would part ways. But he stayed in Chapel Hill long enough to form one of those short-lived little magazines that, in Robert Frost's witty terms, had to die to make verse free. His co-conspirator in this was a lively and

Ezra Pound-like young man named Brown, whose politics were the opposite of Pound's however, and in a time when many marched and picketed theatres and tried to break down some of the racial barriers that still existed even in a liberal bastion like Chapel Hill, Brown would abandon the official march for which some kind of permit had been issued and simply sit in the middle of the town's busiest intersection until the police came to get him. The little magazine, for which Leon served as fiction editor, was called *Reflections*, with Bob Brown's subtitle, "The Free South Review." It went through five or six issues over a three-year period and apparently no full run remains even in the library at Chapel Hill, if library records on the Internet are to be believed. I have one copy of Volume III in which Leon's story "Jones' End" appears. Someone projecting Leon's biography will want to know who the other staff members and "corresponding editors" were, perhaps — and there were a bunch — to take down impressions from Leon's associates during an important if somewhat unsatisfactory period of his early development as a writer.

WHAT THE ROOKE SAID[1]

RUSSELL BROWN

A rook is a crow-like bird, and tradition holds that if one splits the tongue of the crow, it will learn to speak. The fact that it will presumably speak with a forked tongue may be an inevitable side effect of its rather painful initiation into language but that is in no way relevant here. Perhaps it is the novelty of hearing a Rooke speak that so affects Leon Rooke's audience; let us catalogue some of their responses.

1) Rooke receives his first critical attention in Canada when, in the Summer 1979 issue of *Canadian Literature*, Clark Blaise discussed two of his books in a review called "At Home in All Voices."

2) In November of 1980, while visiting Leon and Constance Rooke in Victoria, I begin writing a piece on Rooke's emergence into the Canadian literary scene. (It appeared in the Fall 1984 issue of *Essays on Canadian Writing*.) When I asked Connie, a critic who teaches English at University of Victoria, about *her* responses to Leon's fiction, she replied: "There are no themes to talk about really. All you can *ever* talk about is that control of voice."

3) In November 1981, Stephen Scobie writes on Rooke in *Books in Canada*; the piece is called "The Inner Voice," and he quotes Robert Kroetsch's comments on choosing *Fat Woman* as the best first novel of 1980 "because of Rooke's ear for language . . . that fully realized world of appetite and speech" (8).

4) In a 1981 special issue *Canadian Fiction Magazine* on Rooke, Geoff Hancock, the editor, writes: "His stories began with a character's voice." In that same issue the following exchange takes place near the beginning of an interview with Rooke:

---

[1] An earlier version of this essay was presented at the Association for Canadian and Quebec Literatures in 1984.

Hancock: "Some would say your own work is nothing but voice."

Rooke: "I've yet to decide whether that is an insult. (108) "

If Rooke's critics consistently take voice as the starting point of their considerations of his writing, they have not gone very far towards defining that voice, towards saying what it does and how it does it. Nor have they really attempted to say, to borrow a phrase, where that voice *is* coming from.

Let us listen to the openings of three of Rooke's most recent stories:

We got fifty-two (52) kids in the nursery, the Henny Penny Nursery, only one teacher, and she's retarded. They come to me, the parents of these kids do, and they say, "Sir, Mr. Beacon, excuse us, sir, for butting in like this, but some of us parents, mostly those of us you see right here, what we've noticed is that Mrs. Shorts, running your place, well, sir, to make no bones about it, she's retarded."[2]

Ladies and gentlemen, I want to speak to you about the need for flux in your lives. That is what the man said on Sunday radio, on the show "Your Own Self."

You need flux in it, he said.

My wife was lying in bed next to me at the time. This was a Sunday afternoon, all the kids out of the house, and Sunday afternoons we like to take it easy. We like to take it easy on other days, too, but Sunday is, as you know, a special day and, to make no bones about it, we were resting.

Did he say what I thought he said? my wife asked.

He said we need flux in our lives, I said.

That's not what I thought he said, she said.[3]

The King of England was out courting Anne.

"Anne?" said the King of England. "I thought I was out courting Emy Dealiath of Detroit. How'd you get here, Anne?"

Anne held a wet finger up to the wind and pointed her toes.

"My Mummy put me up to it," she said. "My Mummy said I could

---

[2] "Some People Will Tell You the Situation at the Henny Penny Nursery Is Getting Intolerable," *Matrix* 17, Fall 1983.

[3] "Flux," *Event* 12.2, 1983.

have anything I wanted, 'cepting popsicles. Have I put my foot in it?"

The King, as time went by, was delighted. He still had an ache in his heart for Emy Dealiath, but he was so pleased he took Anne to the castle and introduced her around.[4]

What do these stories have in common? To begin with the obvious, in none of them are we hearing an authorial voice. In the first two stories, the speakers are I-narrators, but even in the third story, where we *seem* to be listening to a traditional narrator, one who is not a character, even this narrator is very different from the traditional, omniscient, objective, and authoritative teller of tales. For one thing, after he makes an opening statement of the kind that narrators ordinarily make ("The King of England was out courting Anne"), the main character violates all conventions of such narration by responding, as though overhearing him: "'Anne?' said the King of England. 'I thought I was out courting Emy Dealiath of Detroit.'" Furthermore the teller of this tale will — a few lines later — say, "Anne had growed up some by this time. She was practically thirteen." (274).Whoever is speaking to us, it isn't The Author.

Dennis Lee has been arguing lately that an important development in poetry for him and for many other contemporary practitioners is what he calls "polyphony," the use of several contending voices within one poem — which may involve the presence of more than one speaker but more usually involves the poet himself speaking in more than one voice, that is, modulating from one way of talking to another.[5] In contrast to this kind of polyphony, Rooke is what might be called, borrowing another term from music, a monodist. "Monodic" music is defined by the *OED* as "characterized by the predominance of one part or melody, to which the other parts merely furnish harmonies," which is the way Rooke's stories are fashioned. When Conrad's stories utilize first-person narrators, we not only hear other voices in the tale, but those voices have their own weight, are equal in strength (in intensity) to that of the narrator. Consider, for example, the way the unnamed speaker at the beginning of *Heart of Darkness* yields to Marlow, and how in turn Marlow

---

[4] "The History of England, Part Four," *Canadian Fiction Magazine* 46, 1983.

[5] See Lee's "Enacting and Meditation" (*Journal of Canadian Poetry* 2.1, 1979), which was revised as "Polyphony" (*Descant* 39, Winter 1982; reprinted in *Body Music*).

can make us hear Kurtz's disciple crying out, "I tell you . . . this man has enlarged my mind" as if first-hand, that is without an awareness of a mediating presence. In contrast, in a Rooke story — such as the one about the Henny Penny Nursery — we hear speakers only *through* that primary narrative consciousness, as if the voices existed inside the voice that is speaking to us. Not reported, not even reflected really, these other voices come to us filtered through that speaker who is talking to us in a way that makes the old questions about reliable and unreliable narrators irrelevant.

> They come to me, the parents of these kids do, and they say, "Sir, Mr. Beacon, excuse us, sir, for butting in like this, but some of us parents, mostly those of us you see right here, what we've noticed is that Mrs. Shorts, running your place, well, sir, to make no bones about it, she's retarded." (227)

This use of a single, dominant voice overriding or engulfing all others in the story makes one think of the way Saul Bellow came to prominence with the creation of protagonists as centres of consciousness out of which the world unfolds — Henderson turning his journey into Africa into an Africa of the mind; Mr. Sammler "become an explaining creature"; and before them both, Augie crying out in his opening sentences:

> I am an American, Chicago born — Chicago, that somber city — and go at things as I have taught myself, free-style, and will make the record in my own way: first to knock, first admitted; sometimes an innocent knock, sometimes a not so innocent. But a man's character is his fate, says Heraclitus, and in the end there isn't any way to disguise the nature of the knocks by acoustical work on the door or gloving the knuckles. (3)

It is perhaps worth noting that the first story Rooke had accepted was in *The Noble Savage*, a literary magazine that Bellow was then editing. To push this connection a bit further, one might consider Rooke's fiction as an answer to the question that Bellow posed in his very important essay called "Where Do We Go From Here?" There Bellow argued that the modernist notion of a "unitary self," a self susceptible to analysis using the methods developed by depth psychology, had to be replaced with something more like what the sociologist Erving Goffman calls the "presentation self." Like the Bellow hero, Rooke's protagonists dwell *in* their presentation of self; they come alive not so much in their authors' dramatization of them as in their own self-dramatizations.

In utilizing these self-dramatizing voices (these self-creating speakers, one might say) Rooke has — again like Bellow before him — turned his attention away from any pursuit of inward essences to the job of cataloguing the externals of role: gesture and flourish, concern for appearance, the playing of self-conceived parts. For this reason the centre of interest in a Rooke story is shifted away from the modernist one of *discovery*, of the finding of new or unrecognized meanings, to — Ah, but here is the hardest feature to describe in a Rooke story, for clearly he has not thought, as Bellow did, that the answer lay in returning to a literature of ideas. If we can never "get under the surface," if the ways of reading stories we learned from James and the ways of reading people we learned from Freud no longer work, then what for must we read, and what are we reading for? "Epiphany" is certainly not likely to be waiting for us; in stories that are so much part of their speaker's consciousness, epiphanies could occur only if experienced by the characters themselves, and — as we will see shortly — that is not what we learn to expect from the kinds of characters Rooke usually chooses. Similarly, character revelation is out; in stories such as these we no longer have the sense of the apparition of external character opening up, like one of those images of Silenus, to reveal the fixed stare of some Platonic self within. Moreover, "subtexts" are largely gone from such stories because we no longer have a stable vantage point from which to perceive them, nor any of the two-character exchanges that the modernists frequently used to generate them.

Nor do Rooke's characters — which is to say, the voices we are listening to — change very much in a Rooke story. The tone, the emotional pitch, the peculiar slant taken — these things vary greatly from story to story, but within any one story these qualities do not develop noticeably. Instead what the Rooke story generally gives us is *more* — not only more pages of the same, but passages in which the intensity of the voice increases, the volume is felt to have been raised, the pressure that seems to lie behind the speech of all of Rooke's characters goes up another notch. Listen, in the concluding moments of the "Henny Penny Nursery" story, to the ascending curve of language:

"Hold on," I said. "Just one dang minute. I'm not opposing your ideas in the least. It's a fine idea and I want to tell you that Henny Penny is behind you 100 percent. We will give you all the advice and encouragement you need."

That quieted them down.

"Funny thing is," I said, "you are reminding me of my very own self, some fifty-three years ago, when I marched in here, head of a concerned parents' group just like yours. I demanded the situation improve at Henny Penny School. You won't believe it but in them times the plight of the little lads and lassies was truly sickening. A real sweatshop. Little three-year-olds making wallets. They knew nothing but misery. Whippings day in and day out. Typhoid, whooping cough, measles. A true dirt hole. But I and my then wife and some of the others, we decided to march. Get organized. We marched in here and laid down the law — to a Mr. Magruder it was then . . ."

"And Mr. Magruder, he laughed. He laughed in our faces. 'Try it,' he said. 'Go ahead and try it. *You*,' he said, talking to me. '*You* take this chair. This desk. Here, take it,' he said, 'it's all yours. I give you one year. Maybe two. I give you as long as it takes you to get *your* kid out of short pants. Once your own kid has moved on you're going to start forgetting about the rats. About the refuse. About the beatings. You're going to forget about it all. You're going to wish you could go somewhere where you could never see another little child through all of your born years. You're going to *hate* the darlin' little rascals. You're going to learn that these little brats, up to and including your own, are the ugliest, rottenest, stupidest, noisiest, most venal, selfish, hurtful, *dangerous* sonsof-bitches ever put on this planet since God was himself an ape. And you're going to want to *hurt* them, to *menace* them, to *wreck* the lit-tle bastards while they're in knee pants, because you'll know that is the only chance you'll ever get. You're going to want to drive home the message once and for all that adults have lives too, that not *all* the world belongs to these sniveling, bug-eyed, innocent, knock-kneed, big-eared fools.'" (234-35)

• • •

If there *is* something close to traditional character revelation in these stories, it comes in such passages — which convey a sense of a speaker on the verge of a breakdown. As a dam might be said to be threatened with breakdown from the pressure of the water it seeks to contain, so the language-constructed "selves" of these characters threaten to collapse under the very pressure of that language. We sense this almost from the beginning of the story, have known it as soon as we heard the odd sound of this voice.

It is inevitable that we think of Faulkner when we listen to Rooke, that giant presence that looms over the writer growing up in the American South, and like Rooke a man hyped on language from a region that keeps recreating itself out of language. There are some features of the "Faulknerian style" that connect Rooke with the creator of Yoknapatawpha — the sense that language is sometimes like a tide engulfing the reader and the material, that this speech will roll on forever carrying everything along with it and uniting this flotsam to that jetsam in unexpected ways — but in particular I think of the style that Faulkner utilized when he wanted to show one particular condition in his character: the falling apart of the mind. The speeches of Quentin in *The Sound and the Fury* and *Absalom, Absalom!* seem to have taught Rooke how to create what we might recklessly generalize as the "Southern Breakdown Voice," a phrase that can carry with it perhaps — at no extra charge — some suggestion of the square-dance breakdown, with its caller moving us all about to the rhythms of his language.

• • •

It *is* a particularly rhythmic voice that we are listening to in many of Rooke's stories. It falls into a phrasing that invites a chanting style of reading, and it depends heavily on repetition of words and syntactical structures:

> We got fifty-two (52) kids in the nursery, the Henny Penny Nursery, only one teacher, and she's retarded. They come to me, the parents of these kids do, and they say, "Sir, Mr. Beacon, excuse us, sir, for butting in like this, but some of us parents, mostly those of us you see right here, what we've noticed is that Mrs. Shorts, running your place, well, sir, to make no bones about it, she's retarded."
> (227)

This is a style that is not ultimately literary in its sources; it is pre-literate because it returns, as Faulkner and most other Southern writers returned, to the oral sources of language. But Rooke has taken for his sources not earlier storytellers but those great North American manipulators of rhetorical language: the carny-barker and the various demagogues, hucksters and salesmen descended from him (recall the opening of "Flux": "Ladies and gentlemen, I want to speak to you about the need for flux in your lives"), and the evangelical preacher — especially the Southern black preacher who sweeps up his listeners and carries them along with the sound of his voice. Which is why I regard "Mama Tuddi Done Over" as representative Rooke:

> HOW MANY OF YOU FOLKS BEEN TO THE RIVER?
> "We been there, preacher!"
> HOW MANY OF YOU POOR SINNERS HAVE BEEN TO THE RIVER?
> "The river, amen!"
> I SEE SOME OF YOU FOLKS HAVE BEEN TO THE RIVER AND I KNOW YOU HAVE BEEN THERE AND JUMPED RIGHT IN—
> "Right in!"
> WHILE OTHERS OF YOU HAVE STOOD ON THE SHORE AND WAITED FOR THE WATER TO DIVIDE SO YOU COULD WALK A DRY BOTTOM RIGHT INTO GLORY LAND NOW AIN'T THAT THE TRUTH?
> "It's the truth!" (41)

• • •

I have said that in Rooke's writing the voice of the story's speaker contains the other voices of the story. Which is true, but what is probably already obvious is that it contains all the rest of the world as well. In itself that might not affect our reading if the world of these stories wasn't so *weird*. But Rooke's stories are mostly fantasies, like "The History of England . . ." in which King Henry VIII and Anne Boleyn dwell in the clichés and effluvia of the modern world; or else they are comically paranoid delusions such as "Flux," in which a man listening to a radio announcer feels threatened by "what I took to be the biggest invasion of flux ever to come into our lives." (33) Or they are (not infrequently) grotesques in which twenti-eth-century nursery schools exist that sound like the kind of surreal night-mare that an undigested bit of beef might give one on a really bad night. While communicating to us from these worlds that range from the mildly askew to the totally bizarre, the speakers in Rooke's stories generally seem not to notice that reality has gone off its tracks; usually they give no evi-dence of even mild surprise over events that would leave us in our worlds aghast. Because of this milieu they report to us from, the sound of these voices is — in a way that the voice in a Bellow story never is — estrang-ing. We are not enlightened by these stories; we are dazzled by them. One of the chief concerns for the writer native to Canada has always been to tell us of locus, but Rooke as border-crosser seems compelled to dislocate us.

In stories that so swiftly depart from any known world, the logic of nar-rative continuity does not operate in the usual way. Listen to the zigs and zags that can take place in a single paragraph in "The History of England . . .":

> One day the King came into the Queen Mother's bedroom. "Mama!" he said. The Queen Mother had grown old and many reasoned she was now on her deathbed. "Call in the Bishop," they said. But the Bishop was in France, on a secret mission, so she was saved that additional discomfort. The Queen Mother's eyes rolled, "Am I dying?" she'd say. "Am I dying? Is the realm in order?" Everyone assured her the realm was in order. But she persisted with her questions: "Am I dying? Am I dying? Is the crab tree in blossom?" The entire court tired of it and more than a few sug-gested the old woman was being a trifle silly. (274-75)

"Anne would play the king his favourite records . . ." begins the next paragraph; and we sense that these stories can, and may, go anywhere. Anything can happen because the speaker can choose to make it so. Rooke illustrates that explicitly in the story called "A Nicer Story by the 'B' Road" (which appears in his most recent collection, *The Birth Control King of the Upper Volta*); there the story proceeds in its usual preposterous manner, telling us of Agnes, a giant fat girl with three eyes who is seduced by God — until we reach a point three-quarters of the way through when the narrator strikes Agnes over the head with a champagne bottle. "Five or six people screamed," we are told, and then the text of the story abruptly divides itself into two columns, one labelled "A" and one labelled "B". "'Why'd you do that?' sobbed Agnes, slumping down between the tables" in column A, while "She picked herself up and began rubbing her head" B tells us. In one of these continuations Agnes dies, while in the other the narrator realizes that "*No one* could ever beat Agnes." In the last three pages the two columns become one (although the story refuses to return to normal margins), so it really doesn't matter whether we pass through this story's divagations by means of column A or column B; we arrive at the same place. And as the narrator says in his closing lines: "Felt I'd *dreamed* this entire business. That I could do anything!" (83)

Rooke's speakers *can* do anything, anything they can dream of doing. Perhaps this is the payoff for the reader of this fiction: he is taken so far outside of the daily that he returns with his wonder renewed.

And if these stories lack the traditional features of the short story, what happens to closure? The answer, not surprisingly, is that we don't experience a traditional kind of closure either, and these stories leave us with a feeling of bafflement that becomes part of their overall effect. And sometimes I think these stories can't possibly give us a sense of conclusion because of the way language and voice have operated so powerfully throughout them.

Rooke's stories don't seem to end so much as just pause for breath.

BIBLIOGRAPHY

Bellow, Saul. "Where Do We Go from Here? The Future of Fiction." 1965. *Saul Bellow and the Critics*. Ed. Irving Malin. New York: Gotham Library, 1967. 211-20.

Blaise, Clark. "At Home in All Voices." Rev. of Leon Rooke, *The Love Parlour* and *The Broad Back of the Angel*. *Canadian Literature* 81 (Summer 1979): 179.

Brown, Russell. "Rooke's Move." *Essays on Canadian Writing* 30 (Winter 1984-85): 287-303.

Scobie, Stephen. "The Inner Voice." *Books in Canada* Nov. 1981: 8-10.

Hancock, Geoff. "The Hi-Tech World of Leon Rooke." *Canadian Fiction Magazine* 38 (1981): 135-45.

——. "An Interview with Leon Rooke." *Canadian Fiction Magazine* 38 (1981): 107-33.

Lee, Dennis. "Polyphony." *Body Music*. Toronto: House of Anansi, 1998. 51-70.

Rooke, Leon. "Flux." *Event* 12.2 (1983): 31-34.

——. "The History of England, Part Four." *Sing Me No Love Songs I'll Say You No Prayers*. New York: Ecco Press, 1984. 272-90.

——. "Mama Tuddi Done Over." *Death Suite*. Toronto: ECW Press, 1981. 9-42.

——. "A Nicer Story by the `B' Road." *The Birth Control King of the Upper Volta*. Toronto: ECW Press, 1982. 71-83.

——. "Some People Will Tell You the Situation at Henny Penny Nursery Is Getting Intolerable." *Sing Me No Love Songs I'll Say You No Prayers*. New York: Ecco Press, 1984. 227-35.

Fat Leon

M.A.C. (Marion) Farrant

She would make a space where even this darkness might thrive.
—Fat Woman

What he sees first and foremost are the holes, invisible, perhaps, to most of us, but holes nonetheless. The holes in our perception and understanding of things. The holes in the blankets we cover ourselves with, hiding out from each other and from life.

Fat Leon is a tall, skinny drink of water but he's called Fat because, in truth, he's enormous. Some would say he's as enormous as the holes he measures and fills.

Imagine this. Imagine some kind of god pointing at Fat Leon and saying, "Okay now, we're going to give an extra dollop of *something* to this here mortal man." And this extra *something* squishes and oozes out of Fat Leon like gravy overflowing a platter. Always has. From his pipsqueak stage to his mature pyrotechnic self. And what Fat Leon does is scoop up handfuls of this phosphorescent, dripping *something* and pour it into vessels of words, causing these words to become numinous, alive.

In a way Fat Leon harvests his own mighty self. And he's not demure about it, that's for sure. Fat Leon is everything but demure. He's a wild spirit wrapped up in skin. And he's doing what he's done for years, measuring the contours of those holes he finds for metaphor and flesh. He's using his tape measure and his ladder and his clipboard and he's measuring beyond what's secret and hidden there, revealing the true depth which is the human heart. And then he pours whatever he's built up inside of himself into these holes, illuminating them for all to behold.

And this is what an artist does. Fills up and empties out. And if you're a supreme filler-upper like Fat Leon, the deeper you dig, the more *something* you get. Filling up. Emptying out. That's how it's done. Thanks to Fat Leon's explosive example, now anyone can see, that's how it's done.

Types of Holes Fat Leon Excels At Measuring and Filling

• Naturally Occurring Holes. *To do with the warp and weft of this life of misery and wonder and the holes in the meanings we give.*

• Excavated Holes. *A wide interest in the holes excavated by others.*

• Reality Holes. *Same as Naturally Occurring Holes but the understanding deepens.*

• Metaphorical Holes. *The shingle hanging outside the door of Fat Leon's imagination says: Open for Business.*

• Character Holes. *This is where the heart of compassion comes into play, this is where Fat Leon does his speaking for others.*

• Holes Dug With Fingers. *An abiding curiosity. There is little that isn't looked at fully.*

• Holy Holes. *He doesn't shrink from these ones, either. Indeed, some of the most satisfying of Fat Leon's tales can be found in Holy Holes.*

• Hidey Holes. *Well, this is where we shove our own poor excuses into the sand around our buried heads.*

• Black Holes. *These are the holes of extinction. Handled by Fat Leon, not a bad thing because it's the extinction of the self. It's putting your own self aside. Fat Leon has said, "One enters other skins. To enter that skin you say to the character, 'Let me become you. Make me over. I do not exist. I do not matter in the slightest. But you do. Use me.'"*

Hole: A hollow place in a solid body, a deep place in a stream.

Amen.

Fat Leon would make a space where even darkness might thrive. Fat Woman, blubbery Ella Mae Hopkins, found out about that. A space above everything else. And around that space a trembling love was flickering, like it does around us all if we take the time to see, showering us with sparks from an eternal fire.

Fat Leon hauls his mammoth heart from the depths of his skinny/fat body and he's using it to rain those sparks down upon us. He's singeing us with his words. Such an artist to mine the hollows of this sorry time! Fat Leon is a literary book-thumping preacher. And he's exhorting us to go crazy, snap our boundaries, behold ourselves, delight and astonish in our lives.

People often ask Fat Leon, "Do you prefer measuring and filling your holes manually or mechanically? Do you camp out at them like it was an archeological dig? And how long does it take to convert these holes of yours into a spell of words?"

These sorts of questions come up. And questions about the kind of measuring tape he uses, and whether he prefers aluminum or wood ladders. And that clipboard that's strung around his neck at all times like a postmodern cross. What of that?

But what we really want to know is how he does it. How does he keep all that love and energy and happiness and pain frothing together like a perpetually boiled jam? And why do his words always taste so sweet?

We want to know why Fat Leon doesn't drown in his own fat self: "I don't have a self," Fat Leon repeats and repeats. Other times he'll tell us this: "It's a gift what I do with holes, the measuring and filling of them with words. I never ask where these things come from."

Ella Mae Hopkins was stuck in her blubber; she was drowning in her own fat self. She plainly needed saving. Some of us do, from time to time. It's true, some of us need saving from our own rutted selves. It took the love of Edward, Ella Mae's husband, to do *her* saving. He nailed shut her bedroom window and her bedroom door, and put in a small opening so he could slide in enough food to keep her going. *"I'm taking matters into my own hands,"* he told her. *"All I mean to do is whittle you down."*

We shoulder each other's burdens all the time and if we do it with love and good humour, we're secret heroes, like Edward. We jump out of our own skins, leaving them behind like the useless, dried up things they are, and we take action in the service of another.

Amen again.

Fat Leon's fatness is not the kind that gets stuck on itself, pound for pound, causing the helpless drowning that would be Ella Mae's fate without the fact and hope of Edward's love. Fat Leon's fatness is the golden goose that's shared around, feeding one and all. And those holes of his are questions, areas of worry and pain and deep, deep love that Fat Leon first measures then fills with his lightning quick words, giving view and comfort.

He tells us this of Ella Mae Hopkins: *She would make her wide flesh be everything, a lake of cream to drown in, a field of earth in which Ella Mae Hopkins and everybody like her, all the world's poor and miserable, might forever cuddle — cuddle and hide.*

One time Fat Leon made my acquaintance. This was during the *Shakespeare's Dog* years of the eighties. When I first beheld him, dressed all in white including the wispy hair and the crooked dazzling teeth, I was afraid, never having come across one so hugely alive. When he read from a book and that wild *something* of his exploded through his mouth, it was like hellfire and ecstasy and pure energy unleashed. And it wasn't even his own words he was reading. It was someone else's. About the shock that comes when finally, irrevocably, we understand the fact of our own mortality. About how this certain writer had placed her kitchen knives face down in the drawer; they were such a temptation in light of that awful reality.

We were a class of fourteen students in a university room no bigger than a spare bedroom. The late September rain ran in rivulets down the one window. Oh, it was a dreary gathering until Fat Leon read. There was just this one class for me. I'd left small children at home risking everything to be there. I was carrying around Alice Munro's famous phrase: Who do you think you are? I wore that phrase like a heavy black cloak and until that class I wore it in secret. Still, I knew there was this ember of *something* inside me, too, which is why I was shyly attending. And what happened when Fat Leon read, first another's words and then his own, and I watched him in the reading, yes the watching was part of it too, was that my flesh was unleashed and that ember in me ignited and a small blue flame began to burn.

Years later he called me up. Thousand and thousands of words later. "I've been following your work," he said. "You've been moving along." It must have been two a.m. where he was calling from.

"Yes," I said, "that's probably true." I'm finding my way. But for years I peered over the edges of those holes of yours, handing you shovels and ropes as required, straining to see the precise measurements you were taking, hoping to be present when you did the emptying out, the filling up, when your magic was unleashed. But somehow I was never there. And then I wandered off, following my own nose, and discovered that instead of holes, it was rivers that interested me more. Ebb, flow, currents, ferryboat rides . . .

This business of creating worlds with words: it's about not telling lies. You begin and you speak directly. You don't hide behind your words. You get equal billing with the words. It's a matched set. It's a combination but it's not locked.

Or, using Fat Leon's example, you say what you have to say, and then you move on. You leave the words, the created lives, and you ride your slow horse past them. With your love you let them go.

Best is when you leave them like Ella Mae Hopkins: *"Oh my life will shine. I will saw my logs and dream my dreams, knowing I am safe here. I am at peace and can know my heart's rest here."*

On a Leap Year Night in Havana, a Man in a White Suit Who Said He Was Leon Rooke

Barry Callaghan

At the centre of the dark stage in the courtyard there was a pin-hole of light. It widened into a white circle wherein a man with white hair who was wearing a white suit stood in the hole in the dark. He was lank and tall, gangly, what they call in tall tale country 'a long drink of water', which is what he was, a teller of tall tales rocking on the balls of his feet in the white light, warming up.

He flung his arms apart and yelled, "AAAAAAAAAAAAAAAAHHH-HHHHHH." Pause. Then again, "AAAAAAAAAAAHHHHHHHHHH." Pause. "I'm summoning the muse," he explained. "Okay, I think I've got her now. CHRISTIANS WELCOME! WIPE YOUR FEET!"

He shuffled his feet furiously. He reached into the dark as if he were scuffling with shadows.

Then he said: "There have been days when I have trod through the city without a bell around my neck, with no gun, and I have spoken with the tongue of sauciness, all as a prelude to my telling you a tale that was told to me in a dream."

He paused, cried WIPE YOUR FEET, and went on: "This tale is about a man with long hair, deep eyes, and a sweet glance, an old man who was a master of the difficult art of pottery, the art of blowing life into clay so that we might hold life in our hands and eat and drink from the crucible of life. In my dream about this man there were three dream catchers who spoke to me, and the first said he had decided not to employ the eighth letter of the alphabet, h, in telling me the tale."

"And wy?" I asked myself.

"And wy not?" I said. "You can see ow muc fun te story will be," a story wic I am now telling you, wic goes like tis:

Te pottery man's name was Noel.

E dressed simply. No one recalled earing im utter a single prase. E gave people e met corn meal and leaves of coca, and e went is own way, e fled all uman company, and worked furiously gatering clay, until one day te Mayor of te faraway town sent im is son to study. Te boy ran ome in terror, covered wit mud, trembling:

— Te Evil One, Te Evil One! e cried.

And told is fater tat e ad been seized by an enormous sadow in te clay tat was still wet from te ands of te potter, a sadow tat struggled to old on to im. Only te artist could set im free from tat grip and e did and tereafter te potter forsook all te townspeople, drawing a circle of silence around imself.

One day e made a serpent of clay tat wistled.

Anoter day e made te Dance of Deat.

And all te time it was said cries of pain came from is cabin.

Ten, one afternoon, aving gone to te river to wet is clay, e eard a flute and saw a man playing in solitude.

— Wo are you, e asked, playing alone out ere were no one can ear you?

— Wo are you, you look like my memory of myself?

— I am Ekoor Noel, te potter.

— I am Yrrab, te flute player.

— Were did you come from?

— I stepped from between te legs of a woman. And you?

— I come up from te clay country, all wet.

And it was the tall man in the white suit who, at that point in the story, rose up on his toes in the circle of white light and started thrashing the air. He leapt out of the light into the darkness and for a moment he seemed to be lost, darting around wildly, doing a dance, as if his bones were coming apart at the joints, but then he leapt back into the light, crying "CHRISTIANS ARE WELCOME," and be forewarned, the second dream catcher in my dream said he was no longer going to use the sixteenth letter of the alphabet, p, and so the man in the white suit hunched forward to report that the flute player had asked,

— Can you make me a clay ead of te woman I once loved?

And te master otter did, making a ead te size of a fist so te flautist could carry it wit im in is ocket.

Te astonised flautist said:

— Wy do you insist on staying ere alone? Solitary? You could recreate te dreams of all te men in te town.

— No. I was only able because of te sound of your flute. It soke to my longing.

— Wat longing?

— I feel an unutterable emtiness, a relentless flame burning. You can suffer and sing your grief on te flute but I see and I imagine beautiful tings and oter tan your beloved's ead, wic is still very crude because it is te clay of our clay, I can never create wat my eyes see, I can never do wat te river does, mirror te trees as tey actually are in teir cool clear dets. I do not ave colours tat reflect te ideas in my soul. I ave tried wit all te juices of te leaves to reroduce nature, but my work is always inert and lifeless. Tere is no one wo understands it, tat te clay is simly crude, so ow could I reresent a man tinking and ondering life's mysteries, ow migt I discover in is face te allor of sleelessness. My efforts are insignificant, my broter.

E led im into is wretced cabin were is aint colours were rubbed into te wall, and it was clear tat one colour was lacking, te colour of te sky at te our wen te sun, in robes of cloud, sinks from mortal sigt beind te mountain ranges leaving a suffused flow of rose-coloured ligt. Te red of te ainter was too glaring.

— Tis not te rigt colour, broter, tis is not te glow of tat very oly our.

— Tat's te colour only te Sun can roduce. Wy trouble yourself by attemting te imossible?

— I wis to do wat te Sun does, wat te day does tat follows te nigt, transforming te darkness, as te rainbow follows te blackness of te storm.

With his arms stretched toward the darkness around and the darkness above, the man in the white suit uttered a sound like the nasal staccato cry of a dying cattle beast, his words breaking down as he became more ecstatic, suddenly whirling on the spot inside the circle of white light, chanting AAAAAAAAAAAAAHHHHHHHHH, WIPE YOUR FEET, pleading that the muse not leave him: And the third dream catcher said the h was a comet whirling in the skies and the p was a stone angel fallen into the riverbed, but to end the story he would not employ the sixth letter of the alphabet, and so, without the f

— Were is te artist, asked te lautist?

E ad a rare seed, a rare tincture to give im.

Te artist decided to try one last time to colour is wall. E gatered leaves and vines to mix wit te seed and e began to rub tem into te wall, adding colours rom crused etals.

— Bring me blossoms o wysteria, e said to te lautist, wo soon returned wit te desired etals.

— Tis is not te rigt colour, broter, but maybe I can make do.

E began to rub te new colours into te wall wit intensity, trying to bring to ass wat e ad so long desired: to aint as it really was te landscae seen troug is narrow window. Ten e stoed. E lacked someting, one ting only, a tone, a colour wic e did not ave.

Quickly, e drew is blade and slit te skin o is and. As te blood surted, warm and red, e mixed it wit water rom a jar and beold, te colour. Overjoyed, e continued to lay in te colour were it was needed til e elt a surge o te oneness o everyting as is blood began to alt in staccato sort-circuits til e sank dead on is bed.

Te lautist saw im, blood gatered in a ool on te dirt loor, and te ainting on te wall, wat te artist ad seen te way e ad seen it, was done. Kissing te cold ace o is riend and weeing, e layed is lute at te eet o te artist, laying te oly ymn sacred to te sunset.

Te last rays o te sun tinctured te artist, is otter's tools, is aints, and ten dissolved into gray, te gray o te dead artist's lis. And e continued to lay is lute til nigt ell, one great lieless sadow covering a silent world.

Into which, as his time on stage shortened, the man in the white suit whispered the last words of his tall tale. He had ceased to wag his arms, ceased to shuffle, and the light he stood in slowly shrank. The darkness inexorably closed around him until there was only a pin-hole of light, and then there was nothing, a complete silence, a complete darkness. He was never seen again.

•   •   •

Over the months, after the fateful evening, there was much speculation: was the man in the white suit Leon Rooke himself, pretending he was an imposter, or — as some said — was he an apparition of the Russian novelist Mikhail Bulgakov, author of *The Master and Margarita*, or, are we to believe the First Secretary of the Embassy who insisted that he was not only present in the courtyard for the tall tale but immediately knew by the accent who the man in the white suit was: the Prime Minister, Jean Chrétien. Lending credence to this possibility is the fact that guests at the Embassy are daily confronted at the front door by a hand-lettered sign that has obviously suffered weather damage: WI E YOUR EET

•   •   •

There is a further, and more persuasive, explanation as to who the apparition in the white suit in Havana was, or more accurately, is (as great writers never die).

It is my contention that Leon Rooke is the reincarnation of another theatrical presence, a tall man who often appeared as the imposter of himself, dressed in white, as a ghost.

To the point, the dance of language never lies: the particular and idiosyncratic prose in which the man in the white suit told the tale of the potter is the exact language of *The Irish Masque at Court*, first printed in the Folio of 1616 on signatures Pppp 2 verso to 4 verso. This masque, also dealing with an ambassador in the audience, was performed in a courtyard similar to that in Havana. Beyond all doubt, Leon Rooke is the reincarnation of Ben Jonson:

The ambassador being set in expectation, out ran a fellow attired like a citizen.

Dennis, Donnell, Dermock, Patrick.

Dennis. For Chreesh's sake, phair ish te king? Phich ish he, an't be? Show me te shweet faish, quickly. By Got, o' my conshence, tish ish he! An tou be king Yamish, me name is Dennish; I sherve ty mayesty's own cashtermonger, be me trote, and cry peepsh and pomwatersh I'ty mayesty's shervice, 'tis five year now. An tou vilt not trush me now, cal up ty clark o' ty kitchen, be ant be shall give hish wort upon hish book, ish true.

Donnell. Ish it te fashion to beat te imbashators here, ant knock'em o' te heads phit te phoit stick?

Dermock. Ant make ter meshage run out at ter mouthsh before tey shpeak vit te king?

Dennis. Peash, Dermock, here ish te king.

Dermock. Phair ish te king?

Donnell. Phich ish te king?

Dennis. Tat ish te king.

Dermock. Ish tat te king? Got blesh him!

Dennis. Peash, ant take heet vat tou shay'sht, man.

Dermock. Chreesh blesh him, I shay. Phat reason I take heet for tat?

Donnell. Chreesh blesh ty shweet faish, king Yamish, and my mistresh' faish too: pre tee hear me now. I am come a great vay of miles to shee tee now, by my fait and trote, and graish o' Got.

Dennis. Phat ish te meaning o' tish, Donnell? Didsh tou not shay, a' Gotsh name, I should tell ty tale for tee? Ant entrait me come to te court, ant leave me vare at shix ant seven? By Got, ish true now.

Donnell. Yesh. But I tank Got I can tell my tale myshelf now I be here, I varrant tee: pre dee hear me, King Yamish.

Dennis. Pre dee hear me, King Yamish. I can tell tee better ten he.

Patrick. Pre dee hear neder noder on 'em; here'sh Dermock vill shpeak better ten eder oder on 'em.

Dermock. No, fait, shweet heart, tou liesht. Phatrick here ish te vesht man of hish tongue of all de four; pre tee now hear him.

Patrick. By Chreesh shave me, tou liesht. I have te vorsht tongue in te company at thy shervish. Vill shomebody shpeak?

Donnell. By my fait, I vill not.

Patrick. Speak Dennish, ten.

Dennis. If I speak, te divel take me! I vill give tee leave to cram my mout phit shamrocks and butter and vaytercreshes instead of pearsh and peepsh.

Patrick. If nobody vill shpeak, I vill shpeak . . .

. . . CHREESHENS VILLCOME!

THE INCOMPARABLE EXPERIENCE OF HEARING LEON ROOKE

ANNE MICHAELS

He begins like a freight train — or a preacher. He starts off slow and low and gradually, with impeccable timing, picks up speed and volume, expression and gesticulation. Most of us here tonight[1] have had the incomparable experience of hearing Leon Rooke read. My first time was in a crowded, smoky bar on Queen Street in Toronto, the second time in the bucolic outdoors of the Eden Mills Festival; the effect was the same. He's a preacher-tornado, antic in the pulpit, increasing in ferocity, depositing the preposterous but never incongruous details of his fiction with lethal precision. After the reading, initiates lean back in their chairs, exhilarated. Everyone else looks shell-shocked; they scan the room, mutely: what was that? Leon, with his liquid lope, resumes his seat, once again looking perfectly harmless, smiles benignly, as if nothing untoward has occurred. He's the professional subversive, the elegant assassin, the mad flame-thrower juggling dozens of flaming arrows around our heads. In his fiction he peels back the smooth skin of social convention, lets the wild darkness scream out, then closes up the wound. Each fiction is an act of kamikaze, a suicide mission, full-tilt into the mean chaos of life. The stories and the novels are dark, terrifyingly aggressive, possessed. Narrated with the bitter humour of the broken-hearted. Where does it hurt? Asks Dr. Rooke. Where we laugh. Where does it hurt? Everywhere. (While other writers might make you laugh until it hurts, Leon will hurt you until you laugh. His characters are often ornery, lost, cruel, rude, sometimes horrid company, always in compelling turmoil. They're battling misery, loss, self-loathing,

---

[1] Anne Michaels read this piece on the occasion of a tribute organized in honour of Leon Rooke by the Harbourfront Reading Series, Toronto, May, 2001.

searching for a scrap of human happiness. It's both their fortune and misfortune that they possess abundant appetites. They contain the energy, the exuberance, the hell-in-a-handbasket verve of madness, the desperate disappointment, and wild hope of near-defeat. Sometimes, the negative power of the bully. Therefore, in Rooke's fictional universe, the small moment of tenderness — when and if it comes — is explosive. Kindness has an effect. It is never taken for granted and sometimes when it occurs, we're shocked. It's as if the narrative suddenly shrieks to a halt and we can hear our own breathing. This eruption of compassion is all part of the master's plan: the extreme control, the heart-piercing, bone-splintering accuracy of the master magician who first saws us in half and then restores us, more whole than when we started. I'm reminded of a Buster Keaton sequence in which Keaton and the heroine are in dire distress, fighting frantically for their lives. The heroine is screaming, beside herself with panic, and driving stone-faced Keaton crazy. He takes her by the shoulders and shakes her, shakes her hard. Then suddenly he stops, looks penetratingly at her, kisses her. Then just as suddenly starts shaking her again. It's a wonderful moment of recognition: the screaming woman is also his beloved. It's like the cartoon moment in which the character, after being chased over the cliff, pauses in mid-air, suspended just long enough to recognize that he's about to plummet. And sometimes, that's just what grace is like. The smallest moment of tenderness or innocent humour, just a breath, almost an accident, in a tide of disability, failure, grief. Extraordinary, rare; ordinary, everywhere. (Think of the last few pages of the masterful story "Muffins.") Are Leon Rooke's characters the damned or the saved? His tornado fiction strikes again, pulling up everything human in its way, leaving everything human in its wake.

Thank you Leon Rooke, for over thirty years of fiction. Thank you for your cool eye, and your very courageous heart.

CHAPTER TWO

CRITICAL CONTEXT

Rooke's Move

RUSSELL BROWN

I

LEARNING ABOUT LEON

FRIDAY AFTERNOON, EARLY JANUARY, 1979

Clark Blaise is at the University of Toronto's Scarborough Campus, reading selections from his forthcoming novel, *Lunar Attractions*. Readings on our campus usually attract twenty or so, but today there are only six in the audience: three students and three faculty members. Maybe Friday afternoon is a bad time; maybe we've scheduled this reading too soon after the Christmas break; maybe my students don't know who Clark Blaise is, even if the critics do; maybe at fifteen below it's just too damn cold outside to care about literature.

At lunch, Blaise had mentioned feeling anxious about his new book's reception and as I listen now it occurs to me that I reviewed his first book, *A North American Education*, in *Canadian Literature*. That short story collection had impressed me but its dark moody voice had bothered me too. Given the acclaim that *A North American Education* received, my mixed review may well have been the only one with some reservations. There has only been one further book of stories since, but in just six years Blaise has become part of the Canadian literary establishment, one of our best-known writers. As he reads I find myself thinking about how and why some authors gain readerships while others do not. With time running out, Blaise flips through the pages of his novel as if searching for something, then reads a bizarre and chilling passage, one that feels like an assault on his listeners: the protagonist caught in a sexual initiation gone horribly wrong, the seductive woman a transvestite. The whole scene has the underwater quality of nightmare and the students move uneasily. "That wasn't *in* the novel originally," Blaise will say later. "I dreamed it one night after I thought I was through — and *then* I knew I had to put it in."

Trying to make conversation at lunch, I had asked Blaise about *Best Canadian Stories*, the annual series that he and John Metcalf are now editing. "Any new discoveries?" He doesn't have to think about the question. He smiles and says immediately, "Leon Rooke." After a moment, he adds "I reviewed his new book, *The Love Parlour*, for *Canadian Literature* — a terrific group of stories. For *Best Canadian* our biggest problem was deciding which of his pieces to use. Every time Metcalf and I thought we knew, he would send us another."

II

READING ROOKE'S WRITING

MARCH 1979

In my mail I find a manila envelope with a Victoria postmark. In the letter inside Leon Rooke thanks me for my interest and says that he has enclosed a story for *Descant*'s consideration, but that we didn't have to use it, that it was probably too long for a literary magazine, and that in any case it was "told in a pernicious idiom not guaranteed to win me instant friendship." If we rejected it, he wrote, he would send us another, but this was all he had on hand at the moment.

That story — "Mama Tuddi Done Over" — was the first thing by Rooke that I had read, and I wasn't immediately sure what to make of it. Its dialect and setting sounded like that of the black American South. The South as seen by V.S. Naipaul, I am tempted to add. That's not quite right, but there is an odd "island" feel to the story.

> The fact is Mama Tuddi have sunk so deep in thought she have failed to observe that the audience is now getting up and filing by the box which hold the remains of Reno Brown, the lid lifted and held up by a red broomstick, the folks who have already had their last look at the boy now crowding around Mrs. Brown to

tell her what their last look at Reno have meant to them, telling her
that he look so peaceful you would swear he was only sleeping,
telling her they never seen him looking so good, he the prettiest
child they ever sat eyes on, he is safe at rest in the arms of the
Lord — hugging her and patting her hands and sort of being
swept along until they come to Mama Tuddi where they bend
their knees and take a close look at her fox tail with the head of
the fox still on it and at her two front teeth which they know now
is real and at her dyed-orange hair and even at her shiny black
purse which have the word Double Ola in big letters on the flap
— then to slouch on by and return to their seats or their standing
place and join in on another verse of 'The Old Rugged Cross',
which is the cross Jesus and Reno and everyone in this room have
to wear until they exchange it for a crown. (21)[1]

Maybe it's a literary dialect, maybe its region is a region of the mind.
Still it pulls me through the story like a boy hauling in a trout, gently at
first, till the hook is set, and then *Wham!* The *Wham!* of this story comes in
the funeral oratory, the speeches that show what this language can *do*.
First Mama Tuddi speaks her piece:

This heah be Reno Brown who adore his mama and his poppa and
who love LeRoy and all you folks. He dead now but Mama Tuddi say
he not dead, he live forever in the Book and in the Mama Tuddi Show.
I now rename this child, I rename him Calvary, for Mama Tuddi can
do what she please and it please me to name him that. Now I say
adios to Reno Brown renamed Calvary from this moment on. (25)

After quite a bit more of this speech, in comes Preacher Teebone, wear-
ing his "expression of doom," to preach the closing sermon and to go Mama
Tuddi one better, catching the crowd up in his flowing rhetoric. The sermon
reaches a crescendo and then it dissolves into song, and that's it for the story
— or almost. There's an ending that I don't quite understand. According to

---

[1] Leon Rooke, "Mama Tuddi Done Over" appeared in *Descant*, Nos. 25-26 (1979), and was
reprinted in *Death Suite* (Toronto: ECW Press, 1981), 9-42. All further references to this work
appear in the text.

the last paragraph Mama Tuddi, although initially antagonistic to the preacher, has, as she listened to his sermon, had an experience at once sensual and transcendent. She is ready to return to the everyday world with a new vision. Though I reread the story, I'm not sure I can say why.

Since I'm new to the *Descant* editorial group I pass "Mama Tuddi" on to another editor for a second opinion. Three months later it's the lead story in Number 25-26, a special prose issue. Within weeks of its appearance we hear that Metcalf and Blaise think they want it for the next volume of *Best Canadian Stories* — but that they are hesitating because of its length. A few weeks after that Stanley Elkin writes to Karen Mulhallen, editor-in-chief, saying that Rooke's story has been selected for his 1980 Houghton-Mifflin volume of best American stories. Karen later swears that after we published "Mama Tuddi" the stories submitted to *Descant* started getting better.

III

RUNNING WITH ROOKE

JANUARY, 1980

A letter from Sam Solecki asks me to review *Cry Evil*, Rooke's new collection of short stories, for the *Canadian Forum*. From never having heard of Rooke a year ago, I now seem to be encountering his name everywhere. The previous week I'd attended a conference at York University sponsored by the new journal *Essays on Canadian Writing* — on Hugh Hood's fiction. Metcalf was there, and afterwards in the bar he and west coast writer John Mills spent a large part of the evening talking about Rooke and his stories. Metcalf had edited *The Love Parlour* for Oberon — the first of Rooke's books to be published in Canada. "I just called up Leon out of the blue, and I said, 'I want to publish a book of your stories.' There was a long pause and then he said, 'Tell me again who this is.'"

It's been a year since I first heard about Rooke, and I still haven't read anything but "Mama Tuddi." So I tell Sam I'll do the review, figuring it's time for me to find out more about this writer. Over the next four days I read his collections of short stories in chronological order: *Last One Home Sleeps in the Yellow Bed* from 1968, *The Broad Back of the Angel* and *The Love Parlour*, both published in 1977, and then *Cry Evil*. There is another book, *Vault*, a novella published in 1973 by a small press, that I can't locate. There have also, according to a blurb on *The Broad Back of the Angel*, been some plays — "seen in Toronto, New York, and other major cities." With no further clues, I have only these four books to go on.

As I read through the collections, I see that "Mama Tuddi" had not prepared me for Rooke's range and technical virtuosity. I am especially taken with the first book, and moved by the stories in it. Even at this distance it seems a stunning debut. The opening piece has a sensuality that's rare in this age of explicitness. It opens provocatively, and builds from there.

> "Did you ever walk through an ice house in the summer," I say, "when it was hot as hell?"
>
> "No," she says, "I never," and cuffs a lock of hair from her forehead and wiggles the toes of one foot under the instep of her second and places her palms on her knees and leans into them, licks her lips and watches me watching her tongue. She grins. Confessing her lie, she lifts a hand and places it over her face and looks out at me through the slits of her fingers.[2]

Connie Rooke later tells me that North Carolina's arch-conservative U.S. Senator Jesse Helms was so offended by this story when it was published in *The Carolina Quarterly* that he went on radio protesting the misuse of public funds to print a tale about "a couple *fornicating* in an ice house!"

Fire *and* ice, I think, because the long last piece in the book is "Brush Fire," a story that makes the experience it recounts (army reserves working on a fire-line in Alaska) so vivid that I suspect it may be based on personal experience. But for all its realism, it takes on the quality of parable in the way really good novellas sometimes do. Its fiery destruction is an apt backdrop for the internal fires that burn in its characters, and the suicide at its centre seems somehow a heroic act in a harrowing world. The American South comes across as a kind of hell, but it also seems only an

---

[2] Leon Rooke, "The Ice House Gang," in *Last One Home Sleeps in the Yellow Bed* (Baton Rouge: Louisiana State Univ. Press, 1968). 3-4. All further references to this work appear in the text.

example of the way we live today — no worse nor better than other places. The story ends with Gode, a character who meets all the offences that the army has to offer him with haughty indolence, drifting off to sleep and beginning to talk obsessively — almost incoherently. Like "Mama Tuddi," this narrative ends by dissolving into a pure flow of language.

> Isn't it of basic significance that, say, art is so abstract today and that they the artists will say no man it's not abstract at all that's just the way it is man — life. And you're looking yes sir at a mirror? Or is that only a fragment of the grand play, the royal dream, the big hoax, the "all-right-America-you-might-not-make-it-in-practice-but-BY-GOD-YOU-GOT-IT-IN-PRINCIPLE!" . . . take this artist I know, Hite; all his canvases show muddled heads and all his sculpture looks like some pig freed from a medieval torture rack. Why? I ask him. Because, he says, man, I'm trying to wiggle into a meaning. Trying to shake that old core, loose, man, I mean that vicious core. And because I'm in pain, man. Because I don't know who told me but the boat left this morning and, man, I AIN'T ON IT AND I DON'T KNOW HOW TO SWIM! Because, man, I'm standing on the pier alone. I'm standing on it AND I'M ALONE! And not only alone but bored too and restless and I'm this way when I wake up and when I go to bed and whether I'm with my best girl or my ninety-seven-year-old aunt. Because my dinner tastes like cold fish and because there's some of yesterday's in my craw and I want to throw up, Jack. Because I'm lonely and I don't care about nobody. And if I work twenty hours a day getting a man's wrist out of a piece of wood or metal to look just so it ain't because I love art or man that much and you can believe that, cat.[3]

The story is also like "Mama Tuddi" in that it doesn't come into focus in the end. But it is (also) all the more fascinating for being elusive. Gode is clearly a liberating trickster but, as he patiently sharpens the shovel with which his workmate finally kills himself, is he saviour or diabolic tempter?

One image remains with me long after I finish this story.

---

[3] Leon Rooke, "Brush Fire," in *Last One Home Sleeps in the Yellow Bed*, 177-78. All further references to this work appear in the text.

> There in front of me was the twin corpse — or what was left of
> them — of two caribou. The fire had burned all the fur and flesh
> away and their bones lay shining in the moonlight in a bed of
> ashes. Obviously they had been fighting, their antlers had
> locked, and they had been unable to free themselves, or escape
> it, when the fire came raging down around them. (150)

I recall that passage often as I read Rooke's next three books. It
embodies the locked-in confrontation in so many of the stories. But when
I try to describe these encounters in my review, I feel I'm reducing the
tales in a way that leaves me dissatisfied. To get around that I try talking
about these in terms of the use of dialogue, and then I think of using the
idea of "dialectic" instead. Perhaps an old-fashioned phrase like "war of
the sexes" would be more helpful, since so many of these struggles are
male-female — but that phrase *really* oversimplifies. I'm *still* moving
around this question as I write now, but ready to try again. Perhaps I
should have put it thus: in most of these stories there are only two char-
acters that matter, and there is an intense emotional pitch, frequently a
savage quality, to their interactions. And *all* the rest — plot, setting, even
the other characters — serve as background against which these two
characters come together in language. Everything but these characters
functions like the flames in "Brush Fire" — to lend urgency to these inter-
actions, and to hem in the main characters, to illuminate them with a stark
backlight.

The story I turn back to as I think about this is "No Whistle Slow," in
Rooke's second book, *The Broad Back of the Angel*, which, according to a
note at its end, was written "in collaboration with Constance Rooke." In
it a university teacher of English called Dr. Conly starts her morning by
both thinking about how much she loves her husband and making a list
of the reasons she hates him. Later she conducts a seminar with her stu-
dents and lunches with a friend. In an afternoon seminar, she suddenly
loses control and, like so many other Rooke characters, falls into logor-
rhoea, drifting from a discussion of Wright Morris' fiction to talking about
her life with her husband. In the evening she and her husband attend a
party given by friends, and the two of them engage in a dialogue (a
debate? *dialectic*?) about fictional situations, all of which are, of course,
versions of their own situation.

This summary suggests the structure of the story, a characteristically loose one, as well as the conflict embodied in it. But what's important lies elsewhere. The impact of this story comes from the *way* it is told — from the technical facility that is especially striking in its quick and easy movement between interior voice and external voices. And it also comes from what the story leaves unstated but implied. Which is much, but once more I'm having trouble saying exactly *what*. Clark Blaise's stories conclude with what might be called "anti-epiphanies" because they refuse to explain, but instead evoke what Blaise has called "the hint of unfathomable complexity."[4] Maybe one has to understand Rooke's tales in that way too.

There's a nine-year gap in time between Rooke's first book, *Last One Home . . .* , and the second, *The Broad Back of the Angel*. I wonder what was happening during those years for a writer who now seems so prolific. Rooke as playwright? A period of writer's block? A time of further apprenticeship and consolidation? "Rooke keeps a lot of things going simultaneously," Geoff Hancock will later tell me. "When one piece is not developing right, he puts it away and works on another. That means he may not send out anything for a while and then may finish a lot of stories at once." Connie Rooke will explain it this way: "Leon's a compulsive rewriter, a constant reviser. Even on galleys, even on page proofs. He doesn't find it easy to turn things loose." Whatever it is, the effect of these three books of stories suddenly appearing in close succession, followed soon after by the short novel, *Fat Woman*, is to give to Rooke's recent career the quality that characterizes the individual stories — a sense of incredible energy arising out of the steady flow of language. As I work on my *Forum* review I look back at Blaise's review of *The Love Parlour* for *Canadian Literature*. Other writers, Blaise suggests, are part of "the old storyland limited," a picturesque train that stops at every small village; Rooke is the Twentieth Century Express, roaring into town, unstoppable in impetus.[5] That train metaphor comes across with more intensity than it did when I first read that review. I'm now carrying a mental picture of a machine-like Rooke, rushing down

---

[4] Clark Blaise, "Author's Introduction," *New Canadian Writing 1968* (Toronto: Clarke, Irwin, 1968), 68.

[5] Clark Blaise, "At Home in All Voices," rev. of *The Love Parlour* and *The Broad Back of the Angel*, by Leon Rooke, *Canadian Literature*, No. 81 (Summer 1979), 118.

shiny metal tracks, unsuspecting readers not realizing they are about to be flattened by all those words, all that energy, all that output.

My deadline is approaching, and I still haven't given final shape to my review of *Cry Evil*, partly because I want to write an ambitious piece, one that could serve as an introduction to Rooke for those readers who, like me until recently, still haven't caught up with his work. But because there is so much diversity, to generalize about his stories in the space of a review is difficult. Especially when each piece of fiction seems like a small *tour de force*. I think about mentioning Rooke's ability to get inside a woman's mind in some of his stories (the best job I've seen any male writer of his generation do), and how that seems to be related to his ability to make dialect stories work, which in turn points back to his overall ability in the use of voice. "At home in all voices," is what Blaise has already called *his* review.

That phrase evokes an image of a ventriloquial Rooke but it also makes me think of Eliot's original title for *The Waste Land*, the line he borrowed from Dickens: "He do the police in different voices." Voice, the great twentieth-century preoccupation, *is* certainly at the centre of Rooke's writing. And yet these stories also seem to inhabit the spaces between the speakers, between their speeches. None of this goes into the review. Instead I write:

> Rooke began publishing in the early sixties, hooked on the sound and flow of language for its own sake in a way that remains identifiably Southern, but since then he has moved on in his writing as well as in his locale. Without relinquishing that original feeling for the power of language, Rooke has now assimilated other traditions and heard other voices; he has responded to newer landscapes and gone on to master new techniques. In fact, of late he begins to give the appearance of one who is engaged in an exploration of the whole range of the contemporary story.
>
> Despite Rooke's versatility, there is something about all his fiction that remains identifiable, characteristic, and uniquely personal. Made out of internalized perceptions, his stories are typically ones in which the central character's mind becomes a reflecting pool through which we glimpse the external world. In the course of the story a few stones are dropped in, and as their ripples spread, the images we thought we had recognized reorganize themselves into intriguing new patterns which coalesce, vanish, and reappear,

before giving way to something else again. The experience of stories such as these is perhaps closest to that of a particularly vivid dream: one is drawn into a dislocating scene, undergoes a puzzling but compelling experience, and is released somehow more troubled than enlightened.[6]

I decide to include some reservations I have about *Cry Evil* — that there may be a little too much self-consciousness in the book, too much of the shadow of John Barth falling over the pages, that I miss some of the joys of narrative of Rooke's earlier fiction. In the end, however, I know I have to qualify this objection:

Perhaps by emphasizing this aspect of these stories I have somewhat distorted *Cry Evil*. Rooke's experiments with technique are never so purely technical as Barth's were, or as others have been since, and there is still emotion embedded in these stories, still human compulsions and neuroses which lie under the words to trouble and intrigue us. There are, after all, depths that wit and cleverness do not sound and Rooke seems to be a writer who cannot but choose to remind us of those depths, even in stories as ingenious as these newest ones.

IV

SORTING OUT THE STORIES

APRIL 1980

I stop at Oxford University Press with some copies of material for an anthology of Canadian Literature that Donna Bennett and I are editing. While there I tell Bill Toye that I think we should include a story by Leon Rooke.

"Who is Leon Rooke?" he says.

---

[6] Russell M. Brown, "Experiment and Compulsion," rev. of *Cry Evil*, by Leon Rooke, *The Canadian Forum*, Aug. 1980, 36. All further references to this work appear in the text.

A week later Toye calls us at home. "That Rooke fellow — Frank Davey has been telling me about him. Frank thinks he should have an entry in the new *Oxford Companion to Canadian Literature*."

I find it hard to choose a Rooke story for the anthology. Drawn back to the *Yellow Bed* volume, I tentatively select "When All the Swimmers Have Gone Home from the Beach." It's beautifully crafted but I'm not happy with the choice: it's an early story, written before he came to Canada, and somewhat unrepresentative. "Mama Tuddi" doesn't feel right either; and anyway, for an anthology it really *is* too long. The following week I encounter Jack David and Robert Lecker at the ACUTE meeting in Montreal; they are there to promote their new press, ECW, which specializes in Canadian literary criticism and research tools. We've hardly begun to talk when Robert asks, "What do you *really* think of Leon Rooke's stories?" Robert is never one to beat around the bush, and it seems to me that he and Jack have been busy for the last while trying to identify all the writers in the emerging Canadian canon. "Think he'll be the next major Canadian short story writer?" While Robert waits for an answer, Jack, as always the more patient and methodical of the two, explains that Metcalf has passed them the manuscript of Rooke's newest collection of stories, and they are trying to make up their mind about publishing it.

Back in Toronto I ask Jack if I can look at the manuscript. I like it immensely — even more than Rooke's previous collections. "Mama Tuddi Done Over" is the lead story, and it reads particularly well in context with these other stories. But one story in particular fascinates me — "Sixteen-year-old Susan March Confesses to the Innocent Murder of All the Devious Strangers Who Would Drag Her Down." In it Rooke has pared away until absolutely nothing is left but voice — and the voices that can be heard within that voice.

> Mr. Reeves I know it's crazy and absurd and out of the question even but I declare myself I yearn I ache I love you Mr. Reeves for god's sake don't let me keep sitting here too fragile in this instance even to remove my eyes from your face O tell me what I should do how I might give myself help me Mr. Reeves because this has never happened to me with those others I shall show you in our lake for I am my father's virgin and have waited here for you but of course it probably happens to you all the time

because you're so perfect women can't help themselves O say something

Mr. Reeves I said and

Lovely tea he said Daddy

though how did I hear for I was dancing all around the room even as I sat brittle and moist with sweat and apprehension in my mother's Queen Elizabeth chair without a hair out of place or a smudge any place and nothing to do with him Daddy until we could circumvent mother's stern presence across the room and advance towards each other over the Persian floor and take each other in our arms.

O crumple me Mr. Reeves I said almost a scream I wanted this so much O melt me within your

but wait Daddy what were they saying my mother and Mr. Reeves that day that hour in our quiet house O what a wasting of time and cruel that time was[7]

This story just rolls along like a wave waiting for a shore to come crashing down on, and when I finish I know my choice has been made. Bill Toye calls the evening after I drop a copy off at the press. "What a fascinating writer this Rooke is," he says.

The "Susan March" story has been published before (in *Wascana Review*), but several others in the ECW manuscript have not, so I call Rooke in Victoria and ask him about their availability for *Descant*. We agree on one, but he says he's revising the version I have: he'll send me the revision. Two weeks later a completely different story arrives. The one I was interested in, his letter explains, is going into a special issue of *Canadian Fiction Magazine* that will feature his work. "It's funny how some people have a year, isn't it?" says Karen Mulhallen when I tell her. "This has been Rooke's year."

---

[7] Leon Rooke, "Sixteen-year-old Susan March Confesses to the Innocent Murder of All the Devious Strangers Who Would Drag Her Down," in *Death Suite* (Downsview, Ont: ECW, 1981), 59-60.

V

LISTENING TO LEON

NOVEMBER, 1980

I'm at another reading on the Scarborough Campus, but this time it's just before the Christmas holidays rather than just after. Maybe timing makes all the difference because none of our students have ever heard of Leon Rooke but a good number come anyway. The evening before, Leon and Connie had had dinner with us, and I got to meet them at last. Rooke tells stories over dinner at least as well as he writes them, but is surprisingly soft-spoken, even seems shy at times. Eli and Ann Mandel, who also came, talked more than he did. Donna found herself feeling so relaxed around the Rookes that she told some of her Texan stories. Rooke is a large man with the kind of bushy white hair that calls up punning descriptions like "leonine." He is older than I had been picturing. I had known he had to be but back when I'd asked Clark Blaise — almost two years ago now — about new discoveries, I'd been thinking of young writers, as though only young writers could be just getting discovered.

The next day, at the Scarborough reading, it is my students who are quiet, not Leon. Nothing from the night before had given me any hint of the kind of reader Rooke will turn out to be. Listening to him read is truly a remarkable experience, one of the most remarkable I've ever had. Though he remains soft-spoken when he pauses to talk about his stories, whenever he reads from them he seems possessed by them: it is as if he himself has his real existence in the language on the page.

He not only reads, he sings sometimes (the next night, reading at Harbourfront, he danced as well), and he shouts, and he chants, and, yes, he speaks the different parts in different voices. I think of Plato's *Ion*, with all that divine magnetism called down from on high, its current flowing through the rhapsode, the reciter of the text, and into his audience. When he reads Rooke no longer seems to be the author of his words. They seem to have picked him out as their means of getting here. When the reading is over the students, who usually ask a lot of questions, are silent. When one finally speaks, she says, "We're stunned." So, I think, am I.

Later that night, in my creative writing class, we continue a discussion of voice that we had begun the week before. But I find our terms of reference have changed. These students were at the reading and they now understand literary voice in a way they had not previously. I can tell that something has happened for them; I can see that they just *know*.

Three months after the Rookes' visit to Toronto, I find myself in Victoria, out there for a job interview, and sitting in the Empress Hotel bar drinking beer with Connie and listening to her talk about Leon as a performer of his work. "You know," she says, "the first time I ever saw him was at a reading in Chapel Hill, and the way he read just knocked me over. Who *was* this man, I thought, who could get into a woman's head that way, who could so catch a woman's voice?"

VI

FULL STOPS AND STRANGE LOOPS

FEBRUARY, 1981

After a word-filled day at the University of Victoria, engaged in my own acts of language-based self-invention, and talking to people in the English department about their Canadian literature program, and reading them a paper I've written on crossing borders in Canadian fiction, I spend a quieter evening drinking and talking with Leon and Connie. Then that's followed by a late dinner and more talk, now with Connie and some of her colleagues from Victoria, then I have that later drink with Connie back at the Empress, where we talk some more. "By the way," she tells me, "Leon's revising 'Susan March' again. He'll send you a new version soon."

It's the early evening at the Rookes' home that stands out in my memory. They live in a big house on a hill and looks out over the water. It's peaceful, a comfortable place to sit and talk. Before I'd met them, Eli Mandel had said, "Oh, you'll *like* the Rookes." And I find that I do.

It's late that night when I finally go to bed, after one a.m. which means it's four a.m. for me because I'm still running on a Toronto clock. At four-thirty — that's B.C. time — I'm wide awake again: my body knows it's seven-thirty in Toronto, the time I usually get up. I lie in the darkness thinking I want to write about Rooke, thinking I know what I want to say. I don't want to write another critical essay, that doesn't seem the right way to talk about Rooke. I want to talk not so much about the stories ("There are no themes to talk about really," Connie had said to me earlier that evening. "All you can *ever* talk about is that control of voice") but about Rooke's *presence* in Canada, about the impact he has had on the rest of us and about how even though he'd immigrated to Canada in the late sixties (Rooke is vague on the exact year) it's only now that we've suddenly became aware of him.

When I'd visited for dinner Rooke had not seemed the intensely compulsive personality his writing would lead one to expect. Maybe there are no trains bearing down after all. Even the blues records he put on the stereo didn't break the quiet mood. While Connie changed for dinner, Leon, who has now taken Blaise's place as co-editor for *Best Canadian Stories*, talked about the experience of reading through all the literary magazines in Canada, and about his having made his selections for the year, and about choosing some from *Descant*. I could see that things had come full circle in the course of two years in a way that appealed to me. "Strange loops" is a phrase that Mandel has, after reading *Gödel, Escher, Bach*, become fond of. "Strange loops" is what he would say now if he were here.

So I sip my Scotch and lean back, watching Leon sitting across the room sipping his. "Well," I say to him, savouring the question, and the closure it offers. "Any new discoveries?"

VII

'AND THEN': A SORT OF EPILOGUE

JULY, 1981

Jack David came by last night to borrow the dust jacket of my copy of *Last One Home Sleeps in a Yellow Bed*, something to do with a promotion for *Death Suite*, the book by Rooke that they're publishing. He tells me that ECW has bought out the remaining stock of that original LSU Press book, but that the copies are all stuck at customs — they can't come across the border because of some foul-up in the paperwork.

Paperwork and words. The piece I'm writing on Rooke is different from anything I've tried before, and I sit in my office today rewriting it completely for the third time. The *Canadian Fiction Magazine* special on Rooke that I'd originally thought I was writing it for has been postponed twice. I'm behind on four other deadlines. There's a mail strike, which makes most of them irrelevant.

Words and paperwork. It seems my life and those of my friends and colleagues have come to be made of such things. There are page proofs for the anthology on my desk begging to be read. Next to them are the galleys of the "Crossing Borders" piece, which will now be an article for *Essays on Canadian Writing*. No Rooke in that essay, but those other border-crossers of his generation: Blaise, and Joyce Carol Oates, and Robert Kroetsch. In the middle of my desk, among these other pieces of paper, are the pages of my typescript on Rooke, covered once more with pencil marks.

But Rooke's books can't cross the border and the lack of mail threatens to leave us not only without paperwork but without that flow of words we've built our lives around, and built our worlds around. It's a stagnant moment in the middle of the year. As I sit trying to think how to end the Rooke piece, I remember a Tuesday night the previous March. *Canadian Fiction Magazine* celebrated its tenth anniversary with a reading at Harbourfront, the readers Metcalf and Rooke. Metcalf read from *General Ludd*, a book he had recently published with ECW press. It had been a funny selection — about Canada Council funding and open plan house renovations — and it had been well-received by the audience, who were mostly in on its in-jokes. After a break Rooke mounted the low stage and leaned his large body over the podium the way a man might drape a coat over the back of a chair. He tipped the podium forward and stood there surveying us. "There's a piece I published in *Descant*," he said, "that I'd like to read from. The whole thing is too long, but I'll read the conclusion, which is mostly a sermon."

As he reads from "Mama Tuddi," not just his voice but his manner and his whole body imitate the preacher Teebone.

> HOW MANY OF YOU FOLKS BEEN TO THE RIVER?
> "We been there, preacher!"

HOW MANY OF YOU POOR SINNERS HAVE BEEN TO THE RIVER?
  "The river, amen!"(41)

Rooke's right arm comes up in the air as if reaching for something —
heaven, perhaps. His face grows red; his white hair sticks out and falls
down over his face; he grows shiny with sweat as his voice reaches out
to us. It is like being present at a church service and, although Rooke reads
out the congregation's lines too ("Save us, preacher"), I feel that there are
those around me who wouldn't mind throwing in a few extra *Amens* as
we listen. Maybe one or two of us do. Leon begins to shout now, his voice
growing more intense, rhapsodic. I feel a kind of movement in my gut,
so intense is the effect. Then I remember that that's what Mama Tuddi
felt in the end of the story, in that conclusion that had puzzled me.

> Something crawls over Mama Tuddi's skin, first up her legs and
> over her knees then wrapping her thighs and hips and finally set-
> tling like a feathery waked-up thing that thinks to play possum in
> her lap. (39)

Rooke rocks back and forth with that right hand still reaching, that voice
still reaching. Then the sermon's over. As he quietly reads that last para-
graph of the story I can't think why it seemed hard to understand before.
  Rooke stands silent, his face covered with perspiration. Then he
breaks into a large smile and leans way over the podium to us, the North
Carolina accent strong.
  "I sure do like the chance to preach," he says.

THE PERFORMING ARTIST

KENT THOMPSON

When you think of Leon Rooke at work, it is best to think of him as a performance artist. Certainly the notion is inescapable if you see him give a public reading, which is less a reading than a dramatization. No hiding behind the podium, head down, for Rooke. No — he is all across the platform, eating up the space, taller than tall in his high-heeled boots, white hair flying, a country preacher on the prowl for souls. He means that, too — which may come as something of a surprise.

But the performance begins at the keyboard, noodling about with phrases and themes — like a jazz pianist, except that Rooke's keyboard is the word processor. The left hand carries the tradition while the right hand plays the always surprising and frequently stunning variations on common ideas or casual phrases — as with "Want to Play House?" which is one of the finest stories in his recent, excellent collection entitled *Who Do You Love?*

Performance comes naturally to Rooke, although the form it now takes is fairly new. His early plays — at least those available to me — are indeed variations on themes and voices, but they lack the disturbing resonance that he develops in his fiction. For example, his play *The Suicide Club* is a variation on a theme from Sartre's *No Exit;* and his *Sword Play* is an extended riff on the peculiarly British ability to be polite and rude in the same phrase, the same breath. It was the sort of activity that might be easily noticed in Victoria, British Columbia, where Rooke was then living. Professional Brits, especially those living abroad, can be quite adept at this sort of nastiness.

But his best voices are found in his prose performances, especially in those fictions that use the voices of his ancestral American South: the voices of the dirt back roads of North Carolina, near the Virginia border.

Less successful, but sometimes impressive, are those performances that rely chiefly on cleverness. And make no mistake about it: Rooke is a very clever man, a very intelligent writer, and very well-educated. His characters, however, usually possess only two of those traits. Like country musicians, they are clever and intelligent — but rarely formally educated.

Rooke's own cleverness (and his education) are evident in the five-finger exercises in *Shakespeare's Dog*, the novel for which he won the Governor General's Literary Award for fiction in 1983. Probably the least successful of his three novels, it tells the story of Will Shakespeare in Stratford from the point of view of his pet dog. What saves the novel from mere cuteness, however, is the recurring interest in original sin, which Rooke shares with Shakespeare. Innocent animal lust is examined in terms of carnal knowledge, which dog and master share. The clever idea in Rooke's hands becomes something more.

And there are examples of Rooke's cleverness and learning in *Who Do You Love?* as well. Some of the stories are very close to mere showing off — "Art," for example, and "Typical Day in a Desirable Woman's Life." "Art" is a story of visual intertextuality — doesn't that sound grand? — in which a fellow purchases some flowers and a cow out of a painting and takes them home to his wife. It is soon evident that the man and the woman are also participants in a work of art (oh, aren't we all? — viewer and viewed alike!), and, alas, the woman hasn't been very durably painted ("why couldn't we have been done in oil," the husband bemoans [43]), and when she spills her drink on herself she begins to dissolve. The story is a crumb thrown to the postmodernist theorists in the universities, and was quickly gobbled up. The story is included in a recently published sampler of postmodernist Canadian fiction, *Likely Stories*, edited by Professor Linda Hutcheon and George Bowering. It is, for Rooke, a very weak story, but even here his ear for the woeful human voice is touchingly exact. The wife's confession to her husband begins, "I am so sorry, she said. I am so sorry. She said that over and over" (42). In Rooke, characterization is always likely to triumph over idea.

Equally clever is his little story for the feminists, "Typical Day in a Desirable Woman's Life," in which the male narrator manages to convince the woman that he is thinking just as she insists he must think — but at the same time, he is privately admiring her lovely body. Even the casual reader might think that the narrator has achieved political correctness. He has agreed with her with such intensity and imagination that she believes that she can fly. Amazing. Her satisfaction takes a familiar form: "Are we past that little quarrel now? she said. Have I enlightened you even a little bit? I am totally enlightened, I said. I am a completely new guy"(111).

Where have we heard these tones before? Rooke can be a *wickedly* clever writer. Shakespeare's dog would have recognized his master turning out some sonnets to get in the lovely lady's pants. Oh, all right: *somebody's* pants.

But, in Gulley Jimson's immortal phrase, this kind of cleverness is just "farting Annie Laurie through a keyhole" — amazing perhaps, and certainly clever, but not art. Empty virtuosity. Much much better is "The People in the Trees," where the cleverness gives way to intelligence, and what begins as a turn on the topic of assertiveness training becomes a moving story about resurrection. And yes, there are undertones of the living Christ in the story. The Christian motif is (perhaps surprisingly) common in Rooke's work. In this story, for example, a fat black woman has come to a care facility (to use a newly common term) to lead an assertiveness-training seminar. What she does chiefly is demonstrate assertiveness — and her demonstration works: the much used, badly used girl who is not paying close attention (she yawns) has a vision of her parents sitting in a tree, and afterwards she washes dishes at the feet of the fat black woman and thus becomes a disciple. The girl leaves the group home (to use another newly common term) to return to her parents. It is a contemporary Christian story. You can find others in the work of Hugh Hood; you can also find examples in the paintings of Stanley Spencer.

"The People in the Trees," in fact, might serve as a bridge to Rooke's best work, which is frequently characterized by theological, Christian thinking. Those Christian premises are clearly evident in the original sin of his most recent novel, *A Good Baby*, but they are also part of the rural life of the central character in his best novel so far, the virtually flawless novel of characterization, *Fat Woman* — which is, in one sense, a story of the attempts of uneducated rural people to solve their problems without the help of assertiveness training or evangelical religion. The fat woman of the title has always been fat: her appetite is just one more example of the weakness of the human flesh. The flesh is weak, and there is so much of it. The novel is touching because we cannot help sharing her humanity — every time we approach the refrigerator for a little comfort from the anguish of the human condition. She has two rotten kids. We understand. And we understand, too, her husband's tough love: he intends to save her life if he possibly can. Already she is so fat that her wedding ring has cut off the circulation of blood in her hand; she is willing to suffer the consequences of human weakness — and her devotion to the symbol of marriage — but he is a pragmatist and rationalist, an expert in making do, and he intends to have the ring cut off. And more: he is going to lock her in her room until she loses weight. He intends to save her life.

It is, in fact, fair to say of Rooke's world that, very frequently indeed, his characters attempt pragmatic, rationalist solutions to theological problems that they cannot understand. In "Daddy Stump," for example, the narrator, a little girl, finds herself in a family cast out of Eden. The mother is dying in the back room; the crippled father is watching Japanese porno films with his buddies in an abandoned house next door; and the narrator and her younger sister are peeking through the window at him and his buddies, looking at the depiction of carnal knowledge. The narrator can know only that carnal knowledge exists; she doesn't yet know what it is, and her response is to deal with one problem at a time, starting with the one nearest at hand: her little sister's bed-wetting. If the narrator must become the mother in this terrible situation, she will, and she does. The narrator is not responding to the depiction of carnal knowledge, which is simply part of the world and nothing but original sin. For her it is merely context. She is responding to the bed-wetting. First things first. Her goodness is an assertion of human innocence in the face of carnal knowledge. This same innocence is asserted in several of the best stories in this collection, sometimes at the cost of determined illusion, as in "Admiral of the Fleet" and the title story, "Who Do You Love?"

But Rooke's virtues as a writer should not be confused with his theological concerns. Another writer might be equally interested in Milton's themes and not be a quarter of the writer that Rooke is. It is not the subject matter that makes one writer succeed and another fail, that makes one writer better than another. It is not even "the story" — the event or series of events by which we refer to the account. We use *events* to remember stories, but the value of stories frequently lies elsewhere. In fact, if you look closely at Rooke's stories, you will see that very little usually happens. Even in "Daddy Stump," which seems to be full of events, the chief action is the running of the two little girls after they have tipped over the barrel on which they were standing to peer into the house of carnal knowledge.

Rooke's particular success is with his knowledge and use of the language of human speech. And it is not merely that he has as we so often blithely say — a good ear. It is much more than that. In common with all good prose writing, his paragraphs are full of pattern, rhythm, and surprise; but in Rooke's case these virtues are caught in the "language really used by men" and woman and children.

In one sense, the language is absolutely authentic. In "Who Do You Love?" for instance, there is an excellent example of psychological authenticity — which is to say that in the boy's voice we hear the way that we make stories when we are young:

> A body was discovered one summer in a stream called the Dye Ditch, the stream you had to cross to reach grammar school, but you went down to look at that place in the ditch where the body was discovered but no one was there, no corpse was there, and after a while you didn't hear anyone speak of it and you never knew who it was had been stabbed in that ditch. The ditch was deep, with steep clay walls, the walls always wet, wet and smooth and perfect, but clay was not a thing you knew to do anything with. You found a shoe in the woods just up from the bank, a shoe with the tongue missing, and you said, This was the stabbed man's shoe and you asked yourself why So-and-So had done it, because of some woman, most likely (6).

It's not merely that we can see the boy creating the story of the death at Dye Ditch that makes this passage psychologically authentic, but also the sequence — he stops to describe the ditch (he will do it more, further on in the story) — as well as the echo in the last line of what he has been told in response to his questions. The sequence is important. That last comment is almost a throwaway — "because of some woman, most likely" — but it is a rewarding surprise in the last line of the paragraph. Fine writing.

But Rooke's writing is also authentic of time and place — and here you have to take my word for it, and trust that I, who share something of Rooke's background, can recognize in the following the authentic American voice of the boonies:

Your grandfather let you walk down the rows with him, he let you hold the plow, and he said, Just let the mule do the work, but you couldn't hold the plow handles and the reins at the same time and the plow blade kept riding up out of the ground. When you came to the end of a row the mule would stop and your grandfather would look at both of you, look and flap his hat against his leg, and say, Now let's see which of you has the better sense. You stood behind your grandfather's chair in the evenings and combed his balding head, but your grandmother said, I've got enough plates to get to the table, why should I get theirs? Why can't she come and take away these that are hers and leave me with those that are mine?

No one asked her to marry that drinker.

Didn't we tell her sixteen was too young?

She made her own bed. There ain't one on their daddy's side ever had pot to pee in or knew what pot was for (7-8).

It's a skill for which Rooke will not likely receive much credit in Canada — for who will recognize it and value it? But it is there, for all that, and I think it is wonderful.

I have only one reservation about the title story of the collection (which plays a variation on the most terrible question a mother can ask: "Who do you love best?"), and that is with the ending, which shifts the focus and makes a little plea for feeling that the story doesn't need. Still, it is one of the best stories in the collection, as is the last one, "Body Count." That story — which purports to be, and maybe is, an interview with an old lady in a nursing home — raises the terrible question we so frequently address to God the Father, if there is a god the father: why is there death? What have we done that is so terrible that we must die? Was it our crime to be born? It is terribly unfair.

And so it is. But it is a fine story because we can't tell from reading it if Rooke really interviewed an old woman in a nursing home and wrote down what she said or if he made it up.

My favourite story in the collection, however, is the stunning and violent "Want to Play House?" in whose title is an echo of two forms of the favourite children's game of carnal knowledge. Sometimes the game involves going into the bushes and taking off your clothes to look at one another like Adam and Eve, because you know, somehow, as a child, that this nakedness and connection is what makes a family. And sometimes the little theatrical game with the same name refers to a performance of home as we know it. Rooke's story hints at the first and performs the second. The two are intertwined. It is a story of playing house in which the little girl insists upon three revisions. It is her story, set in the imaginary kitchen. The little boy — probably her younger brother — is to play the man who comes home after work. And it is a story of rural poverty and despair that ends with a butcher knife. Its language is that of the Bible Belt and the miserable little house or trailer off the dirt road; you can hear the King James Version in both the vocabulary and cadences:

> Okay, I will take you through it step by step, though that's precious little fun for me. I tell you, it is precious little fun for me, and I don't know why I go through it. All right, you are here at this line, which is the door, and you come in and I am sitting at the table crying my eyes out because I am full of woe.
>
> That's right. I have changed my mind, I am not standing at the sink when you come in. Let's play this way instead. I have been full of woe all day and I have got nothing done, nothing is ever done because I am unable to rouse myself from the loathsome woe, and now I have lost all track of the time and don't know which way to turn (60-61).

I cannot imagine better writing, anywhere, than this sample. It is the equal of Flannery O'Connor's best work, and it is Rooke's bad luck to share with O'Connor a common background and similar concerns, because she has had the more powerful literary establishment asserting and demonstrating her virtues. She is accorded the American reputation.

But Rooke at his best is her equal, and he's still writing. Let's not forget either of those facts.

BIBLIOGRAPHY

Rooke, Leon. *Who Do You Love?* Toronto: McClelland and Stewart, 1992.

THIS HERE JASPER IS GITTIN READY TO TALK

JOHN METCALF

In the nineteen-seventies when I began to encounter Leon Rooke's stories in the literary magazines I recognized immediately an interesting new voice. A way of approaching the form new to Canada — though not so new in the States — was beginning to make itself heard. Or *should* have been making itself heard for it was surprisingly difficult to get people to listen.

I remember showing some of the stories in what became *The Love Parlour* to Michael Macklem, the publisher of Oberon Press. Macklem has a doctorate in literature from Princeton and taught English at Yale. He declared the stories incomprehensible but said that if I thought they were good he'd publish them on my say so but only on condition he wouldn't have to read further.

This seeming inability to read Leon Rooke, to connect with his vitality, is puzzling because looking back at *The Love Parlour* now it doesn't strike me as wildly innovative or madly experimental. It remains a good, solid collection but it is not a stylistic trailblazer.

To get Macklem to publish Leon's second book in Canada, *Cry Evil*, I had to write little explanatory notes about each story. Macklem published the book but remained unconvinced. It was with *Cry Evil* that Leon began to move towards the sort of story that was to be his major contribution to the form. With *Cry Evil* we were treated to a display of Leon limbering up for the major work ahead. This is not to say that some of the stories in *Cry Evil* are not already masterly performances. I'm particularly fond of "The Deacon's Tale," "Adolpho Has Disappeared and We Haven't a Clue Where to Find Him," and "Biographical Notes."

Another anecdote about listening. In 1980 Leon published his first novel *Fat Woman*. It is a book that draws with intense imagination on his

Southern roots. Every line of the book is in sync with the rhythms and cadences of Southern speech yet a young Canadian fiction writer, and a good one too, reviewing the book for a major newspaper, understood it as being set in Nova Scotia.

Yet another anecdote. When Leon and I left Oberon Press I wanted to move us to ECW Press because the owners, Jack David and Robert Lecker, were friends of mine and possessed of great energy and dedication to Canadian writing. I sent some of Leon's new work to Jack David who seemed unenthusiastic. Indeed, he phoned me and asked me if I really stood behind the work, if I really considered it the genuine article. I told him very firmly that I did. A short while later, Leon was in Toronto giving a public reading and Jack David went to hear him. Jack phoned me the next day in great excitement. "*Now* I get it", he said. "Now I've *heard* him. I just wasn't getting it from the printed page."

Jack David and Robert Lecker went on to publish two major books of Leon's stories, *Death Suite* in 1981 and *The Birth Control King of the Upper Volta* in 1982.

These anecdotes about the seeming inability to hear Leon Rooke are, of course, merely anecdotes but they do represent, I think, a fairly widespread reaction to his work at the time and need some explanation.

Academic neglect of Rooke's work is easily understandable. Not many academics actually read contemporary writing and many of them were unaware of his existence. Another part of the answer, less silly than it sounds, is that Leon is playful. Not a good thing to be in any of the arts in Canada. Yet another strike against him is that he moved progressively away from normative realism into fable, fantasy, pastiche of genre writing, all in scrambled shapes of his own invention. This departure from realism did not endear him to academics whose hastily cobbled canon really had no room for his shenanigans; shenanigans, furthermore, which were suspiciously American.

But the central reason for his early neglect is that most readers were not hearing what Leon was up to. Their attention was directed elsewhere, to theme, perhaps, or form. They were in a similar situation to an earnest gallery-goer standing in front of a Rothko and asking: 'What does it mean?' The answer is: 'Look.'

To the reader who asks: 'What does it mean?' of Rooke's "Sixteen-year-old Susan March Confesses to the Innocent Murder of All the Devious Strangers Who Would Drag Her Down" the answer is: 'Listen.'

Listen.

Rooke has published four or five plays and many of the stories are essentially *scripts* — monologues or voices talking, arguing. The insistent direction in his work is theatrical. Leon himself is never happier than on a stage, the rhetoric flying high and wide and often over the top. Leon is a performer. Leon is a self-confessed ham. His stories are *performances*.

He is very prolific having published by now some three hundred short stories in the literary magazines. Most are uncollected because on further reflection he felt they simply did not work. Leon doesn't brood for months over the shape and detail of what he hopes will be a masterwork; he picks up his horn and tries out a few runs, a few phrases to see if something is going to happen.

I sometimes think that Rooke's academic acceptance has been slow because academics have been slow to think of Leon as, say, a tenor sax player and the story as a jazz improvisation. If the reader *does* respond in those terms it becomes immediately obvious what Leon is up to.

Leon is leading the parade. He doesn't want a tweed-with-leather-elbow-patches response. He wants celebrants performing along with him. He wants a Second Line. At other times he wants to preach, a big Texas tenor sound, wave after wave of impossibly mounting fervour.

Leon preaching always reminds me of recordings I've heard of the Reverend Kelsey leading his Washington congregation in "Lion of the Tribe of Judah"; the preacher's voice probes at the words, repeats, hums, slides into falsetto, repeats and finds a form and then all rhythmic hell breaks loose, hands clapping, jugs grunting and booming, a trombone's urging. All rather glorious.

Leon has talked about his story-writing practice not in exactly the terms I've used here but in sufficiently close terms to validate what I'm saying. In a book called *Singularities* edited by Geoff Hancock in 1990 Leon contributed a piece which reads in part as follows:

> "I don't have many rules for the writing of short fiction. One of them is, if a thing is going wrong, then start over. If it is going nowhere, then give it up, or start over. If it goes awhile, and stops, then you stop too because maybe you have gone as far as the story wants you to go. Which often means, of course, starting over. The

piece lays down its own laws; that's another thing I mean. That's why many very intelligent, very gifted literary people who want to write, can't. They operate under the fallacious notion that the writer is Creator — God, whereas intervention of another sort is more frequently the case. The thing, at a certain point, and usually at the start, creates itself. It is of value, or it isn't. Does it matter so much anyway, since the story that awaits the telling awaits as well the teller, and as many aren't found as are."[1]

I think what Leon is saying here describes an improvisatory approach to fiction. (For anyone interested in pursuing further how Leon composes, an essay he wrote for my 1982 anthology *Making It New* called "Voices" is vivid and fascinating.)

In a Geoff Hancock interview, in *Canadian Fiction Magazine,* Leon said:

"I've also written ten or fifteen stories that came out of no-where. I sat at the typewriter, typed out one sentence, and that sentence invited another sentence and that demanded a third. Several hours later I had the first draft — even sometimes the final draft — of a story. These stories happen very fast and where they come from or where they're going I don't know until I get there."[2]

Leon's body of work, his teaching, and his many performances over the years have helped to give the short story in Canada a new and different emphasis. In 1982 in *Kicking Against the Pricks* I wrote about the short story in Canada:

"Where twenty years ago Canadian stories stressed content — what a story was *about* — the main emphasis now is on the story as verbal and rhetorical *performance.* Our best writers are concerned with the story as *thing to be experienced* rather than as *thing to be understood.*"[3]

---

[1] *Singularities.* Edited by Geoff Hancock. Windsor: Black Moss Press, 1990, 96.

[2] *Canadian Fiction Magazine.* Leon Rooke Issue 38, 113.

[3] Metcalf, John. *Kicking Against the Pricks.* Toronto: ECW Press, 1982. 168.

Thing to be understood implies that the reader is outside the story and regarding it intellectually. *Thing to be experienced* implies that the reader is inside the story and reacting to it emotionally. Leon Rooke has been one of those who effected the verbal and rhetorical revolution.

In case I have been too fanciful or insufficiently precise in my talking about Leon's work I would like to illustrate his approach by taking a particular story and examining it. The story I wish to consider is "Saks Fifth Avenue" from Leon's 1984 collection *A Bolt of White Cloth*.

Jazz groups play what are called 'head arrangements,' rehearsed, memorized introductions, statements of the tune. The various instruments in the band then improvise. Some sessions sparkle; the head arrangements are crisp, the solos inventive, galvanized. On other nights all that musicians seem able to deliver is competence; solos noodle around, everyone seems to be going through the motions, there is no spark. And sometimes it happens that one of the musicians breaks out of the noodle pudding into something suddenly emotionally charged.

Something like this happens in "Saks Fifth Avenue."

The story starts: "A woman called me up on the telephone. She was going to give me twenty thousand dollars, she said. I said come right over, I'm not doing anything this evening."

No explanation is offered about the money. At the end of the story the woman appears, gives him the money, and the story ends with his counting it. This is the frame of the story, those parts analogous to the head arrangements in a tune.

After launching the story in this way, Rooke next introduces Coolie, Cecil's wife. They bicker interminably. Coolie abuses Cecil relentlessly while polishing her nails and watching television. Cecil meanwhile, at her suggestion, polishes his shoes and muses about this and that.

The shoe polish is kept in an old box from Saks. Cecil wonders where the box came from. It seems that the box is going to form a riff in the story but that direction peters out.

Coolie almost mechanically abuses him.

The writing is tepid, repetitive, banal. This is not because Rooke is not capable of better writing. It is because Coolie and Cecil no longer hear each other.

"Habit: me with my dishes, Coolie with her words."

At the same time, it is also true that Leon is noodling, unsure of where he's going and why. The story, thirteen pages in, is beginning to founder. And then that magical thing happens and Leon leans into the story and starts to blow.

Cecil wonders what it would have been like if he and Coolie had had a child. And in a lyrical outburst Cecil conjures up his imaginary son as together in the kitchen they cook Spezzatino di Vitello. This solo is tight, builds beautifully, and for the first time this story achieves genuine emotion. Then the story slumps again for five pages until Cecil then imagines a daughter. Again Leon plays a fiery solo. Then again the story slumps. The lady with the money arrives and Leon plays one last solo about a little Peruvian girl Cecil's going to give money to and the story then expires.

These three solos occur in "Saks Fifth Avenue" in *A Bolt of White Cloth* on pages 133-134, 139-140, and pages 143. Any reader ought to be able to feel the intensity of these passages, the way they differ from the material that surrounds them.

It is obvious that I don't consider "Saks Fifth Avenue" a success but it serves perfectly to illustrate the improvisational way in which Leon works. He always runs the risk of falling off the high wire but *taking* the risk is a part of writing's attraction for Leon.

"Saks Fifth Avenue" suffers also from being a hybrid, an attempt to mix a rendition of an unhappy marriage with elements of fantasy or fable. We remain unconvinced by Cecil and Coolie as people, baffled by the lady bringing the unexplained money. Leon's work, paradoxically gets 'realer,' more deeply emotional, the more stylized it is, the further he gets away from anything approaching realism.

Of course, there are plenty of times when he gets it right with the very first note and blows fiercely through to triumph. *Then* he gives us such gorgeous performances as "The Deacon's Tale," "Hitting the Charts," "Winter Is Lovely, Isn't Summer Hell," "Mama Tuddi Done Over," and "Some People Will Tell You the Situation at Henny Penny Nursery Is Getting Intolerable."

We all have our favourites in his work.

CHAPTER THREE

SHORT STORIES AND NOVELLAS

Dangerous Crossing: A Reading of Leon Rooke's "The Birth Control King of the Upper Volta"

Simone Vauthier

Toward the end of Leon Rooke's story "The Birth Control King of the Upper Volta," the narrator-protagonist renders a crucial moment in the day that he is relating — and that happens to be the anniversary of Blondin's crossing of Niagara Falls — by projecting himself as a sort of Blondin: "Adlai is on his tightrope out over the swirling water, balanced between rope and sky, wavering and floundering with his balancing pole. Adlai steering for the river's other shore . . . Adlai falling. Adlai crying. Then only the quivering rope and the crashing water there" (37).

What Adlai offers here as a metaphor? a vision? of his acting self can easily be extended as a metaphor of the reading experience in which his narrative involves us. Reading a Rooke story, and this one in particular, is indeed a perilous adventure, one in which we risk either being overwhelmed by the impetuous flow of the narrative or carried away by a responsive flow of wild interpretations. It compels a realization of the spot we are in as participants in the story. For the transitional space of reading is (no longer) a safe place. We are caught "in the middest" between the shore of the word-world and the shore of the world as we know it (or believe we know it) and are obliged to cross back and forth from one to the other. Giving an account of the experience becomes in its turn something of a feat, which must leave the critic frustrated, since there was ever so much more to the crossing than one can explicate. Like Adlai, however, I must make the brave attempt.

What we perceive first is a voice:

> "The most extraordinary thing happened to me today. I woke up
> and discovered I had lost yesterday. Amazing! Not a slither, parcel

or dot of it remained. Yes! The sun was dazzling bright, my entire room was lit up like a store-front. I stretched, I yawned, I kicked off my sheets: oh lovely, perfect lovely! — is what I said. / Absolutely. That's how innocent I was" (7).

An excited narrator is eager to reconstitute his extraordinary experience and to share it with a narratee. As he summarizes his story before launching into it,[1] he interjects confirmatory comments — "Yes," "absolutely" — which anticipate possible remarks from his addressee and, further, his "You'd think I would have a hint," in which a generalizing "you" includes "you and I," takes it for granted that the narratee responds to the events as he himself does. Throughout his narration Adlai goes on confiding in his audience, in the double sense that he tells them about his private life and trusts them to see things much in the same way as he does. "Days, I thought — as you would have yourself — just don't disappear" (11). Although, on rare occasions, he imagines that his addressee may get impatient ("But wait, for here's the news") or may need further explanation ("What do I mean?" [8]), he never conceives of a narratee that would not accept his vision of things, so that he ascribes to him or her his own prejudices; speaking of his Chinese neighbour, he says, "A big country like that, you'd think they'd stay in their rice fields" (14). Thus, he unselfconsciously aims at involving his audience in his word-world. In short, he implicitly calls for a non-distanced reception of his story. What he seeks from others is simply recognition. "Everyone needs noticing is what Greta would say" (8). Though he does not appropriate the saying, he behaves as if he believed it. Yet the details we are given of his life are evidence enough that until that day — and leaving aside his mother — he has received little notice himself. Now, however, the tale of the most extraordinary thing that ever happened to him can be told in exchange for recognition.

On the other hand, his narration is not totally oriented toward others but also toward himself. He tells his story to put together his two selves, the "innocent" self who woke up that morning, and the more experienced self he now has become, in short, in order to understand himself. Such

---

[1] Summaries frequently introduce oral narratives. See W. Labov, "The Transformation of Experience in Narrative Syntax" in *Language in the Inner City*, 363 and ff.

an endeavour requires and implies distance. In this case, however, the temporal distance between the two selves is rather restricted, since Adlai narrates his adventures on the same day. Moreover, from the opening lines, the reader may have doubts about the maturity of Adlai. What with his diction ("extraordinary," "amazing," "Lovely," "absolutely") and his syntax (the exclamative and elliptical sentences), his utterance conjures up the image of an adolescent, and thus we are surprised to learn that Adlai is 47 years old, inclined to infer provisionally that, notwithstanding his affirmation, his capacity for wonder testifies to his continued innocence.

Whatever contract the narrator has been making with his narratee is thereby subtly undermined. And the fiction — as distinguished from Adlai's narrative — programs a more distanced reading. As is often the case with pseudo-autobiographies, "The Birth Control King" makes a double contract with the reader, who must at the same time take on the inner contract passed between narrator and narratee and enter into an outer one with the author. (An element in that outer pact is, of course, the title. "The Birth Control King of the Upper Volta" announces its fictionality in its puzzling referent [who ever heard of such a king?] and in the elaborate materiality of its signifier; "The Birth Control King of the Upper Volta" is more satisfying for phonemic and rhythmical reasons than, say, "the birth-control king of Ghana," and for referential reasons, than "the birth-control king of Great Britain.") Inherent as it is to pseudo-autobiographical narration, the gap between the two readings is more obvious in Leon Rooke's story than it is in a story whose I-narrator does not trust his audience. Here we have to move back and forth from an empathetic to a detached reading.

Clearly, then, the character is intended to elicit contradictory responses — which, I insist, the narrator does not intend. Different readers may be more or less tolerant toward Adlai. His rhetoric, for example, may be more off-putting for some than for others. But it is likely to raise in one and all the question of his reliability. What credence can you lend someone who makes such statements as, "She had fire in her eyes — a torrid spitball" (15) or, "What a whimpering, roaring, blood-boiling feast *love* is! The floor scraped at our elbows. Knees cooked . . ." (27)? Even if we leave aside the question of his language for the moment, the narrator's understanding of people and of events may strike us as limited, to say the least. When, on the telephone, the Pole exclaims, "Oh, it's you, *the* nincompoop" (14; emphasis mine), Adlai is baffled. "It had been my impression that the Pole, more than most, held me in high regard. Respected my talents" (14). His very surprise betrays his simplicity. Similarly, when he muses, "Sweet, dear old mam. Her stick was hard on the behind, but she was ever straight with me" (34), the assessment seems wildly off the mark. Much as she loved her son, Old Mam, it appears to us, was less than direct and candid with him. Even when he comes to his own immediate experience, the narrator does not get his priorities right. "The most extraordinary thing" that happened to him on that August the 11th was not, as he announces, the loss of a day — not even his recovery of it. Partial amnesia is small beer in comparison with what transpires. First, there is his dead mother returning to pay him a visit. Now, since in Adlai's world such an event is not to be marvelled at, he may not feel the need to underline its strangeness to a narratee who shares his attitude. We may therefore grant that his omission of it in the opening summary is natural. Nevertheless, the silence helps build suspense for the reader and reveals the difference between the narrator's world and ours. At the same time, by announcing a single extraordinary event, Adlai obliterates at the beginning the really crucial happenings — the "cure" of Hedgepolt, the landlady's severely retarded son, the "purest joy" of Adlai's vision, which heralds a major change in his *weltanschauung*. Because it proves somewhat misleading, the introductory summary casts doubts upon the narrator's ability to comprehend his own experience.

In addition, as he reports in detail his actions on that bizarre morning, the narrator includes the numerous childhood memories that passed through his mind. All these retrospects are in the form of dialogues between Old Mam, the repository of knowledge, the embodiment of *savoir*, and young Adlai, who is in quest of knowledge about the world, about his origins and therefore embodies *vouloir savoir*. But when Old Mam appears in Adlai's room, the conversation taking place between her and her 47-year-old son has the same ring as the earlier exchanges. The I-actor occupies the same position in regard to his mother and to knowledge; he is still asking questions about his father and inquiring about himself, much as a child would, and indeed speaking in the same tone of voice. (Exemplary is his query, "Did I cry too, my mam?" [16], which in the context is absurd, since he was not born at the time.) Nor does he seem to be aware, any more than a child would be, of the preposterousness of his father's "mission"; according to Old Mam, Old Daddy has gone off to sell birth control to the peoples of the Upper Volta in order to "protect us" and "our very way of life" (16), saving, with each successful attempt, "another white child his rightful spot in the world. Another white boy his freedom" (22). When they speak together of this sacred duty, mother and son innocently use *double-entendre*, which the I-narrator relays just as innocently. So, increasingly, the image being built up is that of a man of arrested emotional development.

On the face of it, then, Adlai is a simpleton, yet he is an endearing one. In spite of his failings, in spite even of the prejudices instilled into him, as an I-actor he shows no real meanness of spirit in his relationships with the people he encounters, and as a narrator he harbours no personal grudge. A fool, yes, but a holy fool.

Eventually, the holy fool proves to have more perception than we at first credited him with. Compelled by Mergentoire, his landlady, to realize that the lost day is the day of his mother's funeral, he finally faces up to his guilt. He remembers that, when Old Mam wrote that her "spot's about used up" (34) asking simply, "Will you come? Can you do that for me?" he did not go: "No, I'd let her dot fade right out" (34). Later, he asks for her forgiveness. Moreover, he is able as an actor to operate a complete readjustment of his attitudes toward the world, and as a narrator to give a lucid account of the complex and rapid shifts through which the conversion was made possible. Although he has renounced his mother's beliefs — and the beliefs that his mother told him were his father's — although he sees her "watchful eye" disappear when he has his new insights, nevertheless, once he is free, it is to her that he speaks of his new-found knowledge: "I sat on, thinking: So many people in the world depend on you. So many. Even if you are nothing — even if you are no one and you don't know which way to turn or whether turning is a thing you're capable of — even then they do. / Oh, mam, they do" (38).

The final sentence may be read in two ways, according to what one supplies as the reason for the emphatic repetition. "Oh, mam, [you may not believe it, but] they do." Or, "Oh, mam, [isn't it wonderful?], they do." Whether in gentle admonition or in wonder, the narrator feels the need to share his discovery with his departed mother, thus reasserting that neither rejection of the dead woman's values nor death itself need put a stop to their dialogue.

With the reduction of the extra-diegetic narratee to an intra-diegetic one, the narrative seems to fold back upon itself. Even as the act of narration enables the narrator to move away from his origins, the ending suggests that the desire to narrate is desire to orient oneself toward origins. What called the story into being was perhaps the desire to tell Mam something. At the same time, the narrative opens out in another way. When the extra-diegetic narratee, with whom we find it easy to identify, is excluded from the final remarks, we are required to slip into another slot; we are made to realize that we are like the people of whom the narrator speaks. For like them we have been depending on Adlai. Although he is truly nothing and no one on the fictional level, where he is only an underdog, and on the ontological level, where he is a mere paper being, we exist as readers only through our participation in his narration.

Whatever reservations we may have, we depend entirely on his storytelling. And even if the reader is uneasy at Adlai's verbal flamboyance, he will have to grant him a capacity to render the concrete minutiae of experience (as in "scrunching up my toes, for there was not enough room for my feet" [11]), a vivid sense of metaphor (as in "beaming their great white teeth . . . all to gobble up our jobs" [10]), in a nutshell, a gift for rendering his world.

What is more, we rely so much on the narrator's representation of his world that we take the curious laws of this world for granted as though they were the laws of ours. (The "reliability" of fictional narrators is a more complex matter in some ways than that of real-life narrators, and, notwithstanding all the attention it has received, the whole concept might bear further investigation.) The world in which Adlai moves and has his being is uncanny and demands from us a special form of engagement.

Adlai lives with his beloved — a calendar photograph of Greta Garbo, which hangs on the door of his "flea-box" of a room. Greta sulks and scolds and wipes mud on the floor, the perfect *hausfrau*. Adlai soothes and praises her and finally makes love to her. These are events that we come to accept on their own terms without regarding them as tokens of a deranged mind. To see Greta as a mere hallucination would, it seems to me, be denying the nature of Rooke's short story. Even at the end, when Adlai dismisses Greta ("Go home, honey. There are people at home who have need of you" [38]), he is not seeing through an illusion but renouncing Greta and what she stood for, what she can still stand for for other people. Leon Rooke's Greta Gustafsson obtrudes upon our consciousness as both a fictional existent — based, of course, on a real person, or rather on a real-life screen persona[2] — and a figure whose existence, conjured up by the protagonist, is metonymy and metaphor of his desire. (Eventual objections have already been anticipated by Leon Rooke, talking about another device of his: "Can the writer work such a double street? Can he have it both ways? Why not?" ["Voices," 261]). Greta's frequent appearances make light of the conventional dichotomy between narrative levels, which opposes the (fictive) real and the imaginary; the literal and the figurative. The short story thus achieves some of the impact that Susan Sontag wants for fiction: "I want the novel to have the same kind of believability that film has. In a film anything you see is *there*, even if you understand that it's a flashback, or it's a dream, or a fantasy. Still it fills the screen and what you see is the only reality at the moment that you see it" (quoted in Bellamy, 124).

When Adlai, after making passionate love to Greta, exclaims, "What a world! What a dream-time!" (27), he introduces the distinction between the levels of the real (world) and the imaginary (dream-time), all the better to negate it through the implicit equivalence of the two juxtaposed exclamations. "What a dream-time" itself fuses the two levels insofar as the compound noun joins time with what is timeless, and insofar as the narrator uses the phrase figuratively, while the reader may be tempted to read it only literally, thus making the love scene an onanistic fantasy. But the two meanings co-exist, and the second should not be given priority over the first. The text thus plays repeatedly on a hierarchy that it keeps reasserting only to destroy. A few lines after those I have just quoted, Adlai wonders: "Greta had wanted *me*? Pitiful me? . . . This dream had wanted me? Uncanny. No, it was beyond truth. Reality couldn't touch this. / But I touched her — one finger along the ribs — and knew that it had" (27).

In a few short sentences, complex vacillations are expressed. The dream that is better than reality is a metaphor for Greta or for Greta's wanting him, yet the usual denotation remains active in the text, much as "uncanny" in the context attenuates yet retains some of its literal meaning. It is the realized dream which is beyond truth and thus becomes unreal.

---

[2] The short story also blurs the distinction between the woman and the film star by playing with her names. First called Greta Gustafsson, she becomes Garbo only in the torrid love scene.

"Reality could not touch this." But the verb *touch* becomes the hinge on which the sentence turns when the narrator transforms an abstract proposition into a concrete statement with a personal subject, *I*, and a personal object, *her*, linked by a verb of contact. *Reality* touches *this* in more ways than one. The narrator only plays with conventional tokens, *reality, dream*,[3] which he conventionally disjoins in order to grope at some sense of their basic conjunction. Dream and reality touch so well that they are reversible. To this extent, the questioning of this particular experience prepares for Adlai's later injunction to Hedgepolt, "dream the dreams," and for the realization of these dreams.

The visit of Old Mam also works toward a similar effect through different means. Old Mam first emerges in the narration as the receiver of a little speech of Adlai on the physical and educational advantages of the outdoors job he would in fact have gladly given up for a desk job. At this point, she is only a mental interlocutor. But then the narrator introduces a lengthy discussion with his mother with the comment: "I could swear my old mam had walked right into the room" (15). This statement, which, because of the modalizer "I could swear," almost negates what it asserts, is the only moment of uncertainty for the narrator-protagonist in respect to this event.[4] While he repeatedly emphasizes the strangeness of her appearance, his involvement with her is such as to preclude all further questioning. Even her departure, when she "fold[s] back into the wall, becoming the wall" (24), is a matter for emotion ("I ran over and kissed the wall"), not for puzzlement. The reader, for his or her part, early surmises what the I-actor does not seem to suspect, namely that the old woman with soot on her face and "mites running in her hair" (17), with her "moldy" smell, "all earthy and wormy" (19), is a visitor from a world beyond ours and a time out of time: she looks "so ancient, so feeble, so ahead of or behind her times" (18). Soon, comparisons and images associating her with "some foul pit or tomb" confirm our suppositions. Partly because of the narrator's unquestioning attitude, partly because of

---

[3] *Dream, Dreamy* are recurrent words; their meaning(s) and placing would deserve careful analysis.

[4] It is the only moment within the particular narrative unit when Adlai seems to have doubts about his mother's presence in his room. But, on the whole, Adlai is often uncertain about his perception of the world.

the narrative role of Greta, which has already conditioned our response, we easily construct the mother as a presence (a presence that marks an absence since, after all, Old Mam appears in her son's room *because* she is dead). Again, what character and reader "see" is "the only reality at the moment that [we] see it." To put it another way, the text does not require us to oscillate, much less choose *between* a natural and a supernatural inter-pretation, an objective and a subjective view of the event; we accept Old Mam's return and at the same time we remain aware that it contradicts our sense of verisimilitude, our image of the external world, while ful-filling some of our own phantasms. The co-existence in the intermediate space of reading of two orders, the real and the imaginary, the inner and the outer, neutralizes the boundary between them.

Let me adduce one last example. When, in the final sequence, Adlai sees thousands of canoes riding the waves, he sits "rocking in his chair — in my chair or wherever my spot was — delirious in the face of this vision, wondering which was vision and which was real life and finally where it, or they, or even myself, had gone" (37).[5] On this occasion, it might seem that the narrator unambiguously expresses his uncertainty as to the nature of his experience. Are we not therefore entitled to regard it as a hallucination? But observe how the narrator weakens the hierar-chy between ontological and temporal levels by putting first "delirious in the face of this vision," as though perhaps the delirium proceeded from the vision and the ensuing wonder from the delirium. The organi-zation of the utterance destabilizes its meaning. Because of its polysemy, language is for the narrator the balancing pole with which he keeps his equilibrium between conflicting possibilities, whereas, for the reader, it is the very locus, rocking like Adlai's chair, where the real and the surreal engender and define one another. "The Birth Control King" constantly subverts the antinomy between the real and the imaginary so that it even-tually creates a new, otherwise indefinable, space, a sort of interface world.

If the reality of the narrator is ultimately something that we perceive / construct as the only reality there is for us during the act of reading, his utterance can be heard on two wavelengths. On the one hand, insofar as

---

[5] The vision also makes the notion of *here*, the spot I am occupying now, somewhat uncer-tain ("in my chair or wherever my spot was") even as it makes *there* problematic when Adlai wonders "where it, they, or even myself, had gone."

the story purports to be the discourse of a locutor, the narrator's propensity to overstatement conveys some of Adlai's character traits, as we have seen. In addition, his hyperbolic exuberance, when associated with his meagre opportunities and his coffin-like room, also appears as the means to go beyond his restricted circumstances, to be, as Thoreau would say, "extra-vagant." Words are his only riches, which he can spend profusely, the medium through which he can dazzlingly reshape the trivialities of a mean life. On the other hand, insofar as this make-believe speaking subject is both the object of the writer's discourse and the controlling trope through which the authorial utterance is organized, Adlai must be seen stereoscopically as a virtual existent and as a hyperbolic oxymoron,[6] which implements Leon Rooke's "extra-vagance," and presumably his own desire to "wander far enough beyond the narrow limits of [his] daily experience, so as to be adequate to the truth of which [he] has been convinced," his desire "to speak somewhere *without* bound."[7]

THE TWO WORLDS OF "THE BIRTH CONTROL KING"

The reader's tightrope stretches between the world inside the story and the world outside it. But the world inside the story also incorporates the world as we know it. When, after quoting the "grim headlines" of the day's newspaper, Summit Talks Collapse / Automakers Lay Off Another 30,000 / Inflation Hits New High. Adlai observes, "My world, I thought, and still there" (12), he might be putting the words into our mouths.

Uncanny as it is that a photograph should come to life, Adlai's Greta is so much like our image of Garbo that we would have recognized her even had she not been named Greta Gustafsson. We would have known her by the hat she puts on ("the one with feathers, plumed like a cavalier"), by her stance ("her shoulders arched back as she paced, pivoting her hips" [15]), by that mysterious, "maddeningly dramatic" look of hers — and of course by that epithet, *divine*. When Adlai recalls her appearance on

---

[6] Adlai is himself fond of oxymoronic phrases — "dreadful love," "the hum was silent," "joyful weeping," etc. — which fuse extremes of experience into baroque unity.

[7] H.D. Thoreau. *Walden* (New York: Rinehart, 1948), 289.

the screen, he describes our memories of Garbo; "Yielding only *to* love, no matter how fatal. Love came first, above her very life. Her every perform-ance insisting that love *was* life. That every risk was worth the taking. *Mata Hari. Camille. Ninotchka. Wild Orchids. The Blue Sea. The Yellow Bed. Anna Karenina* — Garbo. My very own Garbo" (25). My very own Garbo indeed! She is ours too. But hold on. *Mata Hari, Camille, Ninotchka, Wild Orchid* . . . all right. But *The Blue Sea, The Yellow Bed* . . . Did we miss these movies? *The Yellow Bed,* now . . . that has a familiar ring. Got it! *The Last One Home Sleeps in the Yellow Bed,* Baton Rouge, Louisiana, 1968, by none other than that Leon Rooke, who is now slyly trying to get our mytholo-gies mixed up. But the intertextual allusion, of course, refers us to the real world, of publishing, libraries . . . and writing/reading.

The undefined locus[8] of the fictional action stands out sharply against the precise reference to the Upper Volta and twelve other African states. The sceptical reader may not trust Old Mam when she invites her son to "imagine the Upper Volta as it was the day (Adlai's father) set foot there. Two hundred thousand Roman Catholics reproducing all over the place . . . And that's not to mention three million Mossis with the soles of their feet white as yours or mine and every bit as busy. Or half a million Lobis, another half-million Bobis, plus the thousands of itchy Gurunsis" (21). *Imagine* is the operative word here, and the Africa that Old Mam goes on to evoke is obviously a projection of her phantasms. Yet, for all the weirdness of her conceptions, we would be mistaken to reject offhand her information on the peoples of the Upper Volta. There is a majority of Mossis in that country, and sizeable groups of Lobis and Bobos and a smaller group of Gourounsis (or Grunshi, or Gurunsi). The actual world intrudes into the fictional. But the referential data are turned into fictional material through semiotic similarity. This is achieved through rigorous selection — encyclopedias cite numerous other ethnic groups, for example,

---

[8] "I like material that free floats, that puts you in a recognizable place without street signs," says the North-Carolina-born author who considers that the strong sense of place evinced by Southern literature can "also be confining" (Janet Dunbrack, "Man of a Thousand Voices," *The University of Toronto Bulletin* [Oct. 9, 1984]). One might, however, speculate that some of the story's background material comes from the writer's childhood. Because the fear of the rise of racial minorities is not confined to the South of the United States or to North America, the place of "The Birth Control King" can be "recognized" by white readers. The absence of "street signs" points to *our* street.

Samo, Marka, Diouala, Fulani, Tuareg, which were eliminated because they did not fit the pattern — and through a little graphic and phonemic manipulation, since the encyclopedias I consulted all mentioned Bobos and not Bobis. Such checking, naturally, is not required for us to enjoy the text. A reader ignorant of what is one of the lesser-known African nations may even regard the description as fantasy, and delight in its rhythms, sounds and rhetoric.[9] Nevertheless, the fact that the country *is* named is direct reference to the world out there, and I, for one, was led into looking up the Upper Volta because I knew that Mossis and Lobis were real ethnical names and became curious about the Bobis and the itchy Gurunsis. We are, in such cases, explicitly invited to consider the overlapping of fictional and referential elements.

If Greta Gustafsson and the Upper Volta (not to mention birth control) are reality indicators that eventually point to the blurry edges between the real and the fictional, other narrative strategies achieve a similar effect in more oblique ways. Take the black news-hawker. Adlai can read the headlines of his paper but has a hard time seeing the boy straight: "It seemed to me I'd seen him before — him or his twin — standing in the line-up to receive his dole, wearing butter-yellow shoes, a red eye-patch, a watch chain as long as his arm — and streaming off in his big Rolls-Royce with three boisterous women white as white eggs and laughing like mud-flaps" (12). At this point, Adlai still has doubts about the validity of his perception, and wonders, "Was this true or was it my old Daddy sending his vision across the licking water?" (13). So he asks the vendor whether he bought a paper off him the day before: "His black face grinned up at me over his watermelon. 'Not off me, boss. I'm fresh brand-new in the country, first day on the job.' He danced a swift jig along the pavement, playing a mean tune with his harmonica comb. 'I aims to make my fortune, boss,' he chirped. 'Me and my fourteen brothers looking no way but up'" (13). Under Adlai's eyes, the boy keeps shifting shapes because the protagonist looks at him through the distorting lenses of mythical images of the black man. This is a scene that we read through reality models of coherence, sociological and cultural, literary and cinematographic — and probably more characteristic in their particularity of the United

---

[9] Similarly, the list of African nations on page 37 is arranged not according to alphabetical, geographical or historical order, but for textual effect.

States than of Canada. To anyone unfamiliar with these models, the scene must appear surreal, whereas it brings into play stereotypes of the urban black as a parasite upon society (and a pirate, to boot, which is a more original image), an ostentatious dandy, an economic threat, a successful sexual competitor *and* as soft-shoeing "plantation negro" complete with watermelon and harmonica comb. Contradictory as they are, such stereotypes are entertained, even if perhaps in more updated forms, by vast numbers of white North Americans. In their distortion, they still refer us to the actual world. Moreover, the socio-economic rise of blacks in North America, the influx of emigrants from the West Indies into Canada are observable, statistical phenomena, so that the fictional incident has a relation to the world out there. Notwithstanding its representativeness — it cannot be taken as representational — unless we assume that Adlai is hallucinating.[10] In other words, the episode functions figuratively, not mimetically. The fictions that are shown to be the very stuff of the character's life, to the extent that he cannot see what is before his eyes — those fictions within the fiction — refer to, and emblematize those outer fictions that inform, willy-nilly, our lives, preventing us from really seeing the alien Other. So, once more, conventional hierarchies between the real and the imaginary are upset, boundaries are displaced.

The newspaper-boy incident is but a minor scene through which emerge the racist fears that Adlai inherited from his mother's talk and his father's example. Among other things, the irrationality of such attitudes is pointed up by the rumours, which Adlai hears as a child, that he himself may be "tar-brushed" and by the strange darkening of Old Mam's skin, which she ascribes to the "change," or to "the dark thoughts of a lifetime!" (34). The terror of being engulfed by "the black tide," the "numberless hordes," which include "Poles and A-rabs and Indians and even Huguenots" (23) ties up for Old Mam with the doctrine of "the rightful spot."[11] Every one has a "spot,"

---

[10] To see Adlai as mad does not detract, of course, from the story's social relevance, if only we regard the character's "insanity" as symbolic of the madness of our racial attitudes, that is, if we read the narrative mimetically and allegorically.

[11] The figure of the "spot" would also be worth tracing. The West Coast reviewers who have attacked *The Birth Control King* as a racist work (conversations with Leon Rooke, October 24, 1984) give it an interpretation that is very wide of the mark, completely misreading the dynamics of the story.

"saved," "waiting" for him — except that "the black tide" is an ever-increasing danger to this well-ordered plan. Hence the mission of the birth-control apostle. Hence the necessity for every one to be vigilant. Old Mam reproaches Adlai for not having married: "You have let [your] spot, and [your] children's spots, go to some gang of unruly, howling blacks! You've let the blacks take charge!" (23). In this respect, "The Birth Control King" reflects a heightened image not only of racial insecurities but also of certain religious tenets on our appointed place in the divine scheme of things. One might read the story as a satirical commentary on the type of ethnocentric mind that sees the changes in our world as evidence of a paranoid plot on the part of despised minorities.[12] From the beginning, let me add, Adlai, through sharing in those attitudes, evinces awareness of their destructive power. After the encounter with the news-hawker, he does 100 push-ups to work the vitriol out of his system. If the sociological interpretation of the short story is reductive, it is a necessary phase in the reading process. As we move back and forth between the bizarre world of the narrator-protagonist and the actual world, we are compelled to see the latter as a place more crazy than we like to think it. (Or perhaps not crazy enough?) To paraphrase the narrator, this dream — the story — had wanted us? Uncanny. No, it was beyond truth; reality could not touch this. But of course, it does.

BETWEEN / ACROSS TEARS AND LAUGHTER

Traversing the swirling stream of the narrative, the reader wavers and flounders, balanced between comedy and pathos. Comedy sparkles and bubbles at all levels. There is the baroque quixotism of the father's "mission," the funny side of the confrontation between Old Mam and her 47-year-old "little man" who, when scolded, hangs his head and "look[s] dumbly at [his] shoes" (22), or the irony of the protagonist's very existence. Adlai remembers questioning his mother:

---

[12] If I interpret his rapture after the love making correctly ("The first time — The first time ever — My baptism" [27]), Adlai was until then a middle-aged virgin, i.e., in our present society, a figure of fun.

— "Mam? My mam? Did he ever try it out on you?"

— "Try what, my boy?"

— "His birth control."

— "Oh gracious. Goodness gracious. Of course he did. I was the first."

— "But mam!"

— "It didn't take, son. Otherwise, would I have had you?" (32).

The comedy inherent in the situation is enhanced by the arresting use of words and syntax, particularly by the inappropriate verb *take*. Our sense of doublings, and, for instance, our feeling that the relationship between Mergentoire and Hedgepolt duplicates, at least to some extent, that between Old Mam and her son, also contributes a comic note. As for the characters, they are all in their different ways a source of amusement. What with his illusion, not to mention his delusions, with his bewilderment and his resilience, his Hollywood-romantic model of love and desire, Adlai is a delightful clown of an anti-hero.[13] "Lunatic old mam," "wonderful old mam," so self-assured in her narrow outlook on life, so ready with her mythologizing and moralizing, so close with her secrets, is a droll eccentric, while the absent father, the birth-control missionary nicknamed Humpter, is also a leaven of comedy as idolized hero and/or suspected seducer and scoundrel. And the reduction of Garbo to animate and passionate pin-up, cleaning woman and nagging concubine, is a brilliant piece of whimsy.

But as much as from the situations and the characters imagined by Leon Rooke, the comic effects spring from the language of the narrator; that is, from the hidden verbal manipulations of the author. Not unexpectedly, overstatements are a major source of fun, but since the device is a time-honoured one I may be allowed not to dwell on it here. Hyperbole, however, can be used in conjunction with other tropes, which can create rippling interferences. Consider this report on Adlai and Greta's

---

[13] Verbal comedy also includes such linguistic contaminations as the following: "That's the bite of it, son. But eat your carrots, Adlai" (10). The fun also proceeds from the possibility of a two-way reading of the influence; while, diegetically, the literal *eat* (and the situational context of the meal) called for the metaphorical *bite*, which yet comes first, textually, the metaphor seems to generate the literal injunction.

lovemaking: "We locked limbs, we licked and scratched, we yowled and bit and spun. Howl, spit, and claw" (26-27). Exaggeration heightens, while animal metaphors undercut, the scene; a succession of intransitive verbs makes it very physical yet somewhat remote, and the remoteness is increased when the shift to forms that could be interpreted as nouns raises the action to a timeless level of abstraction. That the efficacy of the hyperbole rests on its metaphorical underpinnings is demonstrated when the narrator next turns to machine imagery to convey the power of the encounter. For, then, the effect achieved is less complex because machinery, though a recurrent source of images, is not as functional in the context as animals, and particularly dogs, which are, as we shall see, a narrative, thematic and figurative matrix of considerable importance. What at first reading we accept as hyperbolic colouring, and thus implicitly discard as ornamental, turns out to be one nexus in a complex system of signs. Awareness of this adds to the connotations of the passage and modulates its mock-heroics into humorous irony.[14]

Together with colloquialisms, such as "We had us a good cry," clichés account for a fair share of the comic effects. However bizarre the situation narrated, however idiosyncratic the narrator's utterance, the speech of Adlai and Mam is encrusted with the deposits of a language that speaks them as much as they speak it. At times, the discrepancy between the autonomy that Adlai believes to be his and his dependence on commonplaces is in itself funny (and needless to say is also an indication of the distance between narrator and author). On the other hand, clichés are not used simply in a negative way. They also on occasion make for picturesque, vivid speech. And they are for the characters a way to stylize and give dignity to their lives, redeeming them from formlessness and insignificance.

In addition, the piling up of stock phrases and proverbs — or pseudo-proverbs — exploits the comical possibilities of accumulation. Juxtaposition (e.g., "'thick and thin,' she said. 'It doesn't rain but it pours'" [23]) create incongruities, and so do mixed — sometimes expanded — metaphors (e.g., "It had been the [metaphoric] vitriol that slammed down my old Daddy and made his gums bleed. That had turned him boots up").

---

[14] If hyperbole, on the whole, seems more characteristic of the I-narrator's rhetoric than of the I-actor's, conversely, clichés are more abundant in the characters' utterances, although they can also be found in the narration.

Linguistic transformation of an idiom may pleasingly renew it: "Greta was sulking, giving me first one cold shoulder and then the next" (11). (The exterior context that we provide also contributes here to our enjoyment, as we are made to remember the old dramatic photographs of stars looking wide-eyed at us around one strapless shoulder.) The fictional context may amusingly rejuvenate hackneyed phrases as in the black humour of the passage where dead Old Mam sobs, "My man! . . . My little man. My comfort in this sick old age" (19). In the same manner, clichés take on a new life when we read them as *double entendres,* "A woman wanting a baby she'd fall down in a ditch and let the men poke at her . . . It makes you sick, don't it. Just thinking about it. It does me. But your Daddy was no crybaby. He was not the man to tuck tail under his britches and run. No, he kept plugging. Kept singing the glories of birth control" (21). Since the narrator never displays any awareness of the sexual innuendoes of his or his mother's words, it is up to the reader to make the extension from the literal to the figurative. More than once I caught myself chuckling and wondering: Can this "mean" what I think it means? To ask the question is, in a sense, answer enough. Leon Rooke uses words in such a way that he makes you responsible for and aware of your "dirty" mind. "'Roll me over, dear,' asks Daddy, 'Roll me over in my grave . . .'" Now, tell me, frankly, didn't you expect "in the clover"?

Less comical but still worth a smile are the allusions or parodies, in short, the play of inter-textuality in the narrative: the image that makes the hard-hat labourers "our century's dogly warriors" (28), the echoes of Kipling (the repetition of "the itchy Gurunsis" and "in the distant Upper Volta") or of Poe ("washed up from some foul pit or tomb, some ill and dank un-resting place" [19]), the reverberation of our culture's myths ("How beautiful. How divine" [25]: only one guess allowed). The moment when Adlai projects himself as the masterful, Hollywood-type lover is a hilarious hodgepodge that infuses the style of popular romance with a dash of nineteenth-century naughtiness "piquant" and perhaps a *soupçon* of the metaphysical poets:

> "I want you. Garbo!" I thundered.
> "Dun't talk, idiot!"
> We romped past passion, past love's fury, and settled in for holy worship of piquant — exquisite — lust (27).

One may doubt whether the narrator is conscious of his imitations. But whether he is or not matters little in the end to our own enjoyment of them. And lest I have given the wrong impression of him, I hasten to add that Adlai is far from being illiterate. He tips his hat to "old Darwin the theorizer" (15), and he deploys a wide vocabulary and considerable rhetorical skills. His verbal agility enables him to assimilate various registers and various voices in an utterance that is ultimately as triumphantly his own as our speech can ever be ours.

Working with and against the comic strain, there is a pathetic strain. The two are not only intertwined but are also often mutually generative. The terms of endearment exchanged between mother and son may be at once funny and moving:

> — "Is that true, mam? Am I your pudding and pie?"
> — "You're it, Adlai. The apple of my eye."
> — "I wasn't dropped off on your doorstep? By some man on a black horse?"
> Mam would get cross when I'd ask that (33).

Even the characters' tears, when reported as, "We had us a good cry," or, "It was just like the old days us having that good cry," will elicit a smile. When Old Mam folds back into the wall, Adlai runs over and kisses it, "pining for a sweet farewell," "wanting total forgiveness — full recognition — from her" (24). Nevertheless, his grief is not unmixed:

> Afraid — shivering with fear! — that my Daddy next would walk in.
> Sighing. Unable to admit that what I wanted most was what I never could have. This: that *both* would leave me alone (24).

This sequence of micro-actions develops from the pathos of loss and absence to the comedy of forever haunting presence — enhanced here by the fact that Adlai has never known the father who did leave him long before — from the simplicity of love and the fantasy of ideal love to complexities and ambiguities of parent-child relationships.

On the whole, we tend to perceive pathos and comedy as two poles because the story's and the narrator-protagonist's quickly shifting moods maintain in the reader an awareness of extremes. The pathetic dimension, however, does not lend itself to a formal analysis as easily as the comic one. Certainly it depends, too, on rhetorical devices. Hyperbole again plays a part, and some of the narrator's hyperbolic flights have a tinge of almost nineteenth-century sentimentality, as in the following metaphor: "I might have dozed or daydreamed myself — dappled off on beams of sunlight" (19). Or, one can point to the repetitions of emotive words as in the oxymoronic sentences, "She was simply smiling her sad understanding at me. Smiling her sad, abandoned hope" (23). The recurrence of "my mam," which combines an emotive diminutive with a personal adjective, again strikes a sentimental note. Yet, this is only one of the many functions of the phrase, which brings together socio-cultural and psychological connotations; and, in its many textual returns, it resonates to a sentence uttered only once. "My mam" chimes in with "my little man." Neither Mother, nor Mum, Momma, Mummy et cetera, would have permitted quite the same semiotic effect, which heightens the theme, the relationship between solitary (deserted?) Old Mam and her lonely little man. It should also be observed that the narrator does not shrink from using and repeating words that in this our dry season have almost become obsolete. Like *love*. Like *soul*. Words that radiate feeling. Notwithstanding the display of sentiment, the love that permeates the short story is not of the wishy-washy kind. It is "dreadful love [that] slouches in" (26) as oxymoronic as Old Mam's love is ambivalent — or Adlai's or anyone's. Ultimately, "The Birth Control King" seems to implement the statement of Neville in Virginia Woolf's *The Waves*: "Our mean lives, unsightly as they are, put on splendour and have meaning only under the eyes of love" (152).

Everything considered, the pathetic seems to me to depend a good deal — and even more than the comic — on what the reader brings to the story, *consciously or not*, whereas for the bawdiness to work we have to be aware of the second meaning of the phrases used. Take the description of Old Mam's work boots: "She still wore the same ankle-high work boots [sic] that had mesmerized me in my childhood. They had the rot of thirty years messing about with turnips and spuds, a lifetime of kicking at grass and dandelion. The laces were covered with mold. The socks on her thin bones were both shoved down" (17). One may argue that the emotion is created by the hyperboles ("the rot of thirty years"; "a lifetime of kicking"), by the word *mold* which, in the context, is heavily connoted.

But to me the most moving sentence is in fact the last, in which no word, except perhaps *thin*, is emotionally loaded. Of course, the closing sentence is coloured by the associations of the preceding ones, which evoked a lifetime of hard work, growing humble turnips and spuds rather than sweet peas or asparagus, fighting against useless grass and dandelion. The feelings that a text elicits are always grounded in the words of the page, naturally, but I contend that in such a case the verbal effects build up only a diffuse kind of pathos to which readers respond differently, to which I resonate because of something in my experience.

Part of the emotional appeal of "The Birth Control King" is that, through the idiosyncratic extravagance of the hero (or anti-hero), it fictionalizes not only fears and uncertainties, but also aspirations and hopes, common to all. The adult Adlai's questions are such as haunt most human beings over a certain age: "[I wanted] to say, *Old mam, what's happened to us? For I had lost a day and my life was going nowhere* — but where had hers gone?" (18). And the child Adlai's continued interest in his absent father, in the mystery of his origins, reflects a fundamental concern of the human child. Underlying Leon Rooke's story, one recognizes the main features of the Freudian "family romance," in which Marthe Robert sees the basic structure of narrative fiction, specifically the main features of the Foundling version of the family romance.[15] More generally, the childish and manful struggles of an aging underdog against his sense of loss and failure, his unwillingness to surrender in "a world gone sour"[16] are strangely moving. "The Birth Control King" is oriented toward a reader with both a tender heart and a bawdy mind.

A high point in Adlai's pathetic questioning occurs right after the moment of comedy when Old Mam explains to little Adlai that his father's birth control did not take:

> — "It didn't take, son. Otherwise, would I have had you?"
> — "I'm here, am I not, my mam? I'm *real*"

---

[15] In the pre-Oedipal version of the "family romance," the Foundling, whose birth is clouded in mystery, attempts to escape reality into a world of his own making, whereas in the post-Oedipal fable, the Bastard, whose birth is shameful and glorious, enters into conflict with the father and seeks to impose his will on the world.

[16] See the blurb on the jacket of *The Birth Control King*.

— "Oh you're real, son."

— "Are you sorry, my mam? That I'm here?"

— "Now, son, don't cry! Don't blubber. Hold those shoulders back. Don't you want your Daddy to be proud of you?"

— "Will he be? Will I grow up to fill his fine shoes?"

— "Oh I doubt that. There can be only one of him. And there's this to think about: long before you've come of age the black tide will have swept over all of us."

— "But my *spot*, my mam?"

— "I have upset you, haven't I? There, there. Mam's sorry. Give a kiss to your potty, unthinking old mam" (33).

This memory of Adlai's is not a narrative climax. Rather, it functions as a counterpoint to an anti-climax in the present chain of actions when Mergentoire orders Adlai to quit giving her son expectations. But the remembered scene knots most of the thematic strands that the narration has been spinning: the protagonist's concern with his identity, and consequently his reality, with his place in his mother's desire, the mother's casual but devastating denial that the son can fill his father's shoes and enjoy the allotted "spot" she has promised him all along, the very contradiction at the heart of her expectations for, and desire of, her child. Crucial as they are to the fatherless boy, such concerns are wide-spread, and consequently, the fictional child's fears, the shock he experiences, together with his mother's unwitting betrayal, can reverberate in the reader's imagination.

Poignant moments such as this abound in "The Birth Control King," and I draw attention to one more, which, this time, does coincide with a narrative climax — the retarded Hedgepolt's sudden breaking into speech. This is a particularly interesting sequence because it shows the great risks that Leon Rooke is willing to run — and that his readers must be willing to take. In a first phase, Hedgepolt, whom Adlai has exhorted to brace up, speaks his first words ever, and speaks them apropos, whereas, a few minutes before, asked "who's your mam?" he had pointed at Adlai.

Strangely his face shook loose of its idiocy until at last it became one radiant angel's smile.

"*Dad-dee*," he said.

> Our jaws dropped. Hedgepolt had never been known to speak before.
>
> "*Dad-dee*," he said again. And his arm flopped towards me. Then with more grace than I could believe he swung it around to point at Mergentoire. "*Mam-mee!*," He patted her head (35).

Most readers. I think, will experience a twinge of *reluctant* emotion. Conditioned by twentieth-century literature, we have become wary of sentimentality, and so we do not know quite how to react. What if, after this dubious sequence opening, the story descended into bathos? Leon Rooke saves us from further hesitation not by exercising more restraint but by letting go. (Or, should I say, saves me? Playing the scene for all it is worth, he sweeps me away, succeeds in convincing me of the rapture of that instant.)

If we are made to share in Mergentoire's bliss, our emotion proceeds from identification with Hedgepolt and his excitement at mastering language — which perhaps reactivates buried memories of our own early triumphs. Hedgepolt's rapid progress is itself swiftly and economically conveyed. After naming his parents — and thereby choosing himself a father — Hedgepolt goes on to a second phase in which he names his world "Gret-ta" and dogs, "brutish, snarling dogs." The phrase is as unexpected to the reader as it is to the characters. Hedgepolt not only establishes a link between a simple sign and a person or a thing in his environment, he can now juxtapose words, which are not exactly basic English, and describe what he is seeing through the window. Until then, insofar as the statement because of its diction sounds like a quotation (is Hedgepolt parroting someone?), the breakthrough, undeniable as it is, remains ambiguous. Not so, however, his next utterances:

> "Shoes!" he crowed. "Adlai and Hedgepolt get shoes wet? Walk in muck? See old Mother? Throw flower in grave? Kiss old Mother goodby? Walk home in rain? Adlai hold Hedgepolt's hand? . . ." (36).

Hedgepolt is now using language to tell a story, no matter how discontinuously, and through it to recover the lost day that Adlai so much wanted to forget. Nor is his emphasis on shoes — the first word he introduces — an irrelevant detail. His mother has been worrying about his getting his shoes wet and his catching cold at the funeral (29), and has just been making his inability to "tie his shoes" the sign and emblem of his mental retardation. He "doesn't even know what shoes are for," she has just reminded Adlai angrily (31). Well, Hedgepolt *does* know.[17] Moreover, the story he chooses to tell is a crucial one, since it rounds out the story of Old Mam's burial, an event to which Adlai has never completely faced up. On the pathos of Hedgepolt "wanting to get it all out" is superimposed the pathos of the lonely burial of Old Mam. Compared with the partial relation that Adlai gave ("A black snarling sky. / Rain thundering down. / . . . Wind whistling past my ears like shrieks from a shut-up thing. / Hedgepolt's sticky hand in mine" [29]), Hedgepolt's is a toned-down, more factual version.[18] Yet, it is more moving than the heightened, expressionistic rendering of Adlai. Perhaps because it is more sober, but largely also because of the circumstances and the speaker's nature, which a few stylistic details keep recalling to us. Hedgepolt evokes the past with the present tense, for the act of uttering, of making present through words, is as important as, if not more than, the experiences narrated. The question marks ending each sentence indicate that these utterances are not so much assertions of what was as appeals to his hearers to corroborate his statements, or rather to confirm him in his use of language. This is speech oriented toward the others, so much so that Hedgepolt can eliminate the subject of several of his verbs, confident that his audience know whom he is referring to.

In the third phase, he addresses himself only to Adlai: "*Adlai happy!*" screeched Hedgepolt. "*Adlai happy for his old mother? He happy for Hedgepolt? He happy with world?*" (36). Hedgepolt can now describe (and shape)

---

[17] The shoe motif is also linked to the recurrent motif of traces which ranges from the muddy tracks Adlai observes in his room to the darkening pigmentation of Old Mam through the notes in Adlai's diary.

[18] Adlai's narrative contains two meta-narratives which to a lesser or greater extent duplicate it (and contrast with it) Hedgepolt's account is somewhat more detailed than Adlai's (the flower, the goodbye kiss). Adlai's own diary entry for August 10, on the other hand, records the hour-to-hour routine of the day, omitting all mention of the burial, indeed leaving no time slot for it. The macro-narrative, revealing the paralipsis (Genette, 93-94), denies the reliability of what was supposed to be an authentic, authoritative document. Yet the diary, which at once tells too much and too little, reflects Adlai's narrative, which tells too little and too much.

the mood of his significant Other, lending him not only happiness but generosity of feeling (he happy for someone else). The self-forgetfulness of a deprived being puts, as it were, a seal on this moment of grace, as Hedgepolt's first naming of Dad-dee and Mam-mee expands into a conquest of language and a celebration of love.

Together with his relaying of Hedgepolt's speeches, the narrator records his and Mergentoire's dazed then ecstatic reactions, again resorting to hyperbole.

> He spoke on, radiant. And joy, pure joy, in that moment seemed to serenade my bones. It seemed to seep up through my chair and to surge through me like light through a door. And it went on blazing. It went on rising. It shot up through the long table, rattling the dishes; it pulsed over our heads, and spun; it crashed up into the ceiling and went on rising; it crashed through our very walls and went on splashing and tumbling, whirling like a fireball through the atmosphere (36).

The passage is mostly generated by two semantic fields, or isotopies. The isotopy of light ("like light through a door"; "blazing"; "pulsed"; "fireball"; "shining") takes up, or rather blows up, the seme of the initial word, *radiant*, which denotes brightness and diffusion: a word that itself echoes — and justifies — a phrase we may have earlier objected to, "the radiant angel's smile." This local isotopy combines with the much larger isotopy of water, which governs much of the narrative. Here we have "seep up" "surge rising" "splashing" "tumbling" "whirling" "flooding" and even "crashing" elsewhere associated with turbulent waters. (The water matrix had engendered in the same narrative sequence the image through which Adlai rejected Mergentoire's acceptance of her son's stringent limitations. *"a sea of expectations*, I thought, *a sea for every one"* [30].) Just as on the narrative level of the chain of actions, Hedgepolt's outburst is an existential realization of Adlai's thought, so, on the figurative level, the "radiance" flooding the universe — a metaphor for joy and for understanding — is a transformation of the earlier image and is linked to Adlai's later vision when he sees "deep water and over the face of that mammoth water legion upon legion of matchstick canoes" (36). Thus the hyperbolic flight of metaphors is firmly correlated to the figurative network that reticulates the narrative. And again the verbal "extravagance" is a fitting vehicle for the reporting / the production of a moment of ecstasy and of an experience that is essentially a transgression of custom-accepted limits, the explosion of too restricted a concept of human nature and reality. Leon Rooke's gamble has worked for the reader who lets herself or himself be carried away by the pathos of the scene into some sort of faith in man and in words. In "The Birth Control King" extremes meet, if we are willing to extend our reading selves. Then the comedy and the tragedy of "these / our mean lives" have significance.

THE DYNAMICS OF THE NARRATIVE

The tensions that I have been examining are embodied in a narrative structure. The narrative action unfolds over a very short time span, from the moment Adlai wakes up to the "epiphany" that takes place at the breakfast table. But the narrative, as we have seen, is made to incorporate Adlai's childhood experience. As a result, on the inherent duality of narrating time and narrated time is superimposed a second cleavage in narrated time, between this morning's past — which becomes for us the "present of reference" in Mendilow's term — and the remote past(s). Nevertheless, all the time levels tend to blur into one another because the flashbacks are not always properly introduced as such. Because they often report iterative scenes (Genette, 146-178), telling only once events that have recurred several times over an indeterminate period of time (for example, p.9). Because, during Old Mam's visit, which takes place in the present of reference, mother and son hark back to the same subjects that exercise them in the narrator's flashbacks, standing in the same adult-child relationship. In the circuit of "The Birth Control King," the past is a remanence. Such stagnancy makes unlikely, we think, any dramatic change in Adlai's life.

Furthermore, the narration foregrounds very early its "hermenautic" and "proairetic" codes (Barthes, 25-26). Why Adlai lost a day, or in other words what happened on that day, is the enigma that has to be solved. And since Adlai is "eager to run down to breakfast" (8) we expect him to leave his "upper room" and go down to breakfast and to reality. This double program, hermeneutic and actional, is periodically recalled whenever

Adlai, trying to "figure this one out," wonders and asks about the date (8, 9, 11, 12, 13), when Mergentoire shouts up to him that she is not holding breakfast all day (19, 24), or Adlai hears the boarders' voices floating up from the dining room (9). But the realization of the program is postponed by all sorts of dilatory micro-narratives (memories of Old Mam, interventions of Greta, visit of Mam, love scene with Greta), not unexpectedly, when at last Adlai goes down to breakfast, the code of the enigma and the code of actions merge. Mergentoire provides the first objective clue to the mystery: "How was the funeral?" (28). As she asks more and more probing questions, while Adlai, foraging for food among "the wreckage" on the table, refuses to answer, the narrative entropy increases considerably. What Adlai refuses to confront is no longer enigmatic. We hardly even puzzle at a particular reason for Adlai's amnesia, since obviously the relationship between mother and son was remarkably close and not a little ambivalent. So when we later learn that Adlai ignored Mam's restrained yet pathetic last plea, this is, as it were, a bonus, an added reason for his wanting to blot out her death. Nor is Mergentoire's intervention in the action a surprise, inasmuch as almost from the first she was present in the background as a figure of authority, related to the common-sense world of downstairs, and Adlai needed an outside nudge to recover his memory — or the narrative needed the outside element that could motivate his remembering. For about two-thirds of its length, then, the narration runs a predictable course toward its end.

But — surprise, surprise — this model of storytelling conventions suddenly breaks down, or breaks free. Just as its initial program becomes entropically saturated, the narration regenerates itself by producing a new, unanticipated and much more complex program, which transforms the situation. To this extent, the structure of "'The Birth Control King" is homological with the story of rebirths that it tells. At the same time, the regeneration of the plot, which now confronts Adlai with Mergentoire, so far merely a background figure, and with a character only mentioned in passing as a source of noise, obscures the beginning-middle-and-end pattern. It is almost as if we had two stories, though, in truth, they are intricately related.

The point is that the new program does not deploy actions that could be said to evolve proairetically out of the first, except to the extent that they take place after Adlai has joined his landlady and her son at the breakfast table. The new sequence originates accidentally — though, of course, accidents no more occur in narratives than in modern psychology — in Adlai's attempts to elude Mergentoire's questions by changing the subject of the conversation. His various remarks to the effect that Hedgepolt should start thinking about girls, if they please poor Hedgepolt, incense Mergentoire. "Stop dreaming dreams about my Hedgepolt!" she orders Adlai. "Quit giving him expectations!" (31). From then on, unanticipated events follow in a dizzying succession of euphoric and dysphoric moments. Leaving aside Adlai's interspersed memories of his mother, we may dimly perceive a chronological thread in the series of actions — or project it out of our need for such concentration. Mergentoire's angry assertion that her son is mentally deficient hurts Hedgepolt. His sobs, even if they prove that he is no longer the "vacuum" he used to be, in turn cause Mergentoire to weep and to comfort her afflicted child. "'Your mam loves *you*,' she said. 'Adlai loves you too. We are all one big family.' Her foot nudged mine under the table. 'Tell him, Adlai. Tell him how happy we are'" (35). And Adlai, in spite of his sorrowful reminiscences of a similar scene with Old Mam, manages a smile "for Hedgepolt's sake." "'You bet,' I said. 'She's said a mouthful, son'" (35). It is as if Mergentoire's inaccurate affirmations, "we are a family and we are happy," and Adlai's familiar and familial address, "son," have triggered Hedgepolt's outburst. As if words had caused things to happen. This breakthrough then spreads on the radiance and rapture that eventually lead Adlai to his epiphany, the canoes riding the mammoth water, and "in those canoes a thousand black faces and those faces whooping delight at me the same as I was whooping it back at them" (36). In this vision, Adlai accepts as a happy dream what to his parents was a nightmare. "And nothing poor mam could do about it" (37).[19]

But, once more, extremes touch and the euphoria of welcoming the black tide ("I gave them my biggest *wave*") leaves Adlai wondering "which was vision and which was real life and finally where it, or they, or even myself had gone" (37; emphasis mine). Adlai experiences the familiar

---

[19] Old Mam has already suspected that her son may be turning from her and from her values. There are moments, she says, "when I wonder if you don't think I brought you up wrong. Times when I think you are holding me responsible for so much that goes on in this mean world" (18). See also page 21.

feeling of being unreal. "Had I slipped forward into some future year? Adlai, where are you? Adlai is on his tightrope out over the swirling water, balanced between rope and sky, wavering and floundering with his balancing pole. Adlai steering for the river's other shore. Adlai saying Mam, are you there? Mam, will you forgive me?" (37). This passage is one of the most moving in the story. The sudden shift from joy to despair acts at this point as a reminder that Adlai, being a human, if fictive, being, can but live constantly suspended between (re)birth and death. The abyss still yawns. "Adlai falling. Adlai crying. Then only the quivering rope and the crashing water" (37). The I-actor sees himself from a distance, then disappears from sight — only the Janus-like epithet *crashing* recalls his own fall even as it describes the destructive element. The I-narrator is at the same time obliterated from his discourse, which contains no traces of him as the enunciating subject.

This is the darkest, the most perilous, moment for Adlai. But he is rescued from it by Mergentoire and Hedgepolt's hugging him and the mother's praise "'You've done it, Adlai! Hooray for you!'" (37). Mergentoire, who first acknowledged the miracle with a passive form, "My son is cured" (36), is now ready to recognize that Adlai's interest in, and "grooming" of the boy have not been in vain, that he saved her son. For even sharp-tongued Mergentoire is endowed with generosity of spirit.[20] "You've done it!" In context, the phrase applies more largely to the protagonist's high-wire act over the rapids of despair, which we have just witnessed. Adlai has now found peace and his place. He sends Greta away. He observes Mam's watchful eye "whirling away into the dark . . . I stayed on. Stayed, I say, as if bolted to my chair, as Hedgepolt's head lay warmly in my lap, and Mergentoire leaned against my knees, emptied of her joyful weeping." They are now a family unit because Adlai and Hedgepolt have dared to "dream the dreams," because Adlai and Mergentoire have spoken the inaccurate words, which were the right words, at the right time.

The unannounced narrative program can be summarized only when it has been completed; a reborn Adlai succeeds in coming home, in actual-

---

[20] I cannot agree with Judith Fitzgerald that the female characters of "The Birth Control King" are "abominable women" ("About the Edges," *Canadian Literature* 101 [Summer 1984]: 126). Even Old Mam with her racism and horribly narrow views has courage and dignity and a certain selflessness.

ization of what seems to be a basic narrative plot.[21] Both programs form a sort of diptych, with the recovery of a lost day being followed by the discovery of a lost (or until then never found) inner space of freedom, and paradoxically, of a fixed spot in a network of love. And with Adlai emblematizing in both parts "un ser de deseo tanto como un deseo de ser," to use Octavio Paz's fine phrase, a being of desire desiring to be.

As the plot finds a new life, it reactivates the thematics of the first program, so that, whatever diegetic surprises the last part of the narrative holds for the reader, the short story itself never seems to break apart, but rather appears to develop and harmonize chords that were faintly to be heard from the beginning.

To begin with the more obvious, the new developments serve the didactic function of correcting, within the textual system, the racist notions of the protagonist, thereby increasing the "liberal" reader's identification with him. Notice, however, that, as he stands converted and urges blacks to "come on," Adlai still assumes a certain superiority, acknowledged by the blacks, "We coming, *boss* (37; emphasis mine). More generally, what is destroyed is Old Mam's concept of the self as tied up to a special time-space that is both predetermined and yet liable to be invaded by the Other. The concept has already been subtly undermined by Greta's leaving the screen for a place on Adlai's door and the door calendar for a bath tub, undermined, too, by Old Mam's rising from her ultimate resting ground. But now Adlai discovers for himself that space is less restricted, and invaders less threatening, than he was led to believe. "'*Come on, you, polecats!*' he shouts, '*There are spots for all of us!*'" (37). He is again made aware — and with him the reader — that the boundary between inner and outer space, imaginary realm and actual locus, is fluid indeed.

Less ostensibly, the latter plot energizes again the theme of the underdog coming into his own, by presenting Hedgepolt as a double, even if less favoured, of the protagonist. Both are cases of arrested development. "Hedgepolt looks to be every bit of thirty yet he's still in grammar school," says the narrator (30), while Greta, in a fit of anger, calls Adlai "theece child, theece half-man, theece mental deficient" (25). One, of course, is dumb, whereas the other's verbal exuberance verges on logorrhea, but the con-

---

[21] Interestingly, the hermeneutic code is hardly operative in the second part. There is little enigma in the action proper, which, yet, is the working out of the mystery of being.

trast unites as it opposes them. Both are fatherless — significantly neither is given a patronym in the narration — both enjoy, or suffer from, a privileged relationship with a loving but dominating mother. The parallel is driven home in the juxtaposition of two scenes when Mergentoire and Old Mam try to comfort with the same gestures and the same words the sons whom they have upset by reminding them of their limitations (32-33). And, last but not least, both are "saved" or "cured." Notwithstanding all this, I cannot quite accept Judith Fitzgerald's judgement that "Adlai's identification with the silent Hedgepolt is ultimately what saves him" (126), because it ignores too much what is going in the action and in the narration.

The link that is created in the second half of the diptych between Adlai and Hedgepolt is part of the overarching theme of the mystery of origins, of fatherlessness and fatherhood. In the first leaf, lacking a father's presence and even knowledge of who and what his mythical father was, Adlai is shown as lacking *authority*; he has, in his mother's words, been unable "to take up [his] Daddy's mighty cudgel" (22). (The phallic symbolism may speak volumes to the reader but not to Old Mam.) In the second leaf of the diptych, Adlai's interest in Hedgepolt opens up new possibilities for the boy and for himself. Taking Hedgepolt to Old Mam's funeral, standing hand in hand with him at the side of her grave, is to assign him, symbolically, a grandson's place. Hedgepolt acknowledges his sonship first indirectly, then increasingly clearly, after — if I may be allowed to belabour the point — he has been called son by Adlai. This may be a textual co-ordinate rather than a diegetic cause — as we must remember even if we are tempted into establishing some sort of causal relation, as I did in earlier development. Another connection is made when Hedgepolt accedes to language and its symbolic possibilities. For then he is "cured," that is to say, partly freed from his infantile dependence on his mother. "*My baby's no baby no more!*" Mergentoire exclaims (36). And his rebirth he owes largely to Adlai's affection for him and to Adlai's faith in life, his belief in the world as "a sea of expectations," which contrasts with "poor Mergentoire's" realism, her preoccupation with "small stuff." The question then arises: Should we read the episode as suggesting that mothers give birth and love while fathers give language and with it life? Adlai, at any rate, has reversed his situation. He now is in a position of *savoir*. He has acquired the power of the man whose knowledge has been confirmed by reality. He knew that you must dream the dreams. Once he has been acknowledged as a father by Hedgepolt, he can be assimilated to his father in the very moment when he rejects his father's life lesson. For as he greets enthusiastically the blacks in their canoes[22] the "Upper Volta ears picked up. Their eyes did a double-take. *Is that you boss?* they asked. *Is that you? Is that the King?*" (37). Since he does not decline the address, he does identify with the king, the Father, his father. And we suddenly realize that if we have so far assumed that the birth-control king could be none other than the mythical father, perhaps the title also refers to some avatar of the hero himself. Adlai has achieved a life-long dream of man; he has both symbolically replaced his father and become a better man, in the bargain. The last paragraph depicts a family tableau, with Adlai seated as a *pater familias* in an old photograph, thinking of his enlarged obligations. He is in a position of responsibility and author-ity, and even proud Mergentoire leans against his knees. Yet, as I read and picture this "still" on which the dramatic oscillation of the narrative ends, something tugs at the back of my mind. Is not the Adlai-Hedgepolt-Mergentoire group strangely like a pictorial holy family? And even more specifically like Leonardo's *Madonna with Saint Anne,* which inevitably makes of Adlai not the expected Saint Joseph but Saint Anne. I am pleased to think that there is even this faint suggestion of one more crossing of boundaries in "The Birth Control King" — a crossing of the gender bound-ary, a slight intimation that the child is father and mother to the man.

In addition, the unanticipated turn of events *spot*lights a pattern of oppositions that pulses through the text. Mentions of dogs, romping, squealing, fighting, yowling, recur from the first page to the last (see 7, 12, 19, 24, 30, 34, 38). Such insistence on what might at first appear as "real-istic" background sketching solicits our interpretative zeal. The dogs re-main outside the house and have no part in the action proper apart from making noise. So what can their function be? Symbolic, naturally. One remembers that dogs, which are the companions of the dead on their voy-age to the underworld, are "associated with the symbolism of the mother and of resurrection" (Cirlot, 84). Yet, one may hesitate to load the dogs with such symbolic weight all the more so because they are not associated in any way with Old Mam. Until the last narrative unit:

---

[22] One might interpret his greeting them as his salute to the courage of man, his ever-renewed attempts to overcome his restricted circumstances. *The Birth Control King* offers a constant temptation to read symbolically.

The dogs beneath the window were silent. Or gone. I thought I could see them racing as a pack down the long street to another place. Soon, perhaps, to splay off into green country side. I closed my eyes.

Peace.

Soul's ascension.

And mam's watchful eye splayed off, too. I went whirling away into the dark (38).

The juxtaposition in the narrative of the dog's and of Mam's disappearance is a first correlation. But, there is a more telling connection; the use of a verbal phrase, "splay off," which is already striking when applied to dogs, is positively weird applied to the human eye. Should we then regard the dogs as modern Erynies, pursuing Adlai for some fault, seeking to avenge his neglect of his mother? They do indeed "splay off" *after* Adlai has asked Mam's forgiveness and made his peace with the world.

These symbolic possibilities, however, do not exhaust the signification of the dogs. Early in the narrative, animal metaphors and comparisons start cropping up — "hogging the phone"; "shrill as a rat"; "growling at her son"; "to ferret out wrongdoers"; "my hoofprints"; "spiry as a cat"; "slurp-slurp"; "you'd think I slept above a hog pen." Human beings act like animals, even pet other human beings as they would animals (e.g., "raking a hand idly up and down Hedgepolt's back" [28]). We feel that the dog motif must be related to the animal imagery. But how? As far as I am concerned, the pieces of the puzzle fell into place when I read Adlai's advice to Hedgepolt — the unspoken advice that the jealous Mergentoire is yet able to hear, thus overcoming the barrier between minds. ("You'd think she had stepped right into my head" [31]). "Dare to be God!" is what Adlai had thought. God-dog, dog-God, the inescapable polarity of human nature encapsulated in the unity of a mirror-word. Because of the reversibility of the two English words, we could say with Kafka that "all knowledge, the totality of all questions and answers are contained in the dog."[23] No wonder that at long last daring to be God, Hedgepolt's first description of the outside world should be that of "brutish, snarling dogs."

---

[23] Quoted by Keath Fraser, "Notes toward a Supreme Fiction," *Canadian Literature* 100 (Spring 1984): 117. Needless to say, *God* and *dog* are not reversible in German.

But the very reversibility of God / dog makes it difficult to say where the bar between the two is. Making love to Greta, Adlai was creating his world, his reality, was playing God; but much of the imagery that renders the "ecstasy" of that encounter ("licked"; "scratched"; "yowled"; "howl, spit and claw") reflects the "dogliness" of the experience.[24] Viewed from this angle, "The Birth Control King" is a metaphor of the human condition. It would not do to overburden it with too explicit a philosophy. Yet, underlying the story, there is an outlook that recalls a commentary by Jean-Paul Sartre (566): "God, value and supreme end of transcendence, represents the permanent limit in terms of which man makes known to himself what he is. To be man means to reach toward being God, or, if you prefer, man is fundamentally the desire to be god." Except that "The Birth Control King" also reminds us of the other limit that defines us.

Though the God / dog reversal is itself like a watermark in a banknote rather than like the Queen on the face of it, other forms of word play make up more visible designs. Sets of co-ordinates can be discerned through the narrative. Thus, one may correlate the black newspaperboy's claim that "de *sky* is de limit" (13; emphasis mine) with Adlai's contention that we live in "*a sea of expectations, a sea for everyone.*" (31; emphasis mine). Here semiotic and semantic co-ordinates are aligned. Or one may adduce as an example the pole network. Why should the nameless prospective employer of Adlai's, who exploits cheap immigrant labour (14), be a Pole rather than, say, a Greek or an Italian? From the thematic point of view, any minority group would serve just as well. "Poles . . . What can you say about Poles?" Adlai asks (15). We can answer that Poles enter into a semiotic system that traverses the text. If a Pole failed Adlai in his quest for self-improvement, a pole is what keeps him balanced and moving on his tightrope. Pole is curtailed in Hedgepolt's name[25] and expanded into polecats, the derogatory word turned into a friendly address with which Adlai greets the oncoming blacks who are "going no place but UP UP UP" (the

---

[24] I coin dogliness on Leon Rooke's dogly in "dogly warriors."

[25] Hedgepolt begins his fictional life as a sort of poltergeist who is first heard "hidden away, . . . banging pots and pans" (24). The *hedge* in his name recalls the boundary that separates him from other human beings but over which he eventually vaults. If his name belongs to the problematics of borders and (h)edges, his mother's name, *Mergentoire*, belongs to that of fusion.

pole?). Polecat enters into resonance with the animal names given to the characters (e.g., "you ape") and the animal imagery but it also introduces cat, a slang word for jazz musicians often applied to and used by blacks. In the pole set of co-ordinates are evidenced textual effects — and perhaps the text's capacity for self-generation, or at least the way in which a "sentence invite[s] another sentence and that [demands] a third" (Hancock, 113), in which a word invites a word and invites echoes of itself.

What makes crossing "The Birth Control King of the Upper Volta" so difficult, in fact, is the number of echoes that resonate throughout, dizzying and tantalizing the reader and perhaps leading him or her astray.[26] The problem is also how to end one's movements back and forth. Blondin, after all, only crossed Niagara Falls from one side to the other. But, if in the attempt we become vulnerable, that is because as Adlai says: "Every encounter, including those only imagined, is an affair of the soul. Is cut-throat war."

---

[26] I could have chosen to develop a set of co-ordinates that correlate Blondin's crossing of Niagara, mentioned at least twice, the black's crossing of the ocean — a repeated image — Adlai's balancing on his tightrope, "steering for the river's other shore," all co-ordinates that involve crossing and water. But this would have brought up again ideas that I had already touched upon in other ways and would have emphasized the thematic dimension.

BIBLIOGRAPHY

Barthes, Roland. *S / Z*. Paris: Seuil, 1970.

Cirlot, J.E. *A Dictionary of Symbols*. Translated by Jack Sage. New York: Philosophcal Library, 1962.

Bellamy, Joe David. *The New Fiction: Interviews with Innovative American Writers*. Urbana University of Illinois Press, 1974.

Fitzgerald, Judith. "About the Edges." *Canadian Literature*. 101 (Summer 1984).

Fraser, Keath. "Notes toward a Supreme Fiction." *Canadian Literature* 100 (Spring 1984).

Genette, Gérard. *Figures III*. Paris: Seuil, 1972.

Hancock, Geoff. "An Interview with Leon Rooke." *Canadian Fiction Magazine* 38 (1981).

Labov, William. *Language in the Inner City: Studies in the Black English Vernacular*. Philadelphia: University of Pennsylvania Press, 1972.

Robert, Marthe. *Roman des origines et origines du roman*. Paris: Grasset, 1972.

Rooke, Leon. *The Birth Control King of the Upper Volta*. Downsview, Ont.: EWC Press, 1982.

"Voices." *Making It New: Contemporary Canadian Stories*. Edited by John Metcalf. Toronto: Methuen, 1982.

Sartre, Jean-Paul. *Being and Nothingness: An Essay on Phenomenological Ontology*. Translated by Hazel E. Barnes. London: Methuen, 1957.

Woolf, Virginia. *The Waves*. Harmondsworth: Penguin Books, 1964.

"THE ONLY DAUGHTER" ON THE ROAD: A MOURNING RITE OF PASSAGE

NICOLE CÔTÉ

Fiction is real life coming at you from another angle.
—LEON ROOKE

By disolving the boundaries among genres and by employing a language that is at once mimetic and symbolic, Leon Rooke's art of fiction lies in his ability to explore, through ordeals, issues of transformation and identity.

Fairy tales start invariably with a loss — of order in a country, of riches, of a loved one — that brings about the hero's tribulations and ultimately the discovery of himself/herself. These protonarratives embody a truth about human nature, which, as Lacan has it: "the human object always constitutes itself through the intermediary of a first loss" (Butler, 75). So it is for "The Only Daughter," fairy-tale-like in the impetus of its quest: the mother, on her deathbed, advises her daughter to leave home and journey to meet her father: "Git out fast. Go to him." (24). Counsel from which her daughter recoils: "But I don't want to go." "'Want' ain't got no britches no more she can wear. 'Want' is dropped dead. I can't look out for you no more" (29). The moribund woman, in this beautifully alive repartee, ultimately makes her own death a condition for transforming her daughter's "wants" into necessity. In other words, the mother here assumes the father's traditional role by convincing her daughter to leave home and make her entry into the realm of the social. Thus the story is shaped as a quest that leads the daughter from the (relative) innocence of living an undifferentiated life with her mother to the (relative) experience of becoming a woman and the daughter of her father. The passage from mother to father is regulated by the work-in-progress of mourning, of which her progress along the ever-present road is symbolic.

The narrative, through a focalization intermingling free indirect speech and omniscience, uses flash-backs to provide the necessary exposition: having had no formal education, the girl led an unorthodox childhood, and, despite her piquancy, seems thus all the more vulnerable on her lonely quest for her father. At the onset of the narrative, the girl is walking a dirt road flanked by woods, on which a bus driver dropped her the previous night. Hence, the very unconventional Rooke presents us with a heroine who conforms perfectly to the canons of the low mimetic[1] in that "pathos is increased by the inarticulateness of the vision, and . . . of defective intelligence." In the girl's case, it is rather a defect of exposure to education, which leads her to naïvely reflect that: "it (the sun) moved when she moved, and at what pace she moved, and stopped when she stopped" (22).[2]

The daughter's naïveté also delays her recognition of the father, once she catches a glimpse of him, very late in the narrative. The loving portrait her mother depicted is the source of the daughter's conflict between two opposite images of her father she has to choose from, the ideal father pictured and his reality:

> Was this him? She did not think it could be. Her mama had said he'd be a good height and thin and pretty nice-looking. He'd have a certain glint in his eyes that would make a woman go goose bumpy. He'd have a way about him that let you know he meant to get what he wanted and that you wouldn't mind it . . . Mama

---

[1] Frye, Northrop, *Anatomy of Criticism*, 1990, 38. According to Frye's theory of modes (idem, 34-42), "The Only Daughter" is clearly in the ironic mode: "If inferior in power or intelligence to ourselves, so that we have a sense of looking down on a scene of bondage, frustration, or absurdity, the hero belongs to the ironic mode." Irony arises from the low mimetic, and low mimetic deals with pathos: "Pathos presents its hero as isolated by a weakness which appeals to our sympathy because it is on our own level of experience. ... the central figure of pathos is often a woman or a child (or both ...). Pathos is usually concentrated on a single character, partly because low mimetic society is more strongly individualized."

[2] Aware that she lacks some of the essential skills that a person on her own should have acquired, she is constantly suspicious. The scene of the fare counted by the bus driver is a good example of this redoubling of pathos: "Yesterday she had more but the man on the bus had taken the dollar bill. He had taken the half-dollar too, and had seemed to want to take more, but she had bitten her lip, watching his every move, and thirty-nine cents had been miraculously returned to her palm. "How I know you're not cheatin' me?" she said. "How I know how much this trip is?" "You don't. ... No, you don't. You don't know nothin', I expect."

must of been joshing, for this one was nothing. He was red-dirt nothing. He had a big fat gut and muscley arms all stubby. He wore a rumpled greasy felt hat pushed back on his head . . . It was an ugly face . . . his little pig eyes gleamed. No, this wasn't him. It couldn't be. Mama didn't have memory to beat a bat . . . Him? The idea was so funny she almost laughed out loud. . . Him? The likelihood was plain disgusting. Her mama would never have let herself curl up to nothing looking like that (38-39).

Thus not being ready to meet her father — "Goddamnit," she whimpered, "I ain't ready yet"[3] — she postpones the encounter, and instead begins to acknowledge him by the way of a reconnaissance of his environment: "She was about to step up on the porch and peek through the windows when she heard him coming. He was whistling. She ducked low over the grass, hit the lane, and took off running. For the balance of the day *she searched out the place*, avoiding open fields, steering wide of his house" (41; italics mine). This "searched out the place" suggests that the daughter is really searching for a *common ground* between her father and herself. These grounds being her father's, she is trying to "reconnoiter" her father by literally approaching him.

After the reconnaissance, the girl has a nap outdoors. This magic sleep,[4] in which time seems to stand still as in *Sleeping Beauty*, is followed by stillness earlier presented as foreboding, now as enchanted. Nature — in the form of a bird perched high on a tree — is here not connoted as debased,[5] as it was earlier, but as an object of contemplation despite its apparent sameness: "The same bird was alight, alight but silent, preening

---

[3] This remark, although it can be applied to this later one, is actually made earlier in the story (36), when the girl first recognizes the possibility that the driver of the wagon she saw go by as she was hiding in the ditch might be her father.

[4] "In the afternoon she crawled up in a tangle of vines and slept, pulling the black coat up over her head. It seemed to her she slept a long time, but when she rubbed her eyes awake the same bird was alight, alight but silent, preening its feathers, on the same high limb. It was so blessed still out here even the birds had caught it " (41).

[5] Many passages referring to the natural environment are painted in the light of a soiled or exhausted nature — the story opens with this description: "The walls were eroded by rain and where boulders were packed into the dirt scraggly bushes, leafless now, made vain attempts at renewal" (32).

its feathers, on the same high limb" (41). Since the sameness of nature is iterated, what brought about this change of perspective, or transfiguration, must be coming from the girl herself. This renewal, tapping into the unconscious, seems to be projected onto her environment. The nap changes the daughter's idea of her father: from a total rejection of his body image, she is moved to accept his fatherly qualities. Little by little, she recognizes, from her mother's description, his red hair and freckles (like her own), the house, and qualities other than physical. In this way, she reconciles reality with the ideal, moving from an outward look to an inward one.

How does this change, which allows the mourning daughter to finally consider her unknown parent as a suitable father, come? Let me answer this question in a roundabout way, by going back to the onset of the story. A distinctive feature of the low mimetic is that "pity and fear are communicated externally, as sensations" (38). This is exactly what happens here, as the pain of being "abandoned" by her mother is brought to the surface of her body: from the beginning of the narrative, the plot concentrates on the lonely girl treading along the long dreary road, in pain from hurts caused by her ill-fitting clothing, heavy suitcases, or hunger. Pain is ingrained in the syntax of the narrator-girl, the repetition of the pain motif being associated with superlatives, as these few examples will show: "Her shoulders *ached*. Her legs *ached*, and her arms and hands *worst of all*, though her feet *ached* too." (22); "maybe it was her hands that *hurt the most*." "The shoulder *ache;* shoulder *was worse*." "What was *bad* was the [coat] button . . . Maybe that was *worse*." (23)

The last of the pain appears after the "magic" nap, as if all of her resistance to a forthcoming attachment (to a new parental figure) was in it. It overwhelms her, this time not concentrating on one part of the body, but spreading:

> Her body itched all over. Her flesh was covered with bites, with scratches and welts. Bruises, head to toe . . . You couldn't even see any more where the blisters had been; it was all raw now. That was the *worst pain*, these heels. These feet. These scratches and cuts and being stuck out here (41).

It is significant that the girl's pain should extend to her whole body after she has found her father but has avoided an encounter with him. The rash could be seen as a hypertrophy of a symptomatology the girl develops throughout her journey. Insofar as her body is sending messages to her conscious mind, which rejects them, a non-discursive sign system is produced. Because of its existence outside the language system (which pertains to the symbolic), this sign system will here be considered as semiotic. A brief definition of the dichotomy of the semiotic/symbolic will illustrate this point. Julia Kristeva distinguishes the symbolic as "the order of social and signifying relations, of law, language and exchange" (Grosz, 194). Kristeva links the semiotic to *chora* — "the site of the undifferentiated bodily space the mother and child share" (195). The semiotic is also the site of "the undirected and uncontrolled input of the repressed impulses, energies and spasms of the infant . . . *and later, of the subject in moments of crisis and psychical upheaval*" (195; italics mine). The semiotic always "remains incompletely contained by the symbolic," being manifested in "a materiality that, like . . . the repressed, threatens to return" (196). Insofar as "the semiotic must be renounced and transcended in order for the pre-Oedipal child to acquire a stable social or symbolic position as a unified (masculine or feminine) subject" (196), the dying mother, by sending her daughter, against her will, on a quest for her father, initiates the resolution of her daughter's remaining pre-Oedipal drama at the onset of puberty.

Thus the girl, having led an undifferentiated life with her mother, is now urged to become differentiated, that is, necessarily gendered. Evidence of this lack of differentiation lies in the girl's absence of a name; it also lies in her being associated, in a fixed metaphor, as a part of the mother's body, namely the arms: "My right arm," the mother would say, "is a pretty little girl. She's my left arm, too" (43). This would correspond to the body in pieces (*Le corps morcelé*), which, according to Lacan, precedes the stage of the mirror,[6] where the infant can project an ego on the bodily surface recognized as its own.

---

[6] I would like to introduce this reflection of Butler as an explanatory apology for fusing Kristeva's semiotic stage and Lacan's mirror stage, which stem from apparently totally different premises: Kristeva's passage of the individual from an undifferentiated stage to a differentiated one entails the tearing away from the body of the mother; Lacan's stage of the mirror indicates that the narcissistic relation is primary: "Lacan's effort to offer an account of the genesis of bodily boundaries in 'The Mirror Stage' (1949) takes the narcissistic relation as primary, and so displaces the maternal body as a site of primary identification ... the reification of the maternal dependency as a 'support' and an 'obstruction' signified primarily as that

Insofar as the mother's death initiates the differentiation by urging a quest for the other parent (whose image symbolizes a later stage in the development of the child),[7] the girl seems to invest her body as a transitional object of love, as the concentration on the bodily pain suggests. Judith Butler here summarizes the arguments for the discovery of a bodily ego through pain / illness:

> In [Freud's] essay on narcissism, hypochondria lavishes libido on a body part, but in a significant sense, that body part does not exist prior to that investiture; indeed, that body part is delineated and becomes knowable for Freud only on the condition of that investiture . . . Freud[8] will state quite clearly that *bodily pain is the precondition of bodily self-discovery* . . . In a move that prefigures Lacan's argument in *The Mirror Stage*, Freud connects the formation of one's ego with the externalized idea one forms of one's body. Hence, Freud's claim: "The ego is first and foremost a bodily ego; it is not merely a surface entity, but is itself the projection on a surface" (1993: 58-59; italics mine).[9]

---

which, in the overcoming, occasions jubilation, suggests that there is a discourse on the differentiation from the maternal body in the mirror stage. The maternal is, as it were, already put under erasure by the theoretical language which reifies her function and enacts the very overcoming that it seeks to document.," maintains Butler (1993:71).

[7] Although it seems very difficult to theorize on the semiotic being prior to the symbolic, since it is by definition outside of language, according to Kristeva, it is "anterior to naming (...), to the father, and consequently maternally connoted" (Kristeva, 1980, 133 in Grosz, 1992, 195). Grosz explains: "Although the symbolic is formed through the repression and sublimation of the semiotic it is unable to exist – it has no "'raw materials' or energetic force – without the semiotic, which must be considered logically prior" (195).

[8] In *The Ego and the Id* (1923).

[9] Butler here adds this interesting deduction: "It seems that this imaginary valorization of body parts is to be derived from a kind of eroticized hypochondria. Hypochondria is an imaginary investment which, according to the early theory, constitutes a libidinal projection on the body-surface which in turns establishes its epistemological accessibility. Hypochondria here denotes something like a theatrical delineation, production of the body, one which gives imaginary contours to the ego itself, projecting a body which becomes the occasion of an identification which in its imaginary or projected status is fully tenuous." Concerning this link between illness and eroticized body, Butler adds: "For how is it that the self-preoccupation with bodily suffering or illness becomes the analogy for the erotogenic discovery and conjuring of body parts? In *The Ego and the Id*, Freud himself suggests that to figure sexuality as illness is symptomatic of the structuring presence of a moralistic framework of guilt" (1993: 63)

Since, as Butler maintains, "Freud argues that narcissism must give way to objects, and that one must finally love in order not to fall ill" (1993: 63), the daughter having lost her first object of love (her mother) and having not yet overtly invested in the process of mourning, she is in that in-between state of having to decathect her mother before recathecting a new object of love, her father. This "natural" process is not so easily engaged, since, according to Butler:

> Insofar as there is a prohibition on love accompanied by threats of imagined death, there is a great temptation to refuse to love, and so to be taken in by that prohibition and contract neurotic illness. Once this prohibition is installed, then, body parts emerge as sites of punishable pleasure and, hence, of pleasure and pain. In this kind of neurotic illness, then, guilt is manifested as pain that suffuses the bodily surface, and can appear as physical illness (1993: 63).

The only daughter's pain is not an illness; it has very definite origins in the physical world. The pain is caused by the rubbing of her shoes against her heels, mosquito bites, an empty stomach, et cetera. Nonetheless, the narration's emphasis is constantly put on the all-consuming pain of the girl, so much so that she tries to order her various pains, and to establish a hierarchy of the most painful part of the body.

These pains would correspond to a highly charged libidinal energy that allows for self-discovery, part by part, through a self-invested love. Yet since this narcissistic love is linked to illness — "one must love in order not to fall ill" applies to a love object that is *not oneself* — are we to understand that the girl reverts to self-love through a painful discovery of her body because of the "threats of imagined death" that a new love could present? It seems highly possible, since the fear of the father rejecting his only daughter is overtly manifested early in the girl's quest: "It scared her even to think of him. What would he say when he saw her? Would he chase her off with a stick?" (33); "What if it's him? What if he's got a gun and shoots me dead?" (36); "'What if he don't want me?' she said. 'What if he says I can go rot in hell?'" (37).

But, interestingly enough, these "threats of imagined death" are first manifested as the fear — and desire — of being engulfed, along with her mother, by death. The following passage oozes that fear, in particular, one thinks, because the process of differentiation is not complete:

> When mama went down she'd wanted to go down with her. She'd wanted to be shut up with her and have the lid closed on them. They'd said, no, no you can't, but it seemed to her this had happened anyway. It was happening now. The lid was closing, but mama wasn't raising her arms to welcome her. Mama was stretched out flat, not saying anything. *Come along, child. Come along, child.* Mama's back was turned or she wasn't there at all: black space, cold black air, that's all mama was[10] (41; italics mine).

The imagined iterated vocative *Come along, child. Come along, child* evokes the sheer threat of the loved mother wanting to prolong the embrace over death and thus deprive the child of her life.

The daughter's mourning of the mother, a process of distancing herself from her only object of love, who is now dead, is, as Freud explains, a painful one:

> In what, now, does the work which mourning performs consist? . . . Reality testing shows that the loved object no longer exists, and it proceeds to demand that all libido be withdrawn from its attachment to that object. This demand arouses understandable opposition — it is a matter of general observation that people never willingly abandon a libidinal position, *not even, indeed, when a substitute is already beckoning to them* . . . In the meantime, *the existence of the lost object is psychically prolonged.* Each single one of the

---

[10] Jacques Derrida reflects, precisely in this kind of imagery, on the sudden absence of the departed and the subsequent partial interiorization of the other in order to mourn his/her loss: "Upon the death of the other we are given to memory, and thus to interiorization, since the other, outside us, is now nothing. And with the dark light of this nothing, we learn that the other resists the closure of our interiorizing memory. With the nothing of this irrevocable absence, the other appears as other, and as other for us, upon his death ..., since death constitutes and makes manifest the limits of a me or an us who are obliged to harbour something that is greater or other than them, something outside of them within them. Memory and interiorization: since Freud, this is how the 'normal' work of mourning is often described." "Menmosyne" (trans. by Cecile Lindsay), in *Memoirs for Paul de Man*, New York, Columbia University Press, 1986, 34 (italics mine).

memories and expectations in which the libido is bound to the object is brought up and hypercathected, and detachment of the libido is accomplished in respect of it (244; italics mine).[11]

This "psychical prolongation" of the mother is presented in two fashions: in the carrying of the mother's garments within the two huge suitcases and in the introjection of the mother's words and habits. The size of the suitcases attests to their metonymic value: the sheer weight of the suitcases — filled with memorabilia of the mother — prevents the daughter from progressing. The girl must eventually choose and abandon one of the suitcases in the ditch if she is to reach her father in her long and painful quest:

> She looked hard at the suitcases. They'd got so heavy. My lifely goods, she thought. They weigh more than me. She wondered if maybe she couldn't lighten her load, maybe hide some of it away up here. Maybe take out the best things from the one case and stuff them in the other and go on along with that (32).

In temporarily abandoning a suitcase containing her mother's less important clothes, the daughter is already starting the process of decathecting her mother to liberate the energy needed to meet her father. The opening of the suitcases to choose the mother's "best things" allows scenes and words from her mother to appear. While this choice brings back pain, along with the introjected voice of the mother, it is a necessary step in the mourning process.

In these instances where it is not called — or recalled — but comes impromptu, the mother's voice is differentiated by italics and quotation marks in the text. Quotation marks, a conventional device used to signal the voice of other in the same text, are added to the italics, which here could be interpreted as an introjection of her mother. She is inside her daughter, part of her, and yet other; dead and yet alive: *"You stand right up to him. Call him a jackal to his face, if that's what's come of him"* (33).

---

[11] Freud ends the passage with this remark: "Why this compromise by which the command of a reality is carried out piece meal should be so extraordinarily painful is not at all easy to explain in terms of economic ... The fact is however, that when the work of mourning is completed the ego becomes free and uninhibited again" (1962, 245).

Concerning voice, Derrida affirms that the work of mourning:

> entails a movement in which an interiorizing idealization takes in itself or upon itself the body or voice of the other, the other's visage and person, ideally and quasi-literally devouring them. This mimetic interiorization is not fictive . . . It takes place in a body. Or rather, it makes a place for a body, a voice, and a soul which, although "ours," did not exist and had no meaning before this possibility [of death] that one must always begin by remembering, and whose trace must be followed (1986: 34).

Introjection, as Abraham and Torok affirm, a process first experienced by the infant when its empty mouth is superseded by words of the mother, performs the presence of the absent:

> This void is first experienced through howls and tears, and deferred fulfillment, then as an occasion for calling, a means of making things appear, speech . . . The transition from breast-filled mouth to word-filled mouth is achieved through experiences of empty mouth . . . Thus, the original oral void will have found a remedy for all its wants through their conversion in linguistic intercourse with the speaking community. To introject a wish, a grief, or a situation is to dispose of it through language in a communion of empty mouths. To achieve this transition presence of the object must be superseded by auto-apprehension of its absence. Language, which makes up for that absence by representing presence, can be understood only within a community of empty mouths[12] (1976: 5-6).

---

[12] Abraham and Torok explain the first process of introjection: "Learning to fill the void of the mouth with words constitutes an early paradigm of introjection. Clearly this cannot occur without the constant presence of a mother who herself possesses language. Her constancy – like that of Descartes' God – is the necessary guarantee of the meaning of words. When that guarantee is assured, and only then, words can replace the mother's presence and give rise to new introjections. First the empty mouth, then the absence of objects becomes words, and finally experiences with words themselves are converted into other words.

Thus, the original oral void will have found a remedy for all its wants through their conversion in linguistic intercourse with the speaking community. To introject a wish, a grief, or a situation is to dispose of it through language in a community of empty mouths" ("Introjection – Incorporation." *Mourning or Melancholia*, 1976, 6)

The food-deprived *only daughter* fills the void created with the death of her mother by introjecting her words. Characteristically, the girl has been literally empty-mouthed since her departure, which induces in her an altered state of mind wherein her mother speaks to and through her. It is as if the daughter needed to be deprived of food for this introjection of her mother through language to happen.

The mourning as presented is as complete[13] as it can be when the daughter is at last ready to meet her father. To meet him, she dons the clothes and make-up of her mother. The girl acts as if she wants to accelerate the process of mourning by introjecting all the mementos of her mother's. This process seems to complete differentiation (after all, death awaits the daughter if she cannot separate from her dead mother) and bring about gendering: "The boundaries of the body are the lived experience of differentiation, *where that differentiation is never neutral to the question of gender difference* or the heterosexual matrix" (Butler, 1993: 65; italics mine).

This gendering (feminine clothes and make-up seem to act as symbols, exterior signs of a problematic — perhaps because it is new — gendered self) is re-enacted[14] for her father at the moment she is ready to meet him, that is, ready to recathect a parental relationship, this time with her father. Thus, she also comes to terms with her own womanhood while, through dressing as a woman, announcing the differentiated relationship with her father:

> She felt about inside the suitcase for a pair of stockings — a new pair — and pulled them on. "Bless the navy," she said, for this was what her mama liked to say. "Him with his nylons, going to sweep

---

[13] Derrida stresses the necessity of leaving the mourning work unfinished in order to attain an ethical stance: "is the most distressing, or even the most deadly infidelity that of a possible mourning which would interiorize within us the image, idol, or ideal of the other who is dead and lives only in us? Or is it that of the impossible mourning, which, leaving the other his alterity, respecting thus his infinite remove, either refuses to take or is incapable of taking the other within oneself, as in the tomb or the vault of some narcissism?" (1986: 6). Derrida maintains that an "aborted interiorization" – an uncompleted mourning – "is at the same time a respect for the other as other, a sort of tender rejection, a movement of renunciation which leaves the other alone, outside, over there, in his death outside of us" (34).

[14] Gender, as Butler and other feminists have shown, is performative. Here, in opposition to life, this performance is clearly, theatrically shown.

me off my feet." She drew the hose up over her hips and tucked the extra length inside her panties. Her mama had kept hers up with garter belts or she'd rolled and twisted them somehow and they'd stayed up. Beautiful legs, old mama had. She felt about for a sweater and skirt and slipped these on. She got out a comb and raked that through her tangly hair, making low cries as the comb pulled. She wondered where her bow had got to. She rubbed a finger over her teeth and moistened that finger and set a shape to her eyebrows. She painted her lips with the tube her mama had said she could have. She rouged her cheeks the way her mama had showed her how ... She hooked the purse over her arm and crawled out of her hole[15] (46).

Throughout the whole gendering scene, one will notice how the passage is permeated with the presence of the mother: her words, her mannerisms, the recall of one of her lovers — a marine who sent her nylons by the dozens — her clothes, her way of accentuating her femininity with the feminine props of the era. Thus, the mother now lives within the daughter.

The daughter having made the decision to meet her father, having housed her mother safely *in* and *on* her, is no more in discomfort; her pains recede to oblivion. They are not mentioned, except for the ambient cold, that continues to make her suffer. Ironically, the daughter compares, again in her formulaic hyperbolic syntax, one evil with another: "Being alone in the world was a glory ride compared to being cold" (46). Nevertheless "being alone in the world" can only be "a glory ride" if a parent is in sight. The situation is precisely that of a child who acts out when an older brother or father is around. Nevertheless, the intense feeling of cold might also be an *effect* of being alone: with deliverance in sight, the sheer sense of a new attachment that could end up like the first one, or as a rejection of her, is chilling.

The narrative ends *before* the encounter, after a slow but steady building of the expectations of the reader: "She stretched up her stockings and brushed at her coat. She took a deep breath and knocked on his door. 'I'll

---

[15] This "hole" seems to allude as much to a grave as to a birth canal. Concerning the girl's presentation to the father, there also seems to be some Oedipal seduction at work, triggered perhaps by a fear of rejection.

try it,' she said. 'I'll give him twenty-four hours to prove himself'" (48). A new person has emerged from the mourning: from the "What if he don't want me?" to "I'll give him twenty-four hours to prove himself," there is metamorphosis. The only daughter has become one of Rooke's "resilient, resourceful, independent-minded females coping with the damaged psyche, carrying that heavy baggage of wounds."[16] Not only is she ready to meet her father, — that is, to accept his unlikely refusal — but she now puts herself in a position of authority. She is to decide whether he is a worthy father or not. Perhaps because of the daughter's dauntless posture, the open ending is strangely satisfying for the reader. Whatever the outcome of the encounter, the only daughter will go on. Still, with his open ending, Rooke presents satisfaction (the reunion with her father / a proper ending for the reader) as best when deferred, thus showing that the object of desire is always out of reach.

Although Rooke's position concerning characterization — "It's important for me to see characters in fiction as living human beings"[17] — appears traditional, this study of one short story amongst the bulk of his production shows how consummate his art of the portrait is: the only daughter has a denseness which allows for an in-depth study of her psyche at work in mourning.

---

[16] Rooke in Nancy Wigston "Leon Rooke / Hit Single. Interview" *Books in Canada*, October 1995, vol. 24 no 7, 17.

[17] "Interview," 1981: 111.

BIBLIOGRAPHY

Abraham, Nicholas and Maria Torok. "Introjection—Incorporation." *Mourning or Melancholia, in Psychoanalysis in France."* Ed. by Serge Lebovici and Daniel Widlöcher. New York: International Universities Press (trans. by Serge Lebovici and Daniel Widlöcher), 1980.

Butler, Judith. *Bodies that Matter*. New York and London: Routledge, 1993.

Derrida, Jacques. *Memoirs for Paul de Man.* (trans. By Cecile Lindsay). New York: Columbia University Press, 1986.

Freud, Sigmund. "Mourning and Melancholia," (trans. by James Strachey) *On the History of the Psychoanalytic Movement: Papers on Metapsychology*, Vol XIV, London: Hogarth Press, 1962.

Frye, Northrop. *Anatomy of Criticism*. Princeton: Princeton University Press, 1990.

Grosz, Elizabeth. "Kristeva, Julia," *Feminism and Psychoanalysis. A Critical Dictionary.* Ed. by Elizabeth Wright. Oxford: Blackwell, 1992.

Hancock, Geoff. "An Interview with Leon Rooke," *Canadian Fiction Magazine*, no 38, 1981. 107-133.

Kristeva, Julia. "The Semiotic and the Symbolic," *Revolution in Poetic Language.* New York: Columbia University Press, 1984. 21-106.

Rooke, Leon. "The Only Daughter," *A Bolt of White Cloth*. Don Mills: Stoddard, 1984, 21-48.

Wigston, Nancy. "Hit Single. Interview / Leon Rooke," *Books in Canada*. Vol. 24 no 7, 1995, 17.

Breaking the Reader's Heart: Meaning in Leon Rooke's "The Heart Must from Its Breaking"

Janice Kulyk Keefer

If we are moved by a [story], it has meant something, perhaps something impor-
tant, to us; if we are not moved, then it is, as [story], meaningless.
                                                    —T.S. Eliot (817).

"The Heart Must from Its Breaking" is as typical as any of Leon Rooke's
prodigious number of fictions can be said to be: melodramatic / metaphys-
ical subject matter (dying woman springs from sickbed to defend young
innocent children from the demon incarnate of their vile and evil father),
unusual narrative technique (multiple narrators, inhabitants of a Middle /
Southern American small town), stylistic pizzazz and metafictional der-
ring-do. Yet none of this prevents this 20-odd page text from being pro-
foundly moving and by extension, if we accept the austere Mr. Eliot's
pronouncement, profoundly meaningful. What could have been merely a
brilliant pastiche of backwoods Gothic becomes, as well, a fable dealing
with what, however postmodern we may like to think ourselves, remain the
fundamental issues of human existence: good and evil, life and death.

Pastiche *and* fable — it is important to register the fact that in adopt-
ing a classically postmodern "and / and" approach, by exploiting and,
we might even say, romancing the conventions of the Gothic tale and ghost
story, Rooke keeps himself honest in his relation to his readers whose
hearts he sets out to break at the same time as he teases and busies their
minds. It's not so much that Rooke avoids melodrama and sentimentality
— he courts them in order to ever-so-narrowly skirt them, and it is the
suspense he generates for the reader — the suspense of "what happens
next" at the level of both plot and technique that prevents that "failure of

feeling" which, for Wallace Stevens, is the cause of sentimentality (911). We are deeply and sincerely moved by Rooke's fiction precisely because of our awareness of the sleight of hand by which this fiction proceeds, by its paradoxical strategies of discipline by excess, of reining-in by pouring-out.

Like Vladimir Nabokov, Leon Rooke takes the enormous risk of writing about subjects that can easily become kitsch: very young, very vulnerable children in situations where all the parental love and tenderness in the world cannot protect them from atrocious harm, and where arch-abusive adults are far more likely to figure than guardian angels. I am thinking here of the murdered child in *Bend Sinister* and of the narrator's young son in *Speak Memory*, both of them caught up in the cross currents of terrorism and war, menaced by "fatherly" dictators named Krug and Hitler. Where Nabokov uses complexly coded, high-cultural references and intricately plotted ironies to keep his representations of children from crossing the borders between poignancy and sentimentality, Rooke achieves the same effect by employing elements of the Southern Gothic, the domestic-grotesque, and the wildly erratic.

Take, for example, the two children over whose souls — or mere physical well-being — the good mother and demonic father battle, tooth and nail. The children — for the most part, silent, blurred bundles of innocence, especially the girl — are stock figures — the Babes in the Wood, Hansel and Gretel, Orphans of the Storm. They would, in fact, be the Kitsch Kids, were it not for their bearing such quintessentially Rookean names. The choice of "Agnes," with its spinsterish overtones, its harshness compared to "Amy" or "Marylou" or any such predictable, generic small-town monikers, is a classic example of that "reining-in" of which I spoke. But "Cluey," the small boy's name is pure Rooke — from so far out in left field that any easy sympathy we might feel for the child's plight is deflected by our attempts to puzzle out the implications — if there are any — of the name conferred on him. Not "Joey" or "Johnny," but "Cluey": the effect is to stop us in our interpretative tracks. Of what given name could Cluey possibly be a diminutive? Are we meant to find the "clue" to the puzzles posed by the story in the absent child, his existence only as name? Or does the fact that "Cluey" rhymes with "phooey" warn us against being overzealous in our attempts to make meaning out of a story that surely sets out simply to entertain? By spooking us, as the good old ghost story always means to do . . .

• • •

Hearing Leon Rooke read "Heart" is to think of what it must have been like to hear Dickens mesmerize his audience with his recitations of the death of Paul Dombey, or the perfidy of Steerforth. Reading the text in the hush of your own house, it's difficult to keep the ghosts of Henry James and Edgar Allan Poe at bay. For in its theme — the battle between agents of good and evil for the souls of two young children — "Heart" is a cousin of *The Turn of the Screw;* in its device of multiple narrators, it can claim descent from "The Murders in the Rue Morgue." The combination of devilishly-difficult moral ambiguity and sheer, calm creepiness generated by the story makes it an odd but redoubtable marriage of James and Poe.

The Victorian ghost story, Michael Cox and R.A. Gilbert remind us, is "traditional in its forms and intentions, but energetically inventive and infused with a relish of the supernatural":

> The ghost story's basic dynamics are settled in the reader's expectations at the outset. We know that we are to be shown a climactic interaction between the living and the dead, and usually expect to be unsettled by the experience . . . While it is not necessary for an author to believe unconditionally in the supernatural for a ghost story to come off . . . it is essential that he or she engages fully in the *pretence* of believing (ix, xi).

Is it moral or metaphysical ambiguity that so unsettles us in "Heart"? Whereas the governess in *The Turn of the Screw* is a maddeningly ambiguous character, we are surely not meant or brought to question or even suspect the absolute moral integrity of the heroine of "Heart," the sublimely self-sacrificing mother, Tory. No one, we might observe, takes the father's part — except, it seems, the children. The son, at least, seems to be as much in cahoots with his evil father as is Miles with that "devil" Peter Quint in *The Turn of the Screw.* When the Painter's Apprentice beats Cluey up, Cluey yells out "My daddy will git you!" (259) — and indeed, the apprentice quickly trips, falls and breaks his leg — got but good. There is also an aspect, however inverted, of the Second Coming vis à vis the Father in "Heart." He calls his children out of the church, and they rise and follow him, without fear or trembling, but rather in a spirit of perfect and accustomed obedience. The father is repeatedly referred to as "hardly human" — the children, according to Tiny Peterson "walk into the thing, whatever it was, and then they simply were not there any more" (260). But later, Tiny tells us, in the very process of wrestling with Tory and snapping her back, the "creature" comes closer "to having human form" (261). It remains unhuman in having no language — though the roar it does let out is expressive, Tiny thinks "of hatred, of pure madness at being thwarted" (261) — it does acquire "arms and legs and a face, though that face looked a million years old and like it hated everything alive" (261).

In this context, think of further, disquieting questions this story poses: which of the speakers, the witnesses, are to be believed? For example, was the apparition in the church which beckoned the children outside a whirling light, as The Postman assures us or a miasmal darkness, as the preacher, Timmons insists — a darkness perhaps related to the "dye ditch" in which the Painter's Apprentice once perceived something unhuman and awful that tripped him headlong into that ditch. This dread "something" — how is it connected with Cluey's absent, evil father, who has set out to "git" the apprentice, who has beaten up his son? What credence do we give to the testimony of the farmer and her husband — especially the former's assertion that there were NO children on the white horse's back? Is this narrative an onion peeling away to nothingness where we might have expected a kernel? Is the imperishable bloodstreak marring the fresh white paint of the Sister's house that kernel — irrefutable proof that Tory did indeed wrest her children away from the clutch of their satanic father, or is it merely an embarrassing reminder to the townspeople that though a battle may have taken place between good and evil, blessed spirit and bestial demon, its outcome was not only ambiguous but unknowable, and thus as good as meaningless?

Emptiness is a key word, and a key trope in this fiction. The possible emptiness of heaven is the giggle-inducing topic on which Timmons is preaching in the story's opening sentence. Later, that topic is represented — by Timmons himself — as having been "The Empty Hell" (249). Still later, it is the emptiness of the paralyzed Tory's death bed that leaps into question. The narrative insistently describes Tory's pitifully shrivelled breasts — empty, through terminal illness of any erotic or maternal appeal. But yet if Tory's breasts are empty, her heart is full — so full of passionate love for her children and ferocious courage to defend them — that the cause of her death, as the doctor's last word has it, is heartbreak, though hardly heartbreak pure and simple.

Emptiness also underpins the key metaphysical question this peculiar work of fiction poses: is there, as Marr will stoically pronounce in *Shakespeare's Dog,* only blackness behind us, blackness ahead of us? Or, as Hooker longs to believe, is there a purpose and meaning to our existence, purpose and meaning that pre-exist us and that will reveal themselves to us upon our physical extinction? These are not abstract or rhetorical questions in "The Heart Must From its Breaking," a text whose characters are, on occasion, paralytic with terror, "waiting for Death's hand to grab [them]" (251) and where "the curse of this blood" (258) — not just Tory's, but the blood that makes all of them living and human — is not so much original sin, as the very sin of having been born at all.

No clear answers, no consoling fictions, either, for that matter — the last words of "Heart," spoken by the eminently rational Doctor is "Let these stories stop right here!" (263). Stories as in lies, fictions, parables, postmodern texts? At this point in our experience of reading "Heart," we can no longer distract ourselves with engaging oddnesses or unsolvable puzzles. That *"pretence* of believing" which the writer of the traditional ghost story must perform, has, in fact, become enacted within the reader's consciousness by the last words of this story. We must scratch about to find something to house ourselves within, to fasten on, and when we find it, must make do with nothing so solid as a floor under our feet, a roof over our heads, but with that most unstable of devices, a hinge.

The second sentence of "Heart" tells us how "the wood doors" [of the church] burst open, letting in a "fast-spinning wheel of gold" or a dreadful darkness — take your pick (247). The most riveting piece of testimony — that of Rosie the nurse — involves a window that was never opened all during Tory's sickness (as the Painter later tells us) but out of which, according to Rosie, Tory climbs and through which she regains her bed after her fatal struggle. Doors and windows — fundamentally ambiguous sites and objects, that open and shut, that can be forced as well as locked, that mark the crossover point between constantly shifting zones of safety and danger, ignorance and knowledge.

BIBLIOGRAPHY

Coc, Michael and R.A. Gilbert. *Victorian Ghost Stories*. Oxford: Oxford UP, 1991.

Eliot, T.S. "The Music of Poetry." *20th-Century Poetry and Poetics*, 4th edition, ed, Gary Geddes. Toronto: Oxford UP, 1995. 816-819.

Rooke, Leon. "The Heart Must from its Breaking," *The Happiness of Others*. Erin: The Porcupine's Quill, 1991.

Stevens, Wallace. "Adagia," *20th-Century Poetry and Poetics*, 4th edition, ed, Gary Geddes. Toronto: Oxford UP, 1995. 909-914.

In the Path of Leon Rooke's Sidestepping Narrator: Two Views

Michèle Kaltemback

1. A Man Locked up in a Freezer: "The Blue Baby"

Reading a Rooke story . . . is indeed a perilous adventure.
—Simone Vauthier

As I read "The Blue Baby,"[1] I was reminded of Simone Vauthier's remark[2] that no reader entering Leon Rooke's fictions could for long withstand the pull of a perilous adventure ahead, rest secure in his or her position as an outsider. Rooke's narration, as I saw it in "The Blue Baby," is aimed at us; it drags us into the story, assigning each a part to play. Yet, that part too turns out pretty soon to hold no security at all as we lose our bearings among the shifting identities of the "You" and "I" in the narrator-narratee relationship. Facts pile up with no apparent order. Scenes spring to life for an instant from a nondescript moment in the past and reappear several times with extreme accuracy, creating a whole set of echoes. The narrator takes us along a spiralling quest into an obsessional past, a quest for meaning and identity that will eventually lead us to a standstill.

At the outset of the story we seem to enter a well-trodden ground: the title itself bears connotations of fantasy and childhood innocence, and

---

[1] Pushcart Prize, 1987. David and Maggie Helwig eds. *87 Best Canadian Stories*. Toronto: Oberon, 1987, 7-22. A slightly different version of this story appears under the title "Who Do You Love?" in Leon Rooke, *Who Do You Love?* Toronto: McClelland and Stewart Inc., 1992.

[2] Simone Vauthier. "Dangerous Crossing: A Reading of Leon Rooke's 'The Birth Control King of the Upper Volta'" in *Journal of the Short Story in English / Les Cashiers de la nouvelle*, No. 4, Presses de l'Université d'Angers, (Spring 85), 109.

the initial words evoke a familiar pattern, that of the fairy-tale: "There was a time . . ." (7). This immediately establishes the defined functions of the "I" as the narrator and the "You" as the narratee. A strong first-person voice, asserting himself vigorously throughout the opening page, addresses us with the purpose of telling a story. Yet a few disquieting elements seem to undermine the confidence reflected by the opening statement. The intentions are clear: a tale will be told, which could be an autobiographical one, (set in North Carolina, Rooke's native state),[3] but the narrator has enough trouble deciding on the very events he wishes to report: "There was a time in North Carolina when nothing ever happened . . . There were those times and there were other times. I don't know which times to tell you about" (7).

In fact, the secure structure of the tale soon seems to collapse and we find ourselves on the other side of the border, inside the text. The "I" has been suddenly converted into an indistinct "You." From that point on, the narrative constantly shifts from the first to the second person. Initially, the point of view varies slightly along with this conversion. While the "I" reports thoughts and fears, denoting involvement, the "You" merely watches, reluctant to interfere with the actual telling, still attempting to hold on to its position as an unconcerned observer. A few pages later, however, the "You" appears to have abandoned its passive stance although it is still distinct from the "I" of the first person narration: "The one pecan tree in this place I am talking about was surrounded by a high fence and you could not reach the limbs even with poles and no matter how hard or long you tried" (12). Both the "I" and the "You" refer to the single actor here. In the same portion of the text, we read, "a boy my age fell from the water tower" and "sometimes a black haze would cover the sky . . . You would pass someone holding his nose" (13). There are numerous instances of such overlapping of the first and second person pronouns that refer to the same persona, suggesting that the narrator trusts us, taking for granted our willingness to share his views. Finally, at the outcome of the story, there is no doubt that the "You" is now the narrator. The keys to the narrative construction are the two strikingly similar statements, one presented at the beginning of the story, the other at its closing: "There was a time up

---

[3] To a Rooke reader, this in itself functions as a warning sign. References to actual geographical locations are very scarce in his stories.

north in the Yukon when a man *I knew* locked up another man *I knew* inside a freezer and the man froze" (7), an event reported again at the very end: "*You think* of the man *you knew* who was locked up in the freezer in the Yukon and how he froze" (22; italics mine).

For how long, we wonder, has this been going on and at what point did the narratee trade places with the narrator? Where do we stand as the audience and what did become of the tale? Did our assumption that we would listen to some storytelling mislead us? Or else, could it be that this is the story of a man talking to himself? On the one hand, the narrator calls for a non-distanced reception of his story and lures us into his narrative, taking for granted that we will feel as he does to the extent that we are made to act as he did. On the other hand, as the narratee, we are of some use to him: we bring normality to his world, existence to his tale. Being in the uninvolved position of a witness, we act as a safeguard, as a potential bearer of meaning. Thus, the ambivalent role of the narratee closes the story's gap between the referential and the fictional worlds. As Simone Vauthier pointed out: " . . . The coexistence in the intermediate space of reading of two orders, the real and the imaginary, the inner and the outer, neutralizes the boundary between them."[4] In this interchange of roles a voice emerges, speaking of both the shared intimacy of childhood memories and of an obsessive search for objectivity and meaning.

Eventually, the final turn of the story allows a third level in the reading of the ambiguous "You." The last page reveals a presence of someone of whom we had been totally unaware. Only referred to as "she," the narrator's mother has been lying on her hospital bed apparently from the very beginning and must have died at some stage. The voice says:

> I think about it now because now she lies in this bed with tubes up her nose and tubes attached to her shaved head and she's holding my hand, or rather her hand is limp in mine and you can't hear her breathe. You can't see her chest rise and her lids never move (22).

Perhaps because we expected to be told a tale, we had assumed too rashly the role of an audience. But soon we realize that we are intruding

---

[4] See Vauthier, 116.

into a dialogue between a son and his mother, or rather an attempted dialogue. Some of the second person addresses, such as "I don't know which times to tell you about" (7), may after all not have been meant for us, but rather for the narrator's mother. With a revelation such as this at the very end, the text folds back upon itself and the impassive mother becomes the link that unifies different events in the story. She holds the key to the meaning of the boy's childhood recollections, though she can no longer reveal her secret. With her death, the story ends in silence. And in spite of that, the clue to the story rests with us — we are the ears that overheard the voice, and, as the readers, we must try to draw meaning from the printed page. It seems, whatever position we choose or are made to adopt, we cannot keep our distanced attitude for very long. We must somehow get involved in the urgent quest for meaning.

The text holds numerous echoes, suggesting associations. The presence of the silent mother on her deathbed, for instance, brings back to mind the episode of the blue baby, developed in two separate sections:

> The woman who lived below lived alone and she was so stupid she thought every sound meant a thief was coming to steal her money.
>   She had a blue baby, this baby with an enormous blue head, and all of the light bulbs in her room were blue so that you wouldn't know she had a blue baby (17).

> The blue baby died and went to heaven, but the woman downstairs did not change her light bulbs (19).

Between these two passages, the narrator explains how he used to be left to himself all day long while his mother was at work and how he used to skip school without anyone noticing or even caring. So this curious reference to the blue baby may be read as a metaphor. It brings to light the nature of the narrator's quest for motherly love and attention. Unlike his mother, the mother of the blue baby showed great concern for her child, protecting him from outside aggressions, from a world in which he would be singled out as a freak. She created for him coherent, safe surroundings, which would give him a sense of normality — the blue light brought meaning to the blue baby's existence. Thus, the blue baby's harmonious life may very well constitute the antithesis to the narrator's desperate attempt to structure the elements of his childhood in a way as to make sense of them, to find purpose and reason. But the narrator is doomed to failure because his mother held back the missing information, or never bothered to supply it, and now that she is unequivocally silent, he is left with the silence, forever.

In contrast, the blue baby's mother who brought the blue light into her child's life enabled him to feel one with his world. The blue bulb, then, functions as an analogy for the missing unifying link the narrator is seeking. Unlike the blue baby, he stares without understanding, feeling left out. He shuns other people's gaze afraid of revealing his difference, his colour. His constant fear is to be laughed at, rejected. Buying Kotex for his mother requires, for example, an incredible amount of courage on his part. And his mother's "fat" girlfriend causes in him an endless sense of shame (9). His narrative clearly reflects a quest for an elusive meaning, a need for understanding that would allow him to participate in whatever situation he would find himself in.

The narrator therefore seems to exist only as an eye that registers separate events, which do not make sense as a whole. They are merely listed in rather short sentences and juxtaposed without any logical links. Causal co-ordinators are very scarce. The text, for example, uses mostly additive or adversative ones so that " . . . you still don't know why or how it has happened" (14). In the same way, scenes never lead to further developments, never seem to trigger any consequences. Instead, events exist as isolated fragments referred to over and over again, with a few added details every now and then, as if repetition in itself might finally reveal a hidden pattern. The story, by piling up its unrelated vignettes, suggests the repetitive rhythm of the blues — already echoed in the title's story — and like the blues it expresses the melancholy quest for meaning.

On several occasions the boy's father is mentioned, never by name or anything other than "he" or "him." He is being missed, or at least curiosity is being aroused, but all the information we gather is that: " . . . he was like the nickel that rolled between the floorboards into the utter, unreachable darkness of the world" (8). So much for the father quest! Obsessive images crop up, only to lead to questions and to the ultimate frozen image:

> She's been that way for an hour or more, not moving, and so
> have I, the two of us here, neither of us moving and nothing hap-
> pening, her hand cold in mine and the night darkening and I still
> haven't answered (22).

This final scene epitomizes the whole situation: the boy's understand-
ing of his experiences remains impossible since he lacks the basic refer-
ential element that would grant him existence, identity and recognition
on the part of his mother.

In this context, his erratic search is that of someone who is trapped
in his own meaningless past. The narrator's sense of time seems somehow
to have been disconcertingly warped so that there is no way for him to exit
from an undifferentiated past, one he perceives globally but in which no
chronology may be established. This is how he justifies his search:

> There was the time all this ended, but you never knew when it
> was, so it was as if that time never ended, which is one reason to
> think about it. I think about it because it ended, that is why I
> think about it (21).

This could go on forever in maddening circles. No wonder, the first
story the narrator felt like telling is that of a man who died in a freezer,
a story strangely reminiscent of his own situation. As in a freezer, time
has no significance. The present is reduced to silence and immobility and
only the past is preserved in its totality without any distinctions. Although
the story sets a temporal distance — "there were those times . . ." — it lacks
any referential points in time. Events form separate blocks but are never
organized sequentially, or according to any chronological links.

In the same way, the spatial elements of the story contribute to its
isolation thus intensifying our impression of dealing with a closed world.
A few geographical details related to the referential world may suggest
a reassuring identification. The general background of the story — a
poor rural area with black farmers — could certainly correspond to a
North Carolina setting. The town, an industrial community, has precisely
laid out sections, the names of which are actually quoted several times.
Where there are so few names in the story, we come very close to learn-
ing the exact address of the mother's apartment: "The town was only

seven miles away, but . . . it was quite a town" (17). Or again: "Three streets were paved, all others were gravel, and all the streets were named after U.S. presidents. There was an uptown called Rosemary and a down-town called Downtown, and uptown was bigger, while Downtown was dying, was dead, but was the place you had to go through if you wanted for whatever reason to cross the river" (15). The river here is referred to as a barrier, but in fact it functions as an illusory separation. It delimits the town — the town and country seem to hold very few differences, at least for those who have not been able to make their way up to the uptown section. The mother, "fleeing death" (15) has come to live in that town, but there too, she only encounters death and desolation.

The general atmosphere of the world in which the narrator as a child lives is that of sterility, of unnatural events (the boy who "did it with horses" [15]). It is a place of foul smells (the town stank, the stream called the Dye Ditch which was "some days . . . one vile colour and some days another and at times it was a mix of many" [14]) and of death (suicides and murders are quoted as ordinary, fairly common occurrences). The town very much resembles the interior of a freezer, promising preserva-tion — a form of escape, in a way — but which may eventually turn out to be the cause of death. So, in spite of the precise references, what we have here is an utterly fictional world, set in the narrator's mind, impris-oned in space and time. Beyond the river lies a mental landscape: an ear-lier childhood, a life with his grandparents, referred to only once, practi-cally blocked out from memory and the later developments of his lonely life with his mother.

The actual structure of the text dramatizes this entrapment. The nar-ration keeps coming back to certain obsessive unrelated images: the absent father, the uncaring mother, the fat couple making love in front of the window represent a set of concentric circles. All events revolve around a constant question mark: the few unexplained facts from the past (the father's absence perhaps) that would justify the child's pres-ence in that particular town. In the same circular way, the narrative takes us back to its starting point: the story of the man trapped in the freezer.

The metaphorical freezer, however, could very well have acquired an extra occupant: us, as the non-distanced narratee. We have been made to penetrate the fictional world of the story in order to participate in the quest for meaning and along with the narrator we have come up against death. Thus silence constitutes the outcome of the attempt to reach meaning through words. Yet we are left with a text, but one that does not tell, but rather points at the untold. We as readers are left with the task of supplying the missing links so as to create meaning and thus break into the present, free from the deadly freezer. In an interview with Geoff Hancock, Leon Rooke explained: "I don't like resolving situations because most situations are not resolved . . . I like to leave a situation poised like that."[5] "The Blue Baby" is another striking instance of his technique, which certainly fits his definition of fiction as "real life coming at you from another angle."[6]

2. A Fading Painting, A *Flaked Out* Narrator: "Art"

"Art,"[7] formerly published under the title "I. Paintings / II. Water Colours / III. Hand-painted Flowers; / All You Can Carry, 25c"[8] bears the mark of Leon Rooke's facetiousness. It holds most of the usual characteristics observed by his reviewers; it is "mystifying and playful,"[9] and yet gives us "more than meets the eye."[10] Rooke, "impersonator, or ventriloquist,"[11] has "a matter-of-fact method of saying the strangest things."[12]

In a typically Rookean storytelling manner, we are directly addressed by a first person narrator — a perfect stranger who seems eager to take us into his confidence — and are immediately drawn into the action *in medias res*. We are left with no other choice but to tag along with the narrator at a

---

[5] Geoffrey Hancock. "An Interview with Leon Rooke," *Canadian Fiction Magazine*, No. 38, (1981), p.133.

[6] *Ibid.*, 116.

[7] Leon Rooke. *Who Do You Love?* Toronto: McClelland and Stewart Inc., 1992.

[8] *West Coast Review*, vol. 18 / 3, January 1884.

[9] Michael Taylor. "Courting Indifferences." *Canadian Forum*, vol. 63, April 1983.

[10] Paule Stueve. "More Than Meets the Eye." *Books in Canada*, May 1985.

[11] Stephen Scobie. "The Inner Voice." *Books in Canada*, November 1981.

[12] Barry Dempster. "The Tricks of the Magician." *Canadian Forum*, April 1985.

tremendous pace. We are pulled forward by his steady determination, by his intent to select from a conventional picture-book landscape those elements that he needs. Obviously, the narrator has a purpose in mind; he wishes to produce an effect by rendering the sweetness and the peacefulness of the scene. The sentence, "It was sweet enough with her out of the picture" (39), may then be read in the literal sense. This deliberate picking, even though it goes on in a rapid succession, aims at a visual effect. If the horse isn't available to be used as a complement for the cow, at least the strawberries will add a note of colour and thus balance the bunch of flowers. Even the unavailability of the maiden is conveyed through visual means, the "Not For Sale" sign, and the narrator's careful selection summed up with a verb that carries visual connotations as well: "I plodded on" (39).

Once back home, the same narrator rearranges the cow and the bunch of flowers taken out of their picture book landscape and incorporates them into another very familiar setting. Now all the elements of this new scene are referred to in their spatial organization, inside a limited frame and on a single plane — in fact, in both pictures, we are dealing with a flat all-inclusive space, where each element refers to all the others. This is expressed with double prepositions or with adverbs of place such as "down near," "over to," "out front" (39-40). The reference to a picture crops up again with the mention of a "picture window" (40). Finally we find our bearings, this mysterious "I" whom we have followed rather blindly and who is in the process of artistic creation and wants us as the narratee to witness how he is composing his picture, here in his living room. He *props* his wife *up*, *puts up* her feet, *mixes up* a gin and tonic and *puts on* the stereo for her (italics mine). All these actions are conveyed through verbs, stressing deliberation aimed at winning his wife's compliments: "I pointed out the cow which was tranquilly grazing" (40). And she does appreciate it: "Sweet, . . . very sweet. What a lovely idea . . . The flowers were a good thought, . . . I appreciate the flowers" (40).

In what is otherwise an ordinary conversation, husband and wife embark on a fairly technical discussion about the quality of the painter's craftsmanship. She remarks: "A touch flat, . . . but the lemon wedge has a nice effect" . . . statements, though apparently meant to clarify the message, they actually draw our attention to their dual meaning. The whole composition of the picture, in fact, raises doubts: "I thought about the cow. Wondered if I hadn't made a mistake on that" (41). The central issue of representation continues to remain unsettled in the artist's mind as he wonders whether he should "Go back tomorrow . . . Offer a good price for the maiden, the stream and the whole damned field" (41). Instead of selecting specific items from the referential world, we wonder questioning, shouldn't he just attempt to reproduce it as faithfully as possible? Or else, shouldn't the idea be abandoned, the present picture replaced with a seascape?

Still, as we think we know where we stand and have learnt that the words must be understood in their literal meaning, some puzzling remarks appear in the narrator's confession. He wipes up his wife's wet kiss *before it can do any damage*, admitting he is beginning to *flake* and needs a good "*touch up* job from an expert" (italics mine). Who is this "I" now? He is more like an object, a painting itself, rather than the exterior, all-powerful creator we had been watching up to now. It becomes clear that the "I" has turned into the subject of an artistic creation, stepped into the frame to take his place next to his wife on a second-rate painting, which shows obvious signs of old age and shoddy craftsmanship. Doubtless to say, we have to re-evaluate our standards of perception when the narrator confides: "I just wished the painter had been more careful. I wished he'd given me more chest" (41). At this point, we are standing in front of a painting while one of the characters is addressing us. He is taking part in an intense drama and sharing his thoughts with us.

The drama is first established in spatial terms — the narrator must at all costs resist getting close to his wife. "I shifted quickly away to the far side of the bed . . . away from her, far as I could get" (42). Fear sets in — reinforced by the leitmotiv "away from her" — and we come to the dramatic climax: "we lay in the darkness . . . separated by all that distance" (43). By creating a series of visual notations, representing transformation through the movement of spreading liquid, the narrator builds the mounting intensity of the scene as the characters gradually and literally keep dissolving. First the woman's hand "had gone all wet and muddy and smeary" (42) — the accumulation of the adjectives denoting dissolution here are meant to foreshadow the dramatic progression towards total erasure — until the man, whose own arm was already damaged from the seeping water, "couldn't look at her" any longer. "I looked down at my own hand and saw that the stain had spread. It had spread up to my elbow and in a small puddle where my arm lay" (43). Finally, the whole composition is in danger as "the stain continued widening" (44). The painting eventually disintegrates before our very own eyes!

Parallel to these visual notations, a set of passages, reported in direct speech, brings the two characters to life through their voices. They become increasingly more pathetic as the process of fading evolves. The effect Rooke achieves here is comparable to that of the fade-in fade-out technique in the cinema. As the painting becomes fainter and fainter because of the spreading water, it is replaced by another more theatrical scene. In this scene husband and wife are in a fairly ordinary house, a situation we have no problem placing among our personal references, all the more so as we have been able to spot all the usual pieces of furniture and decoration. The mounting intensity in the characters' voices gives them more acute presence till the drama reaches its climax with the woman's sobs, adding tears and therefore more liquid, which speeds up the spreading of the fatal stain. The scene ends with voices since, once husband and wife no longer exist, new characters come in to add the final touch. They bring confirmation about our conclusions as to the picture of a man on a spoiled painting. Their special interest for the bunch of flowers takes us back to the beginning of the story. It explains the title and suggests questions about the status of a work of art.

Obviously, the relationship between the image and the narrative plays a major role in the development and the structure of this story. The unreliability of the narrator kindles our curiosity, requires our active participation in the creation of meaning. As we are unaware of his nature, that of a painted picture, we must make an arbitrary choice between the various possible implications of some of his remarks. His apparent lack of consistency in this matter is such that we are entirely left to our own devices for a good part of the story. When he tells us for instance "I was beginning to flake a little myself" (41), we might very well infer that he is actually a painted character. However, the commonplace tone of the remark that follows, "we all do, I guess, the dampness, the mildew, the *rot* — it gets into the system somehow" (41), prompts us to conclude that we have been imagining an extraordinary situation behind a rather matter-of-fact statement. Maybe he just meant he was tired, *flaked out*. Here, we find an interesting example of the author's crafty irony. He is making fun of us, of course, by choosing not to disclose the crucial information about his story and letting us create meaning through our mistakes and hesitations, following a narrator whom we can't trust.

The whole process of artistic creation is thus brought to the foreground and questioned by means of that mysterious image. The very fact that we do not know with any certainty whether or not we are seeing a painting is problematic. It poses a question: how can a boundary between reality and fiction be established? How can we figure out the complex relationship among all the actors of artistic creation — author, narrator, narratee, reader and fictional characters? The author — as Rooke frequently shows — can use his narrator to manipulate the reader, because the narrator can act as both the creator, as he does in "Art" by selecting the various elements in the composition of the painting, and as the created object, as he does by becoming a painted character in his painting.

At the end of the story he watches his own image disintegrating, becoming his own public, stepping out of the frame once more to take our place as the recipient of the product of creation. Finally, even the consumers of art come into play with the art dealers and their casual materialistic attitude. Their conversation underlines that a work of art for them is a mere product, a potential profit: "Might fetch a dollar or two, what do you say?" (45). This is to remind us that a borderline between fiction and reality must exist somewhere, that what an artist creates is in the end just an object. Though the circle is closed, we still have trouble telling who is who and what role we have been playing. The narrator, who constantly adopts a new identity and who is finally reduced to a fading picture, lies at the metafictional core of the story.

In addition, the painting constitutes the undisclosed pre-text for the narrative. The entire elaborate construction rests on the presence of this imaginary painting, the unavoidable source of meaning. The series of interwoven images is thus at the centre of the story. First the picture-book landscape, then the framed living room scene, followed by the painting of the man and the woman in their bedroom, and the final bunch of flowers cut out by the art dealers, left to be framed again and sold in a second-hand store. Hence the original title of the story.

The extreme irony in "Art" stems from the fact that once we realize that the narrator is a character in the painting, and when we might finally settle down into a comfortable position as spectators, at last receiving meaning without having to contribute to its elaboration, the story ends.

The image is gone and nothing is left of the narrator. What remains in the fiction is another image, the bunch of flowers, which through a zooming technique has gradually grown from a mere dot on the landscape to occupy the whole frame. It is out of context, cut off from the total composition and treated very irreverently. Of course, as readers, we are left with the printed pages parallel to that bunch of flowers in the *mise en abîme*.

As a conclusion, we might refer to another image holding a similar narrative function to that of the painting in our story, William Gass' windowpane in "In the Heart of the Heart of the Country."[13] Its flat, framed plane blends the outside referential world, the narrator's reflection and his inner-self in the same way as the painting in our story combined the picture-book landscape, the painted character and his inner voice.

---

[13] W. Gass. *In the Heart of the Heart of the Country*. Boston: D. R. Godine Publisher, 1989, 195.

FABRIC OF DREAMS/FABRICATION OF DREAMS: *A BOLT OF WHITE CLOTH*

DANIÈLE PITAVY-SOUQUES

Translated by Alexander C.W. Baird

A dream fabric or a fabrication of dreams? To break out of routines, to re-shape one's existence, these are the possibilities explored by Leon Rooke's volume of stories, *A Bolt of White Cloth*.[1] Opening with a tale of the same title and introducing the reader with important clues, this work is a sustained reflection on the imagination and literary discourse; more specifically, on the relationship between *literariness* and the real and, consequently, the imaginary. If there is something disconcerting about these nine stories, it is their quality of combining fable and delirium to produce what might more properly belong to psychiatry. While representing neither concessions to contemporary literary fashion (including magic realism), nor explorations of certain extreme limiting situations, these stories manage to raise questions about the nature of the individual.

Beyond the desire to entertain the reader, the selection follows a path that explores ever more closely the relations between the real, on the one hand, and the fictive and imaginary, on the other, to lead eventually to a number of questions. Initially the exploratory journey assumes the conventional form of an equal exchange between reader and storyteller: the storyteller needs to be confident, after all, that the reader will follow him into the world of invention. It then broadens out to include an interrogation of what occurs when a fictionalised reality is read or experienced by the reader / creator. In fact, Rooke is engaged in the fictionalisation of the individual's relationship with the imaginary. I offer Sartre's definition of this last term:

---

[1] Leon Rooke, *A Bolt of White Cloth*, Don Mills: Stoddart, 1984.

the imaginary always appears 'against the backdrop of the world,' but the apprehension of the world always reciprocally entails a tacit going-beyond towards the *imaginary*. Each imagining consciousness maintains the world as the nihilated condition of the *imaginary* and, reciprocally, every consciousness-of-the-world summons up and motivates an imagining consciousness determined by the particular *sense* of the situation.[2]

In his work on the novel, Wolfgang Iser proposes a triadic schema that extends the dichotomy of the fictive and the real to include the imaginary. The fictive, which is *derealisation*, manifesting itself in the form of an "as if," acquires a certain reality by virtue of its mediating function, since this, writes Hans Robert Jauss, "confers both force and form onto the otherwise immutable imaginary":

In this way, the fictive act acquires its particularity from its occasioning in the text, the return of the reality of the everyday world and, through this repetition, confers a form upon the imaginary, which raises the repeated reality to the status of sign and the imaginary to the effect of what this sign signifies.

Transgression is revealed in the *irrealisation*, which is the effect of a passage from the world of everyday reality to the sign of something other. In passing from the imaginary as something undefined to a functional determination, the imaginary becomes real.[3]

To focus upon the "waking dream" is therefore not a mere device, but an actual return. This is how I propose to read *A Bolt of White Cloth*.

• • •

To what are we invited to listen? In defining his reader, Rooke defines his text. "A Bolt of White Cloth" opens the collection with the figure of a

---

[2] Jean-Paul Sartre, *L'Imaginaire*, Paris : Gallimard, 1940, p. 238.

[3] These texts are quoted by Hans Robert Jauss in "La perfection, fascination de l'imaginaire," *Poétique*, 61, 3-22, 1985, 2-3.

travelling salesman and his patter. The material he is selling is the spoken word, inexhaustible like the cloth in the story, neutrally white, solid and of good quality. Moreover, and just like the cloth, it can be used for anything. The only thing the salesman asks for by way of payment, touches upon the customer's quality as a listener: the buyer must have suffered and must have loved. He insists on the mundane character of this experience, talking of the simple, ordinary relationships which rule human lives. All that counts is the agreement of those who have suffered to listen with love or empathy. By simply saying "Yes, I'll buy / I'll listen," one already broadens the scope of one's experience; and if the woman in the story claims to have a greater share of suffering than is in reality hers, it is because as soon as one listens or reads, one becomes another. In this way the author also makes the point that the "newness" of the present is illusory, disguising as it does repetition, and more importantly, identity.

This is why Rooke places six stories within a would-be timeless framework, specifically the stories that open and close the book. The atemporality is undeniable in "A Bolt of White Cloth," but in "The Only Daughter" and "Dream Lady" there is an equally deliberate exclusion of the particular, which, when taken into account with the rest of his work, suggests that Rooke-time is neither pagan nor Christian, but rather relative, consisting of a plurality of different temporal series. Added to this is the uncertainty of place. For Rooke, a Canadian, born in the Southern United States and identifying very much with that literary tradition, spacial references always carry symbolic meanings. The stories are intended as texts for the present, while attempting to return to a reality of timeless imagination. In harmony with contemporary aesthetics, they remain open, raise questions, and awaken a sense of philosophic wonder. This should be borne in mind when reading the final lines of the prologue:

> "Wonder where he is now?" we said.
> "Wonder where he goes next?"
> "Where he gets that cloth?"
> "Who he *is*?"
> We couldn't get to sleep, wondering about that (20).

• • •

Rooke's approach is to set out from a world most readers would recognize as real. All of his stories are expressive of everyday life and depict a succession of *banal* incidents, in the sense of being part of a common fund of real-life experience belonging to everyone. But the situations and events which make up these ordinary lives are invariably unhappy. The stories express suffering. To some extent, and it is one of the author's virtues, Rooke gives new life to the well-worn themes of non-fulfillment, emptiness and lack, by carefully anchoring them in everyday life. Through the mouths of his characters — many of the stories are told in the first person — or the narrator's voice, the author disguises suffering under a facade of ordinariness by shifting its focal point. I have picked three ways in which the author does this.

The first involves moving suffering from the emotional to the physical plane. What is most striking, for example, in the description of the little girl's long walk in "The Only Daughter," in spite of the harrowing flashbacks of the mother's death, expressing an almost insupportable pain of grief, is the girl's physical suffering. Rooke's language does not say: "I am unhappy because I have no parents," but only "I am hungry, I am cold"; nor does it say: "I have lost what I loved, I am afraid of the future," but only "these cases are straining the nerves in my back, the handles are cutting into my fingers."

Elsewhere, in "The Woman's Guide to Home Companionship," the innumerable digressions in the report drawn up by the two frustrated wives, weaken the emotional intensity of their complaints. The reader's curiosity about the causes of their unhappiness is continually sidetracked as the two women amass details or lose themselves in observing their anatomy, as when, for example, Violet Witherspoon criticises the imperfect breasts of her friend Vee Beaverdeck, and the latter, after examining her bust for half an hour wonders whether she should consult a plastic surgeon. A thousand concrete details on the precise hour, the places, past times, photographs taken for the purpose of verification, draw out the narrative by providing a surplus of everyday reality.

A third method exploits the possibilities of material objects. The gradual wearing away of a relationship, of a love eroded, are expressed in the accumulated stains on an old dressing-gown, the worn down heels of shoes that have been polished a hundred times, or the badly done housework that must be done again. "Saks Fifth Avenue," for example, is constructed from a proliferation of tiny details apparently taken straight from what is called by common consent "reality." Similarly, in "Why the Heathens Are No More," the wretched existence of an adolescent rebelling against her parents is summed up in the processions of ants which come to her bedroom to finish the half-eaten fruit.

However, when examined closely, these stories express unhappiness: a mother's flight to the city and her comfortless death, a teenage girl's almost autistic withdrawal into herself, a husband's indifference and the confusion born out of a crisis of identity, a mother's abandonment of her husband and children, a childless marriage, madness, solitude. And yet, the more the author strives to ameliorate the tragic side of existence, the more sensitive he makes us to this suffering.

•　•　•

It became clear already in the prologue that the cloth can be used to make anything: curtains, bedsheets, dresses . . . In other words, categories and their compartmentalisations have no place in the story. Words can say anything and everything, they can surmount the taboos of accepted usage, common sense and tradition. Similarly, the fantastic tale and the fairy story are free to ignore the constraints of verisimilitude. As texts, Rooke's stories continually play with this principle of liberty. The writing violates the conventions, and transgresses into the unreal in a variety of different ways. I shall give two examples.

"Why the Heathens Are No More" is structured around a radical reversal of pace, and the opposition lethargy / hypnosis. In the face of the pressures placed upon the adolescent Suzy by her family to come out of herself, to abandon the reassuring world of the cinema and the refuge of sleep, she adopts a strategy of inertia. The narrative makes no headway, becoming bogged down in sentences whose assertive form has more to do with the rejection of action than with narrative progression. Physical movement seems to be held in suspension, as time slows down to pure duration: "I sat at the table with the dry toast in one hand, my other around a glass. I was almost dozing" (62). "'Okay,' he told me in the car. 'Buckle up. Don't want you going through the windshield on your first day of work.' I sat there. Finally he reached over and snapped the belt in place" (63).

Running up against the wall of inertia, the parents' language becomes a concatenation of prayers, cajolings, orders and threats, which creates an atmosphere of continual harassment and exasperation, revealing deep mutual incomprehension.

In contrast to the jerky rhythm, which continually hinders all progression in order to better express the force of the girl's lethargy, the accelerated pace of the last few pages is evidence that, somewhere, a rupture has occurred. As soon as the stranger enters the scene, Suzy, like the text itself, changes. The pleas are replaced by suggestions, orders are carried out, the rhythm begins to move more freely. The antagonism between the two opposing forces is replaced by consensus, and freedom is no longer incompatible with opening up to the world. In a chance remark, Suzy unconsciously offers a rational explanation for this change: "He never stopped looking into my eyes" (p. 67): in other words, the stranger has hypnotised Suzy. A genuine clue, or a trap for the reader? Whichever, the deliberately unobtrusive remark passes almost unnoticed in the wake of the effect of unreality which is produced by Suzy's liberation. Suddenly, everything is possible, no more social or moral prohibitions, nothing is too improbable, freedom alone exists. In this way, the text proclaims the triumph of desire.

On the textual level, the implausible is represented by the abrupt change of rhythm, just as it is represented in the diegesis by the girl's new-found freedom. The act of putting the parent / child conflict into writing undermines its reality, tips it over into the imaginary domain. As this is also the domain of desire, the reader consents more willingly. But, at the same time, the lethargy / hypnosis opposition, the shift from catalepsy to mortal surrender, raises the disturbing prospect of one consciousness dominating another. A menacing shadow lurks beyond the transgressive act.

The aim of "Saks Fifth Avenue" is more complex. It analyses the temptation of fiction, which applies to every form of discourse, irrespective of its subject. The moment one begins to *recount* something, the real disappears and its place is taken by a construction. It is left to the reader to re-establish "the truth." It follows therefore that it is no more scandalous to begin an account of an ordinary evening at home (or an autobiography, for that matter), with a story whose extraordinary subject matter breaks all the conventional laws of probability, than it is to grant some privileged place to what really happened.

> A woman called me up on the telephone. She was going to give
> me twenty thousand dollars, she said. I said come right over, I'm
> not doing anything this evening. Then I went back into the living
> room where my wife was, seated on the sofa with her nail files
> and paint, painting her nails (120).

In fact this is a text about *contingency* as symbolised by the box of
unknown provenance, marked "Saks Fifth Avenue," in which Cecil, the
narrator, keeps the shoe polish. The box is in effect graced with what
Gaston Bachelard has termed "an imaginary aureole." A dialectic is set
up between, on the one hand, the presence of this box, with its disparate
connotations of luxury, mystery (does it form part of the secret life of
Cecil's wife?), banality (imposed by its mundane purpose), and, on the
other hand, the real and imagined events forming the framework of this
tale: the arrival of the lady with the twenty-thousand dollars, the tempting
bargain offers of kitsch merchandise, the son and the daughter, the little
boy and his parents, the adventures of the hero and heroine in a film on
television, the two children from the Third World. Here we seem to have
gone beyond the question of categorical boundaries and moved on to
others about existential contingency. What makes up a human life? What
is a life? What is a human being?

●   ●   ●

Iser's triad rests upon a belief in an immemorial (*unvordenklich*) collec-
tive imagination, the content of which, in contrast to fiction, which has
no bounds and waits only to be defined, cannot be reinvented but only
consulted. If it is the fundamental term corresponding to the imagina-
tion, it is only revealed, that is, it assumes an intelligible form through
the literary act, which then becomes its sign. Just as Barthes has identi-
fied those irreducible objects whose unique function in literature is to
designate the real, and which are therefore signs of the effect of the real,
so Iser sees fiction, which originates in the real, as the sign of an effect of
the imaginary. In other words, the original transgressive act, or the act of
irrealisation which is proper to fiction, is followed by a second irrealisation,
in which the phenomenon gives the imaginary a form and, by so doing,
makes it real. This explains the age-old observation that "it is easier to

sympathise with the sufferings of a hero in a novel than with the sufferings of those about us."

More than anything Rooke has hitherto produced, *A Bolt of White Cloth* displays an overall cohesion which it owes precisely to its rigorous exploration of the various relations which unite the terms of the real / fictive / imaginary triad. In order to delimit the second aspect of the problem, that is, the moment when the imaginary becomes real, I propose to examine the book's progression through this *philosophical journey.*

Collectively, the short stories could be read as comprising a sort of treatise on fiction, with "A Bolt of White Cloth" serving as a foreword. However different they may at first seem, the first two stories have common features that complement each other; they are both closely related to the myth and the folk tale, the two literary genres which have always satisfied the need to experience an ideal of perfection, which the real world, with all its shortcomings, cannot supply. Between them, the two stories plot the opposed axes of the imaginary, the one turned towards the past, the other towards the future. "The Only Daughter" is constructed around the "happy" schema of the return to origins, in this case the father's house, at the end of an initiatory journey with a halt in a makeshift shelter — reminiscent of Robinson Crusoe — with its womb / cave connotations. The challenge thrown down in the last sentence is not so much a reminder of the world's imperfections, represented in the story by the mother's flight, illness and death, as an expression of the desire not to be swallowed up by a happy dream. It is in this way that the imaginary becomes the real — the return can only ever be a construction: "'I'll try it,' she said. 'I'll give him twenty-four hours to prove himself'" (48).

"Why the Heathens Are No More" is based on the no less archaic oppositions of inside / outside, near / distant, familiar / hostile, and presents itself as a gateway to life, an escape route from the enchanted castle. The present tense of the title announces the arrival of a new age of happiness where the wicked can do no harm. The carefully contrasted ways in which Suzy is "seduced" by her two enchanters, first by her friend Richard, and then by the stranger, mirrors a parallel correlation between public and private forms of evil. The one — preserved by Richard in his collection of newspaper cuttings to do with wars, assassinations and totalitarianism — destroying the world; the other, exemplified by Suzy's parents, slowly destroying individuals. When Suzy breaks free from the laws of conventions, it is to protest against what is happening in El Salvador. Once again the imaginary is realised in action, a circumstance not without irony when one recalls the story's opening sentence: "My folks told me that if I left my room things would begin to happen to me" (49).

Continuing this exploration of genres, "The Woman's Guide to Home Companionship" questions the nature of the literary text and is in search of its identity in the same way in which the story's two heroines are in search of theirs. Faced with the apparent "fascism" of language, Rooke decides to ridicule its clichés. If, like the two women trapped by the cultural images disseminated by the media, the author is the prisoner of words, then he must dismantle its combinations and put together others, albeit fragile and ephemeral, to construct — for example — a night of shared despair all in the time it takes to make a speech, to tell a tale. Rooke's novel response to the old problem of the relation between fiction and truth is to import a multiplicity of circumstantial details, measurements, even photographic documents to create a sort of comedy of digressions. Above all, he does not allow the story to be locked into any one precise category, since the two women refer variously to their production as "this story or tale" (72), "a dictation in order to assist the authorities" (72), "this document" (78), "this chronicle" (81), "these memoirs" (84), effectively abandoning all claims to veracity, save to acknowledge the one undeniable truth that every text is the expression of desire: "We have merely been displaying wishful thinking" (84). The real is only ever the imaginary made manifest through the agency of the text.

The question of genre leads to others about purpose. Rooke continues his methodical analysis in the next short story, "Dirty Heels of the Fine Young Children," in which he takes up the idea that through writing one can achieve self-knowledge and adds that it is also a means of communication with the other. These two functions had already been fictionalised by Virginia Woolf and Edward Albee (apparently Rooke's references here) in works in which the characters disguise suffering borne of irreconcilability or absence by playing fictitious roles and which end in scenes of dramatic crisis. Rooke approaches the subject differently by exploiting a particular situation, namely a mother's desertion of her family and consequent absence, in such a way that what is at stake in the fiction becomes paradoxically the mother's presence, in which each character in turn believes. For the father this is a physical presence; for the daughter, Agnes, who has an idealised image of her mother, a moral presence.

In the beginning, the situation is commonplace enough: the grief caused by the mother's leaving drives the father to abandon his position as head of the family and neglect his three little girls who respond in turn by deserting the family home. They then attempt to restore the broken lines of communication by inventing a caring mother who "indirectly" advises the father about how he should behave. At first the father, guilty about neglecting his responsibilities, knowingly goes along with Agnes' game, realising it compensates for the mother's absence. But when Agnes suddenly throws at him: "Mama says you ain't even our daddy!" (91) — echoing Martha's vitriolic jibes in *Who's Afraid of Virginia Woolf?* — the father begins to *believe* his daughter's fiction *because* it represents a profound attack on his own self-image and jeopardises his identity. What has occurred is not, as in Albee's play, a mere breaking of the rules of the game, but a genuine transgression. The fiction has become the sign of the imaginary experienced as real. By dramatising his innermost fears, the very identity of the fiction's intended recipient is put in question, pushing him to the edge of madness. And it is a changed man who now hears Mrs Tucker's question "What kind of father are you?" (95). Returning home, he succeeds in reopening a real channel of communication with his daughter by continuing the fiction, which, no longer a call for help, becomes a game. He even begins to add his own inventions and, in so doing, manages to console his daughters. The intolerable can only be rendered supportable by such fabrications. Agnes believes, or pretends to believe, her father's fiction that her mother has gone to law school, because it preserves her idealisation of her mother and helps to justify her desertion, as it does for the reader. All good fiction tears away the mask of complacency behind which it communicates with others.

"Saloam Frigid With Time's Legacy While Mrs. Willoughby Bight-Davies Sits Naked Through The Night On a Tree Stump Awaiting the Lizard That Will Make Her Loins Go Boom-Boom" is concerned — as one might guess from the title alone! — with reception and the difficulty of catching and holding the reader's attention.

By its very nature, the waking dream is both produced and experienced by the same imagination. What then happens when the imaginary is experienced as being more real than reality itself, when, in spite of the desire not to be taken in, one is mesmerised by one's own dream? The final three short stories are constructed around these musings, exasperated expressions of the desire to lay bare the fundamental contingency of existence: the desire to change one's life, break free from routines, or to escape the sterility of a dialogue where one no longer hears the other.

In "Saks Fifth Avenue," the plot developments of a film watched by one character and another's waking dream are described in parallel. At the end of the story, the distance between Rooke's two characters and their respective fictions has become non-existent. Cecil and his wife Coolie are mesmerised to such a degree that their critical capacities are suspended and they begin to *live this unreality.* There is however a difference between the two cases, stemming from the nature of the two fictions. Coolie, like every spectator, is the victim of the closed form of the dramatic aesthetic: she must passively empathise with the tragic destinies of the characters in the film she is watching, even if this enforced empathy does issue in catharsis. To console her, as her husband does, with the words "it's only a film" is to betray, *a contrario,* a belief in a perfect world. In contrast with Coolie's passivity, Cecil *himself* gets to close the *narrative* (an expression of the idealisation of perfection) which began with the story's very first sentence. He is both its sole spectator and author / creator:

> 'They won't die, Coolie,' I said, 'It's only a movie.'
> I started spreading the money out over the carpet.
> I started counting the money (145).

One notes in these dreams a recurring fascination with twins or doubles.[4] Each male character invents for himself a companion who replicates his wife, who herself may be present or absent. James Ripley, the husband in "The Mad Woman of Cherry Vale," confronted with the necessity of ridding himself of "the madwoman" — who has simply been substituted for his wife — ponders upon the apparent duality: what is the difference between dreaming of another and being another? This penultimate short story sheds a remarkable light on the collection as a whole through its

---

[4] On the double in Rooke's writing, see Simone Vauthier, "Entering Other Skins" – or, Leon Rooke's "The End of the Revolution" *The Literary Review*, Spring 1985, 456-479. On the place of the myth of Psyche in the fairy tale, see Marc Soriano, *Les contes de Perrault*, Paris: Gallimard, 1968.

parallels, albeit in inverted form, with the myth of Psyche. Because he has gazed upon the woman's naked body, because he has discovered she bears the same name as himself, James Ripley must lose her. It is as if the waking dream is simultaneously an attempt at reconciliation with the sensual body *and* the desire to transcend the sensual. An identical ambiguity occurs in "Dream Lady."

In the absence of sex, what *does* return, triumphantly and exercising a veritable fascination, is the gesture. Whether it be in the eroticism of Coolie's fluttering her freshly-varnished fingernails, or in the tenderness implicit in the preparation of a meal for two, "together in the kitchen bumping elbows, getting onions chopped, sauces made, vegetables steamed" ("The Mad Woman of Cherry Vale," 162). The body's seductiveness is bound up with the *magical* transformation of a multiplicity of everyday details: "She started that nail-blowing act again. She'd put on a second coat. Bless you, Coolie, I thought. You are such a wizard." ("Saks Fifth Avenue", 126).

To live with one's body involves repeating the same gesture until it becomes a ritual and a sign of the diffuse and ever-present imaginary. The gesture, ordinary and commonplace, does not change in itself, but once enchanted, has the power to reveal things not usually visible to the naked eye of intelligence. The gesture becomes a messenger between two worlds.

•   •   •

Behind the apparent strangeness of these stories, the author is pursuing a metaphysical project, the aim of which is not to appeal to something lying beyond the bounds of human experience, but rather to awaken the sense of philosophical wonder through which humans grasp their condition.

Some of these texts draw upon mythical schemas (the "deliverance" or the "return to origin" schema); others describe the difficulties implicit in existence, real or ideal. But all are expressive of the individual's essential duality and his desire to achieve some kind of wholeness or reintegration. For Rooke, fiction is the means of achieving this. Its operations incorporate the powerful desire for irrealisation and the ability to give form to the most subtle aspects of the human spirit, while never denying the body's sublimated but indissociable presence.

How Much Do I Love Thee, Let Me Count the Ways: Postmodernity, Language and Love Games in Leon Rooke's "The Guacamole Game[1]"

EVA DARIAS-BEAUTELL

"Can't buy me love," writes Catherine Belsey (72) in her excellent essay on postmodernity, love and desire. In an age of extreme consumerism, in which everything, including pleasure, is susceptible to commodification, love stands out as the only value that is indifferent to market fluctuations. Since it cannot be bought or sold, love "becomes more precious than before because it is beyond price, and in consequence its metaphysical character is intensified" (72).

Yet given the incredulous attitude of postmodern thinking, the metaphysics of love can no longer be considered as valid, without, at the same time, being made suspect. The principle of uncertainty, which constitutes an essential aspect of current critical discourse, doubts the possibility of transcendence. The postmodern emphasis on language has inevitably refocused our attention on the constructed character of reality and experience, including that of love. However, the contradiction implicit in Belsey's statement seems to suggest that this paradox increases, rather than diminishes, the value of love. As Belsey concludes, "no amount of scepticism does

---

[1] I wish to dedicate this essay to Professor Sam Solecki, at the University of Toronto, who embarked me on this project and whose wise advice and disinterested help I have enjoyed all along throughout the process of research and writing. I am also grateful to Professor Branko Gorjup, the project's father, for his enthusiasm, support, and practical help. Finally, my thanks go to the Dirección General de Universidades e Investigación, Consejería de Educación, Cultura y Deporte del Gobierno de Canarias, for a generous research grant that covered my travel and living expenses during three months I spent at the University of Toronto in the summer of 2000.

away with desire, which, if it is the destiny of a signifying organism, is fashioned, but neither produced nor erased, by the specific cultural order which gives rise to our hopes and doubts" (72).

Postmodern love in this way becomes the literalization of the desire for the transcendence that never *is*, and can only be, as such, approached in language, which is a place where meaning is both constantly promised and indefinitely postponed. Love is therefore, says Belsey, the desire that cannot speak. It cannot speak because it is, among other things, weighed down by its own banality, by strong self-awareness of being *déja-vu*; for, how can love speak without repeating the patterns already sanctioned by our culture? Love, then, cannot speak because it does not know how to speak. "If Lacan is right," points out Belsey, "desire inhabits the unconscious, and its motive is a lack, an absence at the heart of identity. In consequence, it is speechless, hollowed within the utterance that is a demand for love. Itself a metonym, a displacement of the want-to-be, desire is unable to name itself: it speaks only in substitutions, in figures, without truly *knowing* what it says" (75).

This essay will explore the implications of the idea of love within the postmodern paradigm of thinking as it relates to identity, desire, and language in Leon Rooke's "The Guacamole Game," the concluding novella in the collection *Oh!* (1997). In it, the two protagonists, Vivian and Thomas, play the title game, which is, despite the obvious gastronomic connotations, both a language and a love game. Rooke's characters play their roles as they attempt to reproduce the main events of a story that *has* already happened at the beginning of the narration. In doing so, they reintroduce these events as the absent referent of the language game. As the narrative evolves and the game progresses, Vivian and Thomas engage in exploring the limits of the very processes of interpretation and representation of reality which they set in motion and are an essential part of. Most important for the present discussion is the characters' exploration of the possibilities of relating to and addressing each other, of speaking (of) love, in an ever more complex world of the postmodern.[2]

---

[2] Gender relations are often explored by Rooke's stories in a number of unexpected ways. In "Sweethearts," for instance, a man and a woman have an argument over the phone before they finally decide to meet and "talk it over," and their fight gives way to a sudden sense of urgency and a powerful image of desire at the end: "Come

The reader of "The Guacamole Game" quickly learns that the plot and the setting are subordinate to language, the function of which is characterization. There are only two protagonists, and they are playing out a drama of near tragic dimension against a set of frames, initially perceived as 'foreign.' The third person narrator moves straight to one of the key structural points of the narrative, introducing the first and the most important of these frames, which is the game itself: "Twenty years they had been playing the game. She made the guacamole, he mixed the masa, deep-fried the tortillas, they played the game" (234).

The expectation of foreignness, raised by the title, is thus met in the novella's opening scenes through the description of a culinary ritual. Yet, the guacamole as game contains a wider meaning, which I will discuss later. For now, let us stay with the guacamole proper, the Mexican dish that the characters prepare as part of the game, and which signals the game's point of departure. In addition, it gives them something to do during the game's intervals: every now and then, they would pause, refill the guacamole bowl and fry more tortillas. The Mexican "theme" and its stereotypically exotic connotations are further played up when Vivian, as part of the game strategy, appears barefooted, without panties, wearing a black sombrero and a silver Mexican necklace (254). This literal sense of the guacamole, which gives the story a fleeting foreign flavour, stands though in a sharp contrast to an otherwise brief description of the novella's setting, a small town in Ontario, Canada. But neither the global — symbolized by the decontextualized Mexican elements — nor the local — tangentially represented by the setting — turn out to be instrumental to the interpretation of the novella's meaning. The non-instrumental character of the setting is evident early on in the construction of the plot. Once the setting is located and named, almost the entire action takes place indoors, inside the couple's living room, where the game is played out. The question of place is

on now, hurry, hurry it up. I want to get inside that coat with you, I want to look into your eyes" (38). In "LR Loves GL," the first-person adolescent narrator, LR, tells us the details of a frustrated attempt at lovemaking with GL, producing one of Rooke's most hilarious beginnings: "When I put it in she said Is it in yet? Now that nearly killed me, that was the worst experience of my life, when she said that" (121). Finally, the married couple of "No Whistle Slow" (1977) attend a party to engage in a language contest about fictional situations which are actually reproductions of their own. In these and many other texts by Rooke, gender relations are usually negotiated by means of language and language games.

thus of minimal significance, if not inconsequential. Rooke's notion of setting, as Branko Gorjup points out, "is a site where a story happens rather than a faithfully reproduced geographic and cultural locale. It is functional, stripped down to the bare minimum, used to anchor the story in place" (Gorjup 1999, 270). The Mexican elements are introduced and marked initially as relevant, but that turns out to be misleading, as they are gradually rendered inappropriate. Such inappropriateness, verging on the slapstick, is graphically depicted when slabs of guacamole begin to fly across the room, landing on the window screens. Or when Vivian's sexy black sombrero bounces off, ending in the guacamole itself (255, 259).[5]

The frame of the guacamole game is double. Its other purpose is to provide the characters with a fixed set of previously agreed-upon rules of conduct. While playing, the opponents' actions are 'voluntarily' constrained by these rules. They repeatedly refer to them, and in case of doubt consult the game's penalty chart (Rooke 1997, 248). This second use of the guacamole game redirects the reader's attention to the story's *real* theme, the theme of how love can speak in an age of self-consciousness and simulacra. It is at the intersection of these two frames of the guacamole game that the theme of love is dealt with, and that the "foreign" flavour of the game extends beyond mere décor. It actually affects a sense of otherness, which is the basis for the characters' mutual exploration of love. In establishing this otherness, Rooke's novella explores identity by using alterity as the necessary condition of desire and love.

To a considerable extent, "The Guacamole Game" relies on postmodern self-consciousness, which makes contemporary fiction, Rooke's included, decidedly ironic. According to Umberto Eco, the postmodern text revisits the past, using irony as its primary tool for investigation; it "demands, in order to be understood, not the negation of the already said, but its ironic rethinking" (33).

---

[5] On this issue, Rooke seems to be self-consciously playing with the expectations of the reader not only of "The Guacamole Game" but of his previous works too, since the Mexican title and the word 'novella' attached to it could draw a misleading connection between this text and "The Street of Moons" (1991), a novella in three stories, set in Mexico and dealing in fact with the interaction between American and Mexican characters. In "The Guacamole Game," however, both the thematic and the generic expectations are soon undercut.

> I think of the postmodern attitude as that of a man who loves a
> very cultivated woman and knows he cannot say to her. 'I love
> you madly,' because he knows that she knows (and that she knows
> that he knows) that these words have already been written by
> Barbara Cartland. Still, there is a solution. He can say, 'As Barbara
> Cartland would put it, I love you madly.' At this point, having
> avoided false innocence, having said clearly that it is no longer
> possible to speak innocently, he will nevertheless have said what
> he wanted to say to the woman: that he loves her, but he loves her
> in an age of lost innocence. If the woman goes along with this,
> she will have received a declaration of love all the same. Neither
> of the two speakers will feel innocent, both will have accepted
> the challenge of the past, of the already said, which cannot be
> eliminated; both will consciously and with pleasure play the
> game of irony . . . But both will have succeeded, once again, in
> speaking of love (32-33).

Eco's passage raises a few important points that require brief com-
mentary. The first to be pointed out is Eco's implicit definition of the post-
modern, not as a movement or a trend, but rather as an attitude. And this
attitude is about self-awareness, associated (in the above case) with a
man who loves a woman but knows the limitations of language for him to
be able to convey his genuine feelings. This calls for self-consciousness,
which is the only way out of an impasse created by too much knowledge.
What must be acknowledged — by way of self-consciousness — is what is
already known, already written and read. In turn, points out Eco, and this
is the second point, such self-consciousness produces complicity among the
subjects involved in a game of language. And, finally, Eco highlights com-
munication as the ultimate goal of both pleasure and play.

In Rooke's novella, the game sets the framework for both: for a self-
conscious playing and for communication. As already mentioned, the char-
acters' playful exploration of love is based on the structures of language,
predicated on the notion of otherness, and is given the shape through the
game itself. Insofar as language is the only possible site for the charac-
ters' discourse and action, it is posited as the other, assumed to be the
only reality, the only way of being in the world. The game, therefore,
while shaped by language is directly related to the question of identity:

Name?
Thomas J. Pabst.
J?
Sorry. James.
Occupation?
Bricklayer. This month it's bricklayer.
Age?
Age, I'm . . .
Count it on your fingers, Thomas James Pabst.
Forty-seven. Eight? I am forty-seven.
Right. Make that forty-nine. Dock me one hundred.

His first docking, getting a free ride on the J, they would
pause to dip the chips into the guacamole, munch the dip, sip the
drinks (234).

What is striking to the reader about the two protagonists is the level
of their dialogue. Although married, they ask such basic and *most imper-
sonal* identitary questions as their name, age, occupation and marital sta-
tus. Thus the game is about pretending, about not knowing what is al-
ready known. It is about the construction of a new identity, each time
for the first time. Failure to pretend to not to know what the characters
know, results in losing the game or falling behind the agreed number of
points:

Address?
Address, you know my address.
The address, please, of Thomas James Pabst and kindly dock
yourself five hundred points for delay of game.
Shit! 209 Saints Road, Estuary, Ontario, Canada, Zip NOB 1PO.
You lose, Thomas James Pabst.
What do you mean, lose? I only said —
You said, 'shit', Thomas James Pabst, in an explosive voice. So
you lose. Mark that another ten thousand in my favour for the
one-minute game (234).

Two pages later, Vivian answers these preliminary questions:

Name?
Vivian Darling-Pabst.
That is your full and entire name?
Vivian *Samantha* Darling-Pabst.
Kindly dock yourself one hundred points (235-236).

No matter how improbable these two scenes are, they underline the unreliability of language, the relativity of identity, and the intricate nature of truth. Vivian and Thomas deliberately conceal part of their names, even at the cost of one hundred points. Thomas lies about his age, but is immediately caught by Vivian who, being his wife, obviously *knows* his right age. Vivian, too, is caught lying on several occasions about a conflict with one of her daughters. Presented as a generational conflict, typical of a classical family romance, it equips the story with a necessary subplot. At the same time, it supplies the protagonists with the essential material for the game, which is the absent reality the characters keep alluding to. The main events in the subplot could be thus summarized: Christina, one of the couple's two daughters, has recently divorced Roscoe Heiss. Vivian, Christina's mother, profoundly dislikes Heiss, with whom her daughter has a baby: "Did you not say *at the time*, quote, and, more specifically, at the time Christina Heiss announced her pregnancy in this very room, quote: 'I would sooner be shot than carry that pig's child?'" Thomas asks Vivian, making full use of his "Interrogator's Role" (250-251). But Vivian hates Roscoe even more because of an incident that happened during a family party, in which the man — later alleging having mistaken the mother for the daughter — tries to kiss Vivian in the kitchen pantry. "That stupid Roscoe Heiss," Vivian cries infuriated by Thomas' insistent digging into the unpleasant event, "put his *tongue in my ear,* licked all over my face, and I don't care what the son of a bitch says, this was not a case of mistaken identity. I am twenty years older, she was nine months pregnant, and if you or anyone else think it was mistaken identity, then I want a goddamn divorce" (259).

The emotional pitch of Vivian's declarations stands in comic contrast to the parody of a judicial process that the game actually pursues. Such questions as "Did you or did you not . . ." or "Is it not true that . . . ?" typical of a cross examination, draw an invisible vector between language and the achievement of an objective truth. In fact, the game is really about

Thomas who sets out to compel Vivian to confess the truth about a recent incident involving their daughter Christina. In addition, the formal pseudo-Elizabethan speech, which the characters use when addressing a special petition, elevates the game to the verbal formality typical of a courtroom: "*I pray thee, kind knight, to repeat the question,*" says Vivian in the prescribed form. "*I impeach thee and cry foul!*" exclaims Thomas later (241).

The effect is not only comic, associated with parody; it enhances the theatrical tenor of the tale as well, revealing an emphasis on performance, which I will discuss later. The legal tone seems to initially confirm the game's search for truth. Yet the search is not carried out in the realm of phenomenal reality but rather in a particular representation of that reality, which is available only in and through the language game.

Such a portrayal of truth, accessible in and through *the law*, is a typical postmodern gesture. The so-called "linguistic turn," a strong feature in postmodern thinking, has radically modified the critic's perception of time and space and intensified the reader's sense of mediation in the world. According to Iain Chambers, "the mediation, the employment and deployment of languages, rather than the objects they supposedly represent" is central to postmodern writing and, "as Wittgenstein put it, it marks the limits of our world" (7). And, continues Chambers, "it is no longer the object, but the encounter with the languages and discourses that orbit around it that counts" (8).

In "The Guacamole Game," the foregrounding of language is reinforced by the characters' self-conscious use of words and phrases and by the metalinguistic comments:

> "The game rule was that you could weave your question down a thousand roads, snake down a thousand alleys, lump in as many clauses as your wit allowed, but in the end you were to restrict yourself to the single question" (238).

As this passage suggests, the rules of the game permit the characters to comment on the syntax and the grammar, even on the use of intonation. Thomas asks Vivian to dock herself ten million points of penalty for "scurrilous language" (251). Later, they play by differentiating literal from figurative meanings as when, for example, Vivian catches Thomas saying that he "broke the radio into a thousand pieces when [he] could not possibly have counted those pieces" (252).

Paradoxically, however, such focusing on the linguistic nature of reality and experience unveils the fragility (or the provisional character) of truth. As it is typical of a judiciary process, nothing must be said in this game that might be considered a fact of truth unless proven by evidence. Vivian, who knows very well the rules of the game, considers her possibilities: "If one answered an opponent's question with a lie and the opponent could prove the answer a lie, then one lost a million points. It was thus a requirement that one have a good idea what information the opponent possessed" (241).

The narrative here reproduces once again the postmodern anxiety about the absence of an unquestionable truth, which could provide the foundations for knowledge. Nevertheless, the principle of performativity associated with postmodern theorizing very often comes to replace the traditional search for truth. In doing so, it introduces a questioning attitude that interrogates all modes of cultural production and the transmission of knowledge. Language, therefore, assumes a crucial role since the principle of performativity can be legitimized only in language. Truth, in other words, is no longer grounded in reality but in its (linguistic) representation. Discussing this inaccessible nature of truth, Jean-François Lyotard (*Sign* 176-177) has introduced into contemporary critical discourse the notion of an "as if" presentation of reality.

Rooke's text implicitly explores a similar view of reality in a number of ways. The reader remembers the game's rule number one, according to which the participants have to act *as if they did not know what they know*. In other words, the characters' ability of role-playing relies on their being able to maintain a simulacrum of reality. Consequently, cases of mistaken or faked identity appear at the centre of the plot and subplot, which turn out to be some of the novella's funniest scenes. For example, in the subplot, Roscoe Heiss apologises to Vivian for having stuck his tongue into her ear, offering the explanation that the pantry was dark and that both the mother and the daughter wore the same perfume (259). Likewise, in the main plot, the opponents continually play with their identities, hiding behind different outfits and disguises. Thomas dons a tuxedo, sporting a red carnation on his lapel (245). Vivian appears wearing diverse jewellery and make-up. Her tendency to adopt faked identities is always justified within the context of game strategies:

"You look stunning," he said.

She was in fact dressed to the nines. Spiked heels, panty-hose, black strapless evening gown, hair twisted to the side and held there by three silver combs. Lipstick, cheek-enhancements, thin silver necklace, earrings resembling minnows.

It could be that the son of a bitch was going to propose tak-ing her out to dinner.

If so, he might have mentioned it before she consumed a pound of guacamole (263).

Notwithstanding the humour, the emphasis on performance — the characters' self-conscious representation of their role-playing — places Rooke's narrative in the realm of simulacrum, of the Lyotardian "as if" presentation of reality. The characters must act *as if* they were someone else. They must display a taste for disguise and mimicry, revealing the story's obvious affinity with the theatre. Actually, "The Guacamole Game" could be performed *as if* it were a play of the kind of *Who's Afraid of Virginia Woolf?* (1962). As in Edward Albee's play, the setting in Rooke's novella is almost limited to the interior space of the house where the Pabsts live and play the game. And, as in Albee's play, the strength of the action in Rooke's novella comes, not from the plot itself, but from the verbal contest waged between the characters.

The narrative power of "The Guacamole Game" resides almost exclu-sively in the way the story is told, specifically in the characters' verbal agility. Setting, action, symbol, and plot are in Rooke always secondary to language. Simone Vauthier, analysing Rooke's "The Birth Control King of the Upper Volta," has observed that the power of his narratives surges from the characters' language, a language that is strongly directed toward the other. The use of question marks, mentioned earlier, help the reader develop a sense of reality, while that reality is being constructed by the parties involved in the game, as well as by the reader involved in the text. Likewise, the lack of quotation marks in the dialogues creates an illusion of immediacy between the speaker and the language, and between the reader and the text.

Rooke is a noted playwright, which explains why his fiction invariably displays theatrical qualities. In several of his works Rooke explores the Shakespearean drama, in terms of language and character. The most obvious and extended example is his prize-winning novel *Shakespeare's Dog* (1983). In "The Guacamole Game" though, the Shakespearean connection is more circumspect, yet easily identified in the characters' language, in the pseudo-Elizabethan lines they sing as part of the game. It is structurally obvious, not only in the division of plot and subplot, but also thematically in the treatment of love and the use of disguise and mistaken identity. The theme of appearance versus reality, typical of the Elizabethan drama, is incorporated in the novella and given a postmodern flavour. As discussed already, "The Guacamole Game" implicitly examines the principle of truth, that very point at which reality assumes an "as if" dimension, becoming an appearance of reality. In addition, the use of Shakespearean language, themes and structures foregrounds a sense of the *déja-vu*, mentioned earlier, as well as the extent to which humans are inserted in and cannot escape their culture.[6]

Occasionally, the dramatic interaction between Vivian and Thomas reaches the intensity of a classical tragedy, especially when love, like in many Shakespeare's plays, turns into a metaphor for the characters' painful awareness of a mutually uncomprehending world, in which all the differences remain unresolved. The passionate confrontation between Thomas and Vivian is, for example, negotiated through a reversal of gender roles, a model often used in Elizabethan comedy to deal with sexual conflicts (see Rose; also Luis Martínez). In this sense the "The Guacamole Game" partakes of a Western classical literary tradition in which the experience of love, as John Bayley has noted, is "a conflict of sympathies . . . which can only be set up by an opposition of characters of the old kind" (39).

The opposition of the "old kind," to which Bayley refers, can be seen in terms of a dichotomy, which the guacamole game sometimes presents, forcing the reader to take sides. The reader may be forced, for instance, to declare his or her allegiance with Vivian in the incident with Roscoe Heiss. Yet, by this point in the novella, her credibility has considerably

---

[6] Anna Pia de Luca (1992) offers an excellent discussion of the conjunction of Shakespearean elements and postmodern techniques in Rooke's *Shakespeare's Dog*.

waned — she has lied or concealed information several times. She has also shown her susceptibility to strong emotions, which carry away her feelings and further erode her ability to impartial judgment. The scenes like the following, in which Vivian discovers to her horror that Christina has a new lover, are telling of her character:

> The man drove a junky car, did not carry the groceries, had not got out to open her daughter's door, wore rumpled clothes, and, moreover, had on his face an ugly moustache. She knew what that meant.
>
> Bad teeth.
>
> So not only was her daughter a floozy, but also a floozy without taste (244).

Vivian's emotional response stands, however, in comic contrast to the illusion of objectivity and impartiality suggested by the game's judicial format. Rooke's characters are as imperfect, misleading and unreliable, as they are human. They are, Gorjup comments,

> . . . like actors in a play: they step into our presence and enact their stories. They invent themselves through the act of telling and engage in the crucial task of attempting to make sense of their lives by rearranging the disconnected and often colliding realities. The effect they have on the reader's consciousness is a lingering sense of disorientation caused by the recognition of having partaken of the drama of life in its naked and archetypal manifestation, of having taken part in an unbearable scrutiny of the assumptions that make or break the individual's ties with other fellow human beings and the spiritual and natural environments (270).

The cathartic quality hinted at by Gorjup is an essential element in "The Guacamole Game," lying precisely at the heart of the text's ability to create theatrical effects. I have already suggested the impressive proximity between the reader and the text and between the reader and the narrator, to which I should add the game's explicit references to the setting as stage. Whenever the characters put on new appearances they change or modify the space they occupy. By putting a new bottle of wine here, a bowl of olives there or a red rose in a vase, they rearrange the scene in which they act.

As a consequence, language is in the broader semiotic sense strongly visual. The characters' body language increases the theatrical effect of the tale: eyebrows expressively arch, a contained smile turns up at the corner of a mouth, legs sweep up and down furiously, feet drum against the floor and arms pull invisible cords in the air. Not only do these elements work at the comic level, but they also intensify the reader's sense of involvement, on which the cathartic effect ultimately depends.

The theatrical in the narrative closely relates to the tale's ability first to engage and then to surprise the reader. In this sense, "The Guacamole Game" is an excellent example of the Lyotardian notion of paralogy, whose working principle involves the recognition of a plurality of languages, intervening locally and provisionally. Lyotard defines paralogy as the power of invention, which "is always born of dissension [. . .]; it refines our sensitivity to differences and reinforces our ability to tolerate the incommensurable" (Lyotard, *Postmodern*, xxv). In the face of the impossibility of reaching a consensus, the pursuit of paralogy offers an imaginative path of communication. "That is to say," states Thomas Docherty in his discussion of Lyotard,

> the point of philosophy is not to look for a truth that can be legitimized or guaranteed through its conformity to an already agreed set of rules for thinking, but rather to push our thinking to the point where we are not prepared for its results, to the point of a kind of surprise or to the point where there is an irruption of that which could not already be accounted for in our prior forms and rules of thinking. (198).

"The Guacamole Game" often pushes the reader's expectation of meaning to the limit, producing confusion and surprise, hinted by the improbable title of the collection, *Oh!* The capacity to surprise or to confuse, however, resides, first of all, in the novella's outer frame; that is, in the reader's lack of information about the game rules. What the reader experiences are the impressions that the language rules are constantly bent in order to allow for new situations to evolve, while the characters play the game. There is a feeling that everything can be realized in language.[7] One can "buy time from the bank" or simply stop the game on a no-fault basis. But the players must signal their intentions and comply with the accepted form, including the required "body language." Thus they yank an invisible cord in the air to announce a pause; drum the feet on the floor six times to signal the end of the game or three times to ask for repentance. Vivian, who is caught lying several times, gets away with it by having recourse to the accepted formula:

> She counted to ten. To twenty. She longed to buy extra minutes from the bank, to drum her feet six times, concede the game, and have this torture be over. But she would not give him the pleasure.
>
> Instead, she drummed her feet three times, signalling repentance, while reciting in a high voice, *Oh, kindest of good knights, I have assailed thee with my lies which encamp upon the wind like a putrid odor, and I wallow unto your mercies and plead contrition from my cup that runneth over.*
>
> That way she escaped from her lies with a penalty of a mere ten million (253).

Scenes like this one, no matter how hilarious, take us back to the relativity of truth. For Vivian, and despite the true-or-false structure that the game at times adapts, it is her knowledge of the rules and her ability to use them, not the supposed authenticity of her answers, which ultimately legitimize her actions. In postmodern theorizing, this is possible because the principle of performativity offers its own self-legitimizing process. Or, as Iain Chambers puts it:

> It is language itself that has become both the palimpsest and fulcrum, not only of immediate sense and aesthetics, but also of an effective ethics and politics. It is the languages of pleasure, of tragedy, of pain, of hope, of freedom, of dealing and difference, of death and beginning, . . . of the 'real,' and not naked reality, that

---

[7] As Douglas Glover writes in his review of *Oh!*, "Rooke breaks the rules, makes up new rules, fractures and twists the story form with breath-taking aplomb, while communicating a generosity of spirit and joie de vivre that is endlessly attractive." (D22). Claire Wilkshire offers a good analysis of the elements of repetition and surprise in Rooke's story "Shut Up."

address us and which we, in turn, address. Thus these languages are not autonomous. They are integral to the 'social construction of reality.' Their power lies precisely in their detailed exchange with what is being continually addressed and constructed through the dialogue itself: our particular sense of time and place. (8)

The more aware of the linguistic nature of the novella's reality we become, the more we are directed toward looking at its process of plot construction. As new rules are revealed in the course of the game, the events of the plot are modified. And as the new events are frequently introduced in the subplot, the reader is forced to keep relocating the puzzle-pieces in the reconstruction of the story, which is always secondary to action and to the process it elicits from the reader. Rooke's writing, points out Vauthier in a similar context, "compels a realization of the spot we are in as participants in the story. For the transitional space of reading is (no longer) a safe place" (10). Besides, an important difference is marked between our two protagonists. While they both seem to know "the facts" of the subplot, it is Thomas, in the role of the interrogator, who maintains the order and who volunteers the necessary amount of information to be released. He is the only one in control of the main plot or the game.

Similarly, the curious arrangement of the narrative point of view increases the effect of surprise and confusion in the reader. While the third-person narrator is closer to Vivian, who provides the centre of consciousness and is actually the protagonist of the *histoire*, she seems to know almost as little as the reader about the order of the events in the narration, or the *récit* — the design secretly planned by Thomas. As a matter of fact, she is constantly surprised, along with the reader, by Thomas' unexpected turns of the screw:

> You have said your daughter, Christina Dolores Heiss, twice today called and each time you slammed the door in her face; is it not true, however, that after your first slamming of the door in her face this same daughter kicked in the screen, made wilful entry into this house, and stood in face-to-face confrontation with you in this very room where we are now speaking?
>
> Vivian Darling-Pabst heard this question through with mounting horror. The son of a bitch had done his homework and now,

within seconds of the game's renewal, had her pinned again (246-247).

Game situations are pushed to the limit, to the point of producing what Lyotard calls a *differend*, a kind of disagreement that cannot be solved by recourse to a higher authority. A *differend* is a conflict that occurs when the terms of discussion are not recognized by any of the parties, when there is no common (third) language for consensus. Therefore, the 'disagreement' is a problem of the structure, or framework in which the subjects are found. It affects the rules of the game, as it were. It is the sign of a failure in the very language of the game, which may be found exhausted in its very possibilities. In targeting the very structure that makes speaking possible, in the first place, a *differend* introduces an insurmountable obstacle in the attempt at communication between two subjects (*Differend*). The impasse situation resembles closely the following scene in "The Guacamole Game":

> He said, Did you or did you not this morning . . . ?
> She interrupted.
> True, she said. I did or I did not.
> He considered her reply. Then pushed his face within an inch of hers and said in a mean whisper, The Bench has only a moment ago warned you that frivolous behavior will not be tolerated. Shall I take this *did or did not* before The Bench or will you kindly, without a single word in your defence, now accept a penalty of one million?
> I hate you, she said (268).

In contrast to the impasse created by scenes like the one just quoted, the game occasionally seems to offer a momentary illusion of consensus. After all, the narrative, at times, seems to say that there are limits to the apparently endless relativity of language. We have seen how the characters act *as if* they do not know; but, in fact, they *do know*. They are caught in their lies and they have to pay their penalties. I have also mentioned that the game can be stopped if any of the opponents "wanted to calmly refuse — equanimity, calmness, being the crucial issue here — to answer a question" (238). Most important, in this context, is the existence of what they call

"The Bench," an imaginary judging entity to which the characters refer repeatedly when found in situations of extreme disagreement, but whose actual participation in the game is constantly postponed:

> Kindly dock yourself thirty thousand for the use of the words *prick* and *stupid prick*, which are appellations not established outside the view of you and your daughter, together with an additional penalty for employing the phrase *going by that name*, since no one disputes Roscoe K. Heiss is his legal name.
>
> *I do thee challenge*, she said in the accepted mode, inasmuch as you have yourself referred to him as a prick on numerous occasions.
>
> *I do thee challenge your challenge*, he said, inasmuch as my defining him as a prick was done in common discourse outside the realm of this competition, which discourse in no way, shape, or form establishes he is a legitimate prick.
>
> *I do thee, stalwart foe, counter-challenge your counter-challenge* out of the commonly-accepted view that as all men have pricks they might be so described as being pricks.
>
> They were then obliged to pull their invisible cords, thus to momentarily withdraw from the heat of battle while they carried their arguments to The Bench. Arguments weighed by The Bench required considerable integrity on the part of the opponents. Otherwise, the game sank into chaos (258).

In moments like these, the game seems to yield to a notion of what Jürgen Habermas calls the 'rational will,' which facilitates the only way out of extreme dissensus. Habermas' theory, radically opposed to Lyotard's notion of the *differend*, is a common sense theory. It is based on an interpretation of discourse as a communication structure, in which the participants must test the validity of their claims and must strive to produce the best argument, excluding all motives but "the co-operative search for truth" (107). A consensus arising from such a co-operative search, according to Habermas, expresses a rational will and confirms a belief in the possibility of acting disinterestedly. Discussing Habermas' proposal, Thomas Docherty points out: "Such an ethical de-mand might be proposed as an initial form of a philosophy of alterity, to the extent that it is concerned to modify the subject's point of view, her or his notion of what is reasonable, in the light of the point of view of the subject's Others" (201). Yet Docherty also notes that such a solution can only be applied after a *differend* has in fact occurred, that is, after the existence of an unsolvable conflict between the parts has been identified. It is here that the Lyotardian *differend* and the Habermasian rational will might complement each other. In order to believe the validity of the latter, it is necessary to acknowledge the existence of the former. In other words, the only way to transcend the situations of extreme dissensus is often by means of renouncing the position of power in the discursive contest.

In Rooke's novella, the solution to the extreme dialectic conflicts the game occasionally enters requires that the power be renounced by either of the two sides. In the end, it is Thomas who gently declines his advantage in the game and cedes his victory over to Vivian by drumming his feet six times, signalling the game's conclusion and granting her a bonus of points that would place them even again:

> You son of a bitch, she said, I do not accept your charity. My penalty is my own.
>
> She drummed her heels and kept on drumming them, since he was still drumming his.
>
> You are not as this game depicts you, he said. Give me your goddamn penalty!
>
> They kept on drumming the heels (269).

Thus, ultimately, the game appears as a demonstration of love. It provides a framework within which the exploration of love between two people could take place; it serves as a site where the reinvention of love is made possible. And in this sense, Rooke's novella, echoing Docherty's postmodern notion of love, offers the only available solution for the two individuals to get out of the impasse created by the *differend*. Drawing on Alain Badiou's ideas about love, Docherty proposes love as the very possibility of being in the world, as the event of production of truth. Love, for Docherty, equals transcendental truth that extends beyond the merely contingent. It does not deny the existence of dissensus but rather makes room for it, it embraces the possibility of radical disjunction between two positions:

> "Love does not rid us of the paradox, but treats of it, engages with it . . . So, rather than love being that which regulates the relation of sexes, love is that which establishes the truth of their un-linking, their *de-liaison*" (205).

In an important way, Rooke's novella engages that radical disjunction between the two positions by marking a sharp division between inside and outside boundaries. The most obvious instance of such division is that between the inner space, the house, and the outer reality, the garden, which is for Vivian an incomprehensible space. She is unable to understand the meaning of Thomas' entry into it during the game intervals. What she sees of the outside world is always framed by the windows and episodic. Thus Thomas' activities outside, between game actions, form a 'supplement' story, which is never fully revealed, but which intensifies and reproduces, in a literal *mise-en-abîme*, the theatrical quality of the tale.[8]

Additionally, the 'garden' story redraws the boundaries between the inner and the outer worlds by positioning the characters visually against each other. Thomas (outside) is intensely self-conscious about his role as a protagonist in the supplemental story, while Vivian (inside) remains closer to the narrative point of view and thus to the reader and the reader's failure to confer meaning on Thomas' actions:

> Now here came the son of a bitch across her lawn again, this time transporting a wheelbarrow load of ready-mix cement, shovel riding the top. Did the son of a bitch have in mind digging a kid's wading pool? So it appeared, because there he was in front of the window with an idiot smile, blowing kisses, pantomiming dig-

---

[8] The garden scenes, literally framed by the windows through which we, along with Vivian, see Thomas, also reveal Rooke's taste for exploiting the connection between literature and painting. Thomas's movements in the garden actually describe his work at painting green sandbox boards, white clouds, yellow play buckets and snowmen wearing black hats (Rooke 1997, 254). Two other stories in *Oh!*, "Fazzini Must Have You Ever at Her Side," and "Raphael's Cantalupo Melon" draw explicitly on such an artistic relation and on the possibilities of a symbolic connection between narrative and painting frames. Michèle Kaltemback's essay in this collection offers a discussion of the function of painting and frames in Rooke's story "Art" (1992).

ging, pantomiming swimming strokes — exhibiting his last hold on sanity (262).

As the beginning, the inner space of the house is associated with cleanliness, while the outside world is implicitly connected to the idea of filth. However, as the story progresses, this is reversed. *Historically*, we are informed that the loser in the game, usually Thomas, must pay his debt by doing household duties, including dish washing, grass mowing, door knob polishing, and window cleaning. After years of playing and losing, Thomas has virtually become Vivian's slave. Although the inner space is still defined as her 'queendom,' it is Thomas who is associated with domesticity, staging a reversal of the usually accepted gender roles frequently found in Rooke's texts. The impact of Vivian's passionate discourse gives full flesh to the text, and it is Vivian who provides the novella's centre of consciousness, being the third-person narrative voice.

The first allusion to the outside world takes place when Vivian goes into the bathroom, after having signalled their first game pause.

> For a long time she washed her face in cold water. She looked at her face and said to her eyes in the mirror, "I know exactly where the son of a bitch is going."
>
> While in there she gave close inspection of his handiwork. The toilet bowl sparkled. The chrome knob was shiny. Even the rust in the holding tank had been removed. The tiles gleamed. There was no mildew in the shower corners. When she turned on the fan it no longer rattled. The blue guest towels with the lace trims

---

[9] Rooke's novel *A Good Baby* (1989) provides an excellent example of such reversal of roles (see Cumming [1996]).

[10] The reversal of gender roles seems intimately related to Rooke's tendency to the depiction of powerful women characters. In the story's conclusion, Thomas appears reading a book significantly titled *The Trials of Judith*, establishing thus a tacit parallel between Vivian and one of the most powerful heroines of Western culture (see Stocker 1998). Rooke's texts invariably depict eccentric, creative, powerful, somehow bossy female protagonists. The girl narrator of "Want to Play House?" (1992) drags the boy playmate around like a puppet, changing the game rules as she pleases. Being the narrator's wife, the strange woman of "A Bolt of White Cloth" (1984) is the story's dominant voice, imbuing the text with a taste of the extraordinary and enabling an allegorical reading of it (see Mathews 1989).

were freshly washed and precisely folded. The basket of fancy soaps in the shape of sea shells had been dusted.

She climbed up on the toilet bowl to inspect the sill in the small window. The sill was free of grime.

The sky through that window was blue.

But blue skies would not save his puny butt.

She got down, examining the mirror for any trace of sludge. No sludge.

About forty thousand points, she thought, in this one small room alone.

This made her feel *much* better (239-240).

The square of blue sky outside, providing a flashing respite from the almost claustrophobic atmosphere of the game, intrudes at this point into the description of the perfect appearance of the room, foreshadowing perhaps a breaking of boundaries between inner and outer spaces. Later, the main events of the subplot, which increasingly disturb the rhythm of the game, mostly happen on the house threshold, around the screen door, separating the house entrance from the parking space where mother and daughter have their fight. As the subplot reaches its climax, the cleanliness of the inside begins to be soiled, as if caused by the tension of the game:

Time! He said. His mouth full of guacamole, which was disgusting, and that he was jabbing his finger at the clock, more so.

To your question have I seen my daughter in the past stated period beyond the two episodes today when I slammed the door in her face, my answer is no.

He was instantly on his feet. A slab of guacamole flew across the room, landing on the garden window, slithering down one of his very clean panes.

Liar! He said. *Knave, I impeach thee!*

In the accepted fashion (242).

The mounting climax is graphically signalled by a series of disarrangements in the initially immaculate appearance of the room. At one point, Vivian's hat falls into the guacamole and she spills her drink on the floor (259); she stands on her toes, yells her answers at Thomas and swings wine and champagne bottles; tortilla chips sail across the room (260). The breaking of boundaries between inside and outside is further staged on the characters' bodies. As they help themselves to the guacamole, they munch, swallow and try to digest the game events and to finally sweat them out. Vivian's neck is soaking wet, her arms dripping (266). To top it all, and to provide the final act of disarrangement, she kicks the table, toppling the champagne bucket and splashing Thomas's lap with ice and water. This creates a pool, a puddle into which they both insistently drum their feet at the game's end (267). Such is the disarranged scenario of their final apotheosis.

By revealing thus the inappropriateness or the simple inadequacy of contextual elements, the progressive transgression of boundaries gradually strips down the plot to the most basic event, that of language, and, most of all, of love. And in so doing, Rooke's text comes close to the notion of love discussed by Docherty above: "It is such love that is aligned with truth and its production. Instead of truth being a function of linguistic propositions guaranteed by reference, truth, in this philosophy, precisely *is* the referent, the referent as event, as history, as the *encounter*" (206). In other words, love as a process at the heart of communication, an ontological love. This notion of love, by definition, resists surrendering completely to the demands of plot (the love story), for there is always something unspeakable about it, something that cannot be said. As Roland Barthes writes: "The other whom I love and who fascinates me is *atopos*. I cannot classify the other, for the other is, precisely, Unique, the singular Image which has miraculously come to correspond to the speciality of my desire. The other is the figure of my truth, and cannot be imprisoned in any stereotype" (34).

It is the *atopia*, inherent in the lover's discourse, and not the plot structure or any other element in the story that produces an incredible sense of catharsis at the end of "The Guacamole Game." The text closes in a traditional way, with a circular conclusion in which the narrative distance increases. Instead of the usual third-person centre of consciousness, we get a series of narrative close-ups, describing simultaneous scenes, and giving us a sense of closure:

> She has closed the door. She is looking at the doorknob, wondering how long she will have to look at it before the knob turns.

It will be a while before the knob turns.

He is seated on the sofa, a towel spread over his lap, white rags nearby, the silver polish out. He is polishing the silverware.

Then he says something that, were she present to hear it, would truly astound her. He is saying, How much do I love thee, let me count the ways. What would most astound her is his utter sincerity (271).

We are finally allowed to breathe, the frame has been renewed, the room rearranged, their love reinvented. With this ultimate act of citation, Thomas invests Elizabeth Barrett Browning's famous line from *Sonnets from the Portuguese* with a new flavour, rephrasing the meaning of his love for Vivian. With it, he also enacts a final inversion of the expected gender roles. But this time in the opposing direction, by inverting the reversal of traditional roles already found in the origin of the famous sonnets, unusually written by a woman for a man, in which Elizabeth ostensibly makes a passionate declaration of love for Robert Browning.[11] The cliché is thus given a new ironic twist that, according to Rooke himself, "revives what's dead in the language and makes you examine all over again what it was that made the cliché powerful and useful in the first place" (Burnham, 5). The use of Barrett Browning's line also emphasizes, at the text's end, the degree of our embedment in the literary traditions and the need to self-consciously acknowledge our act of speaking from within it, the only space from where we can actually speak at all.

"Our interpretations of society, culture, history, and our individual lives, hopes, dreams, passions and sensations, involve attempts to *confer* sense rather than to *discover* it," writes Iain Chambers. "It is in that historical process — in the passage of time *and* being — that there lies our only chance of redemption" (11). With its final image of peaceful domesticity, "The Guacamole Game" returns to the beginning. The improbable language game has provided an arena for the characters to confer sense on their lives — their hopes, fears and passions. As all boundaries are tested

---

[11] I wish to thank Russell Brown for pointing out the source of this quotation to me during a seminar on Canadian Studies held at the University of La Laguna in December 2000. Thomas' sentence differs just in the word 'much' from the first line of sonnet 43 in Barrett Browning's work: "How do I love thee, let me count the ways" (1990/1847).

and broken down, a joyful sense of anticipation remains. The ending is a beginning. It is the language of love and desire, the place where meaning is both promised and indefinitely postponed.

BIBLIOGRAPHY

Belsey, Catherine. *Desire: Love Stories in Western Culture*. London: Blackwell, 1994.

Barthes, Roland. *A Lover's Discourse: Fragments*. Trans. Richard Howard. New York: Noonday, 1978.

Barrett Browning, Elizabeth. *Sonnets from the Portuguese*. Oxford: Oxford UP, 1990 (1847).

Bayley, John. *The Character of Love: A Study in the Literature of Personality*. London: Constable, 1960.

Brown, Russell. "What The Rooke Said." Unpublished Essay. Toronto: University of Toronto, 1985.

Burnham, Clint. "Reading Foreign Writers: An Interview with Leon Rooke." *Waves* 14.3 (1986): 5-7.

Chambers Iain. *Border Dialogues: Journeys into Postmodernity*. London: Routledge, 1990.

Cumming, Peter. "When Men Have Babies: The Good Father in Leon Rooke's *A Good Baby*." *Textual Studies in Canada* 8 (1996.) : 96-108.

De Luca, Anna Pia. "Leon Rooke's *Shakespeare's Dog*: A Postmodern Historiographic Parody." *Atti del XV Convegno dell'Associazione Italiana di Anglistica*. Parma: 1992. 291-300.

Docherty, Thomas. *Alterities: Criticism, History, Representation*. Oxford: Clarendon, 1996.

Eco, Umberto. "'I Love You Madly,' He Said." *The Truth about the Truth: De-Confusing and Reconstructing the Postmodern World*. Ed. Walter Truett Anderson. New York: Tarcher/Putnam, 1995. 31-33.

Glover, Douglas. Review of Leon Rooke's *Oh! Twenty-seven Stories*. *Globe and Mail* (December, 12, 1997): D22.

Gorjup, Branko. "Perseus and the Mirror: Leon Rooke's Imaginary Worlds." *World Literature Today* (Spring) 1999: 269-274.

Habermas, Jürgen. *Legitimation Crisis*. Trans. Thomas McCarthy. London: Heinemann, 1976.

Luis Martínez, Zenón. "Shakespeare's Wicked Pronoun: A Lover's Discourse and Love Stories." *Atlantis* 22.1 (2000): 133-162.

Lyotard, Jean-François. 1987. "The Sign of History." *Post-Structuralism and the Question of Theory*. Eds. Derek Attridge, Geoff Bennington and Robert Young. Cambridge: Cambridge U.P. 162-180.

——. *The Differend: Phrases in Dispute*. Trans. George Van Den Abbeele. Manchester: Manchester UP, 1988.

——. *The Postmodern Condition: A Report on Knowledge*. Trans. Geoff Bennington and Brian Massuni. Manchester: Manchester UP, 1991 (1979).

Mathews, Lawrence. "'A Bolt of White Cloth': Leon Rooke as Parabolist." *Recherches Anglaises et Nord-Américaines* 22 (1989): 105-111.

Rooke, Leon. "No Whistle Slow." *The Broad Back of the Angel*. Don Mills: Stoddart, 1997.

——. *The Birth Control King of the Upper Volta*. Downsview: ECW, 1982.

——. *Shakespeare's Dog*. Don Mills (On.): Stoddart, 1983.

——. "A Bolt of White Cloth." *A Bolt of White Cloth*. Don Mills: Stoddart, 1984. 7-20.

——. *A Good Baby*. Toronto: McClelland & Stewart, 1989.

——. "The Streets of Moons." *The Happiness of Others*. Erin: Porcupine's Quill, 1991. 113-182.

——. "Art." *Who Do You Love?* Toronto: McClelland & Stewart, 1992. 39-45.

——. "LR Loves GL" *Who Do You Love?* Toronto: McClelland & Stewart, 1992. 121-130.

——. "Sweethearts." *Who Do You Love?* Toronto: McClelland & Stewart, 1992. 35-38.

——. "Want to Play House?" *Who Do You Love?* Toronto: McClelland & Stewart, 1992. 59-63.

——. "Fazzini Must Have You Ever at Her Side." *Oh! Twenty-seven Stories*. Toronto: Exile Editions, 1997. 137-140.

——. "The Guacamole Game." *Oh! Twenty-seven Stories*. Toronto: Exile Editions, 1997. 234-271

——. "Raphael's Cantalupo Melon." *Oh! Twenty-seven Stories*. Toronto: Exile Editions, 1997. 104-111.

Rose, Mary Beth. *The Expense of Spirit: Love and Sexuality in English Renaissance Drama*. Ithaca: Cornell UP, 1988.

Stocker, Margarita. 1998. *Judith / Sexual Warrior: Women and Power in Western Culture*. New Haven: Yale UP, 1998.

Vauthier, Simone. "Dangerous Crossings: A Reading of Leon Rooke's 'The Birth Control King of the Upper Volta.'" *Reverberations: Explorations in the Canadian Short Story*. Toronto: Anansi. 1993. 10-42.

Wilkshire, Claire. *Analyzing Voice in the Contemporary Canadian Short Story*. (Unpublished PhD Thesis). Vancouver: University of British Columbia., 1997

CHAPTER FOUR

NOVELS

THE WORKING OUT OF A VOICE: ROOKE'S *FAT WOMAN*

FRANCESCA ROMANA PACI

To the mythopoetic imagination of many ancient and less ancient civilizations a fat woman was easily translated into a goddess, life past and life future melting in her flesh, as a living warrant of survival and permanence. In very poor countries she was, and still is, a sign, even a symbol, of affluence and therefore of pride. To contemporary perception in rich countries a fat woman is mostly a person associated with an eating disorder. All hieratic and pagan glamour seemingly lost, she is a person in need of medical treatment, an object of sociological research, and on the whole somebody who does not conform to the norm. All that would already be enough to disrupt claims of universal significance and to ruffle representational confidence. To Leon Rooke the present crisis of universals proves to be a challenge and an added value. Leon Rooke in *Fat Woman* (1980) defies more than one allegiance, and through (literally) the character of Ella Mae Hopkins enters research on *la condition humaine*.[1] Ella Mae, the fat woman down the road, *chair de femme* and therefore *chair d'homme*, is an important receptacle of pent up complexities, a representation, in fact, of most human complexities, mire, wants, absences, but also of the strength, stamina, hope that make people keep going. Rooke writes from a far less tragic milieu than Malraux, yet Ella Mae, Tchen, Kyo, and the heroic Kalov, being all born with no choice of time, place and rank, have in common 'faith,

---

1 Malraux's *La condition humaine* (1933; English translation *Man's Fate*, 1934) is a book clearly very different from *Fat Woman*, and yet the two authors share a sense of pity for the human flesh, of revolt against determinism, a knowledge of the impossibility of overcoming in the end what seems destiny, but at the same time a compulsion to resist, to fight for sense and value, and ultimately rebirth. None of the very recent 'revelations' of Malraux's 'lies', if any, with regard to his life, can change his literary output and its meaning.

hope and charity,' as well as their own intermittent, even furious, denial of them[2] and the unavoidable, almost incredible resurrection of all three.

Rooke is well aware of the sociological and even of the political aspects of his chosen visual angle and he reaches so far as the instruments of his fiction allow him to go, and moreover he slyly preserves in Ella Mae, albeit in latency, some of the sacral attributes of the goddess. Her very bulk is one sign of that, joined with her being central not so much to her family (mother, father, husband and sons) as to their actions.[3] Rooke's chosen angle forbids too-explicit statements, he cannot tell the audience anything inconsistent with Ella Mae's capability. Also the amount of information that he can convey by very short 'intrusions' of a mindful but prudent omniscient narrator is not large, and, moreover, it can always be traced back to Ella Mae. Intelligence, pity and wonder must be read mostly through her words, accepting Rooke's political stance to be broader than any official politics or idea: a difficult position, easy to lapse into banality, easy to be misunderstood. "Literature," Rooke said in a recent interview, "is meant to serve humanity," in and by as many "roles" as writers can devise. One role is "to speak the speech of those incapable of speaking for themselves."[4] The working out of Ella Mae's voice is one fulfilment of such a momentous statement, the more so because Rooke, who at times enjoys adopting the 'I am no scholar' attitude, knows very well the implicit claim of his words and what side he takes when he says "serve humanity."[5] Throughout *Fat Woman* Ella Mae's voice and the message of an implied author that almost coincides with Rooke merge in the narrative and at the same time stand as

---

[2] In a fit of passion Ella Mae thinks: "What does it avail? What does goodness count — or faith or hope or charity — in a world where wolf attacks wolf and sheep eat off each other and bones are left to rot in open air?" (*Fat Woman*, New York: The Ecco Press, 1986, 174. All quotations are taken from the above edition).

[3] There is at least another 'fat woman' in Rooke's fiction. In the short story "Sing Me No Love Songs I'll Say You No Prayers," Jenny is a "big woman" whom her husband Bingo Duncan loves and admires: "That's right," he says, "she's a good handful, but that's how I like it" (*Sing Me No Love Songs*, New York: The Ecco Press, 1984, 207). The choreography of the story is basically the same, featuring Jenny at the centre of the action and of the family, though the point of view is largely Bingo's.

[4] Branko Gorjup, "Lingering on Posted Land," *World Literature Today*, No 3.1 (April-June), 2003.

[5] In an allegorical battle of ethics and aesthetics for supremacy, Rooke would side with ethics, valuing nonetheless the part played by aesthetics.

two parallel tracks of communication: what Ella Mae sees and what Rooke / implied author sees besides her's, his vision being the creator's vision. As a matter of fact the secret message of the creator is unfailingly the most difficult and the best part of the book.

Ella Mae's story, which is Rooke's first long narrative, is called a novel, but it should be better described as an uncannily effective compound of realistic and of imaginary elements, spangled with, and at the same time sustained by, elements of romance. Reconciliation between romance and realism is not new nor is it any longer bizarre. Rooke's method and result, however, may be said to be unusual for the clear-cut interplay of the two and for varieties of effects, including a brave and often defiant use of tenderness, and, not least, for a story that proves gripping even without the assistance of a grand plot. The first hint of romance comes from the motto, taken from a very popular short poem by the not-very-famous British poet Frances (Croft Darwin) Cornford. The poem, which is in itself a minor mystery, portrays a fat white lady walking the fields in gloves, but it proves more mysterious without its title, *To a Fat Lady Seen from a Train*, and without a short line, "Missing so much and so much?" that is omitted in the motto.[6] The motto itself is certainly not to be over-emphasised, and yet Rooke decided to put it there, omitting the parts he had no use for, or perhaps being himself curious. Why is the lady "not loved," why in the fields, and why in gloves? Why is the grass so soft and shivering? Whys apart, almost every word emanates a flavour of quiet romance, nonetheless for a vivid touch of irony on Rooke's part. A second factor consistent with romance is the setting, the place; not because it is rural or exotic or anything of the kind, but because of its indeterminacy, because it is a sort of any-place, any poor place in the middle of anywhere — not very different from the way spatiotemporal circumstances are presented in fairy tales, legends, and in pseudo-realistic popular fiction.[7] If, as it seems, the

---

[6] Cornford (1886-1960), the granddaughter of Charles Darwin, the wife of the philosopher Francis M. Cornford, the mother of poet John Cornford (who died in Spain fighting Franco), if not a sentimental poet, is openly a poet of sentiment. As for the omitted "Missing so much..." and for the included "whom nobody loves," it is perhaps worthwhile to point out Ella Mae's frenzy towards the end of the book (150-151): "...Fat Woman, you don't mean beans to me..."

[7] Bertholt Brecht valued that kind of fiction, mostly because of the truth that can be conveyed by it. Comprehensiveness and parable fit his attitude as well as Rooke's.

place is the same as where in Rooke's short story "A Bolt of White Cloth" a mysterious man arrives from the East with his magical white cloth, then the romance-like feature points to an imaginative process of investigation and recognition that must be acknowledged as a philosophical exercise in the proper sense.[8]

All the other aspects of romance come from the character of Ella Mae, or better from her vision, in turn due to how she was born out of Rooke's imagination, with her past, her flesh, her love, given and received or denied, her feelings, her inner world, her demotic language, and especially the absence (absence turning into void inhabited by a Serpent) inside her. Yet it must be well understood that Ella Mae is not a character out of a romance, rather Rooke delegates intermittent visions of romance to her as a matter of fact, a wide range of them, including Gothic horror, projection of desire, sentimental bias and even self-deceit.[9] She alternates between bursts of dejection and of hope, pictures herself at heights of misery and of joy, realizes and ignores the actual strictures of her rank and status. Most of her strength is due to her very human, very moving capacity, more than aptitude, for seeing the possibility of romance around her instead of ugliness. She is again and again provisionally rescued by her very lack of discipline and scantiness of culture, while her pent up, unaided, uncultivated, mostly unconscious imagination struggles on blindly waiting for chance and searching for freedom. As a matter of fact, images of imprisonment abound in the book, pivoting around the fat body of Ella Mae, which dominates as an arch-image of prison and imprisonment at all levels. With his "fat woman" Rooke has created one of those incredibly bottomless and multifarious image-concepts (the word symbol sounds both grand and insufficient), one to be compared to Conrad's "Nigger" in *The Nigger of the Narcissus* or Joyce's "Snow" in "The Dead" or to "the dog" in

---

[8] In 1965 Northrop Frye published his *A Natural Perspective, The Development of Shakespearean Comedy and Romance*, a book which is basically a study of romance. Rooke may well know it and appreciate some of the points Frye makes there; especially those concerned with the philosophical, and therefore epistemological, power of romance. And he may know Coleridge's opinion that romance has a positive, enlarging and maturing influence on the mind.

[9] Elements of romance can also be found in *Sing Me No Love Songs I'll Say You No Prayers*, where both the 'what' and the 'how' of the narrative show Rooke's courageous and original choice of the romance mode and of an interesting hybridisation of styles and incidents. Frye may be once more in the background.

Buzzati's *Il cane che ha visto Dio*, that never cease to offer themselves to the endless venture of interpretation.

Both structure and language are deceptively simple. The structure is open, in every sense, the story and the uncomplicated plot develop steadily, generously, giving basic knowledge and details of Ella Mae's life. But the story does not end at the last page, because there Ella Mae's future is left to her to enact. From the beginning to the end the whole story is told in a third person narrative, which is a paper-thin, and yet orderly, disguise of Ella Mae's first person, even the few times when it seems the voice of a conventional straightforward storyteller. It is made paper-thin because the first person is necessary to the appearance of a vigorous realism, it is orderly because order is the guarantee of earnest research. In fact Rooke's consistency of effort in investigating the hows and whys is nothing but scientific. But the term 'order' may be misleading, because here it means both the rules Rooke implicitly sets himself at the incipit of the novel and, on another level, the order of truth in human experience. The incipit indeed decrees that everything we are going to know we shall know in one way or another through Ella Mae, but the order of truth is present as well, and this is a much more complex and debatable concept. There is no doubt that Rooke takes side with the truth of Ella Mae, as much as with the truth of Hooker the Dog, in *Shakespeare's Dog*, because what he vindicates as real is the actual, factual experience lived through by the individual. Individual limitations of any kind are valued as elements of that reality, not as obstacles to the establishment of a vision of any theoretical, or hyperuranian, truth. Truth is what people feel and suffer or enjoy. Rooke is evidently very serious about his philosophical position, and yet shy and careful, as if he would apologise for his rigour and passion, while at the same time he insistently deprecates from his work any tinge of cerebralism. Hence comes his choice of voice and language, and hence comes, years later, a certain subdued playfulness,[10] very moderate, and for all that very crafty, like that one, for instance, we witness at work in the short story "Art" (1992).

The events of the *récit* in *Fat Woman* take place in less than one day, from around midday to one hour or so before midnight, but Ella Mae's

---

[10] While playfulness may be a sort of program-frame of a story, humour is a frequent internal element of Rooke's fiction, part of a character, a situation, a turn of the action.

rambles tell a much longer story. Fragments of the past and of the present spawn a pattern of hours, days, and years, until we are allowed to appropriate almost the whole span of a life and of its context, and to contemplate it from a privileged point of view, as if we were looking at a simultaneous wide-angle representation. Long before the end of the novel the illusion of reality is so strong, that the very pact of fiction recedes,[11] and speculation on Ella Mae's future outside the book becomes almost unavoidable. Page after page the round character of Ella Mae grows into a human being, so credible, so utterly verisimilar as to give rise to both suspension of disbelief and curiosity. Therefore when we happen to find in the short story "A Bolt of White Cloth," published in 1984, four years later than *Fat Woman*, two quick mentions of Ella Mae Hopkins, we relish the reference. When we read: "'You could try the Hopkins place!' my wife called. 'There's a fat woman down the road got a sea of troubles. She could surely use some of that cloth'" and when, a couple of pages later, again we read: "That night in bed, trying to figure it out, we wondered how Ella Mae down the road had done," we give only an afterthought to the interplay of self-reference in fiction, while we are made genuinely hopeful that the white fabric might work its magic for the Hopkins' as well.[12] At this point, Philip Sidney, chuckling and stroking Hooker, would say: "Why, that's Rooke's magic, isn't it!" and so it is.

The illusion of reality is brought forth by a "scrupulous meanness,"[13] made possible by cool, controlled use of a dispassionate technique, applied, so to say, to 'passion.' The character whose flow of thought we are told in indirect speech is firmly established as the 'subject' in the modern sense. Ella Mae is the sentient, the mind in a body, the 'I' central to a given world. This is not in itself responsible for the illusion of reality, it is indeed its very foundation, while at the same time it is the radical cause of Ella Mae being intensely individual, and of her being at the same time more than her

---

[11] We are in fact tempted to break the 'pact' between writer and reader, implicit since Aristotle in the act of 'reading' (he had, of course mainly drama in mind), and forget Ella Mae is a character in an imaginative work of fiction, to consider her a real, living person, our living neighbour.

[12] Leon Rooke, *A Bolt of White Cloth*, New York: The Ecco Press, 1984, 18-19.

[13] Joyce's well known, too-often mentioned, often misunderstood, "scrupulous meanness".

individual self. She is, in fact, both herself and everybody in the class, or category, of beings she belongs to. And moreover, viewed with the general aid of elementary phenomenology, she is every 'subject' in relation to the perception (which includes misperception), vision and description of the world such as the world appears to the 'I.' Her language, which is the language of her inner mind activity, limited and demotic as it is, flows effortlessly, easily comprehensible, lifelike. But simplicity is but the tip of the iceberg.

Even a cursory survey of the sustained description of Ella Mae's experience, both physical and mental, at the beginning of the novel would elicit enough exemplification. Ella Mae is driving her husband's truck into the driveway in front of her house. What we read is a clever chain of "she" and "her" by means of which her reality takes form around and inside her. To Ella Mae this is truth, the only truth she can experience and store, layer by layer, to build her world, but Rooke is in command of a much larger vision and he contrives to convey a good deal of additional knowledge to the reader. Though obviously not all there is to know is communicated, provided that 'what there is to know' could be reckoned, what Rooke obtains by this technique is an even more powerful effect of reality.

The extremes of Ella Mae's station are stated in the first sentence, cleverly made part of the narrative, while at the same time they define the basic modality of the narration: "What she sees . . . on God's green earth" is as a matter of fact all that can be "known to her" of God's round and wide earth. Moreover, in the second sentence a "not reliable," albeit referred to her "heart," hisses in, made more interesting by the fact that she is remembering what her husband keeps telling her. In the following sentences Ella Mae's situation is definitively suggested, if not already established, as one of enclosure: " . . . she knows no better authority than Edward," "the confines of Edward's Ford." Edward, her husband, tells her "Whatever I tell you is for your own good," "You'd best stay home and faint and swoon . . . with me here to provide lock and key," and he thinks that "she has too much air between her ears." On top of all that, Rooke adds the recollection coming over Ella Mae of "the pups . . . that bagful of sorrowful, whiny, wriggling shapes" her father drowned in the creek near their house.[14] Besides, although she does not yet understand the meaning of

----

14 *Fat Woman*, 3-6.

what she sees, there is the image of Edward who is boarding up the window of their bedroom. From the first page onwards "them boards" keep appearing and are alluded to so many times that they become prominent, and develop into a fatal memento, weaving a thematic fabric of foreboding and anticipation that can be assumed to be structural. Ella Mae is afraid of "boarded-up windows," when in the evening from the truck she sees them, "gloomy as Satan," she does not yet know what is waiting for her, but she knows she is afraid: "A sense of abiding dread. What had been plaguing her all day, the foreboding that had been tracking her footprints all week, had manifested itself. It was in there waiting. She had only to walk through the door and it would claim her."[15]

Ella Mae is in every sense enclosed: what she sees is all she knows, she cannot climb up high enough,[16] metaphorically, to look down at herself, she is in no condition to transcend her situation. She is under authority; since the day she was born she was never given the chance of getting a broader knowledge and sense of life. She is not entirely devoid of a desire to exercise her own free will, but she also seems dimly aware that the stars are against her, as they were against her mother: the two linked details of her mother's silver locket and the "silver" she is setting the table with are a masterstroke.[17] All the while Rooke's station being above and outside his work, he knows and sees, and makes us see through her words.

Part of the effect is due to the American Gothic atmosphere, mostly and efficaciously communicated by the frequent recurrence in Ella Mae's thoughts of God and the Bible. The images she calls forth testify to the way she was taught about God and religion, and act no differently than the window of the wooden church in the famous painting *American Gothic* by Grant Wood. There can be no doubt that religion to her is another form of enclosure. In addition to that, her neighbourhood, the social group she belongs to, her difficult economic position, her limited education become

---

[15] *Fat Woman*, cit., 149.

[16] The boarding of the window, that will prevent the "lovely view" from "up" there and Ella Mae's unsuccessful attempt to climb up the ladder Edward left under the window can be read as metaphors in the same cluster of meaning. While the "good china" and the "silver" she sets on the table, and the candles she wishes she had, belong to a not-too-dissimilar cluster, and certainly have the same function. *Fat Woman*, cit., pp. 46-49.

[17] *Fat Woman*, 49.

soon apparent as yet more jails. Her marriage itself can be seen as a sort of prison. Towards the end, once again a prisoner in Edward's truck, she silently cries: "Between God and Edward I never stood a chance."[18] Her house, which is her pride, the sign of her advancement to a higher station in society, and especially her "lovely" bedroom, are to become a prison: the threat looms over her, as already mentioned above, from the beginning of the book.

But, on more than one level, Ella Mae's body is the main representation of imprisonment. She is truly her body, but it is likewise true that her huge body is a prison, that it hides to a certain extent a possibly better inner self, even her possible beauty, the beauty her mother wished for her when she was a child. To an equal degree her body limits her movements and it is a sort of metaphor for the limitations of her rights to the full enjoyment of life on "God's green earth." At the same time her body is the prison, the cage, of a huge raging beast, a serpent, a crocodile, that is the image of her manifold hunger in her frantic nightmare during supper. While all along, her wedding ring, which has become too tight for her fat hand, tortures her finger, making it sore and ugly, and suggesting an interplay of cruelty and restrictions on other levels as well.

The human body is a complex piece of reality for Rooke: it is flesh, it has wants, frailties, rights, and it is equally the temple of the spirit. But at the same time the human body is the prison of that 'pneuma,'[19] of that something in us that is the principle and dignity of life. Ella Mae, the way Rooke made her, does not know anything of the kind, nor can she even dream of thinking of it, yet he makes her feel that there is something basically wrong in the world, something she could not change or control even if she wanted to, and if she were strong enough to try to do something against: "She cried out of a sense of woe, out of the recognition of something wrong having gone on so long that nothing mortal man or woman did now could set it right."[20] At the same time she feels guilty, ungrateful to

---

[18] *Fat Woman*, 160.

[19] Not necessarily in the sense of the 'Holy Spirit' of the Christian tradition, but certainly in connection with the mysteries of metaphysics. Rooke seems to be fascinated by the new metaphysics, especially in connection with language and the influence of language on our apprehension of the world and on our interpretation and judgement, including our sense of being. But this is a long and difficult path to tread.

[20] *Fat Woman*, cit., 75.

God and Edward, she vaguely perceives that she has in some way done wrong to her own body and still does, but she also feels wronged by others, by her destiny, by God. Rooke makes Ella Mae often talk to God, in turn taking for granted his existence, power and goodness, and denouncing that "He . . . turned his back on the human race"; he makes her even proclaim that "the only reason . . . was that there was no God."[21] In the closing chapters of the book God's voice enters her stream of consciousness, and then God finally admits: "Ella Mae, I made a big mistake with you. I made a mistake with you and with all people of your kind. I made a terrible blunder with the starving people of China . . . I did it with all the mobs of humanity who for hatred of their poverty have been wanting since Day One to shoot rather than to kiss my hand . . . So eat, Ella Mae. Eat to your heart's content, for it is the only contentment you will ever get from me."[22]

Her revolt comes of an intimation of the dignity, however obscure, she finds in herself, it comes of an inbred desire of "being of some account" as a human being, of being recognised as part of society, as well as part of a community, a group, a town, a neighbourhood, and a family. The theme of imprisonment and the theme of the "wide world" outside clash and grow, one feeding on the other in Ella Mae's thoughts: ". . . because the whole wide world conspired to make me feel I was of no account and life wasn't worth living."[23] She perceives she has been denied something that she had a right to, that she had been offended precisely in her 'dignity.'[24]

Although by authorial decision she is not a cultivated or even a natu-

---

[21] *Fat Woman*, 67 and 175. Ella Mae's accusation shows undeniable affinities with Yeats's Cold Heaven: "It wasn't God's sky anymore ... the sky was left looking this way – cold and remote and so chillingly placid that all of it went inside you and made you want to cry or beat your head against the wall out of plain hopelessness."

[22] *Fat Woman*, 170-171.

[23] *Fat Woman*, cit., 74. The "wide world" is always far and without: "the ocean blue" and the "foreign countries" Edward saw while in the Navy, China, Australia, Antagonish, Nova Scotia, where you can slim and be happy, the world of the radio man Jack Coombs, and of several others, including her mother's Jewel Tea man. The mention of the Sears Catalogue, 31, is almost heart-wrenching.

[24] The immediate occasion is the Indian Mound she escapes to while waiting for her husband and sons to come home for supper, but her inner debate is clearly of a much longer standing. Hers is a long passionate lament: "...the senselessness, the no-accountness, the long, boring, impoverished wastefulness, waste so thick inside yourself..."; *Fat Woman*, 77.

rally intelligent person, Rooke made Ella Mae far from stupid, developing her personality by an accretion of revealing details, by the constant recurrence of images, words, sentences, commonplaces, or fragments of them that build her case history and posit more than one problem. In connection with class, class-consciousness, rank and status, for instance, not only does she show a certain envy of a successful woman of the community, she asks herself questions too, and almost understands her own reasons for that envy. Even the coincidence of Mozart's *Così fan tutte* and Ella Mae's attempt to get a share of beauty for herself and her family (the table, the silver, the perfume and the make-up she puts on), though being one of Rooke's devices to get through to the reader from above while his character does not register it, adds by contrast and suggestion to Ella Mae's attractiveness: because of that coincidence her effort has a grace and a sort of natural claim that is both beautiful and moving.[25] However with regard to her class-consciousness and her sense of it, the best instance occurs when the whole family together stops to visit Edward's and her old school while driving towards Ella Mae's childhood "homeplace." Ella Mae, remembering teachers and schoolmates, proves to be pretty shrewd. She is almost too intelligent when her flow of thoughts tell the reader: "What a scruffy lot they'd been . . . A sea of big ears, big hands, and feet big from going bare-foot so much. Eyes that, even when dull, gave off a rabid quality, the kind of cunning alertness or rancor of an animal in a cage . . ."[26] That adjective "rabid" alone, containing, as it does, revolt, repressed violence, envy, rancour, but actual waste of power as well, waste of energy, of *élan vital*, of life itself, is more perceptive and acute than a scholarly essay on the matter.[27] She sounds just as shrewd, and unexpectedly well-informed, in her practical

---

25 *Fat Woman*, 68-70. Make-up (pancake powder, lipstick, "a little of that rose eye color") returns later with the mention of the "Avon Lady," 110-111. Incidentally, the Avon Lady, although a common feature of the North American context in a broad sense, may remind the readers who know James Reaney of his *The Killdeer* (1962; revised 1972), inasmuch as an Avon Lady carries out an important social function in the play.

26 *Fat Woman*, cit., p. 122.

27 Aristotle, after his *Metaphysics*, would have said it a waste of 'dynamis'/ 'energeia', 'potentiality' that cannot follow its path, that cannot become actual. The waste, then, is enormous, unpardonable, and, most of all, irretrievable: all those lives spent without fulfilling what could have been, had chance or the stars, decreed differently. In the already mentioned interview with Branko Gorjup, Rooke said: "... we are steered by our stars."

estimate of the value of commodities, when she calculates the cost of an old radio salvaged by her husband: "Edward had worked on it for six months . . . Working in terms of man-hours spent on it at minimum wage, she reckoned this little toy radio had cost near on two hundred dollars."[28]

Furthermore, Ella Mae, who, as already pointed out, is certainly not a well-read woman, has a great respect for knowledge and culture. She seems to know something of "the War", she knows some geography and has a subdued longing for foreign places, and there are some books and even a *Webster Dictionary* in the house. Before going to school she "had never seen a real book . . . outside of the Bible." Now she wants things to be different for her sons: "That's why she and Edward had their *Reader's Digests* and a nearly complete *World Book* encyclopaedia set out in plain sight — so Ike and Theodore wouldn't grow up thinking home was a queer place to find books."[29] Then there are the radio and the TV, both sources of knowledge, although with his usual skill Rooke manages to convey a caveat against their dangers as well.[30] Ella Mae is naïve, even "gullible" as Edward says, but she is really interested in all that she gains knowledge of, and she is somewhat proud of it. She can even afford to let Edward believe that she does not know his "secret", his secret being that "not long ago he had enrolled in the LaSalle high school correspondence course."[31] She admires Edward for that, and remembers his efforts with pride and affection. Actually Edward here and elsewhere does not cut a bad figure at all.

The character of Edward is almost totally seen through Ella Mae's perception. The double track of communication, the narrator's and Ella Mae's, tilts towards the latter, and yet, as usual, Rooke contrives to convey more generous information on Edward. On the whole he has more pleasing traits than faults: he may be too proud of his physical masculinity (but

---

[28] *Fat Woman*, 55-56. Ella Mae is almost too intelligent and well-informed at least in another circumstance, when she blames God's "plan": "Take Adam and call him Exhibit A, and Eve and call her Exhibit B ...", 146-147.

[29] *Fat Woman*, 121.

[30] One example is enough, Jack Coombs saying: "I leave you with my thought for the day. Ask not for whom the cash register rings, it rings for thee!" *Fat Woman*, 59.

[31] *Fat Woman*, 124-125.

so is Ella Mae),[32] he may be too silly or too lazy to reprimand his sons, he may be stupid and cruel in devising the boarding up of his wife, but he loves Ella Mae, is really fond of her, and he has a constructive, practical attitude to life and things (in the proper sense of objects), as well as a feeling for romance, in a popular, sapid way. He conceives romance firmly joined together with love, and love with sex, but it is precisely because of that that he can think of telling Ella Mae: "I see you got the table laid out pretty as a picture. I bet not even the Queen of Hispopatania sets a fancier table."[33] This way what he suggests is that Ella Mae is no less a queen than the Queen of his invented land of Hispopatania. His habit of collecting things discarded and thrown away by waste-makers is imaginative and quite engaging, as is his way of paying compliments to Ella Mae. He is naïve, self-satisfied, unrefined, but certainly he is warm and affectionate. When he tells her that he does not mind her being a big girl, "More for me," or when he courts her with "a licentious wiggle of the hips," or asks "Feel good?" he does not dream of being macho, he just loves and wants to please her the only way he knows.

The memory of their first meeting and of their courtship is vivid in Ella Mae's mind: "He'd come out from a back room slicked up in his tight Navy trousers and the Camels rolled in his sleeve . . ."; and he was kind and considerate: ". . . he'd gone around the room, shaking hands with these ladies . . . finding a nice remark to pass on this one's dress or that one's hair and letting them know how they were all so young and pretty he was liable any minute to drop down at their feet in the worship of them . . ." She is still under the spell of that day, and no wonder, with "his face" that "lit up the room more than sunshine," and with his telling her in front of all in the room "Now this one is a lulu." Rooke makes his vanity real, but his charm is no less real. His "hot kiss . . . in the middle of her palm" is one of those

---

[32] On more than a few occasions Ella Mae shows her pleasure in his "antics." Two or three times she composes in her mind a true 'love Song for Edward', listing his beauties. The best perhaps is the one she recites looking at him in the yard of their old school: "Edward appeared to be enjoying himself ... His face was scorched dark from working in the sun ... Muscles rippled in his white arms, that were slender as any woman's ... He had no backside to speak of ... One of the most endearing sights she knew of was seeing Edward coming out of the bath ..." *Fat Woman*, 123-124.

[33] *Fat Woman*, cit. p. 82.

poignant details, impressive for their power of revealing Ella Mae's and Edward's nature at the same time. The whole scene is an excellent piece of dramatic art, throbbing with life, rich with literary and cultural allusions.[34] There is even a chorus, in an almost canonical classical Greek tradition, when "the ladies" in a circle witness the 'episode': "'Look at Ella Mae,' the black woman sang. 'She's got a face like a sunset and goose bumps all over!' 'I do believe,' another chimed in, 'these two young folks have gone and fell head over heels in love!'"[35] The two verbs "sang" and "chimed in" sound solemnly wise and appropriate.

The book brims with adroit pieces like the ones quoted above, where concepts are lightly touched upon, and yet presented and engineered in a way that makes them carry elements of the whole story. Considering the text in its factual actuality, the mesh of images and concepts results in an extended pattern of cross-references that it is not difficult to follow while reading, but that it is difficult to cut into pieces. Episodes, parts of them, and details cannot be separated one from the other and from the stream of Ella Mae's thoughts without losing some of their strength and meaning, both of which are due also to their contiguity with other episodes and other details, or to the recurrence of the same images, words and details on several occasions. Only after reading the last page of *Fat Woman* is it possible to become fully aware of the value and function of the net Rooke has assiduously woven, because it is only at that stage that a simultaneous view of the 'greater story' is workable in the mind of the reader.

Food is obviously one of the carrying elements, although much less important than hunger. The dreadful poverty she grows up in makes food irresistible to her, hence her hunger, that is so much more than craving for material food. Details concerning food however are special factors of representational insight. Many of them are provided, from the Zesta crackers and Sweet Breeze bread of the first pages, to the elaborate description of

---

[34] The episode is one of the finest examples in *Fat Woman* of Rooke's personal interpretation of romance. Edward's mother can be seen as the widow queen of a small kingdom, proud and humble when she welcomes a wandering princess: "... child, hold yourself up, and come on in. It ain't much ... but it's home" (*Fat Woman*, 114). She has even a court of handmaids, and of course she has a son, the young prince who falls in love with the wandering princess. It would be interesting to study at least part of Rooke's fiction within this perspective.

[35] *Fat Woman*, 116.

Ella Mae's cooking. Her enjoyment of the banana split Edward unexpectedly buys her during their outing is one of the best realistic moments of the whole narrative, rivalled only by the cold cabbage and the chocolate ice cream towards the end: "... I'll just help myself to a mouthful of this cabbage. There are few things better on this earth than good cold cabbage, when it's simmered in ham, with a teaspoon of vinegar sprinkled over the top the way I do it ... Chocolate, the best kind, and going a little runny the way she liked it ..."[36] The sense of taste is aroused, the food is sensual, the passage is actual seduction. Rooke's Ella Mae knows that well when a few pages later she thinks: "food runs through the Holy Book thick as the avenging sword ... Hardly ever had she sat down to the Book without a ravenous appetite coming over her."[37] Rooke does not always make Ella Mae enjoy her food, in fact he seldom does, but whether she enjoys it or not, when he makes her deal with food Rooke achieves excellent instances of savoury realism.

Ella Mae's hunger being more than straightforward hunger carries several meanings: it is reaction, revolt, self-inflicted pain, even habit of pain, for all the deprivation, hurt, injury, damage, poverty of the body and of the mind she had to submit to, at times without even realising she was submitting. Yet Ella Mae is not made totally innocent by her creator, and not because of her "gluttony," as she herself thinks from time to time, but because if she never gives up fighting, at the same time she never makes her efforts last long enough to win her battle and come to her day of renewal. This is not a new topic or theme in literature, nor is it certainly a new problem,[38] it is its treatment in *Fat Woman* that is remarkable, because direct and dramatic as it is, basically simple in its material and harsh imagery, it can be read in a number of different ways. Ella Mae, her hunger and the "Stomach Serpent" are to a certain extent one entity, they belong to the same arch-image. The episode of the Serpent takes place in the kitchen,

---

[36] *Fat Woman*, cit., pp. 164-165.

[37] *Fat Woman*, cit., p. 172.

[38] All aspects considered it is not too daring to see in Ella Mae's lack of self-confidence and will at least a similarity with the same problem of Zeno Cosini, who tries uselessly to give up smoking in *La coscienza di Zeno* (1923) by Italo Svevo. Ella Mae and Zeno are in fact less distant than they may seem on the surface.

when the supper is over but Ella Mae goes on eating and eating ("Ain't missed a beat") until she has a fit and has a nightmarish vision: "She was looking down into her own raw insides, into the giant trough . . . Rank fumes drifted up in waves of stench, as if from a seething pool of rot and filth . . . The entire putrid mass churned at a slow boil, scummy . . . How could a child of God pile in so much?" It seems the description of an ill-kempt, polluted and polluting rubbish dump. "Revolting" still the worst is yet to come: "Something quaked in her, something was alive down there. Some gigantic beast stirring . . . She could see the creature's form . . . moving quickly, changing direction at will, narrow and long, and ugly as a crocodile . . . She looked on, transfixed, horrified, as the huge Stomach Serpent roared to the surface . . ."; and yet the Serpent is "as helpless as she was herself."[39]

While reading these pages the question of what Ella Mae represents arises with new force. She is all the poor, she is all the deprived, she is the epitome of *la condition humaine,* she is human frailty, ignorance, rights denied, injustice of the social system. She may be a warning against the risks of denying the means of knowledge, happiness, even dignity to some people. She is the emblematic product of a 'cold heaven,' of indifferent chance. She can even be interpreted as representing mother earth, rotting because men abuse and destroy her. She can be seen as one with the Serpent, and in turn the Serpent can be seen as a hierophany of all the evils flesh is heir to, or even as a hierophany of the spirit, the 'pneuma' seeking revenge because denied freedom and development. The list could be astonishingly long and assorted. The void the serpent inhabits is not nothingness, it is a void space, a space vacated or not filled, an absence. The serpent is the monstrous product of the insufficient development of knowledge, consciousness, alertness, that were not allowed to grow into any maturity. More than paralysis of the conscience the issue is a hypotrophic state of mind, imagination, conscience, will, that causes degeneration. But Ella Mae may equally be regarded as the embodiment of courage, endurance,

---

[39] *Fat Woman,* 95-97. The symbolism of the serpent is manifold. It is both a symbol of good and evil, of spirit and soul, of human libido and vital energy, of the source of life and of destruction. The serpent can be a dragon, an imago mundi, a genius. There is a cosmic serpent, the serpent of Eden, an ouroboros. The serpent as a labyrinthine form is also a representation of the bowels and of excrements; the intestine has the form of a long serpent.

stamina, stubborn hope, because every time she plunges into grief and despair she manages to surface again. She is indeed "a fine woman."

The end of the book is not the end of the story. Edward's scheme, crude, cruel, and extreme as it is, is a plan of renewal, of rebirth. He wants Ella Mae to go back into the womb of a boarded up room in order to have her be born again. His decision could even be seen as the exercise of the male function. The time of her captivity would be the time of a sort of pregnancy: from the room-womb[40] Ella Mae is to emerge as a new person, a new woman, even a newly made daughter to her husband. Thus the sexual union at the end of the book may be seen as a warrant of continuity, a pledge of a new life.

Edward has no right to do what he does and he is surely wrong, but it may be interesting to notice that he probably decided the course of his actions when he was overwhelmed by the sight of the magnificent, bright orange setting sun they see when they crest the hill: "shocking in its magnificence: a huge, orange ball of sun . . . more awesome than any ever seen. It vibrated with heat and everything in its path was glowing. Edward's face and clothes were bright orange . . . that wonderful orange."[41] Orange, Ella Mae lets us know several times in the course of the narrative, is Edward's favourite colour. The first time they met, one of the women of the chorus commenting on the action compared Ella Mae's blush to a "sunset." The interplay of details and motifs is here fully active, as usual, but the core of the episode is awe, the awe that fills the whole family at the sight of the absolute beauty of the bright orange setting sun. There can be no doubt that this orange sun is laden with symbolic power, more powerful indeed because it is not clearly stated, and that the emotion it yields is the austere passion that the sight of the sublime yields.[42] Ella Mae cries: "It's beautiful!

---

[40] But it can be said too that Ella Mae is herself womb to herself, inasmuch as her fat body potentially contains a similar, smaller, new body.

[41] Fat Woman, 129-130.

[42] The symbolism of the sun is as rich and various as the symbolism of the serpent. The sun represents beauty, light, source of life. It is the heart of the world, and the eye of the world. As it gives life it may give death. Rising and setting it represents resurrection and immortality. In dealing with such a multifarious, overwhelming image/symbol Rooke's touch is indeed beautifully light and effective.

. . . If I was a heathen and saw that, I would fall down on my knees." Edward whispers: "Godamighty . . . Great Godamighty!" and the boys squeal "with rapture." They are all transfixed by a deep emotion they do not know how to express or even understand. Edward reacts by crying, moaning, moving his head and body in a frenzy: "He had lost control. He was sobbing desperately now . . . Saying her name . . ." but after his frenzy he seems ready to do "what I got to do."[43] Right or wrong, he tries to fight "the stars," to overcome a miserable state of the affairs. The authentic realistic, factor is that he is both right and very wrong.

To understand how Rooke contrives to keep realism and romance, symbolism and social analysis, philosophical insight and a taste for story-telling together and alive, the truest critical operation is perhaps tautological in nature, being simply that of reading *Fat Woman* a second time, and maybe a third, because ultimately the meaning of a novel is the novel.

---

[43] *Fat Woman,,* 131-132.

BIBLIOGRAPHY

Rooke, Leon. *A Bolt of White Cloth*. Don Mills, ON: Soddart, 1984.

Sartre, Jean-Paul. *L'Imaginaire*. Paris: Gallimard, 1940.

LEON ROOKE'S *SHAKESPEARE'S DOG*: A POSTMODERN HISTORIOGRAPHIC PARODY

ANNA PIA DE LUCA

Leon Rooke, novelist, short-story writer and dramatist has, since 1969, been living and working in Canada where he has published the majority of his works. Influenced in the 1950s and 60s by the writings of contributors to *New World Writing*, such as Borges and Ionesco, Rooke is now considered one of the most vivacious, innovative and experimental writers living in Canada today. His novel, *Shakespeare's Dog*[1] won the Canadian Governor General's Award in 1984.

With a technique that could be defined as postmodern historiographic parody,[2] Rooke, in this novel, rewrites, re-interprets and thus challenges the official historical version of one of the most obscure periods in the life of William Shakespeare, those formative years which follow his marriage to Anne Hathaway and precede his final departure from Stratford to seek theatrical fortune in London. As biographers do not know when or why Shakespeare actually left home, many contrasting accounts have been given, including the belief that Shakespeare must have shifted from one occupation to another and from one adventure to another before finally deciding to leave.

---

[1] Leon Rooke. *Shakespeare's Dog*. Don Mills, Ontario: Stoddard, 1983. Citations from the novel will be from this edition with the page number included in parenthesis in the text.

[2] In the chapter "Historiographic Metafiction" of her book *The Canadian Postmodern: A Study of Contemporary English-Canadian Fiction*. Toronto: Oxford University Press, 1988, Linda Hutcheon argues that historiography is a poetic construct while fiction is historically conditioned. Thus the role of both the historian and the novelist is similar, that is, "to narrate, to re-present by means of selection and interpretation" 66.

In a postmodern fashion that is a mix "between fact and fiction, between truth and imagination,"[3] Rooke self-consciously and wittily uses and abuses actual historic documentation on Shakespeare's family life and with overt narratorial comment, forcing the reader to realize at the end of each chapter that what he is reading is artifact, transforms that which might have been considered a truthful biography of Shakespeare into a narrative fiction which paradoxically seems more real than the written narrativized forms of history itself. Yet the authenticity of this foregrounded historical setting is immediately undermined and put into question by the seemingly authoritative narrative voice and eyewitness accounts of Hooker, Shakespeare's faithful but excessively bawdy and quarrelsome dog. It is Hooker, a name ironically sounding like an anagram of Rooke, who informs the reader not only of his Two Foot master's early biography but, in particular, of his own personal influence in the moulding of William Shakespeare, the humanist and dramatist. Hooker even saves Shakespeare from untimely death by drowning in the Avon river, permitting him thus to prepare and produce his great works. It is entertaining to remember, however, that the noun "hooker" is also a slang word for the thief or prostitute and such a reading fits in quite well with Hooker's sly tactics and sluttish ways.

Through the voice of Hooker as first-person narrator, Rooke parodies the customs and philosophical concepts of Elizabethan England, such as belief in witchcraft, problems of public debt, enclosure, notions of order and degree or the chain of being, and he inserts, out of context, a pastiche of quotations from Shakespeare's major works such as "Venus and Adonis," *Troilus and Cressida*, *As You Like It* and *Hamlet*, all in a swirl of verbal virtuosity purposely manipulated to resemble the Elizabethan English language.

There have been many historical hypotheses as to why Shakespeare left Stratford and the main plot of the story concerns the legend relating to William's probably having poached deer from Sir Thomas Lucy's park near Charlecote with the result that he was compelled to flee to London to escape the persecution of the Regarders, men who enforced the anti-poaching laws. In Rooke's novel, however, the legend is inverted and it is Hooker who has been identified as the culprit. Because his masters, in

---

[3] Linda Hutcheon, *The Canadian Postmodern*, 73.

particular the "wordy Shagsbier," could not "be bothered with feeding the dog" (9), Hooker is obliged to hunt for food but as a result of his illegal action he fears the tortures of being drawn and quartered by the law enforcers thus leaving his master to have to fend for himself. At the end of the first chapter, Hooker affirms:

> I had not the whatjack to tell him that if Hooker's goose was cooked, then his own would be long-frying. He'd perish a limp squatter in Ludd's town or a rotter in Stratford, and be a play-spinner not ever, once robbed of the advantage of a dog's wide learning (46-47).

During their "man-and-dog" walks "through Arden Wood" (9) Hooker introduces William, who "knew no Latin and less Greek" (52), to Aristotle and he sprinkles "a syllable or two of form" on Shakespeare's wordy "mush" (9). And to Shakespeare's frequent allusions to classical myths Hooker presents his own canine legends with "Canutus" (6) and "Sirius the Dogstar" (9).

From Hooker's perspective we are also introduced to the antics and foibles of each member of Shakespeare's family living in Henley Street in Stratford during those early years. We learn of John Shakespeare's changes in fortune after his marriage to Mary, the youngest of Robert Arden's eight daughters, his not daring to "venture of Sundays to Holy Trinity Church" (13) because of his many debts, his fine for having left garbage on the streets rather than using the common muck hill, of his many trades, from butcher to dresser of fine leathers, from ale brewer to bailiff of Stratford and of his final degrading state in which "he had not pot to pee in nor hardly cause to stand upright" (14), probably because of his "dented pewter tankard that was ever deep with his and Warwickshire's best brown ale" (13).

Hilarious is Hooker's view of his master Will's and Anne Hathaway's love/hate relationship, a relationship that comically parallels Hooker's own with his canine love-mate Marr. Both couple's verbal communication ranges from vulgar back-chat to erotic alliteration in a parody of the plot/subplot sequences in Shakespeare's plays. It is Anne's "harlotrous wedge" (64) that ties Shakespeare to Stratford, prohibiting him greater fame in London. Considered by his family a dreamer, incapable of doing anything concrete except "minting rhyme" and "scratching dandruff from his empty head" (8), Anne boisterously complains of her husband's futile occupation:

> "You'd take meaningful employment," she kept telling him, "if you cared about me or your brats. But, nay, you're all lit up by prince and princess, king and queen, you don't care snit about the real world!" (13).

Shakespeare's mother Mary on the other hand, gently and generously understands William's versifying when she exclaims: "Oh, he's for art" (14). Particularly entertaining are the scenes relating to Hooker's and Shakespeare's discussions on philosophic and moral problems, man's destiny or even order and degree. More often than not, it is Hooker, the idealist, who must knock a humanistic learning into Shakespeare's egoistic head. At times their roles even switch with Hooker imitating man and Shakespeare imitating dog:

> Though I loved him, Will was strict in his conformity. He would rattle no sword at another man's destiny, for all was fair and desirable in his mind's realm: the sop hated equality . . . "We are hooked to our stars, Hooker," the stink would say. "We sink or swim by their glimmer."
> "Untune the lute," under breath I'd utter, meaning it ironical. "Take but degree away and hark Jupiter's bolts that would follow." *He'd hike up his ears at the syllable-roll but stand dumb to their subtlety* (34 italics mine).[4]

In this passage, Hooker criticizes his master's reverence for the Queen, second only to God in that natural hierarchy that puts vermin, vagabonds and dogs at the lowest possible level. Hooker's protestation to "untune the lute," which recalls Ulysses' famous speech in *Troilus and Cressida* where the hero laments the degrading situation in Greece, takes William by surprise but, unlike Hooker, he refuses to respond to the difficulties of

---

[4] Hooker's citation is a parodic misquotation of Ulysses in *Troilus and Cressida* "Take but degree away, untune that string, / And hark, what discord follows!" (III, iii, 109).

the oppressed who live on the margins of society. "'Chaos is odious,' Shakespeare would say, 'Better a thousand vagabonds perish for bread than one strand of our Queen's hair be ruffled'" (34).

In a parody on metafictional historiography Rooke even farcically presents an episode relating to the mystery of William's marriage banns to two apparently different women. On November 27, 1582, William seems to have been granted a licence to marry "Anna Whatetey of Temple Grafion" while on November 28, the issue of a licence appears to have been between "William Shagsbere" and "Anne Hathwey of Stratford."[5] Biographers tend to believe that the first woman mentioned was but a careless clerical misprint but Rooke gives us a much more comical version.

In a flashback account, Hooker recalls how he had accompanied a reluctant Will, now "wilted" and with "hanging head" (73) for having made Anne pregnant, to the registry office to obtain a special marriage licence. The clerk who admitted them had "his eyes bulbous with cataracts that obscured night from day, his hands afright with time's legacy . . ." The man, in fact, was so blind and decrepit that he mistook Hooker for the bride:

> "She's a pretty lass," this fattened hog said, lacing my chin. "Though a mite short, plus being hairy and wide between the legs. Is anyone here to claim the virtue of her?" (74).

But above all he jumbled the names of the forty people who had entered requests that particular day. A certain vicar, Whately, had previously sought tithe payments from lands near Crowle, but his boisterous voice and manners had confused the man in such a way that:

> our dithering, wheezing clerk got mixed Whately with the bride
> our Anne, so that it came out on the license that Will was grant-
> ed privilege to wedlock not Anne Hathaway of Shottery but some
> goose named Anne Whately of Temple Grafton, who did not exist

---

[5] The historical information is in Max Meredith Reese, *Shakespeare: His World and His Work*, (Revised Edition), Edward Arnold, London, 20-21. The spelling of the names is as appears in Reese's text.

in that village or elsewhere in England except in our old duffer's mind (75).

So this is the way it probably went, suggests Rooke, in answer to those moralist biographers who believe that Shakespeare originally intended to marry Anne Whately. At the time however the only persons truly offended by this mix-up were the bride's protectors Fulke Sandells and John Richardson, who "next day thumped down forty pounds surety, thus guaranteeing to poleaxe Shagspere to his weir"(75).[6] Hooker even maliciously insinuates that there were rumours that a hound passing through Shottery "had once witnessed the lusty Hathaway feeding her patch to handsome Fulke Sandells" (70) thus Sandells had reason to cover up and trap Shakespeare.

The whole account of Shakespeare's marriage then, is given a coating, even if ludicrous, of probability and truth and just as we begin to accept Rooke's version of the story he pulls the carpet from under our feet and undermines the whole episode with a parody on metafictional historiographic techniques concerned with the relationship between what historically happened and the process of writing about it. Hooker, in fact transcribes, in foregrounded italics, which include an Elizabethan licence in spelling and pronunciation,[7] the oral record of the words that probably passed between Will, Anne and the curate during the marriage ceremony. In a hilarious parody of the wedding vows, the curate even turns to Will's father and asks:

> "John, wilst thou now go hang bacon of olde hog in the rafters that this union will prosper in the slact tymes and the bad, through plague and pestilence and whatsoever begatting?"
> And John noddid, and dide (76-77).

---

[6] In order to obtain a special marriage licence, William Shakespeare was expected to produce a bond or at least send someone to do so on his behalf. Since William was still a minor, Fulke Sandells and John Richardson were the two Warwickshire farmers, "the sureties, who pledged themselves for the very considerable sum of £40." See M.M. Reese, *Shakespeare*, 21.

[7] In the novel, Rooke even parodies the misspelt name of Shakespeare as "Shagsbere" in the original marriage licence documents. For a list of the variations on Shakespeare's name used by Rooke, see Keith Garebian, *Leon Rooke and his Works*, Toronto: ECW Press, 1989.

The novel also abounds with references to *Hamlet* where Hooker becomes a parodic extension of the intellectual, introspective, idealistic and inquisitive prince of Denmark. Even Joan, John Shakespeare's "sky-struck daughter" (25), wraps sheets around her naked body and "with weeds garlanded through her hair," singing Ophelia's vulgar tunes "with fragile breath that almost became elegy-song" (27), she self-consciously acts out Ophelia's madness, to the grand amusement of William who yells out, "She's not yet for the nunnery" (28), in a play within a play parody intended to cook Anne's goose. Joan's last tune, sung in imitation not only of Ophelia but in particular of Hathaway, "Quoth she, 'Before you tumbled me, you promised me to wed. Now that's so. So, tumbling me, you'll not to London go'" (29) is meant to reveal Anne's blackmailing manoever in keeping Will from his glorious future.

On the same parodic level, Hooker, guilt-ridden because of his having poached Lucy's deer, is visited by a phantom, "a deer vision." The ghost accuses Hooker of murder but before Hooker can plead his innocence the deer gallops away, "in a spangle of golden dust and airy-fairy wind-cloud" calling out to Hooker "Mark me, mark me! List! List!" (58). And as the ghost vanishes into clover saying "Adieu, adieu," Hooker wonders whether the vision was "death, in stag disguise" or just "witch-world doings" (59). This episode not only recalls the ghost scene of Hamlet's father but in a jovial fashion also the many cowboy films where the hero gallops off into the golden sunset.

References are also made to Hamlet's musing over the sleep of death and the fate of man. While walking through Trinity Church cemetery, both Hooker and William comment on the hereafter of the persons buried there. William believes that there is a "fairer sleep" (140) than death and asks: How long, Hooker? How long in the ground ere a body rot, when it went to earth ripe with unused ginger and the countenance still dewed? What counts a life, smelly dog . . . What is to count mine? (140-141).

As is the case with many of the references in this novel to Shakespeare's works, the critical controversy over authorial originality versus authorized plagiarism on the part of an author (here ironically both Shakespeare and Rooke are involved) is challenged and immediately undermined by Hooker who, in the play within the play scene, realizes that Shakespeare had mentally recorded his sister's actions "for liberation in some more tuneful epoch to come" (28), while in the ghost scene he contemplates whether or not to "Tell Will, who might lay down his Holinshed and draw stage action from it" (60).

In a further analysis, *Shakespeare's Dog* is also a disguised parody on the role of the reader decoding the encoded message of the author, and hence on the entire act of the *énonciation*. For while we meticulously try to decipher factual from fanciful biography, intertextual references, linguistic puns, anagrams, portmanteau words and Hooker's "'words' double-turning" (35), we begin to realize that we have become the centre of attention and the real parodic focus of the author. We must not forget that we are reading a pseudo-English Renaissance tale, even a tall tale, reported by an ambiguous narrator, a mangy tail-wagging mongrel, thus creating what Bakhtin calls "an intentional dialogized hybrid."[8] Bakhtin, in fact, argues that in parodic works two languages, two styles and two linguistic points of view come together or are crossed with each other. In our case, the point of encounter is between the language being parodied (the syntactically reconstructed English of Renaissance England) and the language that parodies (the colloquial low-pitched puns and pornographic innuendoes of Hooker).

According to Bakhtin, this second language invisibly serves "as an actualizing background for creating and perceiving,"[9] but if we take a closer look at the text we realize that Hooker, despite his verbal virtuosity, is literally unable to communicate by word of mouth with his Two Foot friends. Thus what we perceive is not a dialogue between ourselves and this invisible narrated text in a labyrinthian search for meaning but between ourselves and our own self-centred performance as readers of parodic artifice. If, like Polonius, someone were to ask us "What do you read?" our answer would be similar to Hamlet's "Words, words, words" (*Hamlet* II, ii, 192-193).

Rooke, in fact, parodies the Elizabethan love for language but his concern with puns and anagrams, in what Linda Hutcheon calls "overt linguistic narcissism,"[10] tends to underline the virtuosity and playfulness of

---

8 Mikhail Bakhtin, *The Dialogic Imagination,* trans. Caryl Emerson, Michael Holquist, ed. Michael Holquist, University of Texas Press, Austin, Texas 1981, 76.

9 Ibid., 76.

10 Linda Hutcheon, "The Language of Fiction," in *Narcissistic Narrative: The Metafictional Paradox,* Routledge, London 1980, 100-101. Hutcheon considers puns or anagrams the most obvious types of overt language "which call the reader's attention to the fact that the text is made up of words, words which are delightfully fertile in creative suggestiveness."

the writer rather than the wordiness of the text. But undoubtedly, Rooke wishes to go beyond this initial humorous reading in order to question the validity of words to convey meaning and the hermeneutic problem of truth. He has scattered hints throughout the novel that Hooker is only a dog and is thus realistically able to communicate solely through canine body language. Hooker's narrated events reverberate with onomatopoeic words in imitation of sounds heard. "Kersplash! Kersplunk! Glug and glug" (109) goes the witch Baxton as she is rolled off a cliff into the water below. In reply to moral or philosophical problems posed to him by Shakespeare, Hooker begins his confutation with a typical dog's response — "woof-woof," "arf-arf" or "bow-wow":

> "Soul's immortal. Here is where I take my first leave with Two Foot, who sees soul as nothing more than cabbage in the pot . . . Soul's nothing according to him . . . We're good fertilizer, Hooker, that's all." Well, I'm master to that scoundrel on this score, and will keep on wrestling him down. Woof-woof. Bend an ear, Shax-poot, I tell him. Listen to Hooker. Your soul is rotten, but it is immortal. Yet the prigger thinks he's genius" (32-33).

On another occasion, when from behind shuttered windows where he had been "minting rhyme" and trying to avoid Anne Hathaway's vexing harassments, Shakespeare turns to Hooker:

> "Has the drab biscuit gone?" he whispered to me. "The viper got her sweetness," he growled *to my nodding*, "yet she's still the viper Hathaway. Let's boil the slut in oil."
> *I barked my feeling passion for his tune.* But the scribbler's nose was already back at work (8 italics mine).

And when Hooker, visibly outraged at "man's inhumanity to dog," (6) cannot get the message across to Will that "what worth was a scribbler if his weight was not put in with the long march of impugned humanity" (36), he takes physical action by sinking his fangs deep into Shakespeare's ankle:

> I'd gnaw the priss without mercy. Grrr. Chomp, chomp. Until in the end he'd beg my favour, weep forgiveness, charge that he

would give thought to mending his reason. "You talk sense, Hooker," he'd say. "Now loosen me" (35).

In the episode when Hooker saves William from drowning, Rooke's choice of verbs gives realism to Hooker's actions. The dog typically "tugged," "whined," "hopped," "licked," and "gnawed" his master to safety and then "ran," "ripped," "leapt," and "streaked" (114) over the open fields to get help.

The most evident proof, however, that Hooker is just a howling dog occurs near the end of chapter three when "like one bedeviled, . . . teeth flashing in hideous growl" (106), Hooker saves the Stratford witch, Moll Braxton, from a horrible burning at the stake. Hooker is fed up with the "provincial claptrap" and the "idiotic superstitions" (106) of a mob who cannot accept those that are different and in a parody of the stream of consciousness technique, Hooker mentally savours ways to persecute them. He relishes seeing these molesters "staked on the commons" or put "in the cockfighting pits, in the bull-baiting rings" where, in a reversal of roles, dogs or stumps could "clap and wager and dance." But this is all wishful thinking for in a final awareness of his own incapability to communicate verbally Hooker comments:

> It was *speechifying* I wanted doing, aye, *as I tell it*, taking no rejoicement at that moment in a canine's *abysmal howl*. Empty triumph . . . Howl and only more howl comes back (108; italics mine).

Hooker then, is intoxicated with the desire to build a better world for man and dog with words, any words. During the course of the novel, his bosom friendship with Shakespeare has given him a quicker perception of the powers and limits of human existence to the point that he becomes more human-like every day. "'There goes Hooker,' cries a youth, 'hind legs dog and front part human'" (56). Even Marr, Hooker's canine love-mate complains of his transformation. "'You've changed' she says, 'You get more like the Two Foots every day.'" But it is Wolf, Hooker's rival in love, who has hit the nail on the head by foreshadowing Hooker's future: "You've turned against dog. Next, we know, you'll be wearing pants. You'll be scribbling too" (10).

This, in truth, will be Hooker's future occupation evidenced by the fact that we, the readers, are reading the written version of his narrated account. At the end of the novel, while still dreaming in the thick of the night that "I was already past my old life and on the road to Londontown" (158), Hooker is suddenly roused from sleep by Shakespeare. Rooke, with a play on the *mise en abîme* technique, has Hooker relive his dream as he and Shakespeare hurry off to London before the arrival of the Regarders. To the warm farewell cries of family and friends who wish both dog and man to "Go and make us proud," Hooker, in a parodic allusion to Victorian narrative conventions, responds: "And so we went — yea, we went — and did" (158); Shakespeare of course to become a great dramatist and Hooker, to find, as in a moral fable, the human capacity to communicate his story through words.

In a farcical allusion to Hamlet, Hooker had once said: "Words. How I hated them. (It ain't words, he'd say, but how they're shook.) As if words, his or mine, would ever have their day" (8 italics mine). That Shakespeare was able to 'shake' his words splendidly and find fame has been proven by the ever-increasing interest historians, writers, psychologists, critics and drama lovers still have for his works today. But even Hooker, at least for some of us, will be fondly remembered. He has presented us not only with a very contemporary and paradoxical historiographic rendition of the life, works and poetic inspiration of one of the greatest writers in history but he has also presented us with a parodic game, for our amusement, of the various narrative, poetic and dramatic conventions found in modern literature. Hooker-Rooke, has given the reader the gratifying joy of co-creation in that multi-levelled process bordering between life and art that is part of contemporary postmodern reading. With words artfully manipulated we can create imaginative worlds that give the illusion of reality or real worlds that conceal the meaning of truth. The ultimate joy, however is Hooker's who can finally say: "Cat will mew . . . and dog will have his day" (146).

Rooke's Hooker: Prolepsis, Natural Law, Decentring in *Shakespeare's Dog*

Michael H. Keefer

We will base our argument on one animal only — the dog, if you like, which is thought to be the most worthless of animals. But even in this case we shall discover that the animal in question is in no way inferior to ourselves . . . falling short of humans neither in the accuracy of perceptions, nor in internal reason, nor (to go still further) in external reason, or speech . . .
—Sextus Empiricus, *Outlines of Pyrrhonism*, Ch. 14[1]

1. The two Hookers

"'Hooker,' it might almost be said, is the name of a book rather than the name of a man . . ."[2] Such, in view of a severe paucity of biographical information, was the opinion of Christopher Morris, whose introduction to the Everyman edition of Richard Hooker's *Of the Laws of Ecclesiastical Polity* framed my first encounter, more than thirty years ago, with that classic of Elizabethan prose and Anglican theology. But readers of Leon Rooke's novel *Shakespeare's Dog* are in a position to contradict Morris's claim — to declare with confidence that "Hooker" is the name neither of a man nor of a book, but of a dog — and furthermore, that there are few if any dogs since the time our two species first entered into a symbiotic relationship about whose life and opinions we know more.

---

[1] I have quoted, with some alterations, from R.G. Bury's translation of Sextus Empiricus, as excerpted in *Greek and Roman Philosophy After Aristotle*, ed. Jason L. Saunders (New York: Free Press, 1966), 163-64, 165-66.

[2] Richard Hooker, *Of the Laws of Ecclesiastical Polity*, ed. Christopher Morris (2 vols.; London: Dent, 1954), vol. 1, v.

Richard Hooker and Rooke's Mr. Hooker are related by more than their shared name. The latter, after meditating on a blazing vision he has experienced of the deer he had poached, surreptitiously devoured, and digested ("Might now they put Hooker's image up on church wall where saint previously had stood? In niches now vacant, in the Protestant zeal to strip wall and window of the Catholic heresy"), pauses to ask himself, aptly enough: "How stand you, Hooker, on ecclesiastical polity?"[3]

The one-day action of Rooke's novel occupies the eve and early morning of the day, some three years after William Shakespeare's marriage to Anne Hathaway in 1582, of his and his dog's departure for London and a theatrical career. We can draw from this the literally preposterous consequence that by the mid-1580s, at a time when Richard Hooker had probably not so much as contemplated writing his *Ecclesiastical Polity* (Books One to Four of that *opus* were published in 1593, Book Five in 1597),[4] its title was already in the mouth of Shakespeare's dog. In this odd prolepsis can be descried a first anticipation of one of the principal concerns of this essay.

2. Prolepsis

Prolepsis is, quite precisely, the rhetorical figure of anticipation, through which the subsequent and secondary is made to come before, and thus to assert priority over that which 'properly,' in due temporal sequence, precedes it. Although overlooked by Harold Bloom in his study of the "revisionary ratios" through which strong writers evade or surmount the anxiety of influence stemming from their initial dependency upon literary precursors, prolepsis is arguably the most powerful such ratio or strategy.[5] The theology of Valentinus, the second-century gnostic heretic, was proleptic in its insistence that the Jewish and Christian orthodoxies which he

---

[3] Leon Rooke, *Shakespeare's Dog* (1981; rpt. New York: Ecco Press, 1986), 60.

[4] Hooker died in 1600; the last three books of *Ecclesiastical Polity* were not printed until the mid-seventeenth century.

[5] Prolepsis does overlap with the first of Bloom's revisionary ratios, "clinamen," or swerve, though by inverting the relationship of priority it makes the precursor swerve from the secondary — now the originary — text. See Bloom, *The Anxiety of Influence: A Theory of Poetry* (London, Oxford, New York: Oxford University Press, 1973), 14, 19-45.

sought to subvert are corruptions of and declinations from a primordial condition of fullness proclaimed in Valentinus' own writings.[6] John Milton, in identifying the narratives elaborated by Homer, Virgil, and other pagan poets as derived from demonic deformations of the originary truth which he recounts, made *Paradise Lost* a proleptic source of his epic precursors.[7] William Blake in turn trumped Milton, proleptically making the earthly doings of his precursor into no more than a material echo of the primordial events narrated in his poem *Milton*.[8]

Harold Bloom exempted Shakespeare from the patterns analyzed in *The Anxiety of Influence* for two reasons that come close to being mutually contradictory: first, that he "belongs to the giant age before the flood, before the anxiety of influence became central to poetic consciousness," and secondly, that he "is the largest instance in the language of a phenomenon that stands outside the concern of this book: the absolute absorption of the precursor."[9] Shakespeare did not play the game; Shakespeare won the game.

Bloom has more recently revised this opinion, to the point of finding Shakespeare's struggle with his great precursor and rival inscribed within the text of *King Lear*: "I tend to find Shakespeare in Edgar, perhaps because I locate Christopher Marlowe in Edmund, but I do not wholly persuade myself."[10] We can with greater conviction discover the influence of another Shakespearean precursor in this same play, notably in one of Lear's most extraordinary speeches, the "prayer" he addresses from his own outcast abjection to the homeless, to "houseless poverty":

---

[6] See *The Gnostic Scriptures*, trans. Bentley Layton (Garden City, NY: Doubleday, 1987), 217-353; and Giovanni Filoramo, *L'attesa della fine, Storia della gnosi* (Bari: Editori Laterza, 1987), 87-137.

[7] See David Quint, *Origin and Originality in Renaissance Literature: Versions of the Source* (New Haven and London: Yale University Press, 1983), 207-14.

[8] See *Poetry and Prose of William Blake*, ed. Geoffrey Keynes (London: Nonesuch Press, 1927), 464-549. Blake first formulated this proleptic strategy in *The Marriage of Heaven and Hell*, 191, where Energy is made to displace the antinomies of orthodoxy in a manner reminiscent of the prolepsis of the gnostics.

[9] Bloom, *Anxiety*, 11.

[10] Harold Bloom, *Shakespeare: The Invention of the Human* (New York: Riverhead Books, 1998), 731.

Poor naked wretches, wheresoe'er you are,
That bide the pelting of this pitiless storm,
How shall your houseless heads and unfed sides,
Your looped and windowed raggedness, defend you
From seasons such as these? O, I have ta'en
Too little care of this! Take physic, pomp;
Expose thyself to feel what wretches feel,
That thou mayst shake the superflux to them
And show the heavens more just.[11]

The precursor in question is none other than Mr. Hooker, Shakespeare's dog. In the first chapter of Rooke's novel, we learn that the young Shakespeare, when left to his own devices, was "strict in his conformity":

He would rattle no sword at another man's destiny, for all was fair and desirable in his mind's realm: the sop hated equality ... Will could see men hanged for stealing a biscuit and smile at this prettily. He would take no umbrage at innocent throats slit or widows set aflame for concocting eel's broth of a Sunday. "We are hooked to our stars, Hooker," the stink would say. "We sink or swim by their glimmer."[12]

Hooker's corrective response to the budding poet's moral aberrations was to "fasten deep bite on his ankle and carry my fangs deeper with every shaking."

"Let go, you trollop!" He'd beat fist on my noodle and whap me with sticks and dance on one leg as he howled his pain out over the borough. Yet I'd hold on. I'd gnaw the priss without mercy.

---

11 William Shakespeare, *King Lear*, III iv. 28-36, in *The Complete Works of Shakespeare*, ed. David Bevington (4th ed.; New York: HarperCollins, 1992), 1195. These lines themselves contain a notable and radically subversive prolepsis, in that they make the justice of the supposedly primary term, "the heavens," dependent upon the justice of the supposedly secondary domain of human agency. See my essay "Accommodation and Synecdoche: Calvin's God in *King Lear*," Shakespeare Studies 20 (1988): 147-88; rpt. in *Shakespearean Criticism*, SC-52, ed. Kathy Darrow (Detroit: Gale Research, 2000).

12 Rooke, *Shakespeare's Dog*, 34.

Grrr. Chomp, chomp. Until in the end he'd beg my favor, weep
forgiveness, charge that he would give thought to mending his
reason . . . "Loosen me, Hooker." The wretch's eyes would water,
and he'd drop down to give me head pats, to play at tickling my
tummy, saying, *"Please,* Hooker! Please! Open your jaws to my ankle
this once and I shall ever hereafter open my heart to humanity."

And only when he made me believe he meant it would I let
my jaws slacken.

"Ooo, I'm hobbled!" he'd cry. "Ooo, I'm lamed. Get me a cup
for begging, Hooker, for you've got me as bleeding-maimed as your
lot of stinking beggars. Ooo, this smarts! Let me lean on you,
Hooker."

And so the false biddy would slouch, hobble, and lean.[13]

Remembering that the names Hooker and Rooke are a near-rhyme,
we may uncover in this Shakespearean precursor a double identity:
Elizabethan dog, to be sure, but also, proleptically, a very contemporary
writer, whose voice retains a distinctive North Carolinian twang.

3. Theologies of natural law

"To impart of holy things to the dogs is forbidden," wrote Clement of
Alexandria in the late second century, "so long as they remain beasts."[14]
Among Mr. Hooker's canine compeers there is a near consensus that he
evades this condition. Marr, his faithless partner, is the first to raise the issue;
her opinion is seconded by Wolfsleach, her accomplice in dog-adultery:

> I gave the harlot a shriveling stare. She took it with a pouty, mad-
> dening grin. "I don't like you," she glomped. "You've changed. You
> get more like the Two Foots every day."

---

[13] Ibid., 35-36

[14] *Clement of Alexandria, The Stromata, or Miscellanies,* II. ii, in *Fathers of the Second Century:
Hermas, Tatian, Athenagoras, Theophilus, and Clement of Alexandria,* ed. Alexander Roberts and
James Donaldson, rev. A. Cleveland Coxe (The Ante-Nicene Fathers, vol. 2; Buffalo: Christian
Literature Publishing Co., 1885), 348

Piddle on the cur.

Wolf limped over to lay his head down on her, whining like a bowlegged toad complaining how I'd broke his legs. To lift a hooded glance at me, saying, "Marr's right, Mr. Hooker. You've gone round the bend. You've turned against dog. Next, we know, you'll be wearing pants. You'll be scribbling too."[15]

If Richard Hooker was a theologian by profession, Rooke's canine Hooker is one by predilection — though to very different effect. Both might be described as theologians of natural law, but while for the Anglican cleric natural law is the frame of order[16] through which a wholly sovereign divine authority governs its creation (and itself), for the dog it amounts to an ethical imperative underlying his passionate commitment to egalitarian justice.

Richard Hooker is a conservative whose defence of an Anglican *via media* rests upon a theology of natural law that had been authoritatively formulated by Thomas Aquinas in the thirteenth century;[17] he voices his resistance to reform of the established church in order that, as he says, "posterity may know we have not loosely through silence permitted things to pass away as in a dream . . ."[18] *Of the Laws of Ecclesiastical Polity* is a magisterial polemic against Calvinist views on church government which had come to threaten key elements of the Elizabethan settlement: episcopal control of and royal supremacy over the church.[19] Its argument hinges on

---

[15] Rooke, *Shakespeare's Dog*, 10.

[16] I borrow this phrase from the title of an anthology now long out of print: *The Frame of Order: An Outline of Elizabethan Belief Taken from Treatises of the Late Sixteenth Century*, ed. James Winny (London: Allen & Unwin, 1957).

[17] Hooker's clearest statement of his understanding of natural law occurs in *Ecclesiastical Polity*, I. iii, vol. 1, 54-61. Compare Aquinas, *Summa theologica I-II*, q. 94, art. 1-6, in *Basic Writings of Saint Thomas Aquinas*, ed. Anton C. Pegis (2 vols.; New York: Random House, 1945), vol. 2, 772-81.

[18] Hooker, *Ecclesiastical Polity*, Preface, vol. 1, 77.

[19] For assessments of the context within which Hooker wrote, and the issues he addressed, see Andrew Pettegree, "The Reception of Calvinism in Britain," in *Calvinus Sincerioris Religionis Vindex: Calvin as Protector of the Purer Religion*, ed. Wilhelm H. Neusner and Brian G. Armstrong (Kirksville, Missouri: Sixteenth Century Essays & Studies, vol. 36, 1997), 267-89;

Hooker's recognition of a link between the insistence of Calvin and his English disciples that the principles of church government must be drawn from scripture alone, and their assertion that any concession of agency to secondary causes, human or other, would amount to a derogation of the absolute sovereignty of God's will.

Since for Calvin the daily rising of the sun and the slightest velleity of any human will are both directly willed by God, natural law has only a residual and perversely negative function in the Calvinist cosmos: like the law of Moses, by which "wee are made more inexcusable,"[20] its purpose is to show that we must bear responsibility for our (divinely willed) damnable condition. Calvin writes of natural law that St. Paul, "where he teacheth that by the creation of the world was disclosed that which was to be knowen concerning God, doeth not meane such a disclosing as may be comprehended by the wit of men: but rather sheweth, that the same proceedeth no further but to make them inexcusable."[21] He sees nature as radically opposed to divine grace — to the point of declaring that the flesh must be mortified until everything we have from ourselves is "annéanty et aboly."[22]

In what may intially seem a similar manner, Hooker writes that "Those things which nature is said to do, are by divine art performed, using nature as an instrument; nor is there any such art or knowledge divine in

---

W. J. Torrance Kirby, "Richard Hooker's Theory of Natural Law in the Context of Reformation Theology," *Sixteenth Century Journal*, 30.3 (Fall 1999): 681-703; and Peter Lake, "Religious Identities in *Shakespeare's England*," in *A Companion to Shakespeare*, ed. David Scott Kastan (Oxford: Blackwell, 1999), 57-84.

[20] Jean Calvin, *The Institution of Christian Religion, written in Latine by M. John Calvine, and translated into English* ... by Thomas Norton (London, 1587), II. vii. 3, fol. 107v (sig. P3v).

[21] Calvin, *Institution*, I. v. 13, fol. 11 (sig. C3). (In the modern translation of John T. McNeill and Ford Lewis Battles, *Institutes of the Christian Religion* [2 vols.; Philadelphia: Westminster Press, 1960], this section is numbered I. v. 14.) In the next section of I. v., Calvin reiterates the point: "But although we want natural power, whereby wee cannot climbe up unto the pure and cleare knowledge of God, yet because the fault of our dulnesse is in our selves, therefore all coulour of excuse is cut awaye from us" (Institution, I. v. 14, fol. 11v [sig. C3v]). For an analysis of the perversity of Calvin's understanding of law, see my article "Accommodation and Synecdoche," cited in note 11 above.

[22] Calvin, *Institution*, III. iii. 8; quoted from *Institution de la religion chrestienne*, ed. Jean-Daniel Benoit (5 vols.; Paris: Vrin, 1957-63), vol. 3, 72.

nature herself working . . ."[23] But this instrumentality operates in terms of an all-pervasive structure of law, which in Aristotelian fashion directs natural agents "in the means whereby they tend to their own perfection," at the same time also "touch[ing] them as they are sociable parts united unto one body . . . bind[ing] them each to serve unto other's good, and all to prefer the good of the whole before whatsoever their own particular . . ."[24] Nature and grace are for Hooker cooperating rather than antithetical forces;[25] likewise, he views nature and reason as overlapping categories.[26]

In this light, human traditions assume a value that Calvinists would utterly deny to them: "The general and perpetual voice of man," Hooker writes, "is as the sentence of God himself. For that which all men have at all times learned, Nature herself must needs have taught; and God being the author of Nature, her voice is but his instrument."[27] Noting that many "principal points" of Christian faith are nowhere mentioned in scripture, but have been deduced out of it "by collection," Hooker raises the question of "how far we are to proceed by collection, before the full and complete measure of things necessary be made up."[28] Having argued that Calvinist principles of church government are for the most part "collections" of this kind, he can urge that it makes better sense to follow Anglican tradition, supplementing the laws of scripture with "rules and canons of that law which is written in all men's hearts . . ."[29]

---

[23] Hooker, *Ecclesiastical Polity*, I. iii. 4, vol. 1, 159.

[24] Ibid., I. iii. 5, vol. 1, 161.

[25] Ibid., III. viii. 6, vol. 1, 312: St. Paul "teacheth ... that nature hath need of grace, whereunto I hope we are not opposite, by holding that grace hath use of nature."

[26] Ibid., I. viii. 9, vol. 1, 182: "Law rational therefore, which men commonly use to call the Law of Nature, meaning thereby the Law which human Nature knoweth itself in reason universally bound unto, which also for that cause may be termed most fitly the Law of Reason; this Law, I say, comprehendeth all those things which men by the light of their natural understanding evidently know, or at leastwise may know, to be beseeming or unbeseeming, virtuous or vicious, good or evil for them to do."

[27] Ibid., I. viii. 3, vol. 1, 176.

[28] Ibid., I. xiv. 2, vol. 1, 216.

[29] Ibid., III. vii. 2, vol. 1, 307.

Hooker's anxious sense of a parallel threat to the structures of the Anglican church and the ideology of natural law gives rise to some of his most resonant prose:

Now if nature should intermit her course, and leave altogether though it were but for a while the observation of her own laws; if those principal and mother elements of the world, whereof all things in this lower world are made, should lose the qualities which now they have; if the frame of that heavenly arch erected over our heads should loosen and dissolve itself; if the celestial spheres should forget their wonted motions, and by irregular volubility turn themselves any way as it might happen; if the prince of the lights of heaven, which now as a giant doth run his unwearied course, should as it were through a languishing faintness begin to stand and to rest himself; if the moon should wander from her beaten way, the times and seasons of the year blend themselves by disordered and confused mixture, the winds breathe out their last gasp, the clouds yield no rain, the earth be defeated of heavenly influence, the fruits of the earth pine away as children at the withered breasts of their mother no longer able to yield them relief: what would become of man himself, whom all these things now do serve? See we not plainly that obedience of creatures unto the law of nature is the stay of the whole world?[30]

The imagery of a loss of nurturance may be expressive of anxieties on behalf of the church, but what this apocalyptic passage most deeply conveys is a fear of social disorder. Loosening, dissolution, and forgetfulness of due order are linked with "irregular volubility"; and the "stay" that prevents weakness, disorder and confusion is the "obedience of creatures" to law. "Equality," C. S. Lewis observed, "is not a conception that has any charms for Hooker," who as he notes found "no equality within us; the first Law of Nature is the law of internal hierarchy: that 'the soul ought to conduct the body, and the spirit of our minds the soul.'"[31]

---

[30] Ibid., I. iii. 2, vol. 1, 157.

[31] C.S. Lewis, *English Literature of the Sixteenth Century Excluding Drama* (1954; rpt. London, Oxford, New York: Oxford University Press, 1973), 460 (quoting *Ecclesiastical Polity*, I. viii. 6 [vol. 1, 179]).

But if "irregular volubility" — speech that escapes the control of institutions and of hierarchies, whether internal or macrocosmic — is a source of deep anxiety for Richard Hooker, it is on the other hand a constitutive principle of Leon Rooke's fictional dog. The canine Hooker shares with his Anglican namesake a revulsion from what he calls "the conscience that called it moral to uphold that we owed nothing to each other." Unlike Richard Hooker, however, he is keenly aware of social injustice and immiseration, and of the violence inflicted upon an Elizabethan underclass of vagrants, beggars, women persecuted as witches — and dogs. Openly scorning dogma, conformity and social hierarchy, he declares: "I wanted railing and ranting. I wanted hot revolution."[32]

This Hooker's affinities, should we wish to trace them, are with radicals and heretics — with the late-medieval pantheist Brethren of the Free Spirit, who believed the soul's vastness to be such that "It fills all things," and asserted that "Every rational creature is in its nature blessed";[33] or with their sixteenth-century spiritual descendents, the Anabaptist radicals who developed a "mystical 'gospel of all creatures,' referring to suffering, the way of all creatures in their kingdom of blood," and who in Elizabethan England became known as the Family of Love.[34] His legitimate successors are the anarcho-communistic Ranters of mid-seventeenth century England, who scandalized the orthodox by such declarations as "If God be all things . . . , then he is this Dog, this Tobacco-pipe,"[35] and who alarmed the political authorities by preaching a natural law of freedom, equality, and universal love:

> Yea, kisse Beggers, Prisoners, warme them, feed them, cloathe them, money them, relieve them, release them, take them into your houses . . . Owne them, they are flesh of your flesh, youre owne brethren, youre owne Sisters . . . Once more I say, own them; they

---

[32] Rooke, *Shakespeare's Dog*, 34-35.

[33] Norman Cohn, *The Pursuit of the Millennium: Revolutionary Millenarians and Mystical Anarchists of the Middle Ages* (2nd ed.; New York: Oxford University Press, 1970), 173.

[34] George Huntsdon Williams, *The Radical Reformation* (3rd ed.; Kirksville, Missouri: Truman State University Press, 2000), 442; cf. 726-27, 1191-1211.

[35] Edward Hyde, *A Wonder and yet no Wonder* (1651), quoted by Cohn, 291.

are your self, make them one with you, or else go howling into hell; howle for the miseries that are coming upon you, howle.[36]

Something much like these religious radicals' pantheistic law of freedom is the burden of Mr. Hooker's differences with "Young William":

> Bend an ear, Shaxpoot, I tell him. Listen to Hooker. Your soul is rotten, but it is immortal . . .
>
> Soul's immortal. A dog's eyes and nose knows it's there. And it seemed to me it was now at play in our backyard. Something was at gnaw under the latticework and I thought that's where it had gone. Then there was a rustle on the snake tree and I reasoned it was searching that space. Dust swirled a small funnel in the yard. Soul again? Getting desperate? Or was it only wind? . . .
>
> No matter. Soul goes where it goes. Taking its greatest strength, I'd say, from dog.[37]

The young Shakespeare holds instead to a doctrine of hierarchical order that has strong affinities with the other Hooker's theology:

> There was a chain of being, Will was like to lecture me, that went from God on high to rocks and reptiles down low. Dog was with brute beast, a shade up. This, the natural hierarchy, as he put it. Reading it off, as he would read a sign on the tavern door. Questioning nothing . . .
>
> Potty, the lad was, licking up his time's dogma as I would lick scented stick or glide my tongue over leg of mutton.[38]

---

[36] Abiezer Coppe, *A Fiery Flying Roll* (1649), ch. 2, quoted by Cohn, 322.

[37] Rooke, *Shakespeare's Dog*, 32-33. Any reader who finds the notion of canine-human colloquies improbable is referred to Thomas Nashe, *Will Summers' Last Will and Testament* (1600), lines 675-78: "To come to speech, they must have it questionlesse, / Although we understand them not so well: / They barke as good old Saxon as may be, / And that in more varietie than we..." (*The Works of Thomas Nashe*, ed. R.B. McKerrow, with corrections by F.P. Wilson [5 vols., 1958; rpt. Oxford: Blackwell, 1966], vol. 3, 254). Nashe is versifying the passage of Sextus Empiricus from which I quoted at the head of this essay.

[38] Ibid. 33-34.

The dog's lesson is that writerly greatness can be achieved only by those who liberate themselves from such commonplaces and align themselves with the radical pantheism of egalitarian justice:

> for what worth was a scribbler if his weight was not put in with the long march of impugned humanity? Soul endured the ravages of fate; soul was immortal. Soul gets by by hook and crook, by quill and by quiver; it seeks out all manner of things, showing its plume in flower bed or grass or animal or even a limestone field . . . The soul's plume lays the grandeur over all of life . . .[39]

Moreover, his dog-theology incorporates and finds its end in a level of the natural that was also explored by Adamite and Familist religious radicals in Shakespeare's time, but that is necessarily repressed in any orthodox natural theology:

> there stood my bloodmate Terry, stirring up all manner of memories pleasant and unpleasant. She was making my dogger yearn to plug up life, to cork up the whole of it so that I might stand back from my tongue-hang and verily ask, What is dog? What is a dog's life? Whereof has he come and whither will he go? . . . So fill up the hole, I thought. Let dogger and hole become one and let time quit . . . Plugging takes a dog back to where it was dog began . . .[40]

4. Richard Hooker and Shakespeare

Although there is little evidence of connections between the writings of William Shakespeare and his older contemporary Richard Hooker, the latter was regularly deployed by conservative Shakespeare scholars of the mid-twentieth century as a tool for locating and fixing the bard's opinions on matters social and political. Hardin Craig, for example, in his often-

---

[39] Ibid., 36.

[40] Ibid., 129.

reprinted study *The Enchanted Glass* (1935), was in no doubt as to Shake-speare's view of social class divisions. Using Hooker to frame the question, Craig assimilates Shakespeare to Hooker's position[41] on class; he then cites Ulysses' speech on degree in *Troilus and Cressida* (treated as though this un-pleasantly devious character's opinions could be unambiguously equated with those of the playwright, and as though the text were a political treatise rather than a play) as confirmation of the substantial identity of the thought of Shakespeare and Hooker — who are finally trotted out together to en-dorse and legitimize the inequities of social class in Craig's century as well as in their own.[42]

Another classic of mid-twentieth-century Shakespeare scholarship, E.M.W. Tillyard's *The Elizabethan World Picture* (1943), which was written as a by-product of his larger study of Shakespeare's history plays, deploys Richard Hooker in a parallel (if more subtle) manner. Passages from the first book of Hooker's *Laws of Ecclesiastical Polity*, the Church Homily *Of Obedience*, Elyot's *Book of the Governor*, the preface to Raleigh's *History of the World*, and Spenser's *Hymn of Love* are used, along with the inevitable long quotation from Ulysses' speech on degree from the third scene of Shakespeare's *Troilus and Cressida*, to establish the contours of a conception of order and hierarchy that "must have been common to all Elizabethans of even modest intelligence."[43]

---

[41] Hardin Craig, *The Enchanted Glass: The Renaissance Mind in English Literature* (1935; rpt. Oxford: Blackwell, 1966), 71 ("Hooker conceived of the social world in terms of orderly progression and saw as a fact the existence of ranks, classes, and degrees"); 72 ("The idea of stability in gradation is in Plato and the Platonists and is fundamental to Shakespeare's political and most of his social thinking").

[42] Ibid., 72-73: "We may still see the social classes that Hooker and Shakespeare saw. We may explain them economically as resulting from control over the necessities and possibilities of life, or socially as resulting from dominance in matters of opinion. We may think biologically of the social degrees and orders of the world as degrees of advantage in environment; or traditionally these orders of society may seem to be religious or political interpretations of man's sense of his own inferiority or superiority ... Hooker accepted, explained, and in minor ways improved a wide hypothesis to account for the universe about us, namely, as the plan of the Creator. That hypothesis rested squarely on unchanging fact then as now."

[43] E.M.W. Tillyard, *The Elizabethan World Picture* (1943; rpt. London: Chatto & Windus, 1956), 10.

Hooker, it turns out, is the central figure: "He has the acutest sense of what the ordinary educated man can grasp and having grasped ratify. It is this tact that assures us that he speaks for the educated nucleus that dictated the current beliefs of the Elizabethan Age. He represents far more truly the background of Elizabethan literature than do the coney-catching pamphlets or the novel of low life."[44] Hooker also provides Tillyard with powerful evidence that "If the Elizabethans believed in an ideal order animating earthly order, they were terrified lest it be upset, and appalled by the visible tokens of disorder that suggested its upsetting":[45] he cites in full the passage about nature intermitting its course and "irregular volubility" that I have quoted above. Finally, Hooker's remark, at the end of Book One of *Ecclesiastical Polity*, that the voice of law is "the harmony of the world" is identified by Tillyard with the metaphor of harmony in Ulysses' speech: "Take but degree away, untune that string, / And hark what discord follows . . ."[46]

That there is much more than this to the historical and literary record might be deduced from Keith Thomas' documentation of the behaviour in church of Elizabethans who "jostled for pews, nudged their neighbours, hawked and spat, knitted, made coarse remarks, told jokes, fell asleep and even let off guns,"[47] or from a sampling of such earthy, dialogical, insubordinate writers as Thomas Nashe, who in defending the memory of Robert Greene (author of "coney-catching pamphlets" and many other things) against the slanders of Gabriel Harvey, Tillyard's academic predecessor at Cambridge, wrote that

> Hee had his faultes, and thou thy follyes. Debt and deadly sinne who is not subject to? With any notorious crime I never knew him

---

[44] Ibid. The slide, within the space of a single page, from the claim that all but the stupidest of Elizabethans shared the orthodox view of social order to an acknowledgment that what is being discussed is the hegemonic ideology of a social elite ("the educated nucleus that dictated the current beliefs...") is typical of Tillyard's mode of arguing.

[45] Ibid., 15.

[46] Ibid., 11-12, quoting Hooker, *Ecclesiastical Polity*, I. xvi. 8, vol. 1, p. 232; and *Shakespeare, Troilus and Cressida*, I. iii. 109-10.

[47] Keith Thomas, *Religion and the Decline of Magic* (1971; rpt. Harmondsworth: Penguin, 1973), 191.

tainted . . . A good fellowe hee was . . . , and in one yeare hee pist as much against the walls, as thou and thy two brothers spent in three.[48]

But as I have argued elsewhere, Tillyard's reduction of a rapidly evolving culture, a complex mixture of residual, dominant, repressed, and emergent elements, into a static and unitary "picture," an authoritarian shadow of the whole, is achieved by deliberately ignoring everything in that culture that contradicts his own heavy investment in authority and submissiveness. The result is what I have termed a "subtractive politicizing" of Elizabethan literature, and a right-wing appropriation of Shakespeare as its central figure.[49]

This Tillyardian subtractive politicizing has enjoyed a remarkably wide and durable success. In 1983, the year in which *Shakespeare's Dog* won the Governor-General's award for fiction, Nigel Lawson, Margaret Thatcher's plump Chancellor of the Exchequer, was quoted in *The Guardian* as fondly citing the familiar lines from *Troilus and Cressida* ("Take but degree away, untune that string, / And hark what discord follows"), and as commenting that "The fact of differences, and the need for some kind of hierarchy, both these facts, are expressed more powerfully there than anywhere else I know in literature . . . Shakespeare was a Tory, without any doubt." As Margot Heinemann remarks,

> To hear Shakespeare cited directly in the context of cutting the health service and reducing taxation on the well-to-do is unnerving . . . We see more clearly what the struggle over the meanings of Shakespeare is really about: or at least it concentrates the mind.[50]

---

[48] Thomas Nashe, *Strange Newes, Of the intercepting certaine Letters, and a Convoy of Verses, as they were going Privilie to victuall the Low Countries* (London, 1592), sig. E4r-v. (I have made some small changes to the spelling.)

[49] Michael Keefer, *Lunar Perspectives: Field Notes from the Culture Wars* (Toronto: Anansi, 1996), 89-95.

[50] Margot Heinemann, "How Brecht Read Shakespeare," in *Political Shakeapeare: New Essays in Cultural Materialism*, ed. Jonathan Dollimore and Alan Sinfield (Manchester: Manchester University Press, 1985), p. 203. Terry Coleman's interview with Nigel Lawson from which Heinemann quotes appeared in *The Guardian* on September 5, 1983.

5. Mr. Hooker and the Shakespeareans

> The history of criticism shows us too ready to indulge a not wholly inexplicable fancy that in Hamlet we behold the frustrated and inarticulate Shakespeare furiously wagging his tail in an effort to tell us something (Stephen Booth, 1969).[51]

Can we now define the central joke of *Shakespeare's Dog*? Ralph Waldo Emerson declared, in the mid-nineteenth century, that Shakespeare

> wrote the text of modern life; the text of manners: he drew the man of England and Europe; the father of the man in America; he drew the man, and described the day, and what is done in it: he read the hearts of men and women, their probity, and their second thoughts and wiles; . . . he knew the laws of repression which make the police of nature.[52]

As Michael Bristol suggests, Emerson was responding both to "Shakespeare's extraordinary transumptive power, his ability to appropriate everything that precedes him," and also to his "extraordinary proleptic and anticipatory power"; the former "creates an appearance of striking and sudden emergence," while the latter gives his work "an absolutely convincing but altogether precocious modernity."[53] In similar terms, one might describe Leon Rooke's novel as a response to the transumptive power of the twentieth-century institutions associated with the reproduction and transmission of Shakespeare: a response to their extraordinary ability to sanitize and prettify the poet, to reduce his writings to the dimensions of an ideology of hierarchy and submission — and, having

---

[51] Booth, "The Value of Hamlet," in *Reinterpretations of Elizabethan Drama*, ed. Norman Rabkin (New York and London: Columbia University Press, 1969), 138.

[52] Emerson, *Representative Men: Seven Lectures*, in *The Complete Works of Ralph Waldo Emerson: Centenary Edition* (12 vols.; New York: AMS Press, 1968); quoted in Michael D. Bristol, *Shakespeare's America, America's Shakespeare* (London and New York: Routledge, 1990), 125.

[53] Bristol, *Shakespeare's America*, 125.

subtractively politicized them, to make them available for use by a mean-spirited neoconservatism.

Rooke's joke is at once a prolepsis, an inversion, and a decentring. Hooker, the theologian whom conservative mid-twentieth-century Shakespeareans had made the basis of their transumptive or metaleptic appropriations of Shakespeare as the figurehead of an unambiguous orthodoxy, is proleptically inserted into the formative stage of the poet's development — as a confirmed politico-religious radical, an active egalitarian, and a dog — and this canine consciousness becomes the centre of the story. Rooke concedes to the Hardin Craigs and Tillyards a Shakespeare who is "strict in his conformity," but at the price of identifying this orthodoxy with immaturity, and of exposing their own favourite proof-text as the young poet's misprision of canine irony:

> "Untune the lute," under breath I'd utter, meaning it ironical. "Take but degree away and hark Jupiter's bolts that would follow." He'd hike up his ears at the syllable-roll but stand dumb to their subtlety. "Chaos is odious, Hooker," he'd say. "Better a thousand vagabonds perish for bread than one strand of our Queen's hair be ruffled."[54]

Proleptic in another respect as well, Rooke's novel anticipates several features of the cultural materialist work on Shakespeare that began to appear in the mid-1980s and quickly established itself as a dominant interpretive tendency. Like Jonathan Dollimore, whose *Radical Tragedy* appeared in 1984, Rooke sets his forehead against "a politically conservative way of doing criticism," seeking to be "intellectually challenging rather than academically stifling, politically engaged rather than spuriously impartial."[55] Like Dollimore again, and like Catherine Belsey in *The Subject of Tragedy* (1985), he playfully interrogates established notions of originary subjectivity and authorship.[56] Like Francis Barker, who published *The*

---

[54] Rooke, *Shakespeare's Dog*, 34.

[55] Jonathan Dollimore, *Radical Tragedy: Religion, Power and Ideology in the Drama of Shakespeare and his Contemporaries* (1984; 2nd ed., 1989, rpt. Durham, North Carolina: Duke University Press, 1993), "Introduction to the Second Edition," xiii.

[56] Catherine Belsey, *The Subject of Tragedy* (London and New York: Methuen, 1985)

Culture of Violence in 1993, he brings to light the complicity of high culture in the perpetuation of oppression and injustice.[57] Rooke anticipates Simon Shepherd's whimsical play with variant spellings of the name "Shakespeare": there are by my count thirteen variants of the name in *Shakespeare's Dog* (from "Shagsbier" to "Shakespizzle") and fully forty-five in Shepherd's 1991 essay "Acting against bardom" (prize forms include "Shapesqueer" and "Shikespewer").[58] Finally, his joking prolepses most definitely anticipates Patricia Parker's discovery, in her essay "Preposterous Estates," of a near-obsessive concern throughout the Shakespeare canon with inversions of temporality and sequence — and hence with disruptions and reversals of the rhetoric that authorizes a particular order as natural, and exposures of "the authority [this rhetoric] creates and the histories it forges."[59]

Shakespeare is not merely displaced from the centre of the narrative in Rooke's novel; he is also decentred in the subtler sense of being revealed, not as a unified transcendent self, the originary source of his own discourse, but rather as a subjectivity summoned into being as an effect of pre-existing discourses. Hooker's initial bitterness, his "dogly vinegar" as he calls it, arises from his recognition that the mental limitations of the "addled" Marr and the "slackard" Wolfsleach proceed (as Michel de Mont-aigne would say) from custom rather than from nature;[60] or, in

---

[57] Francis Barker, *The Culture of Violence: Essays on Tragedy and History* (Manchester: Manchester University Press, 1993).

[58] Simon Shepherd, "Acting against bardom: some utopian thoughts on workshops," in *Shakespeare in the Changing Curriculum*, ed. Lesley Aers and Nigel Wheale (London and New York: Routledge, 1991), pp. 88-107. However, comic invention pales in comparison with the ludic fertility of English dialectal and orthographic variation: while only some half-dozen variants appear in documents from the poet's lifetime (notably "Shagspere" in the wedding bond of 1582), more than seventy variants are attested in early modern Warwickshire and the adjoining counties. See Samuel Schoenbaum, *Shakespeare's Lives: New Edition* (Oxford: Clarendon Press, 1991), 5.

[59] Patricia Parker, "Preposterous Estates, Preposterous Events: From Late to Early Shakespeare," in her book *Shakespeare from the Margins: Language, Culture, Context* (Chicago and London: University of Chicago Press, 1996), 55.

[60] In his essay "De la coustume," Montaigne wrote: "Les loix de la conscience, que nous disons naistre de nautre, naissent del la coustume; chacun ayant en veneration interne les opinions et moeurs receuës autour de luy, ne s'en peut desprendre sans remors, ny s'y

more contemporary terms, that they are discursively produced social con-
structs:

> Oh, the mean blindness of [Marr]: that she didn't know, could never
> see (or care at what she saw), that Wolf, herself, and every other
> dog came to their cribs already maimed. In their spirit, in their
> stringy brains. Maimed by falsehoods, their own deceits, by treach-
> ery of blood and power of tick, by the canon of Canutus and expe-
> ditation's knock-kneed curse — by man's inhumanity to dog.[61]

Shakespeare is similarly maimed. Thanks to the orthodoxies that
have been whacked into him, he lacks understanding of the centreless
soul moving through the natural world that is the basis of Hooker's the-
ology, and lacks sympathy for the suffering and misery through which
this unindividuated soul moves:

> He'd had ushering at Free School, he'd had Hunt and Jenkens and
> even Cotton that had turned out a Jesuit — all trying to thrash-
> whip the classics into him. He'd had red-nosed Alex Aspinall,
> said to be master of art and a man of steep learning, pounding his
> britches. But what had soaked in was all slime and sludge, to a
> dog's true belly. The strutter knew no Latin and less Greek, but
> in these areas he smoked like a chimney compared to what he
> knew of suffering and misery, of the soul and its plumage . . .
>   Half the earth on doom's boat, I thought, and it is sailing right
> by him.[62]

Yet thanks to his exposure to canine discourse — thanks to "the
advantage of a dog's wide learning," and to Hooker's willingness to
"give good ear to [his] mush and sprinkle on it a syllable or two of form"[63]
— Shakespeare has potential for development.

---

appliquer sans applaudissement." *Essais*, ed. Maurice Rat (2 vols.; Paris: Éditions Garnier,
1962), I. xxiii, vol. 1, 121.

[61] Rooke, *Shakespeare's Dog*, 6.

[62] Ibid., 52-53.

[63] Ibid., 47, 9.

One of Hooker's memories of his and Terry's puppyhood is of the disappearance of their "Mam," and their subsequent discovery in a ditch of "what looked like Mam":

> The pile had her fur. It had what was left of her nose.
> "Is that Mam?" asked Terry. She haunched down to whimper whilst I made the vultures spin.
> "Is that Mam?"
> Well, it had her tail. It had her knees. The eyes had been plucked out, but the sockets had Mam's laconic way of seeing things.[64]

Although we are not told as much, it can be deduced that this experience, along with the young dogs' subsequent diet — "Bateless in our hunger as the tick was in his, we did the sneak on deserted thatchtop, barn, and pigeoncote, ate bugs and weech, ate the mossy bark of trees, chawed at log vermin and field rat, pounced on lamed hare and burrowing mole"[65] — was imparted to Shakespeare, to become the basis of Edgar's marvellous poetry of nature in *King Lear*:

> Poor Tom, that eats the swimming frog, the toad, the tadpole, the wall newt and the water; that in the fury of his heart, when the foul fiend rages, eats cow dung for salads, swallows the old rat and the ditch-dog, drinks the green mantle of the standing pool . . .[66]

6. R[h]ooke[r] and the Bard

Mr. Hooker is not just the narrative consciousness of the fiction; he is also made directly responsible for Shakespeare's escape from Stratford domesticity to the London theatres. According to a tradition that surfaced in the early years of the eighteenth century, Shakespeare in his youth was

---

[64] Ibid., 135.

[65] Ibid., 133.

[66] Shakespeare, *King Lear*, III. iv. 128-33, in Bevington, ed., *The Complete Works of Shakespeare*, 1197.

"much given to all unluckiness in stealing venison and rabbits, particularly from Sir [Thomas] Lucy, who had him oft whipped and sometimes imprisoned and at last made him fly his native country to his great advancement."[67] But in Rooke's version, Hooker is the deer-thief, and he and his master set out for London under the noses of the Regarders, the enforcers of the Forest Laws who are in Stratford to maim and kill canine poachers. (Natural law, one might say, impels dog to slay deer; the Forest Laws are part of the same repressive human apparatus that produces hungry beggars and witch-persecutions — and against which Hooker has taken direct action by rescuing the accused witch Moll Braxton from a Stratford mob, and by stealing a leg of mutton for a family of starving vagabonds.)

Rooke plays with another tag of Shakespeare legend to rather different purpose. In 1794-95 William-Henry Ireland, son of the antiquary Samuel Ireland (and in his father's eyes a blockhead), deceived his father and most of the literati of London with an extraordinarily bold sequence of forgeries. Beginning with a mortgage deed and a promissory note bearing Shakespeare's signature, he moved on to forge letters to and from Shakespeare and the Earl of Southampton, a Shakespearean profession of faith, a love-letter from the poet to his "Anna Hatherrewaye," enclosing a lock of hair and doggerel verses ("Is there onne Earthe a Manne more trewe / Thanne Willy Shakespeare is toe you"), authorial manuscripts of the *Tragedye of Kynge Leare* and of *Hamblette* (both heavily bowdlerized), and a previously unknown tragedy, *Vortigern*, which got as far as dress rehearsals at Drury Lane before being exploded by the publication of Edmond Malone's *An Inquiry into the Authenticity of Certain Miscellaneous Papers*, two days before its projected first performance on the morrow of April Fools' Day, 1796.[68] Even when William-Henry produced letters to his father from the purported source of these documents, in which the mysterious benefactor, a necessarily anonymous nobleman, declared that "If your *Son* is not a second Shakespeare I am not a *Man*,"[69] Samuel Ireland did not tumble to the forgeries.

---

[67] Schoenbaum, *Shakespeare's Lives*, 69. This version of the story was noted down by a Gloucestershire clergyman before 1708; a parallel version was printed by Nicholas Rowe in his 1709 edition of Shakespeare.

[68] Ibid., 135-61.

[69] Ibid., 148.

Having swallowed these very fishy documents, he was able at last to engorge the final whale — a Deed of Gift in which Shakespeare, gratefully acknowledging the manner in which in 1604 his "goode freynde Masterre William Henrye Irelande," none other, had rescued him from drowning in the Thames, gives to him and to his heirs "for everre inn his lyne" the manuscripts of five plays, including *Henry IV* (both parts?), *Henry V*, and the previously unknown "kyng henry thyrde of Englande."[70]

Malone thought that the narrative of this happy rescue should be preserved, along with "the old Satire of *Cocke Lorelles Bote*" and the later *Tale of Two Swannes*, under some such title as *The Tale of a Boat, or The Tale of the Swan of Avon Half Drowned in Thames*.[71] The proposed anthology must now include a further text — for fully two decades before Shakespeare made the acquaintance of "Masterre Irelande," the Swan of Avon more than half drowned in the river of his home town, and was dragged from a watery grave by his dog Hooker.[72]

What is to be made of this proleptic imitation of the most bizarre of Ireland's forgeries? William-Henry impudently inserted himself into the life of the idol whose private self he had already been impersonating; wearing the transparent mask of an invented ancestor, he made himself at once the Bard's preserver and his heir (and also, in passing, a forebear of the father who, while praising the forgeries as works of genius still thought his son a dullard).

Hooker (or shall we say R[h]ooke[r]?) is with equal impudence but simpler motives confessing to a lifetime of forgery, of factitious invention, of fiction-spinning. But the Shakespeare family, gathered around the damp shivering dog and their resuscitated Will, the poet-to-be, don't get it: "'*Good* dog, *good* dog,' they kept repeating, affirming it till my ears growed like beanstalks and my eyes swelled up like soup pots and I all but wept tears . . ."[73]

---

[70] Edmond Malone, *An Inquiry into the Authenticity of Certain Miscellaneous Papers and Legal Instruments*, Published Dec. 24, 1795 and *Attributed to Shakspeare....* (1796; facsimile rpt. London and New York: Frank Cass and Augustus M. Kelley, 1970), 211-12.

[71] Malone, *An Inquiry*, 213.

[72] Rooke, *Shakespeare's Dog*, 109-17.

[73] Ibid., 117.

BIBLIOGRAPHY

Aquinas, St. Thomas. *Basic Writings of Saint Thomas Aquinas*. Ed. Anton C. Pegis. 2 vols. New York: Random House, 1945.

Barker, Francis. *The Culture of Violence: Essays on Tragedy and History*. Manchester: Manchester University Press, 1993.

Belsey, Catherine. *The Subject of Tragedy*. London and New York: Methuen, 1985.

Blake, William. *Poetry and Prose of William Blake*. Ed. Geoffrey Keynes. London: Nonesuch Press, 1927.

Bloom, Harold. *The Anxiety of Influence: A Theory of Poetry*. London, Oxford, New York: Oxford University Press, 1973.

Booth, Stephen. "The Value of Hamlet." In *Reinterpretations of Elizabethan Drama*. Ed. Norman Rabkin. New York and London: Columbia University Press, 1969.

Bristol, Michael. *Shakespeare's America, America's Shakespeare*. London and New York: Routledge, 1990.

Calvin, Jean. *The Institution of Christian Religion, written in Latine by M. John Calvine, and translated into English ... by Thomas Norton*. London, 1587.

——. Institution de la religion chrestienne. Ed. Jean-Daniel Benoît. 5 vols. Paris: Vrin, 1957-63.

——. *Institutes of the Christian Religion*. Ed. John T. McNeill, trans. Ford Lewis Battles. 2 vols. Philadelphia: Westminster Press, 1960.

Clement of Alexandria. *The Stromata, or Miscellanies*. In *Fathers of the Second Century: Hermas, Tatian, Athenagoras, Theophilus, and Clement of Alexandria*. Eds. Alexander Roberts and James Donaldson, rev. A. Cleveland Coxe. The Ante-Nicene Fathers, vol. 2. Buffalo: Christian Literature Publishing Co., 1885.

Cohn, Norman. *The Pursuit of the Millennium: Revolutionary Millenarians and Mystical Anarchists of the Middle Ages*. 2nd ed. New York: Oxford University Press, 1970.

Coppe, Abiezer. *A Fiery Flying Roll*. London, 1649.

Craig, Hardin. *The Enchanted Glass: The Renaissance Mind in English Literature*. 1935; rpt. Oxford: Blackwell, 1966.

Dollimore, Jonathan. *Radical Tragedy: Religion, Power and Ideology in the Drama of Shakespeare and his Contemporaries*. 1984; 2nd ed., 1989; rpt. Durham, North Carolina: Duke University Press, 1993.

Emerson, Ralph Waldo. *The Complete Works of Ralph Waldo Emerson: Centenary Edition*. Ed. Edward Waldo Emerson. 12 vols. 1904-05; rpt. New York: AMS Press, 1968.

Filoramo, Giovanni. *L'attesa della fine, Storia della gnosi*. Bari: Editori Laterza, 1987.

Heinemann, Margot. "How Brecht Read Shakespeare." In *Political Shakespeare: New Essays in Cultural Materialism*. Eds. Jonathan Dollimore and Alan Sinfield. Manchester: Manchester University Press, 1985. 202-30.

Hooker, Richard. *Of the Laws of Ecclesiastical Polity*. Ed. Christopher Morris. 2 vols. London: Dent, 1954.

Hyde, Edward. *A Wonder and yet no Wonder*. London, 1651.

Keefer, Michael. "Accommodation and Synecdoche: Calvin's God in *King Lear*." *Shakespeare Studies* 20 (1988): 147-88.

———. *Lunar Perspectives: Field Notes from the Culture Wars*. Toronto: Anansi, 1996.

Kirby, W.J. Torrance. "Richard Hooker's Theory of Natural Law in the Context of Reformation Theology." *Sixteenth Century Journal* 30.3 (Fall 1999): 681-703.

Lake, Peter. "Religious Identities in Shakespeare's England." In *A Companion to Shakespeare*. Ed. David Scott Kastan. Oxford: Blackwell, 1999. 57-84.

Layton, Bentley, trans. *The Gnostic Scriptures*. Garden City, NY: Doubleday, 1987.

Lewis, C.S. *English Literature of the Sixteenth Century Excluding Drama*. 1954; rpt. London, Oxford, New York: Oxford University Press, 1973.

Malone, Edmond. *An Inquiry into the Authenticity of Certain Miscellaneous Papers and Legal Instruments, Published Dec. 24, 1795 and Attributed to Shakspeare...* 1796; facsimile rpt. London and New York: Frank Cass and Augustus M. Kelley, 1970.

Montaigne, Michel de. *Essais*. Ed. Maurice Rat. 2 vols. Paris: Éditions Garnier, 1962.

Nashe, Thomas. *Strange Newes, Of the intercepting certaine Letters, and a Convoy of Verses, as they were going* Privilie *to victual the Low Countries*. London, 1592.

———. *The Works of Thomas Nashe*. Ed. R.B. McKerrow, with corrections by F.P. Wilson. 5 vols. 1958; rpt. Oxford: Blackwell, 1966.

Parker, Patricia. *Shakespeare from the Margins: Language, Culture, Context*. Chicago and London: University of Chicago Press, 1996.

Pettegree, Andrew. "The Reception of Calvinism in Britain." In *Calvinus Sincerioris Religionis Vindex: Calvin as Protector of the Purer Religion*. Eds. Wilhelm H. Neusner and Brian G. Armstrong. Kirksville, Missouri: Sixteenth Century Essays & Studies, vol. 36, 1997. 267-89.

Quint, David. *Origin and Originality in Renaissance Literature: Versions of the Source*. New Haven and London: Yale University Press, 1983.

Rooke, Leon. *Shakespeare's Dog: A Novel*. 1981; rpt. New York: Ecco Press, 1986.

Saunders, Jason L., ed. *Greek and Roman Philosophy After Aristotle*. New York: Free Press, 1966.

Shakespeare, William. *The Complete Works of Shakespeare*. Ed. David Bevington. 4th ed. New York: HarperCollins, 1992.

Shepherd, Simon. "Acting against bardom: some utopian thoughts on workshops." In *Shakespeare in the Changing Curriculum*. Eds. Lesley Aers and Nigel Wheale. London and New York: Routledge, 1991. 88-107.

Schoenbaum, Samuel. *Shakespeare's Lives: New Edition*. Oxford: Clarendon Press, 1991.

Thomas, Keith. *Religion and the Decline of Magic*. 1971; rpt. Harmondsworth: Penguin, 1973.

Tillyard, E.M.W. *The Elizabethan World Picture*. 1943; rpt. London: Chatto & Windus, 1956.

Williams, George Huntsdon. *The Radical Reformation*. 3rd ed. Kirksville, Missouri: Truman State University Press, 2000.

Winny, James, ed. *The Frame of Order: An Outline of Elizabethan Belief Taken from Treatises of the Late Sixteenth Century*. London: Allen & Unwin, 1957.

Leon Rooke Works Wonders

Joan Thomas

These are the sordid facts that launch Leon Rooke's third novel *A Good Baby*: a nasty little man named Truman has been having his way with a teenage girl whom he picks up on a mountain road. Lena, the young woman, is soon pregnant. One November day when her baby is due, Truman picks her up and drives her miles back into the bush, murmuring as he leads her out of the car, "You oughten to be more careful with your next life." The next day a newborn baby is found under a laurel bush, and subsequently, the romantic and gullible Lena is discovered with her throat cut.

The novel *A Good Baby* grew out of a play by Leon Rooke that was performed on the West Coast in 1987. It is consequently, a theatrical novel. The remote mountainous region into which Truman drives Lena is like a set — simplified, self-contained, its characters rising out of mist. It is an abysmal world, where adults are broken by poverty and hopelessness, and children bear the brunt of the world's pain. The legends told around the stove in the general store are a catalogue of real horrors and grotesque imaginings: a man hangs his ten-year-old son from a tree as family watches. A little girl goes missing, and her family finds her body four years later when they think to look in an icebox on their porch. A man commits suicide by decapitating himself, and arranges for his head to roll downhill to a little grave that he has dug for it. Isolation has done to the people in this country what it does in a limited gene pool: it exaggerates the extremes. So, madness is rampant. So also, when human hope and fortitude triumph (as they eventually do), the effect is dazzling. What we have here is, in Mr. Rooke's words, "the world as garden and sinkpot."

The man who finds the baby is a nice young bachelor named Toker who is living in the cellar of his burnt-out house. A year before, he returned home from the tavern to find his mother had locked his sister in the house and his hounds in the shed and torched the property. But in spite of his family's contribution to the tragic history of the region, Toker emerges as though on stage, with no personal past, inventing himself as he goes along.

Toker's first thought is to find someone to take the baby off his hands. He drags it around the country in a fertilizer sack, commenting philosophically on the tick bites around its ears, feeding it tobacco juice off his finger, demanding, "Well, am I its ma? Am I?" As anyone who has had a baby will soon appreciate, this is not a real baby that Toker has found, but the *idea* of a baby. At two days old, she wakes up after a long night's sleep smiling. At three days old she has begun to crawl. This is a baby that glows in the dark.

Toker's attachment to the baby grows, and he becomes more fastidious about her prospective parents. He begins to want to discover the story of the baby's birth, so he sets out with bloodhounds to find the baby's mother. He joins two other people who are tramping around through the hills with similar intent: Lena's sister, who is following Truman with dog-like devotion, and Truman himself, crazed with toothache, having conversations with a god, with a gargoyle face, while he looks for his baby daughter. As the three move inevitably towards each other, Mr. Rooke has some difficulty sustaining tension in the novel; the murder is committed and discovered so early in the book, and Truman is clearly winding down of his own malignant energies.

Truman is a lunatic of the Flannery O'Conner variety (that is to say, grandiose, sadistic, paranoid), which leads one to wonder whether madmen of this sort are endemic in the south, or southern writers are simply more skilled at portraying them. Truman's fury is fuelled by memories of a childhood of cruelty and neglect. The evil in the novel thus rises naturally from the setting — degradation through deprivation. The forces of good are represented best by Hindmarch, an old man whose intuition takes him to people in need, and more fancifully and less humanely (a weakness in the novel, I think, but this is probably a question of taste) by the miraculous baby and by the blossoming love between Toker and a woman who wears a silk bathrobe and rides a white horse.

This novel is such a delight to read that it seems churlish to complain about anything. Its principal delight is its language, which for inventiveness and pleasure probably surpasses Mr. Rooke's ingenious creation of canine Elizabethan in *Shakespeare's Dog*, the novel for which he won the Governor General's Award in 1983. Leon Rooke has written *A Good Baby* with one foot firmly planted in the dialects of the Blue Ridge Mountains (he moved to Canada from North Carolina at the age of 35), and the other in the visceral territory of his private lexicon. Kerflooed, scumadenous, squenchy-eyed — when the perfect word doesn't exist, Mr. Rooke invents it. There is nothing either corny or obtuse about his language, like the language of *Fat Woman*, Mr. Rooke's first novel, it serves as a direct conduit for the primal feelings of the novel's characters.

A Good Baby

ROSEMARY SULLIVAN

Maria: But art has become something bad. I keep telling you that. Today, most art is ugly, because it's not responsible to the people it steals from. Real, honest-to-God true art steals from people. It's a thief. It comes in. It's non-obstructive. You don't feel it. It comes in, and you don't even notice that it's there, and it walks off with all your stuff, but then it gives it back to you and heals you, empowers you, and it's beautiful.

—Maria Campbell and Linda Griffiths, *The Book of Jessica*

It used to be believed that you could describe the world objectively, without ever mentioning the human observer; that "I" and the world could be kept separate. Then it was discovered that the experimenter changes the experiment. Even time is involved. Two events which are seen as occurring simultaneously by one observer may be seen in different temporal sequences by another. We lived in curved time in the zone of middle dimensions.

I read Leon Rooke's *A Good Baby* on a beach backed by desert in the north of Chile. You might say my reading was relative, but then there's no such thing as an objective reading, is there? W.H. Auden used to say: "Let a book read you." When *A Good Baby* read me on a beach in Chile, sun and high summer were suddenly "hell's own darkness out there . . . it was November, an alien month anyhow."

I knew where I was. I was back in Leon Rooke's North Carolina, even as I heard the green breakers breaking. I'd been there once in 1978, though in the summer and not in Rooke's alien month of November; playing a reporter investigating a Sufi Summer Camp, and I knew those blue mountains, and the kind of people they collected; those swamps and rhododendron forests. *A Good Baby* is a landscape so alive you can walk back into it. I did.

I thought, "My God, this writer has nerve." People who read this book are going to talk of his distinctive twang, his cast of characters, bizarre, eccentric, delightful. As if he's invented it, via William Faulkner, and not stolen it from life, as Maria Campbell says, and given it back, like a healer.

And that's what put me back for a second in context. Maybe if I hadn't been on that Chilean beach I wouldn't have thought of it. But I thought of a conversation I'd had with the novelist, Eduardo Galeano, in 1981, when he was in Toronto. We were talking about Latin American novels, and you could see he was piqued. "Why do they go on like that about magic realism as if we'd learned from the European surrealists or something? A stylistic trick! My God, if you're looking for piece dents, we were reading Melville and Whitman and Faulkner when we started out." That's where they learned how to play with time and the speaking voice and to make the form as complex as a character.

> *This then is life,*
> *Here is what has come to the surface after so many throes and convulsions.*
> *How curious! How real!*
> *Underfoot the divine soil — Overhead the sun.*[1]

The vision they wanted was epic, a celebration, and when they looked round, all the material was there to articulate the voice of the South American continent: landscape, myth, and people. What bothered Galeano most about the critics was the word *magic*. To him what the writers were describing was reality. And he told me a story. He was visiting a village in the Colombian mountains. As was his wont, he went into the small local church dedicated to Santa Cecilia; but at the end of the long dim nave, to his surprise, he saw a statue of a male saint on the dedicatory altar. When he asked about the apparent contradiction, it was explained that one day Santa Cecilia got this lump on her shoulder and it travelled down and found its home and after that she was San Antonio. "All those stories we tell are true," Galeano fumed. Reality is not one-dimensional.

How does that get me back to *A Good Baby*? Well, I have a feeling someone might call Rooke's book magic (or diabolic) realism, when its exquisite achievement is that it's slice-of-life reality. Perhaps that shouldn't bother me but it does. I kept thinking as I read, what a good sneak thief this

---

[1] Walt Whitman. "Proto-Leaf," from *Leaves of Grass*.

Rooke is; he steals so beautifully from life — these people are real people, walking along my beach.

Leon Rooke was born in Roanoke Rapids, North Carolina. His North Carolina outback is a husked world, so poor there are no distractions from essentials. There's the local store/gas pump as a centrifugal force pulling to its sparse comforts all members of this universe. At Cal's Place three old men sit together and jaw over the world's stored wisdom: "In Toker's memory so they had always been: ever aged, ever doleful in assembly around Cal's stove, a walled triumvirate of woebegone insignificance — refugees to whom time showed only the most ragged mercy . . . The earth's inaccessible sorcerers."

The Bible is back of all this, threading the metaphors of the locals' conversations: for old Wallace, "Judith Iscaret" roaming the earth in perpetual misery, "and all for the one piddly mischief" sums up our world: "They's not one free soul on the face of this earth." And we see the source of Rooke's own fine rhetoric, so randy, so inflated, so funny, around that stove: "You can't find no plumb line a-tall to mortal man's flimsy script. Now can ye?"

These metaphors, this vocabulary, have stoically evolved over generations in response to the "witchified" landscape that has power over all human expectations, is hated and loved, even as it can erase every human trace. To the inhabitants, it's alive, has rolled over or reared up where the chasms and mountains fall and rise, or turns into a road that has its own intentions and can kill you if it wants. The stories come out of the landscape, the kind Galeano speaks of: a blind man roams the woods, a ghost-legend to most, seeing what others fail to see, but real to the questing child who can predict the future with her visions, which may be visions but are also shrewd anticipations of the reality she's likely to encounter. Childhood riddles and rhymes weave through the meditations of the characters, holding them to their past as we are all held. Evil stalks, as it does in the human heart, with explanations that are only partially adequate. "The mind is an unholy labyrinth, and who knows its trails, its chamber horrors." The only way to get out of it all is "to stroke God's chin, speak nice to his face." Those who fail, fall into the pit of self-pity, unable to shed their hurts; those who climb out do so with love, plowing through to the "shedded hour."

At the two poles of the book stand Truman, a small gargoyle wreaking death and havoc on everyone, and Hindmarch, digging his own grave while he's able and ready, to save the living the bother. It's a jimcracky, hodgepodge of universe, not eccentric in fact, but our own. Not magic realism but something we know because it's metonymic (or universal to use a cliché). The astonishing thing is that Rooke has made it cohere, managed to put everything in.

I heard from someone that Rooke said he wrote *A Good Baby* in a week and took five years to finish it. That makes sense because the book comes in such a sustained rush. Like a dream or a revelation, and this must be the reason he uses the epigram at the beginning: "Whereon do you lead me, bright rider?" I'm not interested in knowing what was in Rooke's own life that he should need to find this good baby, but that the baby comes out of a deep dream place is clear. It's one of those books you feel started as the author's own dream, like Robertson Davies' *Fifth Business*. When Davies told us at a meeting of the Jungian Society of Toronto that his book began one night in a dream of a Peterborough landscape of snow with two boys, a snowball and a sled, I wasn't surprised. That book was earned by a painful searching.

So too is Rooke's. It has an archetypal energy to it that's brilliant: so deeply enfolded that none of the spars are showing. I think of Toker in his hole-house-tomb in the ground, crawling up from the burnt shards of his life, all those journeys, finding his Good Baby, "The baby pitched over on her stomach, only her belly button touching the ground. So it seemed. The arms were pointed wide, the legs straight to the rear. The head straight up. Flying." "She's a world-beater, I can see that." It's not just the baby, but Toker's holding to it, not being bought out, that redeems, that realigns his world, finds him Bathroby, and keeps Truman, the raw organic matter in all of us, at a distance off in his swamp.

But to tell it like this, of course, thins and husks the power, because one feels Rooke is being led by his "bright rider" and not by his head, or by calculated forethought on this journey. Rooke's book, like another great book, Sheila Watson's *Double Hook*, has the resonance of an archetypal allegory that reworks in you, as you read, the pattern of its own breakthrough. Do you prefer the old word *catharsis*? You feel shaken and cleansed when you've come through it.

Landscapes have an extraordinary way of colliding in your head: You can be on a beach in Chile and watch a man drown in North Carolina's swampy blackness. "Scaredy-cat, scaredy-cat, have ye no home? / The bough has broken and you're falling alone." I remember that last sentence, closing the pages, and walking out of the book.

Rooke would like it in Chile, I thought then, though the landscape was other: dry, red, desiccated, and the mountain thrust up like a fist. A man was walking a white horse straight over the Cordillera de Domeyco, mounting in a slow, eternal zigzag. Rooke would see that. And Truman had been here, under another alias. People think of the evil in Chile as having been something spectacular, but it was really the same small-minded phobic mean pettiness, getting so out of hand it swept like a tidal wave up from this beach. Pinochet rattling his medals, Truman baiting his trap with his own flesh, addicted to fear and self-justification. Neither a widge-bit sorry. Here they have a saying: *"De tripas se hace corazon."* From guts you make heart. Toker and Bathroby and Little Girl all had that difference: heart. Reading *A Good Baby* in Chile was a simple contingency. But that the characters are so real, the morality so clean and precise, digging so deep into the human heart that it could give me another handle on that landscape at my back, was a measure of Rooke's vision. "Yes, Maria Campbell," I said, "you're right." Seventy-five per cent of art out there does steal. It takes your stuff and hangs it on the wall and says "Look what I've done." And it's all pure ego. Then comes the book that gives back. "The main healing tool." Maybe not just in the old communities, maybe in the new communities too, the artist is the most sacred person of all.

NOVELS AND DREAMS:
ON LEON ROOKE'S *A GOOD BABY*

DOUGLAS GLOVER

The best novels are like dreams. They come out of the silence of the page like a dream. They structure themselves like dreams, that is, there are clear ways in which the structure of dreams parallels the structure of novels. Like dreams, novels use image-patterning as a device for suggesting meaning: image repetition, association, juxtaposition, and splintering (Viktor Shklovsky's term for the branching pattern created by a repeating image and its associated or split-off elements which also repeat). Like dreams, novels are available to interpretation; the best novels have a central luminous mystery at their core, which tempts generations upon generations of critics and readers to find new structures and meanings beyond the surface of the words. And like dreams, novels are built around (and this is explicable in only the vaguest of terms) the recurrence or insistence of desire which, in order to generate plot, must be resisted; the locus or arena of desire and resistance appears again and again with obsessive regularity in novels, an obsessive regularity which, in real life, would seem eccentric if not pathological. In novels, character is perversion, and the novel returns again and again to the animating desire, which it must resist to the bitter end or even beyond the end of the words on the page.

The front matter of Leon Rooke's novel *A Good Baby* bears the epigraph: "Whereon do you lead me, bright rider?" This epigraph has always puzzled me because, to begin with, there aren't any bright riders in the book. About three-quarters of the way through *A Good Baby*, there is an extremely strange chapter in the point of view of the baby's aunt, a girl who has spent most of the novel trudging through the eerie landscape of Rooke's imagination trying to catch up with her sister Lena and Lena's murderous lover Truman. In the chapter in question, this sister awakes from a trance-like sleep and encounters a blind man on a horse. This blind man has appeared to her once before and in that instance he was leading a mule which never followed the same road twice except on its return journey. If you think about it, this blind man seems like an emissary of death, or he is Death. He just appears, takes the sister to Lena's body, then drops out of the book. This blind man on a horse is the only rider in the novel and this chapter begins with an italicized paragraph: *"Whip me along, bright rider. Whip me along, oh my caretaker, like you done in my dream-house hour"* (227). A paragraph later, there is another italicized passage: *"Hit and bleed me, dark runner. Cozen and devour us here among your dwarf-elders"* (227). Bright rider and dark runner are here syntactically parallel and thus identical. But these two italicized passages seem somehow to emerge out of the page on their own without conventional textual support. No one says these lines; no one thinks them; they are not attached to the narrative in any other way. In a sense they parallel the emergence of the blind horseman who first appeared "out of the mist," "a ghostly mist" (175).

We here enter the dream-like core of Rooke's novel, the place where the planks of conventional narrative prose drop out from under the reader, and words take on a puzzling yet insistent significance and characters do not so much act as surface into the narrative as though driven by some hidden necessity. The novel starts by transporting its actors into this foggy environment. After Lena and Truman have sex and visit the bootlegger in the first chapter, they drive deeper and deeper into the hills, crossing county lines. Lena says, "I never bin up to this country . . . Folks my way says they's backwards up here, though fierce, and loyal to the dog" (16). Truman wonders about "this land he'd ventured into was so switch-backed, so witchified to its cones and to its depths" (17). (It is a place where even the civil and temporal powers signified by the certainty of the daily mail have lost their sure grip — "Mail did git thue once ever blue moon." [29].) And Rooke makes much of "the abiding haze of fog which marked their passage" (18). All of which reminds me of other mythic journeys to the Land of the Dead, that peculiar mirror Other Place where everything we hold familiar is inverted and strange. I think here of Marlow's halting, fog-shrouded journey up that distant African river in *Heart of Darkness*.[1]

---

[1] Joseph Conrad, *Heart of Darkness*. New York: Penguin Books, 1999. All quotations are taken

"What we could see was just the steamer we were on, her outlines blurred as though she had been on the point of dissolving, and a misty strip of water, perhaps two feet broad, around her — and that was all. The rest of the world was nowhere . . ."(72) In both passages, the Rooke page with the bright rider reference and Conrad's fog sequence, the word "trance" appears, as though the fog were a physical manifestation of the mental state occasioned by a journey which crosses, not geographical, but metaphysical borders. And in turn this narrative journey into the fog of trance and dream implies a form that is vague, mysterious and inscrutable. Here again, a passage I adore from *Heart of Darkness*: "But Marlow was not typical (if this propensity to spin yarns be excepted), and to him the meaning of an episode was not inside like a kernel but outside, enveloping the tale which brought it out only as a glow brings out a haze, in the likeness of one of these misty halos that sometimes are made visible by the spectral illumination of moonshine."(5-6)

We speak here of stories that make some metaphoric leap and limn a journey that is not outward but reaches some dark innerscape where meaning is obscure yet luminous. It quickly becomes apparent to the reader of *A Good Baby* that the baby itself is more than a baby. Even Truman, the baby's father who later murders its mother, recalls the luminousness of its conception. ". . . that time with the hat, he'd seen some special light in her face he'd never seen in no female's face before, hat or otherwise, and it was some kind of radiance afloat there. It tickled him, that radiance" (17). This radiance is transferred in the course of the novel to the baby itself. "That baby. Its skin glows some in the dark, don't it? Unhuh. This here's a special baby" (204). This is about all the baby does in the course of the novel, but in relation to plot, the baby becomes the universal object of desire, the empty yet radiant sign to which every human is drawn.

I like to say when I teach that the novel is a machine of desire, that is, the novel is a form which presupposes desire as the engine of plot. The reason we like to read good novels is not because we identify with this or that character's particular desire; it is because we identify with any desire and any character who desires. The novel incarnates a universal plot, which reads something like Freud's clash between the Pleasure Principle and the Reality Principle. You know how this goes: infants begin life with no sense of separation between themselves and the world. What they wish for they receive. But the process of maturation involves the gradual separation of self from the world, the gradual realization that there is a gap between what we want and the getting of it. This radical disconnection is the universal plot: we want and we can't have. The mother withdraws the breast; the world resists desire. Every novel is an adventure of thwarted megalomania, the nuzzling infant searching for the retreating yet radiant object of desire. Desire then leads us into strange places, and in the end it desires only the end to desiring which is death.

A Good Baby is really about a kind of dream inversion of the story of the runaway breast; the baby, in this case, becomes not itself but what everyone desires, a magical love fetish that will heal the sick at heart, replace ancient losses and satisfy the crude and brittle lusts of old men. Comically enough, the baby is indestructible (like the dream of a breast); Toker, the hero of the novel, drags it around in a bag, feeds it on soda, rarely cleans it, yet the baby remains docile, healthy and radiant. Toker doesn't even want the baby — in this novel, those who don't want find love and those who want find only disappointment and ashes. Toker starts out the novel in the Western equivalent of Hindu abandonment. His horrendous childhood has blasted his desire mechanism to bits. He lives hermit-like in the smoky ruins of his burned-out family home, remembering over and over the day his mother killed his dog, burned his sister to death and left town. Released from wanting (though he lusts after a woman he calls Roby, we find out later in the novel that he's a virgin), he dwells in his own Land of the Dead only to find the good baby under a laurel bush and be healed. He keeps trying to give the baby away, keeps telling the baby that "he wont its mother" until in a strange and mysterious scene with Sarah, the invalid wife of the general store owner, he actually learns to "talk" like a woman. "She studied that answer, then said, Yes, yes. I can see another woman might of said that. Now try again. Say somethin else. The sort of thing a woman would" (203). The plot of the novel is built on the curious convergence and recurrence of everyone else's desire for the baby and Toker's desire to get rid of the baby which magically transforms, as he undergoes his own dream gender change and becomes a mother. "I can see you held that baby long enough, you'd holder how a woman would," says Sarah, the storeowner's wife.

There is an odd, dream-like purity to Toker's desire to get rid of the baby and everyone else's desire for the baby. In Rooke's novel, there is hardly anything like conventional characterization. Every person in the novel exists along a single line of loss and desire. Sometimes they're sly about how they pitch their desires, and sometimes they are clearly mad. But that is about the limit of variation. And there is nothing in this novel like a nod to conventional psychological paradigms of character development. Toker's obliterated childhood, his wound, is more mythic than psychological. It leaves him not corrupted but somehow cauterized, burned down to a nub of innocent simplicity. "I do believe," says Sarah, "that in every respect you're nearabouts as innocent as that baby" (203).

Toker's dark double, his evil twin, Truman, is the baby's father, its mother's murderer. Truman is desire incarnate, a shambling beast of desire who lurches awkwardly through the novel trying over and over again to reenact scenes from his childhood. It is Truman who gets to announce what I take to be the novel's surface moral: ". . . they's so much dereliction in the need of things" (14). He is a classic fetishist. Needing to relive the ur-scene of his first sexual humiliation — a brilliant Rookean parody of Humbert Humbert's first love in *Lolita* — he places a crude child's hair bow in Lena's hair, a bow like the one worn by Patience, the girl who taunted him and fought him off in his youth. Truman's desires insist; they recur; they drive him into mechanical and ritualized repetitions so monomaniacal and maladroit that they are doomed to comic failure. Living inside a fetishized (dream) universe, Truman is blind to any portion of reality that might help him achieve even one of his desires: to kiss Patience, to trap a mink (surely, in part, a dream conversion of the word "minx," hence Patience again; "his mind crawling backwards to that time of the mink, when she . . ." [97]), and to retrieve the baby for his own evil purposes. "What's mine is mine. That trap is mine, and that baby is mine. I'll go and gitter" (266).

A Good Baby, like a dream, is a metonymic (read fetishized) world of desire. The plot is barely a plot, less a plot than the simple reiteration of desire. Toker wanders around with the baby trying to find someone to take it while fending off every person who actually wants the baby. Truman bumps along the backroads in his disintegrating car, never getting close enough to do any damage until the final chapter when the dream-like fog which attends the whole novel suddenly seems to condense into a *deus ex machina* flood (how this brings back memories of *Mill on the Floss*) that swooshes Truman out of the book. Truman does not, however, die; it does not escape me that this is a dream-trip down the birth canal and into some other world.

But, finally, a novel is not a dream; novels and dreams only share common structures. Novels need to deal with time in a way completely alien to the world of dream. And novels need to offer their readers at least a superficial plausibility or verisimilitude. Even the strangest novels never completely untether themselves from allegiance to a certain commonsense conception of reality, which is at once familiar and artificial. Again, *Heart of Darkness* is instructive. Marlow makes his mythic dream journey upriver through the fog into the heart of darkness. After Kurtz dies, Marlow himself narrowly escapes death. He has looked, as he says, into the abyss. When he returns to the white city of Brussels, the sepulchral centre of imperial capitalism, and meets Kurtz's Intended, rather than tell the truth, he serves up a beautiful and comforting lie. We can journey into the world of dream, the universe of death, Marlow is telling us, but we cannot tell the truth when we return. The mystery must forever remain a mystery lest the day-to-day fabric of social discourse be forever torn asunder. The traveller can only speak in lies or parables; he can tell stories that radiate a meaning beyond meaning, hinting at what he saw. The beautiful lie Marlow tells sometimes seems like the most terrifying moment in the story.

Rooke's *A Good Baby* proposes a different sort of ending, a kind of neo-Christian redemptive closure, based on the capture of that errant breast-object, the glowing baby. "Jiggers, a baby! the brother declared. A baby will save the world!" (208). Instead of bringing his novel back from the mist-circled hill country, the realm of dream, death and myth, Rooke ejects evil and leaves us in a reconstituted world of gratified desire. He even stage-manages a resurrection of the nuclear family — Roby and Toker cuddling in bed with the baby between them after wonderful sex — when every family in the novel till that moment has been exploded, wracked with loss, or rendered sterile (one insistent recurring motif is the story of the lost child). It is as if, in finding the baby, Toker had won the metaphysical lottery; this brings an amused smile to our lips as does that vision of Truman as a comic book Satan, a bumbling, Keystone imp of Hell. Here dream has become fantasy; it has become mere wish fulfillment; it has become the comforting lie (and I suppose it is true that all dreams are not nightmares).

In this regard, I think *A Good Baby* is a bit at war with itself. I think Rooke's larger allegiance is to the dark side, to the thumping reiteration of desire, to the desolation of loss and the immense carelessness of need. Like Marlow, Truman pities and condescends to women. "They were that fragile in their wantin," he thinks (14). But here women stand in, as a symbol, for hearth and home, for the system of domestic virtues and customs which form the fabric of civilization. "They were that fragile in their wantin" is finally a judgement on us all for we are all ultimately to be pitied for the endlessness of our desire. Kurtz and Marlow see that the end of desire is not gratification but death. This is the truth that cannot be told. That Rooke avoids this truth at the end of his novel does not prevent us from seeing that he lavishes his fiercest eloquence, his most haunting prose, his most insistent patterns, on the enigma of desire, on elegies of loss.

And so I come back to that puzzling epigraph: "Whereon do you lead me, bright rider?" and its companion passage: "Whip me along, bright rider. Whip me along, oh my caretaker, like you done in my dream-house hour." This kind of heightened rhetoric belongs largely in the mind of Truman throughout. Truman is the one character who meditates on a "caretaker." And there is a pattern of italicized passages that insert themselves willy-nilly at the heads of chapters where otherwise they have no place — as if Truman's endless rant, his tent-preacher-from-Hell yammer, is invading and colonizing the rest of the novel. But is this really Truman thinking, or any other character in the novel, for that matter? Or are these moments rather the dream-like emergence of some deeper pattern or interest? What is the dream-hour? Who is the bright rider (dark runner) and whither does he lead us (whip us on)?

I teach my writing students that in a formally correct narrative there are spaces, rhythmic pauses in the action, for what I call thematic passages. These are moments when the text itself seems to slow and gather itself, sifting the past for clues, casting forward for a track into the future of the book. At these moments, the novelist, as composer of the action, can come very close to the surface of his own text. I don't mean the nowadays-diminished device of the authorial intrusion, the textual moment when the voice of the authority weighs into the narrative to guide the reader. I mean it in a more interrogative sense. There are moments all the way through the composition of a story or a novel when the author asks himself, Where am I going? What is this story about? What do my characters want? What is the meaning of this strange and beautiful thing I am inventing? It is very easy, I tell my students, to transfer these authorial medita-tions into the mind of a protagonist. In the interrogative mode, when they are all wondering about the nature of the universe in the midst of being enacted on the page, character, author and, yes, reader become one. And the novel becomes at once most real and most dream-like.

These are the moments when the author comes closest to exhibiting his own struggle to form the fugitive elements of dream, which inspire him, into a narrative structure. But they are also the moments when the author comes closest to revealing the sources of his own animation; the compulsive sifting and tracking of those elements of dream whose whis-pered and fragmentary message is like the sound of distant music. In the midst of telling us how he found Kurtz, Marlow breaks off and says:

> He was alone, and I before him did not know whether I stood on the ground or floated in the air. I've been telling you [you, here, being Marlow's friends on the Nellie, anchored in the Thames] what we said — repeating the phrases we pronounced — but what's the good? They were common everyday words — the familiar, vague sounds exchanged on every waking day of life. But what of that? They had behind them, to my mind, the terrific suggestiveness of words heard in dreams, of phrases spoken in nightmares. (124)

We all know the murmured invitations of desire, which lead us through life. But it seems to me that authors are more preternaturally haunted by the emptiness of desire, by the invisible constraints of form, by the end-less whiteness of the page, and by the endlessness of need as it attaches itself to an infinite series of radiant objects. "Whereon do you lead me, bright rider?" reads the epigraph. "They were that fragile in their want-ing," thinks Truman. "Whip me along, bright rider. Whip me along . . ." These words are full of wonder, pity and compulsion. It is possible that in these mysterious passages in *A Good Baby* Leon Rooke is talking to himself about himself and about his dream which must appear to him, in this narrative guise, as a shining stranger, leading him, riding him, whip-ping him, into fog-shrouded mystery of his novel.

WHEN MEN HAVE BABIES: THE GOOD FATHER IN *A GOOD BABY*

PETER CUMMING

For many feminists, it is a commonplace that men sorely need to be "feminized." "Women can do what men can do," says Gloria Steinem in a television interview. "Now men need to do what women can do." In particular, it is felt that men need to play a much more significant role in the raising of children. Dorothy Dinnerstein, in fact, posits that the fraught sexual relationships and psychological ill health of both men *and* women has one cause: compulsory "primary female responsibility for the care of . . . young children" (4) and one solution: active participation in childrearing by fathers. As the early feminist Bertha Pappenheim prophesied, "If there will be justice in the world to come . . . men have to have babies" (Koestenbaum 17).

However, men's tentative steps towards feminization and "male motherhood" have prompted understandable skepticism about "new men" and "present fathers" in life, literature, and the movies. Rosi Braidotti worries that "male uterus-envy is reaching a peak of paroxysm" (238) and is disappointed in "the 'new men' . . . 'They' are the best male friends we've got, and 'they' are not really what we had hoped for . . ." (235-37). Elaine Showalter, Craig Owens, and others have had second thoughts about *Tootsie*, in which Dustin Hoffman's character Michael Dorsey, after impersonating a woman, confesses to a deceived friend, "I was a better man with you as a woman than I ever was with a woman as a man . . . I've just got to learn to do it without the dress." And Tania Modleski interrogates "male weepies" — as Molly Haskell calls movies in which "women are cast out . . . to make room for Daddy in his new role as male mother" (Showalter 122) — suggesting that men may be appropriating women's roles as a ploy to expand patriarchy's power base: ". . . [M]en can want to *be* women and still hate and fear them" (78).

Granting Modleski's sensible vigilance about whether "representations of masculinity . . . contribute to or . . . undermine the feminist project" (92), I would caution that the urgency of men becoming feminized and good fathers is such that we must be careful not to throw out all men with "Man," good fathers with absent or prima donna ones. As Hélène Cixous writes, "Let's get away from the dialectic which has it that the only good father is a dead one" (1100-01). When, we must ask, is man as father an invader of women's territory, and when is he embracing — finally — the full repertoire of his humanity? Might fatherhood even come to have, as Dinnerstein suggests, a "specific poignance" in which "man's procreativity will seem . . . as concretely miraculous, as fraught with everyday magic, as woman's" (150)?

As a heterosexual male who claims to resist patriarchy and tries to be what E. Anthony Rotundo calls a "participant father," clearly I have a vested interest in exploring better possibilities for men and fathers. This "self-interest," though, need not exclude the interests of others. In fact, with Robert Vorlicky, I fear that everyone loses when men who "embrace feminist ideology" become "invisible" in art and life (276). It is, then, in the spirit of recovering a good father and a truly new man that I examine one of the few texts outside the *National Enquirer* in which men have "had babies": Leon Rooke's singular 1989 novel, *A Good Baby*.

•　•　•

Although Rooke has called Canada home since 1969, it is the twisted backwoods and distinctive accents of a grotesquely dysfunctional rural community in his native North Carolina that ground *A Good Baby*'s confrontation between two men embodying the worst and best of manhood. One man is Truman, a persistent and diabolical incarnation of patriarchy's "True Man"; the other is Raymond Toker, who, although also a most unlikely candidate for a Citizen of the Year Award, grows to be a new man and good father. Though they come from the same swamp — "garden and stinkpot both" (106) — Truman oozes evil the way his rotting teeth ooze pus while Toker develops as a loving human being. One man epitomizes father as sperm factory; the other becomes a nurturing parent. One enacts the Law of the Father; the other, a father's love. One is a walking argument for original sin — his perverse mix of TV evangelist Christian fundamentalism, lust, misogyny, violence, political conservatism, and sense of victimization making him sound more than a little like some "male rights" activists: "Women could . . . moan for they's plight on this earth . . . without never observin they's all males crucified and toothachey on Golgotha cross" (96); the other opens up the possibility for the men, women, and children of his community to "pile better stuff on" (287).

What prompts change in Toker's life is his discovery under a tree of a "good baby," the unfortunate female progeny of none other than Truman — who has "[oiled] the gate" (4) and put in his "tool" (90) — and Lena, a young woman Truman murders. Toker wraps his foundling in a fertilizer sack, feeds her tobacco juice, tries to persuade the community's women to take her, and ultimately learns from the baby how to live, love, and nurture. *A Good Baby*'s refrain "[W]as he its mama? Was he?" (28) eventually results in the feminization of Toker and, through him, the "humanization" of his sorry community.

The power of Rooke's morality play emanates from the dense background of evil and dysfunction out of which the simple human goodness of babies, fathers, and families appears as wonderful as it does improbable. From the first page, the reader is assaulted with images of dirt, stench, rot, smoke, and spit. A farmer named Moss senses a "deformity in the morning" (54); in fact, in this vivid locale, there is deformity morning, noon, and night. And nowhere are the deformities more pronounced than in men, women, and their relationships. The endless talk of the general store elders Wallace, Trout, and Hindmarch revolves around male and female anatomy, male sexual exploits, castration anxiety, and the essence of maleness and femaleness. Apropos the good baby, the sum of their sensitivity is:

> Nicest crease ever I saw, Wallace said. Thatern between her legs.
> Reckon itterd melt in your mouth, said Trout.
> Yessir, she'll break morn one heart, that there one will, Hindmarch added. (68)

The string of women to whom Toker offers the baby — (Bath)Roby (Josephine); Mrs. McElroy; Mrs. Priddy; Sarah, wife of the storekeeper, Calvin; Mrs. Sprockett; Mrs. Looper; (Cherub) Sorrel; the wife of Spigot; and Dolly Bellhop — are as maladjusted as the men. Married couples fare no better. Calvin, the storekeeper, and Sarah carry on "the rigorous soldiering of married life" (66). When Sarah asks for a nipple for the baby's bottle, Calvin says, "I see me one nipple in a year I'm happy. I see me two I'd faint dead to the floor" (69); for Sarah, on the other hand, Calvin has "not climbed over on me in three months" (202).

Truman, not surprisingly, comes from an extremely dysfunctional family. Near the end of the novel, when he is trying — and failing — to understand the stories of old Hindmarch, Truman recalls that his guardian "hadn't never bin a storyteller like this old man. Ye asked that bastard something and he'd slap off your head" (223). Significantly, Truman is missing out on the stories that a *present father* might have told him. More surprisingly, Toker and Roby, who become the good baby's "true parents," come from families no less dysfunctional — making their change in the novel all the more dramatic. Roby's father went crazy, hung her brother from a tree, and kept her mother and Roby at bay until he shot himself. Toker's father "was like to run everybody down . . . But he was the good'un; Mama was worse" (81). Toker realizes his own unlikely potential as a father: "The thing is, baby . . . you heard the story of your own self tole the way our mama and daddy ever day tole it to us, and the wonder is you'd ever even bother to stand up" (103).

If Truman and Toker are doubles, children of the same soil, they are also polar opposites. Truman sullies heterosexual love and procreation, while Toker's courting of Roby has all the earmarks of a teenager's first date: in Sarah's words, Toker is "nearabouts as innocent as that baby" (204). Truman is possessive of women: "How many you given it to?" (11); Toker is not: "If a thousand done hadder, I wouldn't mind bein a thousand and one" (41). Truman is territorial about his baby: ". . . [I]s it hisn or mine is the question I'd ask . . . If she's mine then that fresh-face won't a dog-lap away from my leavins" (93-94); even at the end of the novel, Toker cannot quite believe the baby is his: "What will you name that baby? [Roby] asked . . . I don't know, he said. Is it mine to name?" (278).

Toker's desire for Roby is different from Truman's lust — there is a "maybe" about it, a wish, a hope, something that allows the beloved to remain a subject rather than being reduced to an object: ". . . [T]hat porch knee was bent to put a wrinkle in the green houserobe, with a little air to come thue where he was of a mind to go hisself . . . Maybe some bright day" (25). Toker recognizes the difference between instant gratification of sexual desire and consideration of Roby as a person: "He had a feeling, in that second, that he could cross to her, slide the robe from her shoulders, and the two satisfy whatever was this unspoken thing between them. She would join right in. But he had the feeling too that if he did so, did so now, she wouldn't never forgive him" (244). After a prolonged courtship, Toker touches flour on Roby's cheek (a "feminine" thing to do), Roby aggressively plants a long kiss on Toker's lips (a "masculine" thing to do), and they consummate their pent-up, passionate love.

For Truman, on the other hand, sex is a mechanical process and an instrument of power. His male fantasy is rife with clichéd hyperbole about his prowess and women's hunger for it: "I've known'um would stand on their heads . . . [p]rayin for a minute more of my time" (5). Sex and violence are inextricably linked, and men are naturally superior to women: "They ain't nothin executed [including Lena, tragically] ain't executed in accordance to laws known and writ, or yit to come down" (12). Man gives the command "Do the hucklebuck" and woman "bucked and groaned" (6). It is women's very nature to want men insatiably: ". . . [T]hey were that fragile in their wantin. They were that hungerin in their need to have you do it . . . It was they whole essence . . ." (12-13). Sex is an error in Creation, dirty, unavoidable, and a plague on men because it involves *touching*: "No, he'd not touch women again. He'd done that and propagated his seed as the Book commanded and that ugliness was behind him now. . . . Best ye dribbled your wad into copious snowbank. Thaterd be a better way than touching" (262). Apparently forgetting his dribbling solution, Truman later fantasizes about the sister of his murdered "wife," Lena: "He'd wed her, and spread her, and let God take the rap for whatever eyesore her loins hatched up. *I do*, he tried to say. *I do, and will, and have*" (297). If ever there were a rallying cry for patriarchy, that "I do, and will, and have" is it. Man is action, man is will, man owns woman and *does* with her what he *will*. Man and God are "comminglers" both, women merely the dirty objects of commingling.

It is a kind of miracle that in the same sick world haunted by Truman, Rooke creates a man and baby who transform their community. Not that Raymond Toker is "naturally" good. Quite the opposite: he is "hell-for-leather . . . A draggy-mouth boy" (102); he has "[b]eat up two deputies . . . tore up a bawdy house . . . [p]ut two more in the hospital at a dice-hot game" (119); while his mother set fire to house and family, he was drinking in the tavern, "[l]ike Daddy like son" (112). Toker himself is surprised that the good baby comes into his life: "I do wonder why I was the one set up to find you" (50). But find the good baby Raymond Toker does — perhaps because "unlike some my heart ain't yet been harden" (31). Not only does he find the baby, but in a "magic realism" which is more than metaphor, he *gives birth* to her. While it is Lena who gives *physical* birth to the baby, just as it is her murderer Truman who physically *fathers* that baby, it is Raymond Toker, an imperfect man in a wretched community, who truly gives birth to the abandoned baby. When Toker finds the baby under the tree, he could have, as Roby points out, left the baby there: "Now if I found myself a baby in the woods it wouldn't break my stride one fathom" (31). But Toker does break his stride, and in so doing, begins to construct a new earth, if not a new heaven, in a world that most decidedly needs both.

In short, the unlikely Toker *has a baby*. The fertilizer *sack* is his amniotic *sac*, in which he "carries" the baby to term: "Goddamn baby, you thought it weighed not an ounce till you'd carried it long as he had" (29). From this sac(k), he delivers his offspring: "Toker . . . [extracted] the baby from wet burlap, his hand cupping the baby's icy bottom, tugging the infant forth" (62) followed by the afterbirth: "The blue flesh smelt of moldy fertilizer. And something else too . . . Dead cats, it smelt like" (63). The old men in the store recognize Toker as the baby's mother: "You give birth to it yourself or you have hep? Cackle, cackle. Air your nipples sore?" (63), even though Toker himself is reluctant to admit it: "Could be the little nose needed reaming. But he won't its mama" (73). As a first-time "mother," Toker examines his baby, wonders at his creation: "Was the one leg twisty? The head looked way bigger than the body . . . It didn't have no eyebrows. The top of the head was a pinkish swirl of blue veins" (73). Whose body, one wonders, is Rooke writing here? The male body? The female? The father's? Mother's? Parent's?: "You kept wanting to rub [the baby's head] . . . [Y]ou wanted to nudge your cheek up against it. You wanted to nuzzle it, to let your lips graze . . . You rubbed it and the softness spilled all inside you, made your own bones crumble" (73).

Although the baloney, sardines, Dr. Pepper, and marshmallows Toker feeds his baby would not meet the nutritional guidelines even of this backwoods community, what really matters, as Roby points out, is "have you got the breastworks to feed [the baby]" (26). Of course, Toker doesn't, and yet, in a way, he does: "He swung the baby over to his lap. The nipple [of the bottle] grazed the baby's lips and immediately she pitched her belly, flung her arms wildly, taking greedily to sucking, the eyes bulging, intent on him" (118). Indeed, Toker's promise that the baby will "be breast-cradled by mornin" (60) is fulfilled not by the women he assumes are the only ones capable, but by Toker, whose "milk," significantly, has not yet "come in."

When his baby gets dirty, this nurturing father washes her: "When it gits right ripe in the nose I hightail off to creekwater and let the current take the worst out" (33). While the old men in the store drone on about "Judith Iscaret" and innocence, Toker asks for a washcloth "to cleanse this baby" (72). As the baby wriggles, makes faces, and kicks water, Toker asks what every parent asks: "What's your name, baby? . . . Where'd you come from?" (78). Toker proceeds to play with his baby, "in no hurry to rise and get on with what must be got on with," not realizing that he is doing what must be got on with: "You stuck a finger in the baby's belly she went all giggly. You tickled her feet she went all zany" (163).

In his evil parody of fatherhood, Truman says: "Makes me right mushy . . . [t]o see a baby" (87) and "God's breath. That's what they are . . . Precious as honey in a bee's hive . . . I've got one myself. Yessir, I'm a dingdong daddy of the mountains and slaphappy proud, same as you" (90). What makes Toker's paternity different from Truman's is that it is defined not biologically by the mere act of conception, nor by patriarchy's laws of ownership, but by his very presence as a father. Sorrel casts doubt on the foundations of Truman's kind of paternity, wondering "[w]hy it would matter to a man whose it is, since they don't raise them anyhow" (121). But Toker is raising his child, and that gives him a different, more "motherly," perspective. At first, Toker tries to deny his bonding with the baby, protesting too much:

> Toker wondered what it was he felt about this baby. He hadn't hardly felt nothing this morning, finding her in the woods. Except surprise, he'd felt that. Consternation, he'd felt that. Okay, he'd gone into a headspin, so he had, but anyone would. But he'd carried it all day and felt nothing, othern how to move it over into another person's keeping . . . [A]ll a baby was was worthless . . . He could look at her now and feel nothing. Sorrow for her plight, shivers for her future, some little morsel of grief for the waste and folly, but that was all. (74)

Others know better. "Landsakes, Toker," Sarah observes. "You look plain lovesick" (74). Toker becomes protective, wondering if Roby "should talk this way in front of a baby" (36). At times, he becomes annoyed with his child:

> The baby pulled at his hair, and Toker slapped at her hand.
> Stop that, he said. Then when the baby scrunched up her face to cry he held her to him, rocking the poor lost thing.
> Sorry, he said. Sorry, baby. My mood today is rotten. (181)

With tenderness, he tries to imagine the unimaginable — what life would be like without his baby: "He wondered had she been dead would he of got his spade and buried her. The way you would a sparrow tumbled from the nest. You'd heel out a spot, you'd smooth that spot over with earth. You'd hide it away with leaf and twig" (71).

Although the good baby is the catalyst, Toker is initiated into his role as mother/father by women; in turn, he helps heal both women and men in his community. It is because he has the good baby that he can relate to these others, but it is also through these others that he comes to relate to the good baby. When Sorrel offers to let the baby (and Toker) suckle her generous, though not lactating, breasts, Toker extracts from Sorrel neither milk nor sexual satisfaction, but information about feeding babies. Freed from the rigid gender roles of a strictly sexual relationship — the only kind she has known with men — Sorrel offers Toker woman-to-woman advice: "You git pregnant, she said, your skin you can't do nothin a-tall with. Don't let no one tell you different" (126). In life after "man" and "woman," the two become able to appreciate each other as people: "Sorrel . . . let her one hand fold into his . . . like a child would . . . I love this earth, she said then. I love it to my very most marrow. Don't you?" (127).

Similarly, Toker and Sarah, a woman "worn out . . . by all the killing" of men in her dreams (80), are able to dismantle the gender wall between them. Having just bathed his baby, Toker sees Sarah's bedroom through "feminine" eyes: "He could see a knicknack nailed to the wall . . . dried flowers, or straw . . . white lacy cloth spread over a sewing machine . . . He'd always liked those. He wondered she didn't sew up the hem . . . on [her] tatty robe . . . " (80). In turn, Sarah notices a change in the Toker who holds a baby, a change that persuades her she might risk talking "woman to woman" with him: "I've got to talk to someone, she said. All I can hope is you'll do" (200). When Toker is less than feminine in his response, Sarah bitterly comments, "You was a woman I could talk to you . . . But your gruesome gender wants everything closed . . . Keep it all sealed up and save it, like a Christmas puddin" (201-202). When Sarah tells Toker she was "had at age five by my brothers" and claims that Cal would say it was her own fault, "[t]he same as you are thinkin," Toker responds in a more appropriately feminine way: "I'm not thinkin, Sarah. I'm thunk out, on the vissitude's front. Though I'm sorry you had such trouble" (202). Toker tries to get away from her, and she yanks him down again: "You don't have to like what you hear, she said. All you have to do is listen" (202). Sarah initiates Toker forcibly into womanhood, squeezing his hand to her breast until she cuts off his circulation:

> Talk to me the way a woman would, she said. Try.
>
> Toker squirmed. Not a word came to him.
>
> You're not tryin. Are ye? she asked.
>
> I'm tryin, he said. I'm thinkin I might ask your recipe for scalloped potatoes . . .
>
> She pressed his hand down harder.
>
> What's travelin thue your mind now, Toker?
>
> I was wonderin will my own life be more plentiful, will it have more nourishment, I ever hit forty-two myself . . .
>
> Yes, yes. I can see another woman might of said that. Now try again. Say somethin else. The sort of thing a woman would. (203)

As Carolyn G. Heilbrun points out, the "friendship of a man and woman" such as the one Toker and Sarah discover "is one of the most unexplored of all human experiences . . . " (100). "[W]hat has a man ever known?" asks Sarah. "I don't know . . ." Toker replies. "We are both pioneers in that regard" (205). Indeed, pioneers they are. Writing of recent, male-authored, American novels, Donald J. Greiner notes that "novels reflect culture, and culture in America means separation of male and female" (7). Significantly, *A Good Baby* offers alternatives to this dominant discourse in male-female friendships. The relationship between Sarah and Toker, crossing barriers of both age and gender, becomes an especially hopeful, perhaps revolutionary, beginning point for new relationships between men and women.

Men are also healed through Toker's healing. A seminal — significantly, there is no male metaphor for "pregnant" — scene has a young boy with "[a] long nail . . . protruding from the blackened sole" of his foot come seeking his absent father. Toker is the only man who offers to help the boy, but he misreads the moral of the incident, saying, ". . . That's what comes of bein born without shoes . . . " (187). The boy's blackened "soul," though, results less from shoelessness than fatherlessness. The question is not whether Toker will buy his baby shoes, but whether he will be there for her. Inspired by Toker's example, the other men help the boy too. When Cal distracts the boy so Toker can get the nail out, the boy is surprised not by Cal's offering him candy but by the dramatic change in men who, by becoming mothers, have become better (and present) fathers (187-88). Though no Doctor Spock, Cal even begins offering parenting advice:

> Nine times a day you have to change a baby's bottom . . . Or fourteen, I forget which . . .
> Toker heaved the baby over his shoulder and belched her.
> A good belch make the day, Calvin said. (189)

Toker's feminization, it should be noted, is additive, not subtractive. His discovery of the "feminine" in no way makes him "effeminate." He is not emasculated; rather, he becomes a "new, improved" hero, "a man with more." What Terry Eagleton describes as "the 'feminizing' of the aggressive, ego-centred hero by the gentle, conciliatory . . . heroine" (qtd. in Eagleton, Mary 89) does not apply here: Toker is never aggressive and ego-centred, and Roby, for that matter, rarely gentle or conciliatory. Janet Todd notes "a common habit of female writers — the feminizing of men, either to master them and take away their otherness or to soften their patriarchal potential by allowing them qualities usually assumed to be female . . ." (3). But Toker is not "mastered"; instead, his addition of the "feminine" qualities so long denied men by patriarchy makes him more fully empowered as a human being. As Sarah recognizes, this good baby "radiates a certain power" (205) for Toker: "I can see you held that baby long enough, you'd holder how a woman would. You set there long enough, holdin her, you might could talk to me" (204). In fact, when Sarah hopes that Toker "will do" as a woman to talk to, she grabs his hand and says that a "woman needs a strong man to hold onto" (200). Sarah wants Toker to be a (strong) *man* who can talk to her as a (sensitive) *woman*; what Sarah and Toker are groping towards is the realization that both men and women can be both strong and sensitive.

Interestingly, it is Roby — like many in our world — who initially fails to appreciate the newly developed "feminine" mode of this new man and good father: "Put her down, she said. I can't stand seein a grown man holdin no snot child like it was the Prince of Grace" (231-32).

George Bernard Shaw quipped, "Of the two lots, the woman's lot of perpetual motherhood, and the man's of perpetual babyhood, I prefer the man's" (qtd. in Nicholson i). Toker, though, goes beyond perpetual baby-hood, beyond even the perpetual adolescenthood endemic to so many heroes in Canadian and American literature, to include adult fatherhood in his repertoire. Unlike Truman, for whom a penis is a lethal weapon, and the old men, for whom an erection is a tall tale, Toker discovers ways of being a man which offer an alternative to the remarkable aberration of human development Emmanuel Reynaud describes so well:

> Man turns a little bit of soft, delicate and highly sensitive flesh into the factor which bestows power on him; he is blind to the warmth, the fragility and the hypersensitivity of his penis . . . He tries . . . to desensitize the whole organ . . . to give it the coldness and the hard-ness of metal. What he loses in enjoyment he hopes to compensate for in power; but if he gains an undeniable power symbol, what pleasure can he really feel with a weapon between his legs? (41-42)

For Truman, man's finger, phallus, gun, and speech are all intercon-nected weapons to be rammed down Lena's throat:

> [H]is finger shoved violently into her open mouth. . . His finger was in up to the shaft . . .
> That how you goin to feel . . . Like you done bit off somethin you never seen, big as a hefty log. And that somethin gone git big-ger and bigger till you think it . . . mean to gobble you whole. (10)

How radically different, during Toker's bathing of the good baby, is the baby's trying to pull "Toker's hand into its pumping mouth . . . The baby . . . whooped out great volleys of mirth . . . [T]he baby's big I-don't-want-to-miss-nothing eyes never once left [Toker's] face" (78-79).

• • •

My celebration of the "man who has babies" should not imply there are no problematic gender issues in *A Good Baby*. Toker's romantic, sexual relationship with Roby, for example, problematizes male-female relationships as much as his friendship with Sarah re-visions them. Toker's feminization seems to assume both Adrienne Rich's "compulsory heterosexuality" and the age-old myth of male-female complementarity in its reliance on actual women (the good baby included) for men's feminization: ". . . [H]e wanted to scamper inside [Roby] . . . [t]o git down there and claim some of that softness for his own self" (73). This locks men, yet again, into being vampires, and women, yet again, into being objects (albeit of adulation rather than abuse). Toker is sometimes more concerned with being a "gentleman" than with being a "gentle man," as preoccupied as "moral conservatives" with women "civilizing" men through the exchange of sex. Roby, a woman concerned with Danish furniture and gourmet cooking, civilizes Toker; Toker acts like a "gentleman" because that's how he can get Roby and her "cheese": "This Don Wan business, it had its rewards [Toker] reckoned. It was worth gittin the hang of, it paid off this well" (236-37).

Toker's heterosexual love also assumes the idea of the nuclear family: "Toker . . . went down to stand beside Roby . . . holding himself there as if he imagined someone might any second be coming up from the road to take a Kodak shot of them . . . He had that Kodak man out in the yard, he'd say to him, Hold it a minute . . . Step back a mite and git a snapshot with the baby in it. Git us all three" (243-44). Given the disastrously dysfunctional nuclear families which haunt *A Good Baby*, the envisioning of Toker's, Roby's, and the baby's family as *the* future salvation for the community seems about as likely as a baby who flies. And speaking of flying babies, this good baby actually soars on tobacco juice, without once having colic in the night — a "magic realism" many parents would kill for. Similarly, while the novel's setting and characters bring new meaning to the word "poverty," the political realities of being poor are curiously elided. What, one wonders, is Toker's day job when he is not picking up babies and pretty ladies?

The most resonant questions about Rooke's novel, though, come from Modleski's critique of recent movies "redeeming and celebrating fatherhood" (76). Is Rooke's project in *A Good Baby* crippled, for example, by the same limitations Modleski sees in Hollywood's *Three Men and a Baby*? Although recognizing that *Three Men* "speaks to a legitimate desire on the part of women for men to become more involved in interpersonal relationships, to be more nurturant as individuals, and to assume greater responsibility for childcare" (88), Modleski questions "men's desire to usurp women's procreative function" (77); a "*male* desire to undergo virgin birth, to dispense with the woman's part in conception altogether" (78-79); the sidelining of mature women (78); male bonding being effected "through the agency of a baby girl, rather than through the exchange of women" (82); men "[embracing] the state of fatherhood . . . [but refusing] to grow up" (83); and, most damningly: "That Walt Disney should produce and audiences receive as 'heartwarming,' a film laden with jokes about a female baby as an adequate object of sexual desire for three aging bachelors . . . is certainly disturbing" (78).

Obviously, these comments are pertinent to a novel in which a female baby and her "male mother" transform a community after her real female mother is conveniently murdered. However, Rooke's project, I maintain, is significantly different from Hollywood's in *Three Men*. Raymond Toker assumes the role of parenthood without appropriating the role of women: far from suffering uterus envy, his primary objective from the start is to ditch the baby. He does not ask to be the good baby's parent; instead, he responds to her need. He welcomes women's participation in the raising of his daughter. He does not so much bond with other men through the good baby as he reaches out to share his healing with them. He sucks no one dry, preferring to give back the gift of love to all. Though he has every reason in the world to remain as "weighty and miserable in [his] outlook as them diseased trees" (103), Toker does not refuse to grow up; after he and Roby make love, it is Toker who remembers "Damn! Where'd I leave the baby?" (250). Finally, the "three aging bachelors" in *A Good Baby* who *do* treat the good baby as a sex object are most decidedly not the same as Raymond Toker, the good father I find here.

"Toker" is, in fact, a "giver" more than he is a "taker." Far from being imperialistic, he has a childlike wonder about what it would be like to "understand" an "other": "You took up residence inside anothern's skin . . . you might could know what was goin on. But he had his doubts. It would be foreign territory, he guessed, whether you were inside somebody else's frame, or tryin to see daylight from your own" (200). Against Truman's deterministic world, what Toker opens up in Rooke's "jimcracky, hodgepodge of universe" (158) is the possibility for change. The good baby may be afflicted with mosquito bites, but, through Toker's intervention, she is not hit with "God's fist" (15) from birth. When Lena (in her fatalistic powerlessness) concludes that "I ain't never known nobody was . . . [a]ble to hep hisself. Or herself either," Truman (in his self-centred abuse of power) responds, "I've hepped myself ever minute" (12). Truman misreads "hepping" oneself, for his problem is that he quite literally cannot help himself: he and Lena, man and woman, are determined by the "laws" of God, Satan, nature, human nature, and patriarchy. In such a world, Truman is trapped (albeit with male privilege) in "a picture postcard of aimless dark" (7); worse, Lena is condemned by original sin to eternal damnation.

Against this backdrop of original sin, determinism, and evil, even Truman recognizes Toker's radiance: "Now that fresh-face back yonder, holdin that baby. Could be . . . [he] is knowin somethin I ought to should know . . . But you weren't put in this world to go perfumed and lily-white as a maiden in clover. Now were ye?" (93). Toker, Roby, and the good baby might disagree: "Yes, ye — and we — were." What, after all, does Toker's name signify in this fictional universe? In one sense, "Toker" means that when he first spotted the baby under a tree, he didn't pass her by, but, like the Good Samaritan, "took her." But Toker's name on his road sign is also "mistaken" as "Taper" (19-20); his first name, Raymond ("Ray-Monde," the Light of the World) and his "mistaken" surname suggest he is an image of hope, a possible replacement for his no-good brother LeRoy (LeRoy, the King of Patriarchy). "You gone think the universe done flipped over" Truman boasts of his sexual prowess (6); but the universe flips over and true intercourse between the sexes begins only when Toker picks up this "goddamn wonder" (37) of a baby.

In a world dominated by the "laws" of "Tru-man nature," the possibilities of change embodied by Raymond Toker make *A Good Baby* a profoundly optimistic novel, a fictional world which tellingly destabilizes the "real world" discourses of western culture. As Mikhail Bakhtin writes: ". . . [S]uch a hero casts an energetic reproach at the world order . . . as if he were talking not about the world but with the world" ("From" 798). While Rosemary Sullivan is thus exactly right to highlight the "healing" powers of *A Good Baby*, she may get the novel's function backwards when she argues that "its exquisite achievement is that it's slice-of-life reality" (54). As Rooke himself suggests, ". . . [M]y stuff . . . may be of the real world, but it was not found by me in the real world. I have by writing it put it into the real world" ("An Interview" 130). With his birthing, fathering, befriending, loving, his constructing of his masculine-feminine self(s), Toker's re-vision of manhood and fatherhood becomes a gift to, more than a reflection of, our "real" and pathetically underimagined world. Toker's (and Rooke's) "re-vision" may even give the lie to Bakhtin's contention that "images of virtue . . . have never been successful in the novel" ("Discourse" 344). For much as Truman is one of the most vivid and persistent personifications of evil in fiction, it is Raymond Toker, in his simple goodness and with the help of a good baby who flies, who offers us a humane path through the "stinkpot and garden" of our gendered world.

BIBLIOGRAPHY

Bakhtin, Mikhail. "Discourse in the Novel." *The Dialogic Imagination: Four Essays by M.M. Bakhtin*. Ed. Michael Holquist. Trans. Caryl Emerson and Holquist. Austin: U of Texas P, 1981. 259-422.

——. "*Problems of Dostoevsky's Poetics.*" *The Critical Tradition: Classic Texts and Contemporary Trends*. Ed. David H. Richter. New York: St. Martin's, 1989. 797-98.

Braidotti, Rosi. "Envy: Or With My Brains and Your Looks." *Men in Feminism*. Eds. Alice Jardine and Paul Smith. 1987. New York: Routledge, 1989. 233-41.

Cixous, Hélène. "The Laugh of the Medusa." *The Critical Tradition: Classic Texts and Contemporary Trends*. Ed. David H. Richter. New York: St. Martin's, 1989. 1090-1102.

Clatterbaugh, Kenneth. *Contemporary Perspectives on Masculinity: Men, Women, and Politics in Modern Society*. Boulder: Westview, 1990.

Dinnerstein, Dorothy. *The Mermaid and the Minotaur: Sexual Arrangements and Human Malaise*. New York: Harper & Row, 1976.

Eagleton, Mary, ed. *Feminist Literary Theory: A Reader*. Oxford: Blackwell, 1986.

Greiner, Donald J. *Women Enter the Wilderness: Male Bonding and the American Novel of the 1980s*. Columbia, SC: U of South Carolina P, 1991.

Grosskurth, Phyllis. "The New Psychology of Women." *The New York Review of Books*. October 24, 1991. 25-32.

Heilbrun, Carolyn G. *Toward Androgyny: Aspects of Male and Female in Literature*. 1964. London: Victor Gollancz, 1973.

Johnson, Diane. "Something for the Boys." *The New York Review of Books*. January 16, 1992. 13-17.

Koestenbaum, Wayne. *Double Talk: The Erotics of Male Literary Collaboration*. New York: Routledge, 1989.

Matthews, Mike. Rev. of *A Good Baby*, by Leon Rooke. *The Malahat Review* 90 (1990): 118-19.

Modleski, Tania. *Feminism Without Women: Culture and Criticism in a "Postfeminist" Age*. New York: Routledge, 1991.

Nicholson, John. *Men and Women: How Different Are They?* Oxford: Oxford UP, 1984.

Owens, Craig. "Outlaws: Gay Men in Feminism." *Men in Feminism*. Eds. Alice Jardine and Paul Smith. 1987. New York: Routledge, 1989. 219-32.

Reynaud, Emmanuel. *Holy Virility: The Social Construction of Masculinity*. 1981. Trans. Ros Schwartz. London: Pluto, 1983.

Rich, Adrienne. "Compulsory Heterosexuality and Lesbian Existence." *Blood, Bread, and Poetry: Selected Prose 1979-1985*. New York: Norton, 1986. 23-75.

Rooke, Leon. *A Good Baby*. Toronto: McClelland & Stewart, 1989.

——. "An Interview with Leon Rooke." By Geoff Hancock. *Canadian Fiction Magazine* 38 (1981): 107-34.

——. "Leon Rooke: the Authorized Biography." *Canadian Fiction Magazine* 38 (1981): 145-47.

Rotundo, E. Anthony. "Patriarchs and Participants: A Historical Perspective on Fatherhood." *Beyond Patriarchy: Essays by Men on Pleasure, Power, and Change*. Ed. Michael Kaufman. Toronto: Oxford UP, 1987. 64-80.

Showalter, Elaine. "Critical Cross-Dressing: Male Feminists and the Woman of the Year." *Men in Feminism*. Eds. Alice Jardine and Paul Smith. 1987. New York: Routledge, 1989. 116-32.

Sullivan, Rosemary. "A Good Baby." Rev. of *A Good Baby*, by Leon Rooke. *Brick* 40 (1991): 54-56.

Todd, Janet. Introduction. *Men by Women*. Ed. Janet Todd. New York: Holmes & Meier, 1981. 1-8.

Tootsie. Dir. Sydney Pollack. By Larry Gelbart, Murray Schisgal, and Elaine May. With Dustin Hoffman, Teri Garr, Jessica Lange, Sydney Pollack, Bill Murray. 1982.

Vorlicky, Robert. "(In)Visible Alliances: Conflicting 'Chronicles' of Feminism." *Engendering Men: The Question of Male Feminist Criticism*. Eds. Joseph A. Boone and Michael Cadden.

Leon Rooke's Political Satires

Mike Matthews

A primary pleasure in reading the fiction of Leon Rooke is a thrall of uncertainty about where the experience will lead us — where is he going this time? In any new story, Rooke, always idiosyncratic in style, is likely to be doing something different in subject or genre. Fantasy, surreal extravagance, allegory, and stream of consciousness are only some of the forms or genres of his work. Given a writer of such versatility, a writer whose long-term purpose seems to be to keep readers both surprised and delighted, we can expect entertainment. The comic mode is frequent, and some of the strongest and most enjoyable of Rooke's comic stories are his political satires.

"The creation of any authentic, living character is political," asserted Rooke in the 1980s to Peter O'Brien's question of whether he writes against the world's evils.[1] Explicitly political milieus and characters, and attention to public events and issues have been frequent in Rooke's fiction since that time. The weasel manager of the Henny Penny nursery and the racist birth control messiah in Africa in the 1984 collection *Sing Me No Love Songs I'll Say You No Prayers* show private minds in public places, while the man who sneers at the woman who talks to horses stands, in his corrosive, sexist bigotry, for whole nations of western men.

At the same time, Rooke seems unable to disavow any major character, any personality through whose eyes he has looked at the world. Much of the profound, dark chill which elevates *A Good Baby* beyond melodrama comes from parts of the novel where we are forced by point of view into intimate acquaintance with the mind of the murderous itinerant preacher. "Sixteen-Year-Old Susan March Confesses to the Innocent Murder of All

---

[1] *So to Speak: Interviews with Contemporary Canadian Writers.* Montreal: Vehicle Press, 1987, 292.

the Devious Strangers Who Would Drag Her Down" pulls us, headlong and pell-mell, alongside its speaker, up close, breathing or holding breath in unison with that frantic, hyperextended young woman. Simone Vauthier has observed "the feverish urge to speak that motivates so many of Rooke's characters."[2] And often Rooke's characters will sound like Leon Rooke. Their verbal style will echo the colloquial, regional, sometimes archaic, and also inventive idiom of the author. It is the default style that his characters, speaking or narrating, move into. A Leon Rooke is trying to get into (or is it out of?) Rooke's characters.

But what is Leon Rooke? A tower of Babel perhaps, a compendium of dozens of languages, dialects, accents, and tongues. Rooke has said that he finds it "peculiar that many writers are only willing to write out of one voice. This may be because I don't have a single voice."[3] Above all, Rooke's fictional worlds are inhabited ones, brimming with personality, with idiolects, distinct lingo, rhythms and tropes of singular, audacious beings, and rich with the jostling encounters of their different moods, different selves. Rooke himself is a storehouse, a granary of personalities as well as voices. Personality is a dominant feature of Rooke's fiction, where nearly always a situation is intensely felt — adored, loathed, fought, protested, celebrated. Nearly always a central consciousness asserts its passion, passionately defines itself. Feeling and its articulation is everything; where and when matter little. Time and place in Rooke's fiction are often merely nominal. Where does Susan March live? With her mother.

In 1989, Rooke, twenty years resident in B.C., moved to Ontario. The same year, Oolichan Books, a small but heads-up west-coast publishing company, produced *How I Saved the Province*. According to the cataloguing information on the title page, subjects of the book are British Columbia and United States politics and government, though the longest story "Come Hear the Blind Man Sing" belies that description. Set nominally near the Nass River in northern B.C., it has numerous references to "B———" ("Bennett" in a version of the story published earlier in *Descant*) who, described as a "sonafabitch" and a "thug-asshole," is a shadowy authority-figure and scapegoat who might be read as a former premier of the

---

[2] *Writers in Aspic*, edited by John Metcalf. Montreal: Vehicule Press, 1988, 230.

[3] Hancock, Geoff, *Canadian Writers at Work*. Toronto: Oxford University Press, 1987, 181.

province. Yet no reading so reductively specific is warranted. The story is kin to others by Rooke where a man and woman are hobbled together in an allegorical journey expressing a relationship which is both imprisoning and rancorous, yet committed and unbreakable.

The story "Saving the Province" is the most purely satirical, the least formed to purposes beyond the examination and ridicule of identifiable aspects of public life and politics in British Columbia in the 1980s. From Zundel to "Zalm-bam," from government scams to corporate kleptomania, the targets of Rooke's satire stand in clear light, and receive that mixture of wrath and laughter that brings together in concert the writer of satire and his reading audience.

"Saving the Province" addresses issues and personalities in the political life of British Columbia in the mid-eighties. Its protagonist-narrator is a freelance spin doctor ready for hire by any political interest — preferably on the right side of the political spectrum. Apart from the spin doctor himself, the Social Credit government of Premier Bill Vander Zalm, corporate kingpin Jim Pattison, and Holocaust-denier Ernst Zundel are the major targets of the satire. There are deft thrusts at a number of minor scandals and embarrassments of the day: a cabinet minister who made credit card payments to an escort service, a questionable real estate development in a highly visible downtown area of the provincial capital, and the discovery of the health minister's mother living in miserable conditions in a public long-term care facility — evidence of the minister's heartlessness rather than his probity in not taking advantage. As the spin doctor receives his bag of cash couriered from the Premier's "Think Tank" (the unfictioned Fraser Institute, a quasi-academic cabal of virulently right-wing economists) and prepares the public relations campaign, the satire spirals out into surrealism with references to "gunboats" and a "Reagan mural," and advocacy for the rights of the unborn.

Satire here moves into art. The spin doctor is an unprincipled hog, but his version of the right-to-lifer's credo has robust vitality: "Let the kid burp himself, that's what Zalmbam says, and he's right. But you let him out of the tummy first, we hold the line on that. You give that buster a chance."[4] The gendering of the foetus and the characterization of it as a "buster" raise questions about what sort of child the right-to-lifer seeks

---

[4] Rooke, Leon. *How I Saved the Province*. Lantzville: Oolichan Books, 1989, 30.

to foster and protect. Alarmingly, the cheers anticipated for the Holocaust-denier Zundel will, claims the flack, "pass like a panther's howl through the city."[5] Images of mass murder of the citizens are what the spin doctor offers as ultimate solutions for his government client: "Put a noose around their necks, call it necessary, call it God's wrathful vengeance."[6] Yet the sheer exuberance of this maniac carries the day for comedy.

Rooke's source for the setting of "Dust" is the 1986 International Exposition, the grandiloquent and tawdry Expo 86 in Vancouver. The unbridled, free-enterprise Social Credit provincial government had been in power for what seemed uninterrupted decades, and it knew that circuses were as vital as bread in keeping the favour of the voters. It used the burgeoning city of Vancouver, a prosperous, attractive and increasingly cosmopolitan town, as a showpiece, anticipating that if the Exposition drew most of its attendance from within British Columbia, and even from the city itself, the show would still be a tremendous success. Right they were. Preparations for the Exposition included building projects on the False Creek site, along with renovatory attention to city-centre neighbourhoods. Validating Rooke's satirical thrust in the story, there was indeed a concerted attempt to renovate some of the seedy hostelries in Vancouver's Downtown East-side district and to make them ready for visitors to the city, displacing long-term residents of these hotels and rooming houses. It was perhaps the reports in local newspapers that inspired Rooke, at that time living in Victoria, the provincial capital, with the germ of "Dust." The forlorn narrator, Jack, and his compatriots are in imminent danger of losing their homes to the wrecking ball of the developer or to the "sprucing up" (redecorating and raised rates) that were part of the Expo revamping.

When Princess Diana officially declared Expo 86 open in May of 1986, she did indeed falter and seem near falling as she concluded her brief ceremonial remarks. (It was speculated in the press that the Princess might be expecting a third child.) Rooke's Diana, idealized by the down-and-out narrator's fantasy, stands as a parody of the real Diana, all-too-publicly proclaiming her private needs and woes. Both Diana and her surrounding world of royal status and privilege and watchful, managing officialdom

---

[5] *Ibid.*, 31.

[6] *Ibid.*, 30.

and protocol are satirized. Diana far less, since Jack sees her adoringly and notes, incessantly, that ambiguous "wan" quality which was often projected by the Princess in her public appearances. The salt-in-the-dust hero is to take her "away from all this," and we read her presumed desire to escape from the royal world with sympathy. No such sympathy is invited for "the prince fella."

What makes this story a cutting political satire is exactly those features that carry it beyond the topical and critical. Rooke's mixing of la crème with the scum, forcing into collision the worlds of royalty and commoner, is one of the oldest character tropes in the grand book of story. The pattern of action, tragic or at least pathetic, is also the traditional one. Odds are against the commoner ever winning the princess; down in the mire, the dust, he can only dream of her. She remembers her duty and her place, or, as here, she simply recedes, wilting, into the circle of her consort, her attendants, and the various dignitaries and officials. Conversely, Jack moves from his role as victim and buffoon to the ironist's position, and then beyond that, when he remarks that Diana's clothes might be seen as "a colossal forging of human sin and a crime which would cause God to thunder and drop to his knees in screaming rage."[7] This is no longer the Jack who is dreamily infatuated with the "wan" Diana, who beseeches him to "love me, Jack . . . polish my basin, Jack."[8] He is no longer Jack who "snoozled my lips against her neck."[9] Rooke has, smoothly and without signalling, shifted gears and moved into the fast and furious lane of direct invective.

In "Up a Tree" Rooke uses the title phrase to literally denote the perch which a wife, a woman never directly present in the story, takes as a refuge: she's been chased there by the police, by the barking of a neighbour's dog, and by her own alarm at the state of the world, in particular the state of U.S. foreign policy in Central America as observed in the actions of such figures as President Ronald Reagan and funds-smuggler Oliver North. Taking that title phrase further, Rooke torques it into meaning something like "beside herself," "at her wits' end," "out of her mind."

---

[7] *Ibid.*, 11.

[8] *Ibid.*, 19.

[9] *Ibid.*, 17.

Out of their minds also are those nearby or gathered below around this treebound citizen: her husband, neighbours, the dog whose barking drove her higher up the tree, the police, the President of the United States, and a media reporter questioning anyone he can collar for a statement, without regard for relevance or sanity. The woman whose alarm and whose putative threat of dire action began the whole thing is not heard from on her own behalf, and is seen only by her husband, up the tree: "Her eyes are glazed, she moans a lot."[10]

Where "Saving the Province" focuses on the freewheeling and conscienceless political fixer, and "Dust" on the displaced down-and-outer victimized by both cold officialdom and his own overheated fantasies, "Up a Tree" moves gradually in ever-widening circles of alarm and implication from the hysterical tree-climber to the U.S. national capital, with the focus moving erratically from person to person, in a crazy rhythm of "he said no; what I really said was" driven by the relentless but directionless (and ultimately pointless) inquiry of the roving reporter. The story ends with President Reagan's demonic fantasy of digging a new Panama canal in Nicaragua, closer to home, and with the Duke, John Wayne, checking in with a sound-bite from beyond the grave — deft application of a traditional feature in satire, the dialogue of the dead.[11]

The pell-mell rants and expostulations from the various single-tracked minds we encounter through the story convey the idea that politics encourages and reinforces deafness in citizens and their representatives alike. As often in Rooke, and particularly in these political satires, we hear a polyphony of self-obsessed characters with an unholy mix of private and public concerns on their minds, none of them able to usefully make a connection with the next person, if only because the media microphone or notebook has been pushed in front of their faces. In this mad world, Slipper the dog is hardly more of a solipsist than the humans around him.

Who Goes There (1998) asks its question over and over as it surveys a cavalcade of crooks, politicos, hangers-on, functionaries, floozies, thugs, and oddball bystanders enmeshed in a skein of schemes and counter-

---

10 *Ibid.*, 42.

11 Guilhamet, Leon, *Satire and the Transformation of Genre*. Philadelphia: University of Pennsylvania Press, 1987, 39.

schemes, revenges and retributions, in and near Washington D.C., sometime recently. Its humour arises from the aplomb with which Rooke presents the scruffy, low-rent, matter-of-fact brutality of American politics and life in the nation's capital. So quietly and silkily has the author woven various topical issues and references to contemporary personalities into this novel, and so oblique and cater-gaited is his approach to his characters and themes, that explication of the satire is a formidable challenge. Even with an extensive acquaintance with recent American political history one is bound to miss many allusions, many nudges. Clearly, at least, the story is set somewhere in the early days of the Clinton administration. Clinton and his First Lady make appearances. With casual aplomb, Rooke gives us transcripts of conversations which link the President intimately with murderous racketeer Zippo Giocametti. This is extravagant joking, almost beyond satire. What goes, here? The title sounds an ominous note. "Who goes there?" is a query of identity. Friend or foe? It suggests war, sentries, military camps, the opening scenes of *Hamlet*. Something is coming, something not yet eager to make itself known. Is it a threat, or just a joke? All laughter is nervous; or, as Mavis Gallant suggested, humour is the other side of anxiety. In the darkness and grotesquery of Rooke's political satire, threat and laughter are side by side and close at hand.

Yet satire in *Who Goes There* is only one band or stripe in a broad-spectrum examination of what one not entirely atypical neighbourhood on this planet might look like if viewed from a vantage point somewhere above the earth by sharp, super-telescopic eyes. Political satire set in the U.S.A. of the nineties is twinned with the older, perhaps perennial story of the American encounter between innocence and experience. The innocents are more than usually helpless, some mere victims who happen to be standing in the way at the wrong time, or unwitting intruders like Muriel Goering, who gets her "butt casked" for rudeness; or an "insultin' mouth" gets plastered into a showcase wall behind a portrait of General Lee on his white horse, surmounting fine Italian tilework.

The experienced are more than usually disabled, like Jude, the psychotic war hero with his leg harnesses, walker, and cocaine habit, or at odds with themselves, like Wally the doorman at Senator Cutt's apartment building: "Wally's bones seem to be at war one with the other."[12]

---

12 Rooke, Leon, *Who Goes There*. Toronto: Exile Editions, 1998, 84.

Some are at cross purposes with themselves or with the roles they inhabit. Zippo Giocametti, for instance, is an unlikely sort of gangster, a conscience-ridden softy, dilatory in his attention to the business of being a menace to all who cross his path. Instead of being feared, he is hen-pecked, bossed around by parents, by children, by the women in his life. He is held in contempt by his underlings, and patronized by his chief lieutenant. Altogether he is the Mafia don as Walter Matthau would have played him, hangdog and apologetic. Zippo spends the latter half of the novel confined to his bed, shot in the head, hallucinating, and probably dying.

No matter how filthy, unlikely, or low on any conceivable totem pole, Rooke's point of view shifts to include them. The utmost example must be the dying perceptions of the thug Lootz, shot in the head by Governor Orth. His bemused, dying-of-consciousness reflections give way to a view of things from just his eye, which sees a bug. Finally, it is simply the bug's view as, spraddled on the just-dead eye, it sits and shits and eats.

The rescue of Tabita Banta, the teenage intern, is just one strand in a skein of flowing and releasing movements in this novel. Many characters are freed from entrapments or entanglements, pulled out of something. Tabita has been a captive, part sex slave, part mannequin to model the "shapeless house dresses" of Senator's Cutt's dead mother. Previously she worked in her father's Eat-Rite food store in some "tidal burg," a subterranean world of monsters and morons. Recollection of the place is obliterated by that of a hurricane and a "slam-black cistern-type thing" in which important scenes of her childhood were set. A target for cruelties so outrageous and so casually presented that they are comic, she is used and abused by the Cutts and Chudds and Judes of the world. As a vehicle for satire, she fulfills the role of innocent victim, but she is mute as well as innocent; like Bud and Idena, she suffers injury and indignity with little protest. Like Bud and Idena, she endures and escapes.

Many others are buried, entombed, smothered, shut away in darkness or oblivion. Most obvious of these is Tabita's tormenter, Senator Cutt, walled up with Muriel Goering behind General Lee. Bud wraps motel-proprietress Vivian like a mummy in a sheet and stuffs her in the trunk of his car. Literary images of enclosure and captivity appear as the tilers, preparing to seal up Muriel and the Senator, recall from high-school literature classes Poe's "Cask of Amontillado." The reference to Poe, besides operating literally to inspire the entombing of the tilers' victims, also invokes that theme so extensive in Poe: incarceration, entombment, burial alive. A movie allusion furthers the theme. *A Place in the Sun*, a 1951 drama featuring Montgomery Clift, Elizabeth Taylor and Shelley Winters, based on Dreiser's novel *An American Tragedy*, provides at its climax a harrowing scene of drowning, eerily augmented by the calling of a loon. Alonzo, Giocametti's driver, strives to recall the name of this movie from memory's oubliette. Army veterans Jude, Bud, and Wally are parties to Chantelle Peru's class action suit against the federal government for leaving them in Vietnam after the war's end. The men bringing suit represent the American servicemen often characterized as "buried" in Vietnam by a careless, peacetime America, forgetful of valour. Wally recalls a twenty-three-year captivity, including a scrub-down in "a pot" as preface to forcible confinement with a village girl for procreative purposes.

As the story approaches its conclusion with Bud, Idena and Tabita on the run from the Friends gang, on their way to cave country, Idena reflects that in one of her "own earliest reincarnations she had been Divine Sepulchral Princess"[13] locked in the tomb of a dead god, a phallic deity, as a sex slave, "handmaiden to a prick god — locked away inside a tomb when the god died . . . in the pre-Essene period, long before the many sons of the one God walked the earth."[14] Her vision of entombment includes images of coprophagia and of insects marching through the tomb carrying in their jaws bits of the flesh of Idena and her companions. The Egyptological absurdities of this vision are not more detailed than Idena's recollections of another life, this one as a slave in the cotton fields of the pre-bellum South. Idena is aided in her fantasies of previous identities by her capacity for occult vision generally. She sees blood coming from Senator Cutt's mouth in a newspaper picture, and she consults with a vision figure. Uncannily, her visions include the perception that a woman's body has been sealed up in the same wall as the Senator's. A rescuing angel, she paradoxically sees herself always as captive.

Also stifled, Bud and Tabita, for all their experience in violence and violation, are waifs, adult children hobbled and hemmed in by small rules about dainty conduct and proper language learned from the Miss

---

13 *Ibid.*, 232.

14 *Ibid.*, 232-33.

Chudds of their upbringing. As they drive out of Washington at the end of the story, Tabita is chastised for unladylike talk, and she retaliates:

> "I'm never coming to this fuckin' city again," she said.
> "Dint I tell you?" Bud said. "Don't use that word."
> "Don't say *dint*, Bud."
> "Okay."[15]

If these reflexive attentions to a decorum that might be far beyond Tabita and Bud achieve comic effect, that effect comes from our sense of all the grotesque and scarring experience these people have gone through, and of their determination to persist in finding their own way down the road, getting the words right or not.

What then is the nature of Rooke's satire? Satire tends to be single-minded in its purpose and functional in its means to that purpose, its styles, characterization, plotting, settings. Protagonists are endowed with innocence and with conventional attitudes to the issues that the fiction explores or exposes. Rather than undergo the tests and changes that can define character and make story, characters in satire are pre-tested, pre-shrunk to hold a reliable shape. They are the neutral or the conventional everyperson ready to register, like Lemuel Gulliver, naive incredulity and reflexive chauvinism when challenged by new worlds and new experiences. Gulliver and Candide are the classic innocents; closer to our own time, Nathanael West's credulous Lem Pitkin or Terry Southern's clueless Candy are helpless dupes of vice and venality in the grotesque worlds that their creators seek to shine a searching light upon.

Characters in Rooke's satires, on the contrary, will yowl and scratch and fight to reach some understanding of the dirty tricks the world plays on them. Whether they are the villains or the dupes of the villains, they insist on giving an account of themselves, having their say. Leon Rooke's characters are impelled into the world on the wings of their own voices; they are created by the words they utter. They will not squat as backcatchers in the baseball game of life. They want to pitch woo or woe, make love or war.

Above all, Leon Rooke's satirical fiction shows us these plights and passions, these dynamics, and it celebrates energy and change. It invites

---

15 *Ibid.*, 246.

us, however amazed, amused and aghast we may be at the antics of a spin doctor, a raunchy royal, a demon president, a dead Duke, or a gangster with more Hamlet on his mind than murder, to applaud the sheer vitality of those who return from the grave, from limbo, or from the recesses and refuse bins of life to continue their journey. It is no surprise that Rooke's most recent novel is a road novel; the surprise is that he didn't write it sooner.

Voice, Play, and Performance in The Fall of Gravity

Neil Besner

When loquacious, inventive, drink and love and adjective-besotted Raoul Daggle and his precocious, imaginative, and sad, forlorn, half-abandoned but beloved eleven-year-old daughter, Juliette Daggle, set out from their "gated community, that infamous polyester enclave known as Daggle Shores"[1] (53) in a (speechmaking) Infiniti 130 for the Year 2000 in pursuit of Joyel Daggle, sad and sainted, loving, maligned and misunderstood mother and wife on the lam, thus initiating, no, setting in motion, no, I say, throwing down once again Rooke's gauntlet, wait, how is this sentence now beginning to move before our very eyes, unrolling itself sonorous and mock-ominous, tumbling towards a precipice from which, once approached, once beginning that long Rooke's tumble, Rooke's stumble into story — from which there will be, evermore, yea, for all time, now, after the Fall, no return, nor a return from these our fictions, yes, yours and mine as well, dear reader — when, I say, yea, pronounce and utter, this pair, that is, Raoul and Juliette, united in their love lost, seeking the fair Joyel (Joy-Elle?) across the clichés, glazed phrases, highways and byways of the mute (and also as petty and loquacious as the aforementioned Raoul, who covets our ears as much as, more than our eyes) and vilely or contemporaneously fallen, mundane but increasingly, and increasingly bountiful, wintry desert of middle Western America — throwing off stories, these three pilgrims pulchritudinous, tall tales, sombre allegories, gravitas and caritas, as if they were pinwheels, or those sparklers small and large so beloved of Fourth of July revellers in that America to which I just alluded, the America just

---

[1] Rooke, Leon. *The Fall of Gravity*. Toronto: Thomas Allen, 2000. All references to page numbers in parentheses are to this text.

south of the North in which lies the "Winnipeg, Canada" (201) to which Rooke herein cutely alludes, and where, at present, Rooke really resides — interrupting the allegedly primary narrative and narrator, this Rooke, to speculate fruitlessly on the perpetrator of said story, on realism and its discontents, on speechifying, and inevitably, on what must get left out — o yea, then, verily, pale readers and riders, we, yes, you and I, storymongers to our grave ends, we must, willy-nilly, set out too, in accompaniment at first willy or half-willy or unwilling, along a comedic, epic, performative, picaresque, and impermanently hopeful road, gathering incident and accident with the above-mentioned, temporarily separated trio giving off ghostly and gathering and ultimately snowbound intimations of the trinity.

Why?

Draw breath, like cummings' speechifying politician, and raise a glass of water. Have patience with me, dear readers. Entertainment for the first three hundred nights, pleasure for the next three, by which time, the next three hundred nights' piqued instruction and moral sermonizing will pass, let it pass, there are one hundred and one nights to come. And imitatio is to performatio, mebbe, as criticism is to story. No disrespect intended, no intention to vex, on the contrary. *The Fall of Gravity*, Rooke's most recent novel (2000), invites friendly mimicry. It flaunts its stories and inventions, alternating between the mock-divine afflatus of its grandiose extravagances and their counter-stories and self-deflations, all the while urging us onward on its middle-Western-American via dolorosa, cajoling, slyly winking and then bellowing in the reader's general direction. The strategies of *The Fall of Gravity* are, first, performative: Rooke wants us to listen to a gathering of voices (in dialogue, monologue; in direct address, in sidelong reflection) that perform writing as if it were speaking, constantly and insistently reminding us that to write and to read are potentially fatal but always, in the silence of the reading room that Rooke constantly wants to disrupt with shouts, hoots, and hollers, such ungainly if not certainly unmanly goings-on — are always, I say, necessarily one written half-step away from the body, from the voice and the ear.

The vocation of voice in *The Fall of Gravity* is restorative. This is the novel's key and governing impulse: to restore the (tarnished) sanctity of the family, and ultimately of the family of man, fled from each other, this contemporary incarnation, out of their hideous gated community and into the midst of a culture everywhere fallen and everywhere getting shakily to its knees; and after a year of misadventure on the road, emerging from all of the social, historical, and ideological detritus that has accumulated around them and us (we are forever reminded that we are reading, and therefore that we are accomplices) to gesture towards the hope of a midwinter reunion amidst the blizzard of competing and falling and fragmenting ideologies — religious, scientific, technological, not to mention marital — that beset their progress and ours across America. At the same time, as Rooke righteously and recurringly reminds his rapt readers, each of the three major characters is, as are we all, within the novel or without it, prone to, drawn towards, saved by, but also dogged by, loving invention and imagination and storymaking, always threatening to lead them (and us) awry, but also, necessarily — without the sacred disruptions and iconoclastic rebellions of individual and collective invention and imagination, runs this novel's credo, without burgeoning story to counterpoise against the dull facticity of the mute grey highway, we are doomed, yea, to a more perpetual damnation than any herein limned — leading them, finally, to the novel's last and most sacred word, "home" (271). *The Fall of Gravity*, in other words, is a comedy and a metafiction and a morality play, an allegory and also a picaresque novel; but the picaros, unlike, say, an Augie March, insist more explicitly on our coming along, give us the come on . . .

But before all this, *The Fall of Gravity* is writing that is forever trying to recover and to restore voice — and to revive, by its performance of same, the healing powers of wordplay. This is not to say that the novel is simply a self-referential funhouse; on the contrary, it has abundantly too much to say about the too-real world it too-faithfully evokes and provokes — including, as a major restorative element, the reemergence of the suppressed and / or de-historicized story of the aboriginal North American presence that recurs therein (trailing playful allusions to the hijinks of another trickster, Thomas King) as a mock-vengeful technological monster Crazy Horse, the centerpiece of a travelling road show, preceded by a legion of harbinger-deer and antelope that mysteriously recur, beckoning and indeed summoning the Daggles onward through a tumultuous, mock-apocalyptic snowstorm towards the last of the many (aptly and ironically named) Best Western gathering places and watering holes that punctuate their pilgrimage.

All of this comes to us via Rooke's variations on the powers, mock and true trials, triumphs and failures of voice. Rooke has always revered the word and all its works, yea, including literature: beneath the mock-despairing proclamations of his narrators, man or dog, there has always been an abiding respect for the powers of speech, posing as writing, to move his readers, poised as audience, in and out of the world, back and forth from word to world, which might be why as of 2000 Rooke has performed over 800 readings of his work, and why in this novel so many of the speechmakers and proclaimers from pulpits low and on high are parodied, mocked, defrocked and debunked. Therefore, dear reader, let us consider, more briefly, I promise, than the foregoing bombast might indicate, the performances of speech and play in *The Fall of Gravity*.

Repetition and incantation have always been kith and kin. In this text, the former is a pale and shallow derivation but also, in writing, precursor to the latter. Throughout *The Fall of Gravity*, Rooke's repetitions — of place names (like the repeatedly misnamed and invoked "Anne's Ardor," pronounced and denounced by narrator, by Juliette, and by Raoul, [seven times, e.g., on page 1] or "Hell, Michigan" and the "Hell Café," [3, 6, 10, 13, 20], first locus of fallen ex-priests); snatches of song lyrics (Raoul's blues, "sugar, sugar, where has my sugar gone," or variations thereon [as, e.g., on 29, 30, 45], this last time, intoned by none other than the Infiniti 130 for the year 2000, or, in another variation [67], sung in a Daggles Estate rec-room, on a CD "borrowed from Daggle and never returned" by "a black woman, black as the ace of spades, blacker than the blackest pit, backed by the Echoes of Eden of St. Paul Baptist Church circa early forties" — please note, patient reader, the effect of the patent play on cliché, also the black / back counterattack); longer stories (most notably, Raoul's story of the "Delshi man, residing in Pintou, Guelph province," [126-28, 208-11] who, unwittingly, it seems, perhaps out of his mind with love?, beats his wife to death as she lies beside him, but who is succoured by his twin brother the police chief of the whole of Pintou, Guelph Province, and who — "that terrible Delshi man in Guelph Province" [129], Raoul tells Juliette, is, he'll "bet every penny," secretly married to Joyel Daggle, seeing that Joyel was a "hot ticket, known all over Pintou, Guelph Province"): all of these forms of repetition in concert move the narration towards its eventual literal shape, the road trip, but begin to make of this drive an oral, storytelling saga, fuelled as surely by the gathering impetus of these circling and spiralling recurrences and variations as by the gas that the Infiniti 130 for the year 2000 guzzles thrumming down the highway. These repetitions, in other words, predict other recurrences at the level of plot (such as the recurring appearances and reappearances of Crazy Horse and his place-names, such as Crazy Horse Falls, [e.g. 9, 102, 160-61, 183, 187, 192, 195, 213] or of the fallen priests [e.g. 1, 5-8, 15-16, 20, 28, 107, 246, 248] which gather a layer and level of significance each time they reenter).

But the first recurrences as well as the last in this novel are of voice, are oral; uttered; and one salient account of the origin of all speech, of the word, is holy, but in mankind, fallen, and not to be taken seriously, as suggested by a novel of this title; but if gravity is lost, the freefall post-Newtonian world might be in trouble; and who knows, this far into the post-Fall, how the comic and the tragic and the merely mundane are now to play out; and, but, therefore, the longest monologue has to be Rooke's God's, and it is (145-48). As befits any God of Rooke's Who would aspire to narrate in *The Fall of Gravity,* Who would have the requisite temerity, not to mention the nerve, He must needs enter sidelong, emerging from within the voice and glance watching over Joyel Daggle; His is one of many voices that slide and sidle towards approximations of coherence by indignant cumulation and repetition, gathering wrath, voice akimbo as if it were five pairs of arms, He and His and Him morphing mid-speech into "Me" (146). With apologies: let a page-long quotation stand as exemplar of this narrative tactic; thus will you hear, dear reader, how restrained, nay, modest and subdued, I have actually been in comparison: and so will you see, too, how His voice modulates, fuelled by His own mounting chagrin at His creatures' pettiness; (yes, one of the novel's intents is to Mock the Male, and who better to parody through His own Voice than Mister Holy He Himself?) Note the repetitions, the inversion of cliché to mock literal readings (i.e., "God help them," 145), the intentional mixing of vernacular curse with literal invocation (i.e., "Jesus Christ, isn't that enough to bring on hard rain," 146), the enumeration of middle-American junk food to mock the fatuous silliness of middle-American grace-saying ("Cheez Whiz, chips, Twinkies, Kraft macaroni," 145); note the ever-gathering strength of variation on repetition: these are the rhythms of declamation AS invention, ensuing phrases issuing from their predecessors as if they were progenitors, and they are:

Joyel hits hard rain soon. God is weeping because not even He could create a perfect world. He is weeping because He has made a thousand mistakes, because not everyone loves Him, because a billion people in nearly as many languages bombard Him minute by minute with requests for favors, because billions insist on giving Him news of this and that disaster, miracle, triviality and most asinine thought, as though He had turned stone-blind, couldn't read minds, had a need for such contemptible clutter. He's weeping because these billions feel obliged to thank Him for every little bite enters their mouths, Cheez Whiz, chips, Twinkies, Kraft macaroni. God help them, He must count the very hair of their heads, must never sleep, must lead them not into temptation, must intercede at every sporting match, every public unveiling whether sewer or citadel, even little schoolchildren's piping voices assail Him, people on their knees beseech Him morning, noon, and night, as if He had nothing better to do with His time than a common retiree or pensioner, as if His kingdom is little more than an elevated Daggle Estates. Jesus Christ, isn't that enough to bring on hard rain, His gale of tears, buckets and buckets. Let the earth slide off into the seas, let the oceans percolate, let Joyel Daggle, who hasn't addressed Me once, not once, this vile woman who has forsaken husband and child, the explanations existing in abundance, as many as My blades of grass: he beat her, which he did not, he ridiculed her, which he did not, he was unfaithful, which he was not, he refused to help around the house, which he did not, he was tightfisted with money or threw it away at every opportunity, which he did not, he did not love her or she him, which is an utter untruth, they had a lover's spat, no not that either, she has lost her mind, there's a good possibility, she needs this year of recovery, needs to find herself, get her act together, there's another feasible explanation if you're accepting of such psychobabble, she's running from something or someone, not from husband or child, did I hear something about a bespectacled son of a bitch in a Harry Rosen brown suit (145-46)?

Now, God's voice in this novel resounds from heights that have corresponding depths; the fallen priests that populate the novel provide a recurring and comic but also a sad counterpoint to God's haughty sermonizing from early on. And Rooke's book-long sermon about the depths to which organized religion has fallen is also the occasion for some of the novel's funniest wordplay, and indicative, too, of the ways in which language throughout the novel flaunts its purposefully marshalled ambiguities to wickedly funny effect. Consider this early description, tongue held firmly out of cheek, of the head of the delegation of fallen priests:

> And will you, dear reader, will Juliette ever learn that this old man also is an orphan, deserted by both parents, truly a baby left on a doorstep, a ready solution in those olden days when doorsteps were more plentiful, then raised by the School of Our Boys of St. Paul, but that was a long time ago and is mentioned here . . . because the old fellow will go on thinking until his last breath that betrayal of those crafty buggers who reared him, spanked him whether he was a good or a bad boy, yanked him this way and that and a thousand times said, Bend over, yet for all that still remained true to their Savior, never veered from the tenets of divine faith, always there to hoist the chalice, what would they think of him now, our Lord God casts these burdens upon you only that you may be made fit to enter paradise, that's the one bit of guilt the old priest can no longer live with, granted his thinking is muddled (15).

The "crafty buggers who reared him" is a good example of a phrase signifying twice, the meanings snorting and cavorting alongside each other and nudging the reader into complicity; there are many other examples of wordplay deft and dire in the novel, often pointing with mock indignation masking compassion, masking derision, masking further denunciation, to the sad ploys of the righteously fallen characters who beset the Daggles on their way.

But where does all this portend? What of Rooke's high flights of archaic diction, his swooping into and out of street talk, jive talk, loose talk, mock talk and back talk; what of his sly allusions to other texts (e.g., "Kristan Shanty," 19, or is it I who am too text-besotted?); what of Rooke's names in general, e.g., what of Joyel's alias Jane Dearborne, and all the roadside deer, how their story is borne; what of the recurring yellow vestments, beginning and end, of Joyel (18, 259) and the faux-Joyel, mid-story (135); what of the daughters adopted and true, Juliette and the sad abandoned interloper (yellowish name of Amber, 246) arrived late in the story, having travelled down another lonesome road, fled from home and hearth? What of the "New Indian" (247) who tours Crazy Horse's innards, the giant technological belly, cavernous with rigs and pulleys; what of the final climactic coming-together amidst the beat of tom-tom, as the twinned conventions of Minnesota inventors (246) and fallen priests converge on the Last Best West(ern), science and religion at each for a last lost go-round, where Juliette and Raoul and Joyel and her recently adopted daughter have all foregathered to attend the show; what of the final, comma-less, rousing invocation, ". . . oh my brothers and sisters oh my daughter oh my father and my mother oh all of you in sunlight and in peril we are past Eden we are past the Gates of Hell past the Shores of Darkness every act is crucial including the least of them the elixir is within us shake vigorously and apply daily do not use in conjunction with other medicines we are New Indians fallen priests old warriors lovers afoot over hard trails now coming home" (271)?

And above all, why isn't there at least some more *explication du texte* happening here, goddamit, isn't the critic s'posed to be, gawdamit, way-cool and lowdown into it, get down outa town, gimme some inside info, some insight, in-cite me, outasight man, *explain* this novel, *tell* us something, enuff ranting and raving and goings on, jesus christ it's a hard rain's gonna fall on *you* on *all* of us, give us a *reading* for pity's and mercy's and clarity, and charity's sake.

No can do, sorry, mea culpa and all that hoopla, I for one take the view, subscribe to the position, am firmly of the belief that the novel comes first the critic comes next, yes I know that is heterodox but what can you do these days, even the critics, most of all the critics are unreliable liars and frauds, cunning and deceitful, strutting their esoteric stuff, problematizing and all that jazz, here we are at the end of all of this and all I can leave you with is a series of dumbass *questions*? Eh?

A Word in Appreciation of Leon Rooke's "Mustard-Cutting" in *The Fall of Gravity*

Keath Fraser

Wherein is proposed, because so much of this novelist's voice and vigour are invested in the fall of gravity, designed as the natural law of fiction, that his reader thanks Heaven for the death of earnestness as portrayed in LR's Lolita-inverted novel, of such bel canto language that inevitably overlooked will be smaller domestic observations, e.g. "I wasn't cutting the mustard" (225), henceforth acknowledged as building stones for a veritable cathedral, idioms from the mouths of his salt-of-the-earth characters born of the same language the author was, an idiomatic King James version of our progress unto death, the bracing and embracing diction by which he refurbishes their lives and ours, putting to rest forever the dotty dictum advanced once by Mary McCarthy, that no one ever wrote a novel after the age of 60, inane to repeat except to exalt Rooke's virile imagination as it carries on resisting the world's pallor, predictability, above all injustice, with a dynamic mustard-cutting ever mindful of what the novelist hopes we will take to heart, i.e. "Life has got so complicated. You have to be a child to know how anything works, (192)" so that on our way out of his story we are left gazing up at the stained glass letting in the light, his words, "You got to have faith, you got to have vision, (266)" still ringing in our . . .

. . . Now we're cooking. In the Beginning, as the man in the pulpit knows, was the Word. But a word since worn to idioms, the genes of language. (That's why I'm no longer into the gin," says Raoul Daggle. "My genes have been rearranged." (262) In this regard, Rooke's the horse's mouth. His default language is shamelessly idiomatic.

So how is his common language made uncommon?

From the stones of cliché, homily, and proverb arise LR's fiction of arch, columns, and flying buttress. His high-falutin' riffs are invariably supported by idiom and refurbished through irony. Thus are his idiomatic characters refurbished too: "All the same, a runaway Joyel Daggle certainly appears to be, although hardly, if you'll forgive the expression, the garden variety . . ." (49) Forgive the expression? The narrator's still at it a couple of pages later, causing us to wonder about refurbishment: "Joyel Daggle, we may say again, has not been exactly panting to get her two bits onto the page. Quite the contrary. She has been running from us, we might say, as she has been on the lam from her husband and child." (51)

Rooke's language begins incorrigibly in the commonplace. It builds on its lowest common denominators, inevitably defying the fall of gravity in the manner of a Gothic cathedral. Yet his reverence for language, and no one is more reverent than he, means nothing if it refuses to be iconoclastic.

Once inside his novel we're tuned in, "as the phrase goes," to the fact that — "if the matter might be put that way," you know, "as folks used to say" — you will need to have your "head screwed on right" in order to "[s]hake a leg" (unless, that is, you want to find yourself "flogging a dead horse").

Come again?

Unfairly, one puts put things in a nutshell to stress LR's linguistic genes.

You can't *forgive* an idiomatic expression any more than forgive a carved stone.

As a rhetorical device the idiom is this novelist's basic unit of composition. It's deployed comically, yet sympathetically. Caricature and compassion, parody and mercy originate in the colloquial. If his characters, including narrator, sometimes sound like burlesques of spiritual rebirth, it's for a reason. Without his reverence for their high language, as well as low, Rooke's unique cathedral of southern Baptist persuasion, with its fond regard for the Joycean sermon, would fall flat.

Let us deconstruct his novel, then, as follows:

The new novel, a road novel, goes all the way back to . . .

Listen, this author has been travelling since he left home — a tautology in evidence from his earliest stories, and recurrent in "Gypsy Art" — on the opening page of his earlier story collection, *Oh!*: "At home Fazzini's parents were ever bickering at him. 'Grow up,' they said. 'Avail yourself of every opportunity. Let not the smallest blade of grass go unnoticed.'" In other words, hit the road. So Fazzini struck off on the road, eager for any adventure. (9)

So how is his common language made uncommon?

By hitting the road, if you will forgive the expression, in search of wife and mother in a pleasingly circular, picaresque novel called *The Fall of Gravity*.

Domestic equals idiomatic. It adds up to a recurrent pilgrimage of Chaucerian characters.

Out of this trip Rooke creates the revivifying language of his wider world, grounded in an ardour for home, albeit a lost even irreconcilable home. Home's the wellspring for an unbonding couple, pubescent daughter, cartooning hijinks, Biblical perorations, a love triangle, nuclear family, and the journey *back* to home via its longed-for reinvigoration.

The Canterbury tale of marriage is (as usual) a grounded tale in Rooke's fiction.

Thus via the ordinary does he takes the mickey out of any earnestness latent in the archetypal narrative — his characteristic tall tale: "Why make so much of the improbable when all the evidence suggests it is the improbable that makes so little of us, why make exaggerated claims for mystical presences when the perfectly ordinary is so mysterious as to make us dizzy with wonder." (54)

Here, for example, speak Raoul and Juliette, the husband and daughter deserted by Joyel.

"And all those lost moments add up until one day you discover that what has been lost adds up to more than was possessed in the first place. Do you get what I'm saying?"

"I think so. We're really talking now, aren't we, Papa?"

"Yes, we are. Your mother and I had the notion, picked up somehow, that ours was to be a great love, that we were the picked party. God had picked us, the Pope had picked us, Fidel Castro, hell, Christopher Columbus had picked us, someone somewhere had picked us, and we were to be the fucking example. Damn right, too, it was what we both wanted and expected, we didn't care who had picked us, we were a pair in step one with the other, paving the golden trail. Others could have 'okay,' they could have 'good enough,' but that was their bag, not ours. So that's why I think she took off. Because in that respect, the only one that mattered, I wasn't cutting the mustard."

"Not the mustard again, Daddy, please?"

"I apologize, I'm here mouthing off, but, honey, I believe every word. I let her down a thousand ways. I was not up to the high standards. I was a guy who let the daily grind usurp my honorable intentions. I was a guy who, without even realizing it, had come to accept 'okay' could cut the mustard. (225)

So much in *The Fall of Gravity* depends on mustard-cutting. On this particular writer's red wheelbarrow. Without the colloquial to light a fire under his Infiniti, Raoul might as well pack it in and forsake the wife who's forsaken him. He's a guy who has dreamed "the daily grind" into higher existence.

His idioms ground what they exalt, support what they lift. A cathedral's vault includes the ceiling as well as cellar.

Raoul's not the sort of character to attract universal admiration among opinion-makers in literary capitals. One is reminded of a recent interview (*January Magazine*) in which Kazuo Ishiguro laments the linguistic grayness of "international" fiction, among which he includes his own novels, composed regrettably in the awareness and avoidance of what isn't translatable into other languages.

Not ("perfectly ordinary") Rooke's novel, however.

Who cares if "cutting the mustard" is meaningless in Japanese? His characters would be bloodless without idiom. And if idiom by definition resists translation, tough beans. No homogenizing "international" prose for this author. With his down-home voice, Rooke lifts realism from the page and encourages it to soar into the fluting.

So how is his common language made uncommon?

Commonplace language is a language usually reserved for realistic novels, for the life under siege, who knows why, nor does Joyel Daggle know why at this moment she feels like singing, feels like breaking loose in a brand-new manner, realistically speaking, yes, that is how she feels, the song comes and her musical notes soar over the fields, there is the deer once again loping alongside, I was dead now I am alive, I was entombed and now I am not, I sang false notes and then they were not, I loved but I did not, I would but I could not, I will because I am, I must because

I should, I will because of them, because which of us will, let us kneel to our Buddha, let us sing for there is air, let us break bread where there is none, let us bathe in the pool and shout at each other our foreign names, let us slay the demons, let us . . . (197-98)

End of chapter.

Verse, too, you conclude.

Let us thank our lucky stars for a writer just as sympathetic to us as that other feminist, the Wife of Bath. Long among authors, whom his fellow authors admire, may LR wear the cat's pyjamas.

FOREWORD TO *THE FALL OF GRAVITY*

RUSSELL BANKS

It's impossible to say that this or any other of his dozens of novels, collections of stories, plays, and poems is typical of Leon Rooke's work, except in a few ways, which I will try to elucidate later. The point is, in a nearly forty-year-long career so far, Rooke has explored and exploited the possibilities and prohibitions of just about every imaginable literary form and genre. He's tilled his row in nearly every field on the American literary plantation, from the Southern, comic-gothic Back Forty to the bleak foothills of expressionism and noir; from the scrubby backyard of minimalist realism to the carefully mown, metafictional front yard. He's even cultivated a place for himself among the flowers of poesy (his poems have thorns, however, and can draw blood).

This novel, *The Fall of Gravity*, comes from the front yard. It's in the metafictional mode, reminding one of the best of Robert Coover and Donald Barthelme, but with an emotional forthrightness rarely associated with those two masters of irony. Certainly, like them, Rooke is ironic, even satiric, and very funny (the title, after all, taken as a pun, signals the rise of levity, and indeed, it does rise and rise, all the way to sidesplitting hilarity). And at an important level, the novel, like much of Coover's and Barthelme's work, is about its own process: we observe the story as it invents itself; we listen to it comment on its own observations; we learn as we read that the narrator is as unsure of where he is going as we are. (The author, however, seems mightily sure.)

But there the similarity to the work of the so-called metafictionists ends. It ends because *The Fall of Gravity*, like nearly all of Rooke's work, is profoundly melancholic. It's a postmodern, elegiac romance set in the heart of the American heartland about the death of marriage, the fission of the nuclear family, and the terrible loneliness that follows. There is no single protagonist; there are in fact three: a father named Raoul, a mother named Joyel, and their teenaged daughter, Juliette. But one might consider the broken marriage itself as the protagonist. The story begins shortly after Joyel has left her husband and daughter and, in the grand American tradition of Huckleberry Finn and Jack Kerouac, has lit out for the territory, hit the open road, gone to follow the elephant. Raoul and Juliette are in lackadaisical pursuit of her, but like Huck and Jim on their raft, they, too, are in flight from hearth and home and, in an oddly ambivalent way that is utterly familiar to any parent, are in flight from each other as well.

The narrator's point-of-view alternates from one of these characters to the other, as they struggle both to flee their desiccated family unit and reunite it. All three are equally sympathetic and annoyingly self-absorbed; all three suffer from a terrible longing to belong and a terrible longing to be free. Simultaneously, they seek fission and fusion. And, of course, in the end they manage neither and, instead, end with a third, unpredicted thing. Raoul tries to explain it to Juliette in one of their late-night on-the-road conversations:

> "I think that's why she took off. Because in one way or another I kept breaking everything we had of value. And here I'm not talking about value, per se. I'm talking about the squandered moment, about how every moment you're not demonstrating your regard for everything precious is a moment lost in the annals of human endeavour. And all those lost moments add up until one day you discover that what has been lost adds up to more than was possessed in the first place. Do you get what I'm saying?'"
>
> "'I think so. We're really talking now, aren't we, Papa?"[1]

Really talking. That's one of the things that Leon Rooke, here and in all his work, does best: his writing talks. It has a voice that's stronger and sharper and more ingratiating to the human ear than any writer working in English that I know. And in *The Fall of Gravity* he's at the top of his form. Not since J.D. Salinger has a writer created a more convincing voice for a precocious adolescent. Rooke's narrator seems to float into each character's skull, then instantly emerge speaking in the character's voice

---

[1] Rooke, Leon, *The Fall of Gravity*. Toronto: Thomas Allen, 2000.

instead of his own, before floating on to the next skull, where he does the same thing. It's not puppetry or mimicry. It's a kind of aural conjuring that nearly dislocates the reader, causing us to ask, Who's telling this story, anyhow?

Well, the truth is, Leon Rooke is telling this story, and he's large enough, skilled and gifted enough, and has a sufficiently generous heart to embody all his characters, male and female, young and old, and even to embody his narrator, that artifice, the stick-figure that most novelists either forget is as much a character as any other or, if aware of his presence, turn him into a self-admiring pomposity. By contrast, Rooke's narrator is the reader's friend and confidant, a fellow one can trust, even if he sometimes appears not to know where his story is going or what it's really about. Not to worry, friend. With this novel, from start to finish, you the reader are in the best possible company and the safest possible hands.

CHAPTER FIVE

INTERVIEWS

Leon Rooke's *Fat Woman:*
On Being Delivered

KAREN MULHALLEN

The following interview was conducted more than a decade ago, but it seems to me now to address some ongoing concerns and strategies of Rooke's fiction. Leon was born fully formed, right out of Pallas', or was it Zeus', forehead. He began as a frontrunner, innovative, funny, poignant. And he's never let up.

Rereading the tape transcripts I often found how far off the mark I was as interviewer. Rooke is a deeply thoughtful and wily writer and he runs rings around me in this conversation. His mastery of style, his shifting voices and moods and plots and atmospheres in his tales, is a real barometer for the brilliance of his mind. But he's a kind man, and let me run on, without ever taking me down. I think there's another interview within this text, so I have decided to let the reader be the judge of the direction of Rooke's responses to what now seem to me to be my own questions and statements which miss the mark. Rereading the novels and short stories, I am still dazzled not only by their ingenuity, which is widely acknowledged, but also by their deep and moving humanity. Leon Rooke and voice. That's the real subject.

Our conversation took place in a little Art Deco building on Victoria Street in Toronto. I'd been hired to create a new course in Canadian Fiction for a local radio station. Eventually they got cold feet. Couldn't figure out why I hadn't included Margaret Laurence. Hadn't heard of Rohinton Mistry or Jane Urquhart. Didn't know why Ted Chamberlin or Alberto Manguel might have something interesting to say about the writers, and thought Michael Ondaatje and Josef Skvorecky were a bit too far out. Timothy Findley was right off the graph. You get the idea. They fired me, destroyed the master tapes, and refused to let anyone else run the dubs and the programs. All that happened only a few months after Leon and I talked and looking back I wonder whether they weren't planning as they taped our conversation that it would never ever air. It's full of lacunae, of the most intriguing kind, which makes me wonder whether it was me and Leon meandering, which is entirely possible, or the sound engineer bent on disaster.

Here we are, on a hot July morning, Leon and I, crammed into a little studio. He had positioned his long and lanky form, clad in an open-collared white dress shirt and blue jeans, opposite me on a straight back chair. I was dressed for work, very dressed, but had carefully removed all clanking jewelry. In the booth we began to discuss *Fat Woman* as the engineer was setting up. I remember as if it were yesterday Leon saying quite distinctly "Honour the fat woman. Salinger says that somewhere, and that's where it all began for me." Nothing after that has stuck in my mind, and the tapes begin in *medias res* with Rooke's wonderful laugh. And his *ha ha hah* is everywhere through the interview. It's an inclusive humane laugh, one which invites us to just join in the celebration. You can hear it, as you go.

KM: What I wanted to say to you right away is how hard it was for me to think of questions to ask you. You write with such diversity, which makes your texts difficult to characterize. One of the things that strikes me is your interest in people who are marginalized, and there are so many ways of being marginalized — obviously class being the most common one. The people, like Ella Mae in *Fat Woman*, are country poor.

LR: Yes, right . . .

KM: . . . and that's a specific class that is not as apparent in Canada. There are country poor here, but it is quite different than it would be in the southern states. And American southern poor would be different from the country poor in an agricultural country like France. Perhaps what I want to say is that country poor is different in different countries.

LR: Yes. The one thing that interests me about Ella Mae and her husband Edward and a good many other people like them who are living marginally — and we've never lived such a marginal life — is their need, their feeling that their lives must somehow be justified, that there must be a reason for their existence, some sense of contribution, however marginal one is. So I think Ella Mae, like Hooker, the dog, in *Shakespeare's Dog*, is the same sort of thing. Like Hooker, she's got considerable vigour and energy.

KM: He's the law-giver, isn't he? In the Ecclesiastes sense.

LR: He lays it down. That's right. But he's doing the same, going the same way as Ella Mae — he's justifying his existence. He's saying yes, my life matters.

KM: Except that he's on top. He feels the dark forces, but he can run.

LR: He is on top, but he also knows that he is a dog, and as a dog he is held in extremely low esteem.

KM: And he started as a lower class dog too didn't he? A dog born on the edge of the . . .

LR: . . . bogs, the marshes which are more highly valued in his little bailiwick than dogs are. Dogs' lives don't serve any purpose. If you look at dogs in that period, I guess the only dog which served any purpose at all was either a hunting dog or a lap-dog for . . .

KM: The nobility?

LR: For the nobility.

KM: In fact, I don't think that even lap-dogs were terribly popular in the Elizabethan period.

LR: That's right. So despite Hooker's arrogance, that he's the fellow who runs the town and holds it all together, there is opposed to that his sense of worthlessness — the worthlessness of it all. The same with Ella Mae who probably feels too that her little house would just fall apart if she didn't hold it together. And there are those two atrocious children of hers that somehow ride her.

KM: She's ambivalent about her children, isn't she? She sees their awfulness and yet she loves them.

LR: She does with the children what she does with most of the things in her life — she turns them over in her mind and says yes, they treat me atrociously, they are really mean little brats. But she always comes back and gives them the benefit of the doubt after those cartwheels going on . . .

KM: She's like Billy Liar, isn't she? In the Keith Waterhouse novel, the eponymous hero Billy Liar has two modes of thinking. Ella Mae also has number one thinking and number two thinking, and number two thinking is when you get out the machine gun and kill them all . . .

LR: That's it. You do that and then you have to come back and you can be benevolent and everything is . . .

KM: Number one thinking . . .

LR: . . . golden, and the daisies are popping up again. So what she has that I admire a great deal — something so necessary for people to have — is a sense of renewal. She can mourn and sob about her troubles, pull them all into that interior space where we take such things, and somehow in the process emerge from it with the sense that even if you know you're going to emerge only to be beaten down again, you come back. You rise to tackle the whole business of life again. That I quite admire in her.

KM: That's right, even when she's down in the marshes, running away. There's no one in the house and she starts thinking of this terrible Edward, this horrible man, seeing him at the kitchen window. Yet she's filled with love and she runs toward the house. She turns right around. She literally pivots on her heel and rushes back in a whole wave of acknowledgement and love. And she is made lighter as she runs. She runs very quickly, whereas she'd gone down to the marsh heavy-footed.

LR: Yes . . . heavy-footed and covered in dark?

KM: She was weighed down with dark feelings. And when she goes down, she goes down to that Indian mound area. It's almost as if she's going down a kind of midden heap of history, in a way, and then turning around and running back again. You are interested in this life force in animals as well as humans. Do you think that it is important to you because it has the potential to rise higher? Is it the extremes which interest you? It's a long haul for someone to feel good when they are that far down in the mound.

LR: That's right, it's a very long haul and, in her case, it's a haul that goes all the way back, one might assume, to her birth. She's just not had an easy time of it ever. And then she's always had that ability to come back and that's what I found so wonderful about her.

KM: Where does she get so much to eat? She is very poor and yet she is very fat, even when her mother was thin. Was her mother giving her all of her own food?

LR: Well, I don't know. I'd say she probably has got a little garden out back. I forget whether she does, but if she doesn't, she should have. And she probably does a lot of canning and preserving, and she's got a pantry full of all these old things she's put up from her garden over the years. There's no end of . . .

KM: . . . possibilities for ingestion?

LR: That's right. That's right.

KM: There's no Dairy Queen out there in the country. But that is what she turns to in the city. The kind of things she ingests are interesting to me — the Dairy Queen, and the chocolate bars. The things that she craves aside from being sweet are also cheap, aren't they?

LR: They're cheap, but for her life they represent luxury items.

KM: Like the slice of pie in her purse?

LR: That's right. They would not be things that she had grown up with. When she was a little girl, there wouldn't have been a Dairy Queen, and she probably wouldn't have had five cents for a chocolate bar.

KM: So they're a sign of her rise in social status, like the two-storey house?

LR: Yes.

KM: Edward gives her a two-storey house with a real bed and a dresser and she clings to those things, doesn't she?

LR: Right. They matter considerably to her. And the one reason they do matter, I am sure, is because they represent a rise out of the class that she perceived, at the beginning, herself to be in. So humdrum and dreary as it is, it's a rise. She has a refrigerator that runs and hums.

KM: Edward's truck is decrepit, it is held together with bubble gum. To get it going he has to start a fire in the carburetor, but she sees it as an antique, doesn't she? He's told her that it's a real classic. The reason people are staring is because they all want it, and she seems to buy that view of that old truck. And so you assume that that may be like other things in her life — like the TV he has salvaged from the junk yard. Maybe she has a clearer view than other people who wouldn't think it was a precious object.

Some of the status symbols in her life are to the reader junk and salvage. The reader has one edge on them, they aren't fresh and shiny, and therefore lack status. But for her, they have status. There's something very poignant, the physical objects in her life.

LR: Well, there's something I rather like about that. I like Edward's sense of the possibility of building one's life out of all those things that other people have discarded, or have decided are finished, don't work anymore, don't offer anything. That's a notion I find quite intriguing.

KM: People working in the salvage of civilization, digging around in the garbage?

LR: Yes.

KM: That is like the Indian mound and the midden heap. All these things which people have discarded really do have an importance and a use and can be recycled.

LR: Yes, that's right. But the other reason why I had that Indian mound in there was an attempt to establish a connection between the life of Ella Mae and of people like her and the lives of the vanishing tribes who were . . .

KM: Do you see Ella Mae as one of the vanishing tribes? Do you see the country poor as a vanishing tribe?

LR: I don't see them as vanishing by any means. One might wish so. But no. What I would diligently strike a supportive note for is the idea that yes they may be poor but their lives matter. Their lives matter to them.

KM: And they matter to us too.

LR: Yes, they certainly do. There's that wonderful, and wonderfully invigorating, section at the end of J. D. Salinger's *Franny and Zooey*, the last of the Glass family stories, when Franny comes home from college in the throes of a terrible breakdown, practically in a coma because the world has let her down. It is populated by morons, everything is bogus, and she has given up all hope because excellence, truth, all of life's enhancing measures exist in a surround of fraudulence, deceit, hypocrisy, stupidity and chaos, and she is quitting the battle. So her brother Zooey performs a bit of hypocrisy himself. There's a telephone in dead Seymour's room — Seymour dead in Florida all these years through unforgivable suicide — a telephone not once used in all those years since his death . . . Zooey gets on the phone pretending to be Buddy, Buddy the hermit, another brother, and goes on to remind Franny of something Seymour had told him back in those days when the Glass children were doing their 'Wise Child' radio show. 'Shine your shoes,' Seymour told him, and Zooey was furious, 'it's radio, for godsake, who can see our shoes?' 'Shine them anyway,' Seymour said. 'Shine them for the Fat Lady,' Seymour said. And a picture formed in Zooey's mind of this old sick very fat woman seated in a rocker on a porch somewhere, swatting flies from her head as she listens to the radio, a nonentity, a no one, voiceless, a person whose life you might say was not worth spit. Shine your shoes, be excellent, for her. That's who you shine your shoes for. Franny remembers a similar episode, when Seymour told her to be funny — 'be funny for the Fat Lady.' Furthermore, Zooey reminds Franny, there isn't anyone out there, including the morons, who isn't the Fat Lady. Now that is an extraordinary notion, and to a degree my Fat Woman is Salinger's creature personified. Living a life where every breath is a last-ditch effort, like Edward's truck which is tied together by wires, by string, held together through the most fragile of means, the whole of their lives like that, fragile, each breath sinking them deeper into dust. But I think Ella Mae is a very beautiful person, heroic. I love her.

KM: I love her too.

LR: And she won't give up, that's what I love about her.

KM: She doesn't give up, although I found the ending difficult. Not the imprisonment of her, because you know from the beginning Edward is going to imprison her. You know what he is doing, and you wait for her to figure it out. It takes her about two pages. And then, after that, in the whole novel, there is her denying that that's what he's doing. And then there is her facing what he's doing. Because she says, within a page or two, when she sees the boards, I guess he's going to board me up. So, you know, you watch her dance around it, and you wait for it to happen over and over. I think you wonder will this be the scene where he boards her up?

LR: That's right.

KM: And the piece of plywood is in the hall from page two or three of the novel too, so you know he's going to put the piece of plywood over the bedroom door once she's asleep.

LR: She just can't believe it; it's too horrible.

KM: She can't believe it. But in a kind of funny way you think that she yearns for that, almost yearns . . .

LR: Well, that's right . . .

KM: There's a kind of dance with the darkness . . .

LR: It's out of her belief that she probably deserves it, a sense that "my life doesn't matter."

KM: She is gluttony, Ella Mae, and maybe that's why she feels she deserves this . . .

LR: So do it to me?

KM: Yes, do it to me. How could it be any worse than it is. And I'm married to this man. Now it seemed to me, that Ella Mae begins by saying Edward's wonderful and she deserves everything, and then midway through the novel she starts oscillating between him being wonderful, and him being the reincarnation of bad Daddy, of an unacknowledging God. And Preacher Eelbone, and all of these people who have somehow denied her integrity. At the end, what I found difficult was when he is making love to her, saying it feels good, as if some of this is going to be the compensation. It's in the last couple of lines, where he tells her you're lucky because I still find you desirable.

LR: Yes, it's a very mean moment.

KM: Now the scene where he pretends to be a dog and goes up her skirt. That's a kind of ambiguous scene as well, because it's fun and it's playful . . .

LR: It could go either way . . . that's right.

KM: He's a mean cur. He hasn't given her any other affection, and suddenly he's down there being the mean cur. Edward is a kind of a sexual icon. He has the maleness. The first time we meet him he kind of pulls on his crotch, yanks at his overalls. So all through the book you think, he is the man, he's got the balls. She's the repository. It's all that stuff about giving or leaving her a little door.

LR: Ha ha ha ha. This sense of humour is certainly not a mainstream sense of humour. He's a bit eccentric. But the thing about the ending, perhaps . . . I think what I do as author with that book is that I project a time beyond that ending. I know that she is going to come out of that room. I know that while she is in that room all of those things that during the course of the novel she has been going over in her mind, all of those things are going to find a nice resting place. She's going to emerge from that room much more pleased and satisfied with herself.

KM: So you do see it as good for her finally.

LR: Now, while I think the method is wrong, it's a terrible thing he's done to her, but whatever is done to her, she will always in her own way master, and conquer. She's indestructible. That's what I feel.

KM: Because the spirit is so big in her?

LR: That's right . . . and the most ghastly things that I put her through, she will overcome, she will not be defeated by someone so small, so small-minded as Edward. But that's largely a condition that exists beyond the pages of the book. When I was writing the book I toyed around with the idea of making those overtures more overt — the sense of the exit that awaited her, the decency of it.

KM: A resolution transcending the present?

LR: But I felt that because of the way she'd been characterized, my understanding of the kind of character she was, that maybe I had false expectations, that most readers would see that she's not going to be annihilated by this terrible thing that he's doing to her. She's not going to be annihilated, she will come out of that room one way or another. And I doubt very seriously that she's going to wait for Edward to say now you can come out. She's going to find a way of getting out.

KM: So the scene where she has the stomach serpent. Where she eats and then suddenly she faints . . . and the serpent is there. It's the serpent of her gluttony, of her pain. Later Edward is the serpent. Is that what she has to conquer to come out of that room, that serpent?

LR: Yes, that's right.

KM: That feeling that she isn't deserving is the serpent too, isn't it?

LR: In my mind, that serpent represents two things: one, the serpent is symbolic of the life she was born to, that one is born to.

KM: Is destiny the serpent?

LR: That's right. The serpent is there for you and it's going to claim you. And lucky is the person who is going to escape it. Some do, but most don't. It's the sort of situation where you're born into a life and there is no open sky, there is no exit. You are walking the same furrow that your mother and your father walked; you're going to find yourself with the same kind of jobs, the same sort of education that they had. It is simply a deprived existence.

KM: Do you think that's true to life?

LR: I think it's changed considerably now. There is much more fluctuation, fluidity than there used to be, but I think that it still operates.

KM: You mean a dog is a dog. He may be Shakespeare's dog, but he is still a dog.

LR: That's right.

KM: And "the Regarders" are still coming for him.

LR: So that serpent which fills Ella Mae nourishes her, with the same sorts of things her mother and her father were nourished by. She intakes the same stuff, she eats up the same food and is thereby expected to be the same kind of person. You're in a walk of life and that's the walk of life you're going to stay in. Unless you're very lucky and somehow find a way out. So the serpent represents that, and also the serpent is just more of the male world fencing her in, forcing her to follow the path.

KM: The path that is somehow ordained by the sexes, as well as by class, and family and environment?

LR: Yes.

KM: But Shakespeare's dog will go to town, although of course Hooker's still a dog, isn't he?

LR: Yes, that's right: he has the freedom of the town; he can roam the fields, but it is at his peril. Because those fields are posted and if he goes and brings down the King's deer then he is in deep trouble.

KM: Men in black come for him.

LR: And maybe that same sort of thing happens in Ella Mae's world. If you overstep those bounds, if you venture into the more privileged section of town. It's as though a sign is posted saying stay out of here, unless you come in to work in a kitchen, maybe . . .

KM: How is it that you know these animals and these people who live at the edge of town?

LR: I don't know.

KM: How do you know them so well?

LR: I think I grew up with it. I grew up in a very small town, which carried the stamp of those people who owned the town — quite an impoverished town. Certainly, there was a sense that almost everybody was going to stay, very few were going to get out. And as I grew up, there was certainly an awareness that most people didn't want to get out. They knew nothing else; that was the world that nourished them and beckoned to them. In those times families were much tighter and tended to stay nearer to the place where they were born. I knew from probably the age of seven or eight that I wasn't going to stay there. I just didn't like it that much.

KM: How did you know that?

LR: I don't know. I've often wondered how I knew that. I grew up with that sense and I knew the town. I didn't know when it was going to happen, but only that it was going to happen. It was a very curious little town, a town that really did defeat people. By the time they were forty years old they often looked like they were eighty, and that was because they did the same thing everyday. Humdrum, boring, ill-paying jobs. There was considerable sunshine and mirth that one got from one's family and friends, but there was no larger sense of being, no larger world where there was rich colour and zest and fire and energy and rewards, proper rewards to one's life.

So Hooker's rantings, and those sorts of things that Ella Mae talks about as well, have to do with just that sense of how lives become deprived, what it is that constitutes a deprived life. Just the sense that that condition is not mandatory, that one should rail against it, and should say that is not good enough, it does not have to be that way. Which is what, I guess, in a sense, makes Hooker the dog and Ella Mae blood brothers, blood sisters.

KM: You were working on the two novels very close to one another. Did they overlap when you were writing?

LR: Yes, I think they did.

KM: I have been thinking about that short story of yours "The Problem Shop." There's a character there called Ar-Salar-Saloam. Isn't there a photographer called Ar-Salar-Saloam?

LR: Oh Lord is there? Don't tell me.

KM: I think there is, and I remember wondering what is Leon doing to this photographer.

LR: No, I didn't know there was a photographer with that name.

KM: Ar-Salar-Saloam is also one of the dispossessed of the earth, isn't he?

LR: That's right. He's told in the opening paragraph that your life does not matter. You're a reprehensible human being; you're so contemptible you should be taken out and strung up.

KM: Yes, the judge says that to him. He steps down from his ex-cathedra and just speaks as one human being to another, saying you're nothing. And the rest of the story is really him coming to terms with that and going beyond that, isn't it? That is learning that that is a judgement that he does not have to live with.

LR: He does not have to accept that judgement. That judgement is in error. In the first place, the judge has no business saying that to him. So Ar-Salar-Saloam is offended, as certainly he ought to be, by that, but at the same time it is the first time that anyone has negated him so strongly, so he is forced to think about what kind of life he's leading and what the future might offer. And this leads to a fortuitous plot. He comes to a kind of problem shop.

KM: He just happens to come across a problem shop and a man who puts on a naval uniform who just happens to have a boat?

LR: Yes, he just happens to have a boat.

KM: Which just happens to have a crow's nest, so he can climb up high and look down . . .

LR: . . . on the fish . . .

KM: . . . and look down on the world.

LR: Well, that's right.

KM: Yes?

LR: I think the story ends with the line "Fish! Fish . . . Heaven, my Captain! It is all here! . . ." It's actually set in Victoria as the boat is moving out of the harbour, and he's looking back at the city, which looks quite lovely. It's a beautiful city.

Going back to the idea that to a certain extent we have to assume responsibility for our own lives, that we can't just say I was born to this and I will accept it because my father was a bastard and my mother was difficult, and therefore I am a bastard and am difficult. We assume we have inherited all those things from which we have no escape. We may be taught to believe that the world is an ugly place and that the spirit is stingy and that life treats us in a niggardly fashion and all of that.

One is responsible for one's own life maybe, and if one works hard one can cast off and oppose those things that are inherited. So that's what Ar-Salar-Saloam recognizes at the end, through the help of this man Captain and his big boat and the problem shop.

KM: Including the woman who thinks she's the anti-Christ.

LR: Yes. She's got a real problem.

KM: What are you doing with all these religious figures of people who have an intense relationship with some sort of Christianity? And Ella Mae has that too, doesn't she?

LR: Yes, Ella Mae, too.

KM: She has a vision of Jesus coming down to her. And then there's the woman who thinks she's the anti-Christ, rather than the woman who is clothed in the sun who would be the anti-type to the anti-Christ. So my question is, Where do all these things come from? What is this business about?

LR: I don't know.

KM: Did you train as a minister, Leon?

LR: Ha ha ha ha!

KM: Come on, 'fess up!

LR: No, no, I didn't, but I did go for the first two years to a Baptist college.

KM: You weren't a divinity student?

LR: No, I wasn't interested in it. Really, I just went there because it was in a beautiful part of the mountains, a lovely place.

KM: Where was it?

LR: It was in western North Carolina, near Cherokee.

KM: So is the sense of the living presence of God part of that place?

LR: I think it is. But I was not much interested myself in it, though I did grow up aware of its being around me. And now that the years have gone by it's kind of interesting to look back and say that there was a period when it was there. Then we said God is dead. At the same time, they were saying that the novel is dead. The intellectuals were arguing that question back in the late sixties and early seventies, and maybe even earlier than that. And it was only a couple of years later that some of us may have thought we had discovered that God was dead. In the meantime, there's the religious revival — Jimmy Swaggart and Jerry Falwell down in Virginia with his Moral Majority. Suddenly what had been argued as dead was electing state senators and representatives. Those people who were born again were all over the place. That climate is something I'd been more or less alert to and interested in.

KM: Do you think there are ongoing human concerns and that whatever the intellectuals decide is in a world apart? Do people sense that God is around and that they are caught by class and environment? Are these the givens of human existence, and is the way the human spirit fights against its fate a given? Intellectual debates come and go. It seems to me that this is what you are saying over and over again in the stories, in the tales whatever the length of them. There are enduring things about the human spirit.

LR: I like to think that some of these things are abiding.

KM: Including the need to transcend, the movement toward some kind of resolution? I just reread *Shakespeare's Dog* last week and it is so very moving. I wept at the end. I thought this is everything I would want in a book, this book, and it's about a dog. But it also made me wonder about why you write about this dog. The dog is clearly human. I don't know whether you know Virginia Woolf's *Flush*, which is the biography of a dog. I think it was Lytton Stratchey who said that *Flush* is not so much the biography of a dog, as the biography of a woman who thinks she is a dog.

LR: I'll accept that.

KM: I thought the same about your novel, is it about a dog, or is it about an author who can conceive of being a dog himself?

LR: One thing that some of us who like dogs like about dogs is the sort of appetite they have, the line of inquiry, those eyes that are always sparkling. They seem to be open to the world. Not all dogs certainly, some close down as many people do, but most dogs have that appetite for life and a definite line of inquiry. They're willing to make fools of themselves and to be found in undignified positions. So it's not such a foreign persona to enter, I suppose, and maybe one of the crucial differences is simply that they are lower to the ground. So they see things very differently from the way we see them.

KM: This is spoken by someone who is six foot three! You imagine yourself one foot off the ground!

LR: I think one could build an argument on the idea that most of us do feel we are in a sense the artist in the universe, the one around whom things spin. It's like a kid. Kids feel, or I suspect that they feel, that adult lives spin around them. They are the centre of existence, and really they hold things together. Probably those atrocious kids in *Fat Woman* feel that they keep that house running. They manage it. Maybe because they are never there, they are always doing something or other.

KM: Well, they do feel that until their dad hits their mom, and then their world collapses, and they become again dependent children.

LR: So one might view the dog Hooker as the artist pulling all the strings, keeping everything together. Without him it would all dissolve and things would fall away into random impulses.

KM: But Leon, you are evading my question.

LR: Well, what was that question?

KM: It was about empathizing, identifying with narrators who are not necessarily human. There are the ants in "Bennett," the extraterrestrial ants. In other stories there are spirit dogs, unidentified objects, and you speak in all these voices. It's as if you live in a populous world which isn't necessarily human. Through these voices are you saying that these things have the same status as human beings? Is that how you feel?

LR: Well, I don't know that I feel that way, or would state it that strongly. In fact I don't think that they have the same status.

KM: But they have an authenticity and importance?

LR: I think they do have an authenticity. But what interests me is to try to learn what they know that I don't. What does a dog know that I don't know?

Now I would agree that to tell a story from the point of view of extraterrestrial ants, or otherwise, might be a bit extreme . . . but when one approaches the stuff from these unusual angles maybe the line of vision is unusual, and through that one can find something a little different about it. I want to see it with a freshness that one wouldn't see if one said well I'm so and so, this and that kind of person, and I'll look at it straight on. If you look at it just straight on, it just disappears, and maybe it won't be there any more. This may be what I am doing with some of these odd approaches.

KM: You mention Salinger, and you said that you also knew Virginia Woolf. Are there writers, or are there books that have been really important for you, ones which have a freshness of vision?

LR: There are a few. As you know I write a lot of short stories, and I've always loved Chekhov — he's been extremely important to me. Nobody's better really at the short story. From time to time I go back and I reread all of Chekov. And Salinger was certainly one of the first American writers that I read who wrote with an idiom that I found direct and contemporary. He's dead on and the writing is alive. Also I think Salinger's probably better with the human voice than anybody I know. Gordon Lish is doing a lot of it now with his novels, and there are, of course, other writers who work out a voice, or can assume a voice, and do it with absolute purity.

KM: You see the world, the environment through the voice, don't you?

LR: By and large, although I certainly don't dismiss a more objective point of view. There is such a difference between a story that's told in the third person objective point-of-view, and one that is a first person rendering. The same story can be told but the point-of-view just makes it so much more different. And I think neither's to be discarded. They are both valid.

KM: You do a kind of disguised first person narrator in *Fat Woman*, don't you? I think you called it that yourself at one point "first person disguised . . . as third person?"

LR: That's right, it is.

KM: So somehow the reader feels she is both outside and inside simultaneously which I think is marvellous, because you do pull the world in, but the reader also understands what Ella Mae feels, or what Hooker feels about the world. There are always moments when there's a kind of crazy veering off and looking around the outside.

LR: That's right, and then you see the temporary might of the external world. This is a lovely technique. I love it a lot.

KM: So it's a kind of spirit speaking through the voice, and you can hear it stronger in the first person?

LR: The wonderful thing about voice is that it is "okay, here I am who I am, and I am not you. I am not any of those people out there." I think if we allow ourselves to be delivered unto another body, unto another personality quite foreign, quite distant, quite removed, not at all like ourselves, because we are interested in their story and we are interested in what they have to tell us about themselves and what that then tells us about each other . . . In fact I would love the idea that all writers were interested in writing out of something other than and someone other than the self. I don't think the self just from a writer is that important in terms of what we are going to write. I'm afraid when I'm 80 years old I'm going to write about no one but myself, but how dreary, how dull, how monotonous. I would want to climb walls after just a year or two, maybe even after a month of that, because my story is not that interesting. So if we recognize then whose story is interesting, and everybody's is, and it's just a matter of the writer's job to find a way to make it interesting. If we enter the voice and let the person speak through the voice, whether this finally works its way onto the page or not, this is the exercise to find out what the story is. I think that that is the authentic approach, if one gives oneself permission to enter other skins. Either right away or very soon after one has made the effort that person will begin to talk and often talk in a way that has nothing to do with the writer's self. It is someone else.

KM: And it is someone who has conceived herself. If you can imagine this other person that person becomes real.

LR: The person becomes real — you lay down the line, like "I was at the seashore yesterday . . ." Okay, you don't know who "I" is, but maybe that line is me, maybe "I the writer" was at the seashore yesterday. "I was at the seashore yesterday". . . what's the second line going to be? The second line is probably going to steer it either towards me so it's recognizeably me, author, or towards you."You were at the seashore yesterday" but I am pretending to be you at the seashore yesterday. So by degrees it becomes clear that it's not me, it's you. Now what was Karen doing at the seashore yesterday? She really doesn't want me to know.

KM: Looking for you . . .

LR: Well; I'll let her tell me . . .

November, 1989

LINGERING ON POSTED LAND: CONVERSATION WITH LEON ROOKE

BRANKO GORJUP

BG: In a 1985 interview, you confessed that one strong reason why you left the U.S. for Canada was your romantic sense of Canada's unpolluted and uncorrupted space. You used the word "beckon" — a word Destiny would carry around in its magic bag. You said that Canada "beckoned" you because of what seemed at the time "to be a future . . . that wasn't oppressed by dark clouds overhead." Years later, how would you reconsider these statements? Has Canada been a cloudless place for you as a writer?

LR: That Destiny goes about with a magic bag is an enchanting thought. A lot of people will be asking where that bag has got to, while the lives of a good many other people are an indication of its existence. I am not so much within enchantment's power, however, or so much the addled dreamer that I am not aware, from time to time, of a darkening firmament. But, yes, I pretty much hold to those old views.

BG: I'd be curious to hear you describe what "the dark clouds" might have stood for at the time you were about to leave the States, and what those occasional instances of a "darkening firmament" might have referred to while you were setting up home in Canada?

LR: I have not renounced the United States. I am alert to the genius of its eccentricities. Almost always I feel a wonderful buoyancy while there, whether in New York City or San Francisco or down South. It is a remarkable, and remarkably vibrant, show the people put on. Life as theatre, let's say. But when my wife and I left, the moral sky was indeed suffering an inconsolable blemish. I am speaking of the Civil Rights period. We Shall Overcome, and all that phrase might conjure up for you. Heroic blacks —

and those blacks were outnumbered ten thousand, a hundred thousand to one, you would have thought. Even in my enlightened university town, referred to by enemies as the "red, festering sore," street marches, sit-ins and the like were a regular occurrence. Yet never would more than 200 people join these marches, ninety-eight percent of them black. A docile citizenry lined the streets and watched blearily. This, as elsewhere churches were being bombed, people murdered, jailed, beaten, stung by cattle prod, set upon by dogs, assailed by fire hoses, humiliated at every turn. So, on the one hand, we had the exhilaration of a Movement which would not yield; on the other, a demonic opposition and, more frightful still, an apathetic public standing dumbly by, content to let History write the book. These are the heavy skies to which I allude, and Vietnam has not even been touched upon. Good ole' Hanoi Jane. Then, hello, Canada! Hello British Columbia! All that water, all those trees, those mountains, those gorgeous skies. My first dark day? At our table, Trudeau was revered — a truly exemplary human being. But here suddenly was the War Measures Act. Here suddenly was a Social Credit premier, "Wacky" Bennett, affirming his ability to "plug into" God with the same ease that his wife plugged in her electric skillet. Waiting in the wings, son Bennett, later of stock market fame, and that good-looking fire hydrant, Vander Zalm. My sense of Canada as an innocent, airy Brigadoon underwent speedy revision. Lunacy was not absolutely unheard of, and dark clouds might arise occasionally. As they did recently, with the massive outcry over rusted ships piled high with unwashed immigrants sneaking their way from Hainan Province, China.

BG: Since you settled here in 1969, you've witnessed extraordinary changes taking place in this country. In the intervening years, Canada has emerged from cultural anonymity to identity. It has transformed itself from being decidedly monocultural, in spite of the Anglo-French connection, to becoming multicultural and multi-racial. Its experimentation with cultural plurality and diversity is now praised around the world and perceived as the prime cause for Canada's currently strong literary visibility. How true do you think this statement is? Do you believe that multiculturalism is good for the country and for its literary culture?

LR: There exists that hideous cliché which informs us that the evidence is in the pudding. Yes, I agree with your statement, although prime cause might be stating the matter a bit too forcefully. A major factor in that visibility, certainly. And surely our multiculturalism is to be praised. The one thing that my wife, Connie, and I found weird and strange and somehow not right when we moved to Victoria in 1969, was its absence. In that sense, Victoria is a far, far better place now.

BG: As a Canadian author of American origin, do you feel that this apparent climate of openness, brought about by cultural pluralization, has benefited you as a writer in any particular way? Can you describe your experience of being an immigrant writer in Canada, as well as a writer who comes from a culture that has dominated the world for the last hundred years? Has your status as an American Canadian ever been problematic?

LR: Canada has been very hospitable to me, lately in smallish doses. This probably has more to do with the kind of writer I am than my country of origin. The pride of Americans is such that they can never forgive, or understand, anyone who abandons their shores. The very thought seems to inflict personal injury. But in all the decades that Canadians have been debating the "brain drain" issue, I have never heard one express any personal "wounding" because a party of these parts has elected to go elsewhere. So this is pride of another kind. My theory is that Canadians understand that the building of a country is a continuing process, whereas Americans are satisfied that their nation-building was completed long ago. That's one reason recent events in Florida, à la Bush and Gore, came as such a huge shock, almost as though the Almighty had deserted them.

BG: I'd be interested if you could elaborate on your remark about hospitality being lately dispensed "in smallish doses"?

LR: A slip of the tongue.

BG: Humour me.

LR: Oh, you know, Branko, that literary reputations rise and fall, they slip and slide, you're down one minute and up the next. Or not up the next. There is no next.

BG: For a writer like yourself, who occupies more than one imaginative space, what does the meaning of a "national" literature imply? In your opinion, how does a literature become national? What makes it national? I was mesmerised reading, in a recent review of your latest novel, *The Fall of Gravity*, the reviewer's entreaty: "Leon, please come to Canada. You've lived here since 1969 . . . but you keep setting your novels in the U.S." How would you respond to this reviewer?

LR: That she made this extremely intimate appeal in a very public organ, *The Vancouver Sun*, touched me deeply. It was heart-warming, really. The issue she raised — what, you're a writer who doesn't know where his books are set? — I don't believe I had ever considered much, for the simple reason that I am occupied by what is yet to be done, and scarcely at all by what has been created in the past. So, yes, she yanked my leash, and I would like to set the next novel here, if only to make her happy. As to a national literature, I imagine a nation's literature becomes national at about the same rate as its drift is towards the universal.

BG: But what makes it national?

LR: Little spiders spinning big webs.

BG: Yes?

LR: Well, one thing that does not make it national is utter dependence on where a work is set. It is probably factual to say that, just about in any nation's literature, whether English, Irish, Italian, Japanese or American, we will find that most writers are writing of people and affairs particular to the country they occupy. It is obvious, though, that those who are not doing so are also contributing to a national literature. A national literature is to be cross-referenced with a mature literature, and mature with universal. You cannot have one without the other. Only in recent decades in this locale has it become permissible — even desirable and profitable, an advantage — for the Canadian fiction writer to explore his or her own country. Whereas in Australia, practically from the beginning, they were defining their own land. And thus they had a mature — a national — literature long before we did. But if talented little Molly Crabtree, out there in her little railroad shack on the Long Straight [Australia's transcontinental railroad–ed.] writes all of her books about an imagined city called Hocus Pocus, a city having not the smallest claim on anything Australian, she, too — Molly, the Little Spider — is among those forging a national literature.

BG: Shouldn't we all, instead, like your Molly, strive for a transnational literature, which eludes any strong specificity by way of a national sentiment, a literature that's easily comprehended by the largest possible number of readers? Or should we see transnationalism, at this point in time, as a devouring monster called literary globalization? A unifier of taste, which in writing means a skilfully produced, internationally approved, antiseptic, unchallenging fiction, associated by many critics today with the literatures written in the so-called "international" English?

LR: No less a talent than Ishiguro has bemoaned the presence of this "international" language, including, surprisingly, himself. If all of the world's major presses fall under one ownership, which is our drift, then the writing you describe would seem to be a logical outcome. Could one argue that, despite their vast differences, in Coetzee's *Disgrace* and in Ishiguro's *Remains of the Day*, there is a sameness in the language each employs? Maybe, maybe not. It isn't an argument I'd care to make. But hold on. The "specificity by way of national sentiment," of which you speak, isn't apt to disappear any more than is the teacup or the yellow wheelbarrow. And we will always have those terrifyingly bad blockbuster international potboiler pop writers to steer us faithfully on our course.

BG: Over the years, critics have commented on your voice, more precisely on the endless variety of voices your characters are capable of assuming. Since a voice manifests itself through language, you have been also described as a wizard of tongues. Where did your interest in language come from?

LR: As a child, I virtually did not speak outside my home. But I was listening, one ear to earth, the other to air. Then I discovered books, and an amalgamation occurred.

BG: And what did the ears catch listening, what did the air say and what the earth? And which were the books you discovered? Do you remember any of them?

LR: Mine was a fraught family, and the times were not conducive to a happy survival. So drama was afoot, and the ears caught an air and earth chock-full of accusation, justification, betrayal, mystery. Plus those stories peculiar to the region itself, ghostly tales handed down and passed around like a bowl of soup at the table. Books? The first book I bought and paid for myself, ordered for two dollars and postage from Black's Readers Service, was Tolstoy's *Collected Stories*. I was fifteen.

BG: It must be important to you that a language is a product of place and history, defined by an environment stretching in time. Kent Thompson describes your idiom in terms of "patterns and rhythms and surprises" that are authentic of time and place. He is referring to your Southern diction, the subtleties of which, he maintains, are likely to be lost on most of your Canadian readers. Yet much of your writing is not delivered in the Southern idiom. *Shakespeare's Dog* is the best example. And then there are all those "Italian" and "Mexican" stories, which follow a different linguistic trajectory. And one can certainly add your latest novel, *The Fall of Gravity*. Can you describe how the language works for you?

LR: It may be merely this simple: many writers are content to follow their own footsteps, tracking the same path, writing the same book, over and over. I am not one of these, and this leads me into an exploration of new patterns and rhythms. An example. Currently I have underway a novella set in Glasgow, Scotland, and told entirely in what purportes to be the amazing street vernacular of that city, a vernacular spoken nowhere else on earth, which is its appeal to me. Now I, alas, have never been to Glasgow. I have been consulting with Michael Elcock, a Scots writer friend out on Vancouver Island, wanting to know how close I've come to the real thing, and Mike has made the following astute observation: It may be, he says, that you are only utilizing this dialect in order to keep yourself beguiled; it may be that once you have completed the novella to your satisfaction you will decide to drop the Glasgow peculiarities. But will I be that sensible?

BG: Obviously, you're not much bothered by those who find appropriation of another culture's specificity, whether speech or theme, a transgression. What would you have to say to these people?

LR: Rarely when I see posted land do I venture upon it. Crucial here is who is doing the posting. We all know the appeal of forbidden territory. Often, there are false guardians, is my point. The appropriation of voice issue had its day, not a good one. Let a writer go where he or she wishes, in acceptance of the legitimate risks involved. The very word gatekeepers employ, "appropriation," is a loaded and suspect word. Surely there are times when venturing into a culture not one's own is an honourable pursuit, and "appropriation" is the last word that should apply. But, yes, there are territories I would not encroach upon.

BG: Can you give a few examples?

LR: Caribbean talk. Gulag talk. The native reserves are not mine to speak of, either.

BG: How is Caribbean talk different from the Glasgow street vernacular in relation to its culture, into which we step by reading the writer using it?

LR: It is a matter of believing one is keeping the faith, Branko. Let me underline that. Keeping the faith. Being faithful to the culture entered. With Glasgow, for the moment, I believe I am. Keeping to their faith, I mean. It's a test, really, to see if I can. But with Caribbean, I would be the tourist.

BG: Why so? Because you feel culturally closer to Scotland than to the Caribbean world?

LR: Quite the contrary. Listen, we are steered by our stars, by impulse, by strange contradictions peculiar to our nature. I couldn't do justice to the

Caribbean world and would have to offer a lot of tall explanation to Caribbean writers I admire.

BG: "Steered by our stars?"

LR: You don't think we are?

BG: Since your settings are sketchy and general, however with some signifiers to anchor the tale down, our knowledge of the locale where action takes place is also minimal. I suspect that the way to a broader understanding of the place your characters inhabit is through their language. But that's tricky, too. Aren't your settings more like theatrical sets? Serviceable, convertible and provisional, the sites where human drama and comedy visit and pass through in time?

LR: The novels, less so, but for many of the short stories, yes. It's like a *Seinfeld* show. Cut to Exterior shot, a building façade, certain windows dominating. Sound: Voices. Cut to Interior shot, the gang yapping. Don't we always know where we are? Those characters in Beckett's play, buried up to their necks in sand, where are they? Up to their necks.

BG: If not in sand, you get buried in snow or you sink into mud, into one of the miasmic sinkholes lurking in the dark corners of your fictional landscape. Or you get, as Ella Mae in *Fat Woman*, boarded up in your room. Who are these people who end up in such tight spots? Why are they there? Ella Mae is there because she's fat, but not only for that reason.

LR: Let's reverse our thinking for a second. If Edward, her husband, got boarded up, it would be a different novel and, to my mind, a less yeasty one. It is women, over the years, whom men have attempted to "board up." That Ella Mae is the single party holding her family and personal universe together is Edward's terrible oversight. His blindness. She must suffer because he is suffering. But what, in practical terms, has put her in this tight spot? Had miserable Edward not got fired from his job, the pair would have likely lived lives normal to their time and place, safe from tight spots of this extremity. But people find themselves in spots of this ilk all the time. Elements are at play beyond our control. Misfortune strikes. The guilty may not be punished, so the innocent must. And the most available innocent is usually beside us, in the home.

BG: Why is suffering for your characters, and everything that falls under its jurisdiction — from punishment to pain to humiliation — a prerequisite for an improved life? How much of the Christian notion that the road to happiness leads through the vale of tears is present here? The most cited example of this transformation is your story "A Bolt of White Cloth."

LR: I, by no means, hold the view that these are prerequisites. I've often wondered why so many writers privately lead fine and privileged, luxurious lives, yet bring such a sour attitude to the lives others live, as they do to life generally. Even so, the vale of tears exists, and people trudge through it. But the view that they must is a repugnant one. There is a confusion here: a great many of my characters, to achieve the improvement you mention, are willing to put themselves out on a limb, to put themselves at risk. That limb can be troublesome. Someone — or society as a whole — frequently comes along to saw it off.

BG: To me, your work is, among other things, almost always deeply concerned with social issues: from poverty and its twin brother, ignorance, through abuse of power — be it political, religious or chauvinist — to racial intolerance and consumeristic amnesia. Yet very few critics have seen it as political. Would you consider yourself a political writer?

LR: Decidedly so. Often explicitly. At other times, I stalk a quieter trail. Humorous elements also confuse the critic. It can't be about much if it is funny. Then, too, critics associate "political" with "realistic" and my writing is not strictly bound by that category.

BG: Can writing change the world?

LR: It already has.

BG: In which way? If it has, as you say it has, this puts a special burden on the shoulders of a writer, doesn't it? What is, in your opinion, the role of the writer?

LR: Okay. Deep breath. Literature is meant to serve humanity, and that service involves betterment, which means change. It also has a sizeable role in propping up the flagging spirit. In bringing the news. These are the easier and natural roles, hardly a burden, because it is in the nature of story itself, the telling and the reading, that these are accomplished. We have already spoken of defining or revealing a people or nation, and this too is not a burden, since no writer, except one gone round the bend, is going to set out with that objective. Such depiction occurs with the conglomerate. (What an awful word!) Other roles: to appease the innocent dead. To speak the speech of those incapable of speaking for themselves. Oh, it's a list that goes on and on.

BG: But writing can also change the world for the worse, can't it? Writing can trick us into believing things we later discover morally reprehensible or untrue. One can think of a number of books that turned the last century into a slaughterhouse.

LR: And the Inquisition had its books. But here you are speaking primarily of political, social, religious or scientific texts. In the realm of stage art, surely Euripides, Aeschylus and Sophocles did little harm. Petronius and Apuleius sound pretty modern, and harmless, today. They still prop up the spirit and bring a smile, establish kinships, which is literature's march.

BG: Yes, they are pretty harmless. Yet writers and poets have disappeared, been silenced because they wanted to change the world. Osip Mandelstam perished in Siberia. The Nigerian writer Ken Saro-Wiwa was executed as recently as a few years ago. Salman Rushdie lived in hiding for years. Virgil ended up being exiled to the boondocks of the Empire. Plato wanted no poets in his utopian Republic, thought them too risky. Why so much fear of writing?

LR: The names exist by the thousands. Scores are imprisoned this minute. Isaac Babel was so dangerous he had to be murdered twice. This minute, in Ottawa, there is the case of the schoolboy slapped in jail one month, trial pending, for writing a story in which a schoolboy threatened violence against his school. Writing it, for Chris'sake. It isn't only in the less open states that society's keepers enact their measures. Such crimes are almost always explained as being done to maintain the security of the state. Done "for the public good." In our time, no less than in Plato's.

BG: Who is afraid of Leon Rooke?

LR: Not a single soul, that I know. Although last summer, *Shakespeare's Dog* the play was banned in Boston.

BG: Why?

LR: An offence against public morality, so said the single party who closed the show.

BG: Umberto Eco, in an essay called "The Force of Falsity," discusses the presence of the untruth in our lives, humankind's blind trust in systems of words, which he calls "false tales." The question here is, why do we accept to be governed by so much untruth?

LR: Because if we didn't, chaos would rule? Because we have come so far with these untruths that we are now ourselves composed in and of these untruths? How else to explain the utter ridiculousness, the craziness, of so much that we, as a society and personally, believe? But don't forget that the blind trust Eco speaks of cuts both ways: a lot of these untruths are no more dangerous than the pillow we sleep on. In fact, are that pillow. Could we survive on a diet of pure truth? Doesn't our evolutionary mental journey suggest that untruth, even with an informed citizenry, is preferable?

BG: One of the great themes in your fiction is that of self-authentication, of jailbreak, whether physical or mental. Your characters begin in some sort of cage, dreaming or plotting escape. Many succeed, some don't. Who makes their choices? The question I'm asking is one I've always wanted to ask you: which kind of universe are your characters given to occupy? Is it Godless? One of relativity and accident? Or one run by some power, which can be, as in the Adolpho story, horrid, or, as in "The Bolt of White Cloth," benevolent?

LR: They make them. The characters. Usually. Or attempt to. Sometimes they resist the choices it appears they are being compelled to make. That's my sense of how matters stand, but after nearly 300 stories, I would have to look at each individually. Personal attitude and belief are the great determiners. Existing also in whatever space we occupy are inexorable blind forces which have not a whit's interest either in our attitudes or our beliefs.

BG: Would it be inappropriate to ask about your personal attitudes and beliefs and the ways in which they have determined your fiction?

LR: Totally inappropriate, but I'm an accommodating guy. My attitude is one of immense optimism, enthusiasm and buoyancy, tempered at times by a darker side. A sense of how Uncaring Fate at any moment may blindside us, with fatal results. One might see hints of this in looking at the body of work, but otherwise . . . otherwise, I am pretty diligent about keeping myself out of other people's stories.

BG: Your work is often oppositional, staging the ancient battles between good and evil, pulling into itself both Biblical imagery and those associated with the worlds of fable and tall tale. How important has the Bible been to your creative process?

LR: As a youth, I immersed myself in its lore, and responded to its cadences.

BG: How would you describe stories like "Art" or "Raphael's Cantalupo Melon" in which art — painterly art — is the subject? What attracts you to the visual representation of experience and to its intersection with the world of words?

LR: Those of us working in one medium are in the family of those working in another. The stories mentioned are a gesture of appreciation, a greeting, a way of honouring the comradeship. Of course, my times in Italy, with you and my wife pushing me into every museum, church and gallery, focused my attention.

BG: Many postmodern critics have responded positively to your seemingly endless capacity for deconstruction, to your ability to soften the lines of closure, to create self-reflexive tales in which the demarcation line between the narrator and the narratee is blurred or erased. Do you think of yourself as a postmodern writer? Is there a postmodern sensibility?

LR: Sure, I'm postmodern. My sensibility is shaded, not directed by it.

BG: How do you describe a postmodern writer like yourself? How different would you be from one that isn't? Can someone living at this point in time not be postmodern?

LR: Certainly they can be. Probably most of our writers have no postmodern tendencies whatsoever, especially in this country where strict realism, fidelity to the one way of doing things, remains the preferred route. With the exception of many of our younger writers, for whom, as you suggest, postmodernist winds are inescapable. What I find attractive about the postmodern is this: no simple adherence to old, legislated, often outmoded rules, but loyalty instead to a vision intent on breaking new ground. Which means a fusion of the old and new.

BG: How and why did you make your shift away from realism? Your early stories, like the wonderfully suggestive "If Lost Return to the Swiss Arm," were written in a realistic mode. Didn't you start out as a realist?

LR: In fiction, perhaps so. But I was writing a lot of stage plays at that time, plays owing a big debt to avant-garde artists like Ionesco. What this view ignores also is the unpublished work. Our magazine editors had a realist's orientation, and only stories following the party line found acceptance.

BG: You don't think that realistic fiction is compatible with our postmodern sensibility? Why not?

LR: I am not so foolhardy as to argue that realism is a sinking ship. Realistic fiction and the postmodern are kissing cousins, of the same family, even if they no longer speak to each other. Realism is fine, useful, some stories demand it. Others, not. Why should writers deliberately cripple — that is, limit — themselves?

BG: This is a good point for me to introduce a question on the theatre. You just said that you wrote a lot of plays during the early stages of your career as a writer. But you have never abandoned playwriting altogether. Every now and then you're back at it. How does the theatre enter into your creative process? Did you originally set out to be a playwright? An actor? Why?

LR: I had thought I would support myself by working as a journalist, so that led me, in university, to journalism school. For a while I worked as a newspaper stringer, often covering, say, an evening assignment and having twenty minutes to write the story and phone or wire it in. I liked the pressure of those deadlines, the hurly-burly of having to work so fast. But the school itself was, well, I'd have to say it was a bore. I was always enviously looking over my shoulder at those in the Drama Department. There was life there, and vibrancy, an obvious love for and excitement about what they were doing. I'd already had a few plays produced, and was writing others, so I switched over. Acting, yes, some, but these ambitions remained largely under wraps. In the plays I was writing, I was already performing in my head all the parts, working up a sweat. Funny how that duality of being, acting out the parts even as you are writing them, can exist simultaneously. That waylaid some the desire to actually get up on stage and perform.

BG: Any person who has seen you read could not have failed to notice a strong connection between reading and acting. The theatre has, so it seems, deeply entered your attitude to fiction as an act of communication, as an act of communion. Tell us something about Leon Rooke the performer.

LR: I have definite failings. I never rehearse. Usually I don't even decide what I am going to read until I am striding to the podium. When I lose sight of lines on a page, I don't mind improvising. Often, I will alter a text drastically to accommodate what I perceive as the sensibilities of my audience. I always foresee utter failure. These are all terrible sins.

BG: The theatrical is not only present in a performative sense, but also structurally. Many of your stories depend for plot and action on game-playing, in which the characters are engaged in acting out their roles, as, for instance, in "Want to Play House" or "The Guacamole Game." Two of your novels, *Shakespeare's Dog* and *A Good Baby,* have been recast as plays. Can you elaborate on this fascinating aspect of your fiction?

LR: Actually, Theatre Passe Muraille's Paul Thompson directed a Caravan Stage Company production of *A Good Baby* that toured British Columbia long before it became a novel. The novella, "The Guacamole Game," was written in eighteen hours, all in one sitting. That's writing as theatre, casting your characters onto a supercharged stage, all aimed at getting to that final curtain.

BG: Are you ever involved in the production of your plays? Didn't you recently go to Miami, where you saw the theatrical production of *Shakespeare's Dog*? Were you there as a consultant? And now *A Good Baby* is also a feature film. Did you work on the film script?

LR: Not on the film script. That was the New Yorker Katherine Dieckman's *Baby.* Let's say I was supportive, but didn't intrude. For *Shakespeare's Dog,* which Canadian playwright Jeff Pitcher adapted, I went down to St. Petersburg for a workshop before the play went into rehearsal. Paul Kirby (the director), Jeff and I worked closely on Jeff's script. I was interested in bringing a strong musical component to the show. They agreed. That meant I had to write some songs. Otherwise, we had deep discussions about plot and character. Then at the close of the season, we all assembled in Miami to see the show, which Jeff and I had not seen before, and we hashed matters out again, since the show is being remounted again this year. Tour by tall ship, quite spectacular. So, yes, I frequently find myself very much involved.

BG: In two of your latest novels, *Who Goes There* and *The Fall of Gravity,* you seem to have raised the ironic tone to a higher pitch. The language is not only more humorous, but also more hyperbolic and bombastic, associated with the literary modes of satire and parody, which seem more appropriate to the subjects of the novels. Don't you find satire and parody limiting?

LR: Indeed I do. They are lesser vessels. That's why I offer, *I hope*, compensating measures. Tone in a sentence is everything. The apparent irony may be illusional.

BG: How would you describe illusional irony?

LR: Language as the lizard changing its colours. A lingering sighting is required.

BG: The experimental gusto in your fiction is impressive. You subvert, invert or simply rearrange used literary forms and conventions — as this latest side-stepping into the fields of satire and parody shows — giving them new lease on life, while, at the same time, suggesting their limits, which are those of fiction. What is it that you are parodying in *The Fall of Gravity*? The quest? The picaresque? The American "on the road" tale?

LR: I will not accept "parody." We need another word. Let's look at what we have in *Gravity*: a flock of priests who have fallen from heaven, grown men dressed as chickens, the Pope nightly on TV confessing to the crimes of the church (all historically verifiable, by the way), a Widowhood Gulag, God lecturing us on the merits of two famous paintings, a City of Lost Women, together with much else that might lead us to think *parody*. But parody, no. If parody, we would be obliged to ignore the commentary of the novel's main character, the ever-intrusive narrator, just as we would have to ignore the role of those thousands of deer striving through whiteout, through what mercy, that we might arrive at our rendezvous, where nourishment at last is to be found. And ignore, too, the New Indian in whom resides all possibility. When the narrator says, "Oh, come all ye faithless," he is deriding no one, but in fact is referencing those possibilities. *The Fall of Gravity* is chasing but the heart.

BG: Yes, I see. When I spoke of parody, I was thinking of a literary mode, of the ways in which *The Fall of Gravity* parodies — is, on a certain level, also a demonic vision of a pastoral America — the dream, the vision of the "failed" America. All that roadside accumulation of junk, and what it stands for, is staggering. This is not to ignore the novel's affirmative journey along which all the possibilities can be found.

LR: I see what you mean. Even so, *my* emphasis would be on the latter.

BG: You sound sure of this.

LR: I am in a defensive stance, I guess. Likely, this will pass.

BG: Another collection of stories is being published in April. Are they new?

LR: Painting the Dog. It contains only one new story. Some of the others included date back nearly forty years. Putting together the collection had its humiliations: how much easier it would have been to assemble *The Best* BAD *Stories* of this writer.

BG: I certainly wouldn't agree with your last statement and would hate to leave off our conversation on the note of self-deprecation by one of our short-story masters. Instead, I'd like to thank you for being so forthcoming with your answers and ask you, why has Heidegger been hovering so much above your imaginative magnetic field?

LR: Being and Time. Being and nothingness. His two great questions. What are they? *Why* are they?

April, 2003

CHAPTER SIX

BIBLIOGRAPHY

PREFACE / 341

ABBREVIATIONS / 343

PART ONE: PRIMARY SOURCES

PART TWO: SECONDARY SOURCES

PREFACE

The present bibliography had its beginnings more than twenty-five years ago. "A Preliminary Bibliography of Works by Leon Rooke," prepared by J.R. (Tim) Struthers, Leslie Hogan, and John Orange, appeared in *The Canadian Fiction Magazine* in 1981 and provided me with an excellent starting point. Although limited in scope, documenting only primary sources and covering just the first two decades of the author's career, this pioneering bibliography was remarkable for its accuracy and scholarship. Two years ago, additional work was done by Neil Besner, in collaboration with the present author. Subsequently, I took on responsibility for the completion of a significantly expanded project.

I have attempted to organize here the original and additional material in a practical and straightforward manner, imposing stylistic uniformity, and including an exhaustive selection of secondary sources — scholarly articles, translations, book reviews, newspaper articles, etc., — which, I hope, will open up a more direct route to the critical reaction Rooke's work has received over the past four decades. Name, subject, and title indexes have been added for a more expeditious perusal.

Undoubtedly, Leon Rooke is one of Canada's most original and talented writers. He is important both for the extraordinary quality of his writing and for his profound influence on younger writers. Rooke's output is also impressive: he has published six novels, seventeen short story collections, several plays, and numerous individual stories in literary journals and magazines across North America and elsewhere. His work has been translated into several languages, including French, Spanish, Italian, Dutch, Croatian and Slovak. With this bibliography, the large body of work by and about Rooke is now for the first time assembled for readers and scholars of contemporary literature. Of particular interest, I believe, will be the remarkable fund of secondary sources — especially of reviews — which reveal the extent to which Rooke's work has been critically appreciated and consolidated in the minds of his peers.

In working on this bibliography, I have continually encountered people who responded to my inquiries with generosity and commendable speed. Leon Rooke himself has fed me precious information, allowing me to examine his files, replying to endless questions, and helping to solve puzzles of various kinds. I express my warm thanks to him. I would also like to record my gratitude to my predecessors — J.R. (Tim) Struthers, Lesley Hogan, John Orange, and Neil Besner — for their invaluable contributions, which are now, metamorphosed, integral parts of the present bibliography.

Branko Gorjup

ABBREVIATIONS

ROOKE'S BOOKS

Date of publication is in parenthesis; entry number is in square brackets.

A	*Arte. Tre fantasie in prosa.* (1997) [A24] [E36-38]
BBA	*The Broad Back of the Angel.* (1977) [A5]
BCK	*The Birth Control King of the Upper Volta.* (1982) [A12]
BWC	*A Bolt of White Cloth.* (1984) [A14]
CE	*Cry Evil.* (1980) [A7]
CL	*En chute libre.* (2002). [A27a]
DS	*Death Suite.* (1981) [A9]
FG	*The Fall of Gravity.* (2000) [A27]
FW	*Fat Woman.* (1980) [A8]
GB	*A Good Baby.* (1989) [A16]
HO	*The Happiness of Others.* (1991) [A18]
P	*How I Saved the Province.* (1989) [A15]
K	*Krokodile.* (1973) [A3]
LP	*The Love Parlour.* (1977) [A6]
ML	*The Magician in Love.* (1981) [A10]
M	*Muffins.* (1995) [A21]
NAS	*Narciso allo specchio.* (1995) [A22] [E7-21]
OH	*Oh! Twenty-seven Stories.* (1997) [A25]
PD	*Painting the Dog: The Best Stories of Leon Rooke.* (2001) [A28]
SD	*Shakespeare's Dog.* (1983) [A11]
SMNLS	*Sing Me No Love Songs I'll Say You No Prayers.* (1984) [A13]
SP	*Sword/Play.* (1974) [A4]
V	*Vault.* (1973) [A2]
WDYL	*Who Do You Love?* (1992) [A19]
WG	*Who Goes There.* (1998) [A26]
YB	*Last One Home Sleeps in the Yellow Bed.* (1968) [A1]
Z	*Narcis u zrcalu.* (1997) [A22a] [E23-37]

Other Abbreviations

abbr	abbreviation, abbreviated
assoc	association
anniv	anniversary
BASS	annual Best American Short Story anthology
CFM	Canadian Fiction Magazine
doc	documentary

ed, eds	editor, edited by, edition
enl	enlarged
forwr	foreword
illus	illustrations
incl	including, incorporating
inter	international
interv	interview
introd	introduction
nd	no date of publication
no	number
np	no place of publication, no publisher
p, pp	page, pages
n pag	no pagination
perf	performance
pref	preface
print	printing
proc	proceedings
prod	producer
pub	published
rev	review, reviewed by; revision, revised, revised by
rpt	reprint, reprinted by
ser	series
sim	simultaneously
spec	special
supp	supplement
trans	translator, translators, translated by
Univ	University
UP	University Press
vers	version
vol	volume

PART ONE

A

BOOKS

A1 *Last One Home Sleeps in the Yellow Bed*. Five stories and a novella. Baton Rouge: Louisiana State Univ Press 1968. 178 pp. Hardcover
CONTENTS:
1   The Ice House Gang (see C19)
2   When Swimmers on the Beach Have All Gone Home (see C21)
3   The Alamo Plaza (see C12)
4   Last One Home Sleeps in the Yellow Bed (C24)
5   Field Service Four Hundred Forty-nine from the Five Hundred Field Songs of the Daughters of the Vieux Carré (see C22)
6   Brush Fire (see C3)

A2 *Vault*. Three stories. Northwood Narrows: Lillabulero 1973. 33 pp. Paperback
CONTENTS:
1   Conjugal Precepts (see C40)
2   Dinner with the Swardians (see C41)
3   Break and Enter (see C38)

A3 *Krokodile*. Toronto: Playwrights Co-op 1973. 40 pp. Paperback

A4 *Sword/Play*. Toronto: Playwrights Co-op 1974. 35 pp. Paperback

A5 *The Broad Back of the Angel*. Thirteen stories. New York: Fiction Collective 1977. 201 pp. Hardcover and paperback
CONTENTS:
1   Wintering in Victoria (see C52)
2   No Whistle Slow (see C61)
3   The Magician in Love: Love and Ethics (see C46)
4   The Magician in Love: Love and War (see C62)
5   The Magician in Love: Love and Trouble (see C54)
6   Friendship and Libation (see C67)
7   Friendship and Rejuvenation (see C58)
8   For Love of Madeline (see C34)
9   For Love of Eleanor (see C50)
10   The Third Floor (see C42)
11   Iron Woman (see C68)

12   Dangerous Woman (see C65)
13   The Broad Back of the Angel (see C66)

A6   *The Love Parlour*. Eight stories. Ottawa: Oberon Press 1977. 157 pp. Hardcover
      and paperback
      CONTENTS:
      1   If Lost Return to the Swiss Arms (see C11)
      2   Leave Running (see C51)
      3   If You Love Me Meet Me There (see C45)
      4   Memoirs of a Cross-Country Man (see C31)
      5   Call Me Belladonna (see C65)
      6   For Love of Madeline (see C34)
      7   For Love of Eleanor (see C50)
      8   For Love of Gomez (see C69)

A7   *Cry Evil*. Ottawa: Oberon Press 1980. 157 pp. Hardcover and paperback
      CONTENTS:
      1   The Deacon's Tale (see C77)
      2   Fromm Investigations (see C83)
      3   The End of the Revolution and Other Stories (see C80)
      4   Friendship and Property (see C73)
      5   Biographical Notes (see C71)
      6   Adolpho's Disappeared and We Haven't a Clue Where to Find Him
           (see C78)

A8   *Fat Woman*. Novel. Ottawa: Oberon Press 1980. 226 pp. Hardcover and
      paperback
A8a   ——. New York: Knopf 1980. 226 pp. Hardcover
A8b   ——. Toronto: New Press 1982. 174 pp. Paperback
A8c   ——. New York: The Ecco Press 1986. 179 pp. Paperback
A8d   ——. Toronto: HarperCollins, Oberon Library Series reissue 1994. 226
           pp. Paperback

A9   *Death Suite*. Eleven stories. Toronto: ECW Press 1981. 175 pp. Paperback
      CONTENTS:
      1   Mama Tuddi Done Over (see C16)
      2   Winter Is Lovely, Isn't Summer Hell (see C91)
      3   Murder Mystery (The Rocker Operation) (see A9)
      4   Sixteen-year-old Susan March Confesses to the Innocent Murder of All
           the Devious Strangers Who Would Drag Her Down (see C70)
      5   Lady Godiva's Horse (see C82)
      6   Murder Mystery (Do Something) (see C96)
      7   Deer Trails in Tzityonyana (see C86)
      8   Standing In for Nita (see C85)

9   Murder Mystery (The Strip) (see A9)
10   Hanging Out with the Magi (see C97)
11   The Problem Shop (see C94)

A10 *The Magician in Love.* Novel. Toronto: Aya Press 1981. Rpt 1983. pp. 90. Hardcover and paperback

A11 *Shakespeare's Dog.* Novel. Toronto: Stoddart 1983. 3 rpt 1993. 176 pp. Hardcover.
A11a ——. New York: Knopf 1981. 4 rpt 158 pp. Hardcover
A11b ——. Toronto: New Press 1984. rpt 1994. Paperback
A11c ——. New York: The Ecco Press 1986. Paperback
A11d ——. Large print ed Toronto: Reference Press 1995. 204 pp. Hardcover and paperback
A11e ——. Spanish trans Barcelona: Laia Literatura 1985. n pag. Paperback
A11f ——. Dutch trans Utrecht/Antwerp: Spectrum 1985. 137 pp. Hardcover
A11g ——. 20th anniversary ed. Introd Shelagh Rogers. Toronto: Thomas Allen Publishers 2003. 210 pp. Paperback

A12 *The Birth Control King of the Upper Volta.* Eight stories. Toronto: ECW Press 1982. 148 pp. Paperback
CONTENTS:
1   The Birth Control King of the Upper Volta (see C117)
2   Sing Me No Love Songs I'll Say You No Prayers (see C18)
3   A Nicer Story by the 'B' Road (see C103)
4   Why Agnes Left (see C88)
5   Shoe Fly Pie (see C102)
6   Hat Pandowdy (see C101)
7   Hitting the Charts (see C90)
8   Gin and Tonic (see C119)

A13 *Sing Me No Love Songs I'll Say You No Prayers: Selected Stories.* Sixteen stories, eight previously unpublished. New York: The Ecco Press 1984. 290 pp. Hardcover and paperback.
CONTENTS:
1   Friendship and Property (see C73)
2   The Shut-in Number (see C128)
3   Break and Enter (see C38)
4   Mama Tuddi Done Over (see C16)
5   The Man in the Green Bathrobe (see C139)
6   The Woman Who Talked to Horses (see C130)
7   In the Garden (see C119)
8   Agnes and the Cobwebs (see C115)
9   Conversation with Ruth: The Farmer's Tale (see C55)
10   The Birth Control King of the Upper Volta (see C117)

11   Why Agnes Left (C88)
12   Sing Me No Love Songs I'll Say You No Prayers (see C18)
13   Some People Will Tell You the Situation at Henny Penny Nursery Is Getting Intolerable (see C118)
14   Narcissus Consulted (see C106)
15   Lady Godiva's Horse (see C82)
16   The History of England, Part Four (see C114)

A14   *A Bolt of White Cloth.* Nine stories. Toronto: Stoddart Publishers 1984. 176 pp. Published simultaneously by The Ecco Press, New York. Paperback
CONTENTS:
1   A Bolt of White Cloth (see C132)
2   The Only Daughter (see C133)
3   Why the Heathens Are No More (see C134)
4   The Woman's Guide to Home Companionship (see C135)
5   Dirty Heels of the Fine Young Children (see C124)
6   Saloam Frigid with Time's Legacy while Mrs. Willoughby Bight-Davies Sits Naked Through the Night On a Tree Stump Awaiting the Lizard That Will Make Her Loins Go Boom-Boom (see C136)
7   Saks Fifth Avenue (see C125)
8   The Madwoman of Cherry Vale (see C137)
9   Dream Lady (see C138)

A15   *How I Saved the Province.* Novella and three stories. Lantzville: Oolichan Books BC 1989. 132 pp. Paperback
CONTENTS:
1   Dust (see C187)
2   Saving the Province (see C146)
3   Up a Tree (see C194)
4   Come Hear the Blind Man Sing (see A15)

A16   *A Good Baby.* Novel. Toronto: McClelland & Stewart 1989. 299 pp. Hardcover and paperback
A16a   ——. New York: Alfred A. Knopf 1990. 298 pp. Hardcover
A16b   ——. Vintage Contemporaries ed. New York: Random House 1991. 300 pp. Paperback

A17   *Daddy Stump.* Limited ed. Magnum Readings 2. Ottawa: Magnum Book Store 1991. 12 pp. Paperback

A18   *The Happiness of Others.* Eleven stories and a novella. Rpt from earlier collections, with one story previously uncollected. Erin: Porcupine's Quill Press 1991. 263 pp. Paperback

CONTENTS:

A19   *Who Do You Love?* Twenty-six stories, twelve previously unpublished. Toronto:
      McClelland and Stewart 1992. 200 pp. Paperback
      CONTENTS:

20   Sorrows Drowned (see C214)
21   Neighbourhood Watch (see C176)
22   I Want to Know the Answer (see C163)
23   Blues Roots *or* You Tear Me Apart (see A19)
24   Covici's Guilt (see C211)
25   Smoke (see C212)
26   Body Count (see C213)

A20   *The Boy from Moogradi and the Woman with the Map to Kolooltopec.* Limited ed.
        Food for Thought Readings 3. Ottawa: Food for Thought Book Store 1993.
        16 pp. Paperback

A21   *Muffins.* Photo/text with vinyl recording. Erin ON: Porcupine's Quill 1995. 48
        pp. Paperback

A22   *Narciso allo specchio* (*Narcissus in the Mirror*). Fourteen selected stories. Italian
        trans Carla Plevano and Francesca Valente. Como/Pavia: Ibis Editore, Italy
        1995. 258 pp. Paperback
        CONTENTS:
        1   In caso di smarrimento restituire allo Swiss Arms (If Lost Return to the
                Swiss Arms (see C11)
        2   Non cantarmi canzoni d'amore e io non ti rivolgerò preghiere (Sing Me
                No Love Songs I'll Say You No Prayers) (see C18)
        3   Adolfo è scomparso e noi non abbiamo la minima idea di dove
                trovarlo (Adolpho's Disappeared and We Haven't a Clue Where to
                Find Him) (see C78)
        4   Il racconto di Deacon (The Deacon's Tale) (see C77)
        5   Narciso allo specchio (Narcissus Consulted) (see C106)
        6   Il re del controllo delle nascite nell'Alto Volta (The Birth Control King
                of the Upper Volta) (see C117)
        7   L'unica figlia (The Only Daughter) (see C133)
        8   Arte (Art) (see D54)
        9   Una pezza di tela bianca (A Bolt of White Cloth) (see C132)
        10   Vuoi giocare a casetta? (Want to Play House?) (see C209)
        11   È il cuore che va curato (The Heart Must from Its Breaking) (see C193)
        12   Ammiraglio della flotta (Admiral of the Fleet) (see C197)
        13   Papà Stump (Daddy Stump) (see A17)
        14   Il ragazzo di Moogradi e la donna con la mappa di Kolooltopec (The
                Boy from Moogradi and the Woman with the Map to Kolootopec)
                (see C216)

A22a   *Narcis u zrcalu* (*Narcissus in the Mirror*). Fourteen selected stories. Croatian trans
        Biljana Romić and Branko Gorjup. Zagreb: Konzor, Croatia 1997. 278 pp.
        Hardcover

CONTENTS:

A23   *Oh, No, I Have Not Seen Molly.* Limited ed chapbook. Toronto: Harbourfront Reading Series, booklet no 7, 1996. 16 pp. Paperback

A24   *Arte. Tre fantasie in prosa (Art. Three Fictions in Prose).* Bilingual Eng/It ed. Trans Francesca Valente. Lugi: Edizioni del Bradipo, Italy 1997. 72 pp. Paperback. Cover design Arnaldo Pomodoro

CONTENTS:

A25   *Oh! Twenty-seven Stories.* Unpublished novella and 16 stories. Toronto: Exile Editions 1997. 272 pp. Paperback

CONTENTS:

A26 *Who Goes There*. Novel. Toronto: Exile Editions 1998. 272 pp. Paperback

A27 *The Fall of Gravity*. Novel. Toronto: Thomas Allen & Sons 2000. 276 pp. Hardcover

A27a *En chute libre.* (*The Fall of Gravity*). French trans Richard Crevier. Foreword Russell Banks. Paris: Phebus 2002. 300 pp. Paperback

A28 *Painting the Dog: The Best Stories of Leon Rooke*. Seventeen stories, one previously uncollected. Toronto: Thomas Allen & Sons 2001. 276 pp. Paperback
CONTENTS:

9   The Birth Control King of the Upper Volta (see C117)
10   Painting the Dog (see C243)
11   Wintering in Victoria (see C52)
12   Sing Me No Love Songs I'll Say You No Prayers (see C18)
13   The Woman Who Talked to Horses (see C130)
14   Dust (see C187)
15   Lady Godiva's Horse (see C82)
16   The Only Daughter (see C133)
17   Pretty Pictures (see C158)

B

BOOKS EDITED

B1   *Best Canadian Short Stories, 81*. With John Metcalf. Ottawa: Oberon Press, 1981. 192 pp. Hardcover and paperback

B2   *Best Canadian Short Stories, 82*. With John Metcalf. Ottawa: Oberon Press, 1982. 256 pp. Hardcover and paperback

B3   *The New Press Anthology # 1: Best Canadian Short Stories*. With John Metcalf. Toronto: General Publishing Co. 1984. 260 pp. Paperback

B4   *The New Press Anthology # 2: Best Canadian Short Stories*. With John Metcalf. Toronto: General Publishing Co. 1985. 246 pp. Paperback.

B5   *The Macmillan Anthology No. 1*. With John Metcalf. Toronto: Macmillan of Canada 1988. 298 pp. Paperback

B6   *The Macmillan Anthology No. 2*. With John Metcalf. Toronto: Macmillan of Canada 1989. 346 pp. Paperback

B7   *The Writer's Path: An Introduction to Short Fiction*. College and Univ text. Inter short fiction. With Constance Rooke. Toronto: Nelson Canada, 1998. 1056 pp. Paperback

C

CONTRIBUTIONS TO BOOKS, ANTHOLOGIES, PERIODICALS, MAGAZINES AND NEWSPAPERS

FICTION

C1   "A Christmas Fable." *Tomahawk* 25 (Dec 1958): 6-7.

C2   "Never But Once the White Tadpole." *New Campus Writing* no. 3. Eds Nolan Miller and Judson Jerome. New York: Grove 1959. 184-95.

C3   "The Line of Fire." *The Noble Savage* no. 5. Eds Saul Bellow, Keith Botsford and Aaron Asher. New York: World 1962. 183-253. Rpt in *YB* 95-178 as

"Brush Fire." Also in *Editors: The Best from Five Decades*. Eds Saul Bellow and Keith Botsford. New York: Toby 2001. 811-875.

C4   "Winter Has a Lovely Face, Isn't Summer Hell." *New England Review* 1 (1962): 10-13.

C5   "Those Days Around the Tree-town Corner Now." *Carolina Quarterly* 14.3 (1962): 45-50.

C6   "The Walrus Feeders." *Carolina Quarterly* 14.3 (1962): 52-56.

C7   "The Beggar in the Bulrush." *Reflections* 2.1 (1962): 40-56.

C8   "Not Far from the Borders of the Indian Ocean." *Carolina Quarterly* 15.2 (1963): 39-63.

C9   "If You Went to the River Why Were You Not Baptized." *Carolina Quarterly* 15.3 (1963): 7-15.

C10   "A New Strike Out Record for Every Day." *Carolina Quarterly* 15.3 (1963): 79-83.

C11   "If Lost Return to the Swiss Arms." *Carolina Quarterly* 16.1 (1963): 18-32. Rpt in *O. Henry Prize Stories*. LP 5-23, NAS 2-22, Z 23-40.

C12   "The Alamo Plaza." *Red Clay Reader* 1 (1964): 15-22. YB 36-56.

C13   "Jones' End." *Reflections: The Free South Review* 3.1 (1964): 5-12. BASS citation.

C14   "The Olive Eaters." *Carolina Quarterly* 16.2 (1964): 5-12.

C15   "The Day Begins." *The Young Writer at Chapel Hill* 3 (1964): 5-13.

C16   "The Strange Affair of Reno Brown and Mama Tuddi." *Epoch* 14 (1964): 3-20. Rev as "Mama Tuddi Done Over." (See C74, D10). BASS citation.

C17   "The Woman from Columbia." *Carolina Quarterly* 17.1 (1964): 43-48.

C18   "Sing Me No Love Songs I'll Say You No Prayers." *Epoch* 15 (1966): 111-131. *SMNLS* 193-226, *NAS* 23-38, Z 41-72, *PD* 185-222. BASS citation.

C19   "The Ice House Gang." *Carolina Quarterly* 18.3 (1966): 5-9. YB 57-71.

C20   "Further Adventures of a Cross-Country Man." *Carolina Quarterly* 19.2 (1967): 105-114.

C21   "When Swimmers on the Beach Have All Gone Home." *Louisiana Magazine* 2.1 (1967): 19-25. YB 10-35. BASS citation.

C22   "Field Service Four Hundred Forty-nine from the Five Hundred Field Songs of the Daughters of the Vieux Carré." *Lillabulero* 1.4 (1967): 15-29. YB 72-94.

C23   "The Continuing Adventures & Life Trials of Aunt Hattie." *North Carolina Anvil* 15 (Apr 1967): 7-8. First in a series of eight, seven written by Rooke.

C24   "Last One Home Sleeps in the Yellow Bed." *Last One Home Sleeps in the Yellow Bed*. Baton Rouge: Louisiana Univ Press 1968. 57-71.

C25   *Load Every Rift With Ore*. Novella. *Carolina Quarterly* 20.3 (1968): 5-47.

C26   "Lost Kafka Manuscript." *North Carolina Anvil* 5 (Oct 1968): 5.

C27   "Ancistrodon Priscivorus: Albion Gunter Jones and the Water Viper/Number Five in a Series of River Stories." *Carolina Quarterly* 21.2 (1969) 4-16.

C28   "The Hatted Mannequins of 54th Street." *Carolina Quarterly* 21.2 (1969): 65-82.

C29   "A Short Story Celebrating the Day of Public School Integration, New Orleans, La." *North Carolina Anvil* 19 (Sept 1969): 3.

C30   "Numbers One through Thirty of One Thousand Notes while Passing between the Silent Borders of Your Country and Mine." *Canadian Fiction Magazine* 4

(Fall 1971): 6- 23.

C31 "Memoirs of a Cross-Country Man." *Prism International* 11.3 (1972): 64-74. *LP* 51-64. *HO* 113-129.

C32 "How the Woman's Generation Movement Freed Heleda Bang from her Tortures and Brought Midnight Oil to the Old Folks on Oak Bay Avenue and a Raging Sunshine Oh Yes to My Heart." *Western Humanities Review* 26 (Spring 1972): 127-38.

C33 "Why I Am Here Where I Am Talking to You Like This." *Epoch* 21 (Spring 1972): 313-26. *Epoch* annual fiction prize.

C34 "For Love of Madeline." *Southern Review* 8 (Oct 1972): 919-34. *BBA* 94-110, *LP* 81-98. Rpt in *HO* as part of the novella *The Street of Moons*.

C35 "Quiet Enough My Life of Late." *Fiddlehead* 92 (Winter 1972): 59-65.

C36 "Hot Property." *Dramatika* 1 (1973) n pag.

C37 "More Hot Property." *Dramatika* 2 (1973) n pag.

C38 "Break and Enter." *Vault*. Northwood Narrows: Lillebulero Press 1973. 25-37, A5.

C39 "The Girl Who Made Time." *Grain* 1.2 (1973): 32-46. Rpt and rev in *The Best of Grain*. Eds Caroline Heath, Don Kerr and Anne Szumigalski. Regina: Saskatchewan Writers Guild 1980. 93-109.

C40 "Conjugal Precepts." *Event* 3.2 (1973): 61-72. *V* 1-8.

C41 "Dinner with the Swardians." *Canadian Fiction Magazine* 11 (Fall 1973): 19-32. Rev in *V* 10-23.

C42 "The Third Floor." *Wascana Review* 8.2 (Fall 1973): 39-44. *BBA* 137-143.

C43 "Harry the Tiger Enters His Fiftieth Year." *Fiddlehead* 96 (Winter 1973): 49-65.

C44 "Five Oral Reports on the Death of a Friend." *Quarry* 23.1 (1974): 49-54.

C45 "If You Love Me Meet Me There." *University of Windsor Review* 9.2 (1974): 41-47. *LP* 42-50, *HO* 83-90.

C46 "The Magician in Love." Excerpt from the novel *The Magician in Love*. *Lillabulero* 14 (Spring 1974): 102-104. Enl as "The Magician in Love: Love and Ethics." A5.

C47 "Fine Water for a Sloop." *Antigonish Review* 17 (Spring 1974): 47-59.

C48 "Why a Judaeo-Christian Philosophy that Knows So Much about the Nature of God Knows So Little about the Nature of Jack B. Woodcraft III." *Western Humanities Review* 28 (Spring 1974): 149-64.

C49 "The First Day of the World." *Malahat Review* 31 (July 1974): 104-24. Rpt in *An Ounce of Cure*.

C50 "For Love of Eleanor." *Southern Review* 10 (July 1974): 631-55. *BBA* 111-136, *LP* 99-126. Rpt in *HO* (113-182) as part of the novella *The Street of Moons*.

C51 "Leave Running." *Epoch* 24 (Fall 1974): 82-93. *LP* 24-41, *HO* 43-58.

C52 "Wintering in Victoria." *Canadian Fiction Magazine* 15 (Fall 1974): 66-78. *BBA* 9-23, *HO* 183-196, *PD* 167-184. CFM Annual Prize.

C53 "How the Raiders Are Doing." *Antigonish Review* 16 (Winter 1974): 17-30.

C54 "From the novel *The Magician in Love*." *Carolina Quarterly* 27.1 (1975): 64-70. Rev as "The Magician in Love: Love and Trouble" in *BBA* 57-73.

C55 "Conversations with Ruth." *Wascana Review* 10.1 (1975): 60-66.

C56   "Jettatura." *Ohio Review* 17.1 (1975): 89-103.
C57   "A Girl and a Dummy and the Dummy's Best Friend." *Antigonish Review* 21 (Spring 1975): 11-23.
C58   "Friendship and Rejuvenation." *Canadian Fiction Magazine* 24-25 (Spring-Summer 1975): 103-08. *BBA* 86-93.
C59   "Manifesto A." *Canadian Fiction Magazine* 18 (Summer 1975): 95-100.
C60   "The Magician in Love." *Oasis* 15 (1976): 29-36. Nineteen stories not elsewhere published.
C61   "No Whistle Slow." Written in collaboration with Constance Rooke. *Southern Review* 12.3 (1976): 482-495. *BBA* 24-41.
C62   "The Magician in Love." *Iowa Review* 7.1 (1976): 23-29. Rev as "The Magician in Love: Love and War" in *BBA* 47-56.
C63   "The Girl Who Collected Husbands." *North Carolina Review* 27.1 (1976): 34-56.
C64   "Kiss the Devil Goodbye." *Fiddlehead* 105 (Spring 1976): 88-104.
C65   "From the Love Parlour." *Antigonish Review* 26 (Summer 1976): 55-70. Rev as "Dangerous Woman" in *BBA* 169-183. Rev as "Call Me Belladonna" in *LP* 65-80. Rpt in *77: Best Canadian Stories*.
C66   "The Broad Back of the Angel." *Statements 2: New Fiction* Eds Jonathan Baumback and Peter Spielberg. New York: Fiction Collective 1977. 182-194. Rev in *BBA* 184-201. *HO* 215-246.
C67   "Friendship and Libation." *BBA* 74-85.
C68   "Iron Woman." *BBA* 144-68.
C69   "For Love of Gomez." *Southern Review* 13 (April 1977): 370-391. *LP* 127-157. Rpt as part of the novella *The Street of Moons* in *HO* 113-182.
C70   "Sixteen-year-old Susan March Confesses to the Innocent Murder of all the Devious Strangers Who Would Drag Her Down." *Wascana Review* 13.2 (1978): 57-65. Rpt in *80: Best Canadian* Stories.
C71   "Biographical Notes." *Canadian Fiction Magazine* 30-31 (1979): 53-75. *CE* 97-130.
C72   "Hello, I'm Jane Doe." *Hesperus* 1.1 (1979): 3-14.
C73   "Friendship and Property." *79: Best Canadian Stories*. Eds Clark Blaise and John Metcalf. Ottawa: Oberon Press 1979. 95-121. *CE* 71-95.
C74   "Mama Tuddi Done Over." *Descant* 25-26.10.3-4 (1979): 7-40. Rpt in *Best American Short Stories*. *DS* 9-42, *SM* 58-95.
C75   "Civilities." *Ion* 1 (Spring 1979): 10-16.
C76   "Murder Mystery." *Antigonish Review* 37 (Spring 1979): 11-15.
C77   "Oral History: The Deacon's Tale." *Fiddlehead* 121 (Spring 1979): 27-39. Rev as "The Deacon's Tale" in *CE* 5-23. *NAS* 69-92, *Z* 98-116. Rev in *HO* 13-30.
C78   "Adolpho's Disappeared and We Haven't a Clue Where to Find Him." *Malahat Review* 50 (Apr 1979): 193-213. Rev in *CE* 132-157, *NAS* 39-68, *Z* 73-98. Rev in *HO* 59-82.
C79   "Building a Fire under Peterson." *Antigonish Review* 38 (Summer 1979): 21-25.
C80   "The End of the Revolution and Other Stories." *Crazy Horse* 19 (Fall 1979): 73-90. *CE* 47-70, *HO* 91-112.
C81   "Addressing the Assassins." *Prism International* 18.2 (1979–80): 22-25.

C82　"Lady Godiva's Horse." *Prism International* 18.2 (1979-80): 7-21. *DS* 73-92 *SMNLS* 250-271, *PD* 247-270.

C83　"Fromm Investigations." *CE* 24-46.

C84　"The Selling of Heaven." *Scratchgravel Hills* 3 (Spring 1980): 18-22.

C85　"Standing In for Nita." *Fiddlehead* 126 (Summer 1980): 3-15. *DS* 112-128.

C86　"Deer Trails in Tzityonyana." *Canadian Forum* 701 (Sept 1980): 25-28. *DS* 99-112.

C87　"85 Reasons Why I'm in the Fix I'm in." Written in collaboration with Constance Rooke. *Descant* 32-33.12.2-3 (1981): 132-143.

C88　"Why Agnes Left." *Event* 1 (1981): 5-10. *BCK* 85-92., *SMNLS* 186-192

C89　"Ibena." *Quarry* 30.2 (1981): 15-19.

C90　"Hitting the Charts." *Canadian Fiction Magazine* 38 (1981): 5-12. *BCK* 119-130.

C91　"Winter Is Lovely, Isn't Summer Hell." *Canadian Fiction Magazine* 38 (1981): 13-20. *DS* 54-58.

C92　"The Magician in Love." *Canadian Fiction Magazine* 38 (1981): 21-28. *ML* A10.

C93　"Slocum in Slocum." *Canadian Fiction Magazine* 38 (1981): 143.

C94　"The Problem Shop." *Canadian Fiction Magazine* 38 (1981): 29-43. *DS* 156-175.

C95　"Sisyphus in Winter." *Canadian Fiction Magazine* 38 (1981): 44-54.

C96　"Murder Mystery (Do Something)." *Canadian Fiction Magazine* 38 (1981): 55-59. *DS* 93-98.

C97　"Hanging Out with the Magi." *Canadian Fiction Magazine* 38 (1981): 60-73.

C98　"Shakespeare's Dog." *Canadian Fiction Magazine* 38 (1981): 74-105. National Magazine Fiction Award Finalist.

C99　"Conversations with Ruth: The Farmer's Tale." *Canadian Forum* 706 (Feb 1981): 2-21.

C100　"The Doorstep Syndrome" or "Nineteen-year-old Susan March Confesses to the Wanton Humiliation and Wilful Destruction of All Her Numerous Parents." *Dandelion* 8.2 (1981-82): 15-22.

C101　"Hat Pandowdy." *BCK* 101-118. (1982): 101-118.

C102　"Shoe Fly Pie." *BCK*: 93-100.

C103　"A Nicer Story by the "B" Road." *Fiddlehead* 134 (1982): 41-47. *BCK* 71-84.

C104　"Free for the Asking." *Erindale Review* 1 (1982): 9-11.

C105　"Return of the Magician (In Love)." *Descant* 38.13.4 (Fall 1982): 85-91.

C106　"Narcissus Consulted." *Malahat Review* 61 (Feb 1983): 132-142. *NAS* 93-110, *Z* 117-128. BASS citation.

C107　"The Cat Killer." *Antioch Review* 41.4 (Fall 1983): 421-429.

C108　"Shakespeare's Dog." *Canadian Forum* 726 (1983): 18-21, 25. Photo cover.

C109　"Licking Up Honey." *Scrivener* 4.1 (1983): 22-23.

C110　"Going for Broke." *Scrivener* 4.1 (1983): 24.

C111　"The Pope's Emissary." *Scrivener* 4.1 (1983): 24.

C112　"Beloved in the Bath, This Is My Beloved." *New Quarterly* 3.3 (1983): 43-47.

C113　"Beloved in the Bath, This Is My Beloved." Continuation of the "Beloved" story in *Negative Capability* 4.1 (1984): 71-76

C114　"The History of England, Part Four." *Canadian Fiction Magazine* 46 (1983): 30-42. *SMNLS* 272-290.

C115　"Agnes and the Cobwebs." *True North/Down Under: A Journal of Australian and Canadian Literature* 1 (1983): 17-25. *SMNLS* 133-143.

C116　"Flux." *Event* 12.2 (1983): 31-43.

C117　"The Birth Control King of the Upper Volta." *Antaeus* 49-50 (Spring-Summer 1983): 226-245. *BCK* 7-38, *SMNLS* 152-185, *NAS* 110-122, *Z* 129-162, *PD* 121-156.

C118　"Some People Will Tell You the Situation at Henny Penny Nursery Is Getting Intolerable." *Matrix* 17 (Fall 1983): 2-6. *SMNLS* 227-235.

C119　"In the Garden." *Antaeus* 48 (Winter 1983): 124-138. *SMNLS* 114-132. Renamed as "Gin and Tonic" in *BCK* 131-148. BASS citation.

C120　"Foot-in-Field Story." *Rubicon* 2 (Winter 1983-84): 64-68.

C121　"Manuscript Pages from a Work-in-Progress." *Rubicon* 2 (Winter 1983-84): 61-63.

C122　"Water is Flowing Over the Bridge." *American Voice* 1.1 (1984): 3-4. Rpt *Best Fiction from the American Voice*. Pushcart Prize nomination.

C123　"Working Blind." *Writ* 15 (1984): 52-60.

C124　"Dirty Heels of All the Young Children." *Grand Street* 3.2 (1984): 136-150. *BWC* 86-100. Pushcart Prize citation.

C125　"Saks Fifth Avenue." *Grand Street* 4.1 (1984): 39-63. Rpt in *A Grand Street Reader*. *BWC* 120-145, *PD* 87-114.

C126　"Paintings, Water Colours, Hand-painted Flowers." *New West Coast Fiction* Ed Fred Candelaria. West Coast Book Number Five. Vancouver: WCR/ Pulp Press 1984. 38-43. Pub sim as *West Coast Review* 18.3 (1984).

C127　"Party at Fellini's Before Beginning the Movie." *Fiddlehead* 138 (Jan 1984): 7-14.

C128　"The Shut-in Number." *Quarry Magazine* 33.2 (Spring 1984): 26-32. *SMNLS* 28-36.

C129　"Let Me Not to My True Mind Disdain Euphoria." *University of Toronto Review* 9 (Spring 1984): 11-13.

C130　"The Woman Who Talked to Horses." *Yale Review* 74 (Spring 1984): 410-417. *SMNLS* 104-113, *PD* 223-232. Pushcart Prize citation. BASS citation.

C131　"Bennett." *Descant* 50.16.3 (Fall 1984): 94-112. *SP*. National Magazine Fiction Award finalist.

C132　"A Bolt of White Cloth." *Antaeus* 53 (Autumn 1984): 169-179. *BWC* 7-20, *NAS* 123-154, *Z* 197-210, *PD* 23-38.

C133　"The Only Daughter." *BWC* 21-48. *NAS* 123-154, *Z* 163-190, *PD* 271-302..

C134　"Why the Heathens Are No More." *BWC* 49-71.

C135　"The Woman's Guide to Home Companionship." *BWC* 72-85. *PD* 7-22.

C136　"Saloam Frigid with Time's Legacy while Mrs. Willoughby Bight-Davies Sits Naked Through the Night On a Tree Stump Awaiting the Lizard That Will Make Her Loins Go Boom-Boom." *BWC* 101-119.

C137　"The Madwoman of Cherry Vale." *BWC* 146-164.

C138　"Dream Lady." *BWC* 165-176.

C139　"The Man in the Green Bathrobe." *SMNLS* 96-103.

C140　"Typical Day in a Desirable Woman's Life." *Grand Street* 5.1 (1985): 73-77.

WDYL 105-111. BASS citation. Pushcart citation.

C141 "The Yale Chair." *Paper Guitar: 27 Writers Celebrate 25 Years of Descant Magazine.* Ed Karen Mulhallen. Toronto: HarperCollins 1985. 386-406.

C142 "The Bucket." *Now Magazine* 4.8 (1985): 21. Rept as "The Bucket Brigade" in WDYL 132-134 .

C143-44 "Leon Rooke: Two Stories." "The Bucket" and "Ordinary Mortals." *Cross-Canada Writer's Quarterly* 7.3-4 (1985): 36-37.

C145 "Ordinary Mortals." *Descant* 48.16.1 (Spring 1985): 48-49.

C146 "Saving the Province." *This Magazine* 19.2 (June 1985): 33-34. P 22-31.

C147 "The Judge." *Magic Realism and Canadian Literature.* Eds Peter Hinchcliffe and Ed Jewinski. Proc of the Conference on Magic Realism, Univ of Waterloo, 1986. Waterloo: Univ of Waterloo Press 1986. 88-91.

C148 "The End of the Revolution and Other Stories."Rept in *Literary Review* 28 (Spring 1985): 438-455. See C80, D34, K9.

C149 "A Rough Customer." *Columbia Magazine* 10 (1986): 47-65.

C150 "The Arsonist." *Waves* 14.3 (1986) 8-12.

C151 "Love Child." *Waves* 14.3 (1986) 13-15.

C152 "How the Prime Ministers Live." *This Magazine* 19.6 (Feb 1986): 20-22.

C153 "In Jail with the Bennett." *Random Thoughts* 5 (Mar-Apr 1986): 8-9.

C154 "Apology for Not Getting Back to You Sooner." *American Voice* 3 (Summer 1986): 3-8. Rpt as "Apology" in OH 170-174.

C155 *Bennett.* Short novel. *Descant* 54.17.3 (Fall 1985): 39-104. Rev and enl from the 1984 printing.

C156 "Don't Leave Me, Heinz." *Canadian Forum* 764 (Dec 1986): 20-22.

C157 "Safe Passage through Dark Nights." *Canadian Forum* 764 (Dec 1986): 22-23.

C158 "Pretty Pictures." *TriQuarterly* 64 (Winter 1986): 60-62. Rpt in *Harper's Magazine* (July 1986): 31-32. WDYL 94-97, PD 303-306.

C159 "The Sugar Derby." *Prism International* 25.3 (Jan 1987): 30.

C160 "The Composers." *Grain* 15.1 (Spring 1987): 50-56.

C161 "A Story for Constance." *Fiddlehead* 151 (Spring 1987): 23-25.

C162 "Sweethearts." Shorter vers in *Mississippi Review* 15.3 (Spring-Summer 1987): 104-106. Rev in WDYL 35-38. Rpt in *Mississippi Review On Line* and *The Bedford Anthology*, Boston, 1997. http://www.mississippireview.com/1996/9602rook.html Rev in *Prairie Fire* 7.4 (Winter 1987): 49-51.

C163 "I Want to Know the Answer." *TheQuarterly* 2 (Summer 1987): 14-19. WDYL 164-170.

C164 "Light Bulbs." *Grand Street* 6.4 (Summer 1987): 117-122. WDYL 14-21.

C165 "The Best Good Girl Ever." *Event* 16.2 (Summer 1987): 70-76. Rpt in *Tesseracts 2.*

C166 "LR Loves GL." *Exile* 12.1 (Summer 1987): 92-104. WDYL 121-130.

C167 "Cornfields." *Review: Latin American Literature and Arts* 38 (July-Dec 1987): 66-71. Rev in WDYL 84-93.

C168 "Mama Tuddi." *Chattahoochee Review* 1 (Fall 1987): 89-93. Rpt as "Mama Tuddi Tried" in WDYL 98-104.

C169 "Cooked Pig." *Fiction International* 7: 2 (Fall 1987): 1-2. *Snapshots: The New*

Canadian Fiction. Rev as "RSVP" in *OH* 175-176.

C170   "The Primitives." *Whetstone* (Fall 1987): 8-9.

C171   "Grace Troup." *Whetstone* (Fall 1987): 62-66.

C172   "Shut Up." *Quarterly* 3 (Fall 1987): 102-108. *WDYL* 112-118.

C173   "Blues Roots." *Mississippi Review* 15.1-2 (Fall-Winter 1987): 27-29. Rev as "Blue Roots" or "You Tear Me Apart" in *WDYL* 171-178.

C174   "Those Who Can't Cut It With Mary." *Descant* 59.18.4 (Winter 1987): 59-61.

C175   "The Blue Baby." *TriQuarterly* 68 (Winter 1987): 51-59. Rpt in *Best Canadian Stories 87*, *Pushcart Prize XIII*, *Fiction of the Eighties: A Decade of Stories From TriQuarterly, # 78*. Rpt as "Who Do You Love?" in *WDYL* 1-13, *PD* 39-52.

C176   "Neighbourhood Watch." *Waves* 15.3 (Winter 1987): 16-23. *WDYL* 152-163. Author's Award, Best Story of Year.

C177   "The House of the Sleeping Drunkards." *Story Quarterly* 23 (1987): 1-4. Rpt in *The American Story: The Best of Story Quarterly*. Rev in *OH* 165-169.

C178   "Dippings." *Grain* 4 (Winter 1988): 38-39. Rpt in *Singularities*.

C179   "Statement." *Grain* 4 (Winter 1988): 38-39. Rpt in *Singularities*.

C180   "Bites." *Chattahoochee Review* 2 (Winter 1988): 99-101. Pushcart Prize nomination.

C181   "Eustace among the Gypsies." *Antioch Review* 56 (Winter 1988): 37-44.

C182   "Picture Window Baby." *Carousel* 6 (1989): 9-10.

C183   "Wife Talk." *Carousel* 6 (1989): 11-15.

C184   "The Willies in Watusi Land." *Canadian Fiction Magazine* 67-68 (1989): 187-200. *WDYL* 49-54.

C185   "Play Greensleeves." *Exile* 13.4 (1989): 156-160. Rev in *OH* 177-179.

C186   "Whereon Do You Lead Me, Bright Rider." *Columbia Magazine* 14 (1989): 195-209.

C187   "Dust." *The Moosehead Anthology*. DC Books. 1989. 99-109. *P* 9-21, *PD* 233-246. Rpt in *Moosemilk, The Best of the Moosehead from 1977-1999*.

C188   "Raleigh's Party in the New World." *Canadian Author and Bookman* 65.4 (Summer 1990): 6-7. Rev in *OH* 73-75. Okanogan Fiction Award.

C189   "Veterans of the Uprising." *Writ* 21 (1989): 110-118.

C190   "The Willies." *Grand Street* 8.3 (Spring 1989): 57-61. *WDYL* 49-54.

C191   "Choirmaster's Report on Dissension in the Holy Father's Ranks." *Quarry Magazine* 38.3 (Summer 1989): 5-6. Rev in *WDYL* 140-143.

C192   "A Good Baby." *Brick* 37 (Autumn 1989): 32-35.

C193   "The Heart Must from Its Breaking." *Exile* 13.2 (Winter 1989): 14-29. Rpt in *Best Canadian Stories 1990*. *HO* 247-263, *Z* 215-232, *PD* 65-86.

C194   "Up a Tree." *P* 32-45

C195   "Tale of the Slaughter of Innocents," *Quarry* 40 (1990): 152-53.

C196   "Bank Job." *Gazette Literary Edition*. Univ of Western Ontario [London, ON] 1990: B6-B7.

C197   "Admiral of the Fleet." *Border Crossings* 9.1 (Jan 1990): 50-51. *The Macmillan Anthology No. 3*. Eds John Metcalf and Kent Thompson. Toronto: Macmillan 1990, 170-175. *WDYL* 64-70, *NAS* 203-220, *Z* 223-238. Western

Magazines Awards Finalist.

C198 "The Blue Baby." Rpt from Winter 1987 issue. *TriQuarterly* 78 (Spring-Summer 1990): 400-408.

C199 "Turnpike." *Descant* 69.21.2 (Summer 1990): 59-70." Rpt as "The People in the Trees" in *WDYL* 22-34.

C200 "Swingers Swinging," *Descant* 69.21.2 (Summer 1990): 84-87.

C201 "Drivers," *Quarterly* 16 (Winter 1990): 22-23. *WDYL* 119-120.

C202 "The Second Child." *Main Street* 1.1. *Souvenir Edition.* Eden Mills: Writer's Festival, 1991. 6.

C203 "The Emporium Closes Its Doors at Midnight." *Canadian Storytellers*, Vol. One. *New Directions From Old.* Ed J.R. (Tim) Struthers. Guelph: Red Kite Press, 1991. 151-154

C203a "Langston." *Canadian Storytellers*, Vol. One. *New Directions From Old.* Ed J.R. (Tim) Struthers. Guelph: Red Kite Press, 1991. 158-162.

C204 "The Unhappiness of Others." *Exile* 15.4 (1991) 5-16.

C205 "The Mercenary's Daughter." *This Magazine* 24.8 (May 1991) 38-41.

C206 "The Woman from Red Deer Who Went to Johannesburg, Set Herself Afire, And Leapt Four Floors to Her Apparent Death." *Malahat Review* 100 (Sept 1992): 152-164. *OH* 33-47. BASS citation.

C207 "The Heart Must from Its Breaking," *Exile* 16.4 (1992): 5-16. Long vers in *OH*. Without headings in *HO, PD*.

C208 "Red Meat." *WDYL* 55-58.

C209 "Want to Play House?" *WDYL* 59-63. *NAS* 199-202, *Z* 211-214, *PD* 1-6.

C210 "Unreliable Narrators." *WDYL* 131-132.

C211 "Covici's Guilt." *WDYL* 179-182.

C212 "Smoke" *WDYL* 183-186.

C213 "Body Count." *WDYL* 187-200. Author's proof indicates the story may have originally appeared in *Epoch*.

C214 "Sorrows Drowned." *WDYL* 144-151.

C215 "The Heart Must from Its Breaking." Printed from the abbr radio vers. *North Carolina Literary Review* 1.2 (Spring 1993): 110-119. Also in *North Carolina Literary Review Online* with illus by Stanton Blakeslee and Lee Misenheimer. *Best Stories of the South.* *NAS* 199-202, *Z* 215-232.

C216 "The Boy from Moogradi and the Woman with the Map to Kolooltopec." *Ploughshares*. Eds Russell Banks and Chase Twitchell. (Winter 1993-94): 60-75. *NAS* 237-253, *Z* 251-268, *OH* 56-72.

C217 "The Woman with the Electrified Heart." Cover and inside photos. *Quarry* 42.3 (1994): 35-49. Also on line in *Euphoria*, Brown Univ/Princeton Univ. *OH* 181-195.

C218 "Old Mother." *Malahat Review* 109 (Winter 1994): 93-95. *OH* 30-47.

C219 "St. Pete and the Chamber of Horrors." *Third Coast* 1.1 (Spring 1995): 117-128. *OH* 151-164.

C220 "The Six Blind Boys of Santa Ocuro." *Blood and Aphorisms* 18.25 (1995) 33-34. Rev in *OH* 145-150.

C221 "Raphael's Cantalupo Melon." *Exile* 20.1 (1996) 5-13. *OH* 104-111, *A* 33-63.

C222 "Old Eden Mills Old Folks Reunion Party." *The Eramosa Anthology*. Eds Katherine L. Gordon and Joshua Willoughby. The Eramosa Writers Group 1996. 104-112.

C223 "At Heidegger's Grave." *Carousel* 7 (January 1996): 54-76.

C224 "The Lithuanian Wife." *TriQuarterly* 96 (Spring-Summer 1996): 62-69. *OH* 48-55.

C225 "If We May Not Save the Living Let Us Save the Dead." *This Magazine* 30.2 (Sept-Oct 1996): 36-37. *OH* 212-214.

C226 "Legend of the Flaming Moths." P. K. Page spec issue. *Malahat Review* 117 (Winter 1996): 29-32.

C227 "Bury Him at Home." *Writing Home, The PEN Travel Anthology*, Toronto: McClelland and Stewart 1997. 269-273. Rpt as "The Bell" in *OH* 208-211.

C228 "The Woman from Red Deer Who Went to Johannesburg, Set Herself Afire, and Jumped Four Floors to Her Apparent Death." *Exile* 21.1 (1997): 125-139. *OH* 33-47.

C229 "Fazzini Must Have You Ever at Her Side." *American Voice*, Kentucky Foundation for Women 43 (1997): 3-6. *A* 19-32, *OH* 137-140. In *Best Fiction from the American Voice*. Pushcart nomination.

C230 "Sidebar to the Judiciary Proceedings, The Nuremberg War Trials November 1945." *Malahat Review* 119 (Summer 1997) 57-66. *OH* 18-29. *Exile* 21.1 (1997): 11-23.

C231 "More You May Not Expect from Runte." *Prairie Fire* 17.4 (Winter 1997): 76-83. *OH* 196-207.

C232 *The Guacamole Game*. Novella. *OH* 234-271.

C233 "Hot." *OH* 141-144.

C234 "Reprieve." *OH* 180.

C235 "Adventures in Fairyland." *OH* 215-233.

C236 "Wy Wn Ty Calld Yr Nam You Did Not Answr." *OH* 112-115.

C237 "The Weepers of Vicenza." *OH* 116-136.

C238 "The Judge: High Plains Art." *OH* 76-80.

C239 "There Are Bodies Out There." *98: Best Canadian Stories*. Ed Douglas Glover, Ottawa: Oberon Press 1998. 113-134.

C240 "Gypsy Art." *Antioch Review* 56.1 (Winter 1998): 37-44. *OH* 9-18.

C241 "The Fall of Gravity." *Border Crossings* 17 (July 1998): 44-48.

C242 "The Fall of Gravity." *Dark Leisure* 3 (Fall 1999): 23-25.

C243 "Painting the Dog." *Toronto Life* 34.12 (Aug 2000): 84-87. *PD* 157-166.

C244 "The Fall of Gravity." *Exile* 24.1 (2000): 41-73.

C245 "The Situation with Regard to Henrietta Amani," *Blood and Aphorism* 40 (Dec 2000) 55- 58. 10th anniv spec issue.

C246 "Crazy in Love with Everyone All the Time." *Exile* 25.1 (2001): 78-97.

C247 "The Yellow House." *Best Canadian Stories 2001*. Ed Douglas Glover. Ottawa: Oberon Press, 2001. 9-14.

C248 "Paris for Beginners." *Event* 30.1 (Spring 2001): 97-103.

C249 "A New Relationship with Yoghurt." *Fiddlehead* 208 (Summer 2001): 7-18.

C250 "A Good Radio Voice." *Descant* 113.32.2 (Summer 2001): 9-24.

C251 "My Philippino Bride." *Descant* 115.32.4 (Winter 2001): 20-21.

C252 "The Making of Saints." *Writual* 5 (2002): 65-71.

C253 "How to Write a Successful Short Story." *Antioch Review* 60.3 (Summer 2002): 367-376.

C254 "The Winds of Change, The Winds of Hope, The Winds of Disaster." *Daedalus: the Journal of the American Academy of Arts and Sciences* 131.4 (Fall 2002): 112-119.

C255 "Polar Arms." *Blackbird* 1.2 (Fall 2002). Blackbird online magazine of literature and the arts. Virginia Commonwealth Univ., Richmond. http://www.blackbird.vcu.edu/v1n2/fiction/rooke_l/index.htm

C256 "Ikat the Spirit and Ikat the Kimono." *New Quarterly*. Symposium Issue: Wild Writers We Have Known 21.2-3 (Winter 2002): 209-216.

C257 "Bad Men Who Love Jesus: Queening Isn't What It Use to Be." *Bad Men Who Love Jesus!* Ed Leon Rooke. *New Quarterly* 86 (Spring 2003):18-20.

C258 "Bad Men Who Love Jesus: Seventy-seven Brides." *Bad Men Who Love Jesus!* Ed Leon Rooke. *New Quarterly* 86 (Spring 2003): 21-25.

C259 "Aaron & Mae." *Bad Men Who Love Jesus!* Ed Leon Rooke. *New Quarterly* 86 (Spring 2003): 248-250.

C260 "*A*R*T at Banff Centre." Writers' Trust of Canada pamphlet. Canada Book Week. (Apr 2003).

C261 "The Last Shot." *En Route*. Air Canada (May 2003): 49-56.

C262 "Lamplighter Bridegroom 360." *Fiddlehead* 208 (Summer 2003): 151-158.

C263 "Saddam's Dog." *Exile* 272 (Summer 2003): 48-51.

C264 "Cupid and Psyche." *Exile* 27.2 (Summer 2003) 129-139. Multiple CBC radio broadcasts (e.g. The Arts Tonight Festival of Fiction, 11 July 2002, This Morning Sunday Edition, Richardson's Roundup).

C265 "Son of Light." Novella. *News from The Republic of Letters*. Ed Keith Botsford. New York: The Toby Press, new ser 12 (Fall 2003): 103-34.

C266 "J.D." *Antioch Review* 6.1 (Winter 2003): 44-48.

C267 "Magi Dogs." *World Literature Today* (May-Aug 2004): 60-62.

POETRY

C268 "A Servant of the Night." *America Sings*. 11th Annual Anthology of College Poetry. National Poetry Association, 1954. 7.

C269 "Ode to the Toad." *Free Lance* 3 (First half 1955): 24.

C270 "Pink Edition." *Flame* 3 (Spring 1956): 18. Readers' Choice Award.

C271 "Raven from the East." *Flame* 3 (Fall 1956): 17. Readers' Choice Award.

C272 "Biography." *Existaria* 4 (1957): 13.

C273 "Brown." *Carolina Quarterly* 14.29 (Spring 1962): 13-14.

C274 "What's to Become of Us?" *New England Review* 1 (Spring 1962): 7-8.

C275 "The Pick-Axe." *Skeleton at Sixty*. Ed Barbara E. Turner. Erin ON: Porcupine's

Quill,1986. 96.
C276 "You're Divine" *Writual, New Art and Writing* 3 (1999): 13.
C277 "Forget Lawyers." *Writual, New Art and Writing* 3 (1999): 14.
C278 "Life of a Progressive Party Civil Servant Called Out of Retirement in Benefit of a Busy Nation." *Prairie Fire* 24.3 (Fall 2003): 89.

Numerous other poems appeared in small journals and college magazines, some of which were written while in high school and printed under heading "Today's N.C. Poem" in the Raleigh *News and Observer*.

DRAMA

C279 "The Death of Martin Luther King: A Thursday Evening Play in One Act." *North Carolina Anvil* 13, Apr 1968: 4-5.
C280 "Cakewalk." *Event* 9, No. 2, 1980: 101-32.

D

REPRODUCED ANTHOLOGY CONTRIBUTIONS

D1 "If Lost Return to the Swiss Arms." *Prize Stories 1965: The O. Henry Awards*. Eds Richard Poirier and William Abraham. New York: Doubleday 1965. 109-223.
D2 "If Lost Return to the Swiss Arms." *Chapel Hill Carousel*. Ed Jessie Rehder. Chapel Hill: Univ of North Carolina Press 1967. 89-107.
D3 "Wintering in Victoria." *76: New Canadian Stories*. Eds Joan Harcourt and John Metcalf. Ottawa: Oberon Press 1976. 99-114.
D4 "For Love of Eleanor." *Here and Now: Best Canadian Stories*. Eds Clark Blaise and John Metcalf. Ottawa: Oberon Press 1977. 114-34.
D5 "When Swimmers on the Beach Have All Gone Home." *Transitions II: Short Fiction; A Source Book*. Ed Edward Peck. Vancouver: Comancept 1978. 101-20.
D6 "If Lost Return to the Swiss Arms." *Stories Plus: Canadian Stories with Authors' Commentaries*. Ed John Metcalf. Toronto: McGraw-Hill Ryerson 1979. 167-80.
D7 "Devious Strangers." *80: Best Canadian Stories*. Eds Clark Blaise and John Metcalf. Ottawa: Oberon Press 1980. 149-61. Previously entitled "Sixteen-year-old Susan March Confesses to the Innocent Murder of all the Devious Strangers Who Would Drag Her Down" (See C70).
D8 "Dinner with the Swardians." *Magic Realism*. Ed by Geoff Hancock. Toronto: Aya Press 1980. 111-24.
D9 "Mama Tuddi Done Over." *Best American Short Stories, 1980*. Eds Stanley Elkin and Shannon Ravenel. Boston: Houghton Mifflin 1980. 272-301.
D10 "Stalled." CBC *Anthology*. 11 Oct 1980.

D11   "The Girl Who Made Time." *The Best of Grain.* Eds Caroline Heath, Don Kerr and Anne Szumigalski. Regina: Saskatchewan Writers Guild 1980. 93-109.

D12   "Hanging Out With the Magi." *Illusion One: Fables, Fantasies and Metafiction.* Ed Geoff Hancock. Toronto: Aya Press 1983. 67-82.

D13   "Sixteen-year-old Susan March Confesses to the Innocent Murder of all the Devious Strangers Who Would Drag Her Down." *Canadian Short Fiction Anthology* Vol. 2. Ed. Paul Belserene, Vancouver: Intermedia Press, 1982. 58-65.

D14   "Biographical Notes." *Elements of Fiction.* Eds Robert Scholes and Rosemary Sullivan. Toronto: Oxford Univ Press 1982. 771-794.

D15   "Sing Me No Love Songs I'll Say You No Prayers." *Rainshadow: Stories From Vancouver Island.* Eds Ron Smith and Stephen Guppy. Lantzville-Victoria: Oolichan Books/Sono Nis Press 1982. 25-52.

D16   "Deer Trails in Tzityonyana." *West of Fiction.* Eds Leah Flater, Aritha Van Herk and Rudy Wiebe. Edmonton: NeWest Press 1982. 291-302.

D17   "Standing In for Nita." *Introduction to Fiction.* Eds Jack David and John Redfern. Toronto: Holt, Rinehart & Winston of Canada 1982. 415-421.

D18   "The Problem Shop." *Making It New.* Ed John Metcalf. Toronto: Methuen 1982. 239-256. Photograph of the author by Sam Tata. (See C94).

D19   "Winter Is Lovely, Isn't Summer Hell." *Making It New.* Ed John Metcalf. Toronto: Methuen 1982. 229-238. Photograph of the author by Sam Tata.

D20   "Voices." *Making It New.* Ed John Metcalf. Toronto: Methuen 1982. 257-261. Photograph of the author by Sam Tata.

D21   "Sixteen-year-old Susan March Confesses to all the Devious Strangers Who Would Drag Her Down." *An Anthology of Canadian Literature in English.* Eds Donna Bennett and Russell Brown. Toronto: Oxford, Vol 2, 1983. 355-363. Also subsequent ed.

D22   "Shoe Fly Pie." *Shoes & Shit: Stories for Pedestrians.* Ed Geoff Hancock. Toronto: Aya Press 1984. 87-90.

D23   "Paintings. Water Colours. Hand-painted Flowers." *New: West Coast Fiction.* Edmonton: WCR/Pulp Press 1984. 38-43. (See C126).

D24   "A Bolt of White Cloth." *Canadian Short Stories.* 4th ser. Ed Robert Weaver. Toronto: Oxford Univ Press, 1985. 183-196.

D25   "Adolpho's Disappeared and We Haven't a Clue Where to Find Him." *Canadian Short Stories: From Myth to Modern.* Ed W.H. New. Scarborough [Toronto]: Prentice Hall 1986. 356-372.

D26   "Saks Fifth Avenue." *A Grand Street Reader.* Ed Ben Sonnenberg. New York: Summit Books 1986. 127-151.

D27   "A Bolt of White Cloth." *The Arch of Experience.* Eds Ian W. Mills and Juidith H. Mills. Toronto: Holt, Rinehart and Winston of Canada 1986. 336-345.

D28   "The Judge." *Magic Realism and Canadian Literature: Essays and Stories.* Ed Peter Hinchcliffe and Ed. Jewinski. Waterloo: Univ of Waterloo Press 1986. 88-91.

D29   "Gin and Tonic." *The Art of the Tale: An International Anthology of Short Stories, 1945-1985.* Ed Daniel Helpern. New York: Elizabeth Sifton Books Viking-Penguin 1986. 638-649.

D30 "The Woman Who Talked to Horses." *The Oxford Book of Canadian Short Stories*. Eds Margaret Atwood and Robert Weaver. Toronto: Oxford Univ Press 1986. 263-269.

D31 "Bennett." *86: Best Canadian Stories*. Eds David Helwig and Sandra Martin. Ottawa: Oberon Press 1987. 186-212.

D32 "The Blue Baby." *87: Best Canadian Stories*. Eds David Helwig and Maggie Helwig. Ottawa: Oberon Press 1987. 7-22.

D33 "The Blue Baby." *The Pushcart Prize XIII* (1988-1989). Ed Bill Henderson. New York: Pushcart Press 1988. 292-301. Penguin ed 1989.

D34 "The End of the Revolution and Other Stories." *Writers in Aspic*. Ed John Metcalf. Montreal: Véhicule Press 1988. 201-220.

D35 "The Problem Shop." *The New Canadian Anthology*. Ed Robert Lecker and Jack David. Toronto: Nelson Canada 1988. 385-401. (See C94).

D36 "Bats." *Tesseracts 2, A Science Fiction Anthology*. Eds Phyllis Gotlieb and Douglas Barbour. Victoria: Press Porcepic 1988. 165-73

D37 "Dust." *The Moosehead Anthology*. Montreal: DC Books 1989. 99-109.

D38 "I. Paintings II. Water Colours III. Hand-painted Flowers, All You Can Carry, 25C." *The Last Map Is the Heart. An Anthology of Western Canadian Fiction*. Eds Allan Forrie, Paddy O'Rourke and Glen Sorestad. Saskatoon: Thistledown Press 1989. 221-225. (See C126).

D39 "Admiral of the Fleet." *The Third Macmillan Anthology*. Eds John Metcalf and Kent Thompson. Toronto: Macmillan of Canada 1990. 171-173. Author's photograph.

D40 "A Bolt of White Cloth." *An Anthology of Canadian Literature in English*. Rev ed. Eds Donna Bennett, Russell Brown and Natalie Cooke. Toronto: Oxford, Vol. 2, 1990. 523-530.

D41 "Statement." *Singularities*. Ed Geoff Hancock. Windsor: Black Moss Press 1990. 96.

D42 "Dippings." *Singularities*. Ed Geoff Hancock. Windsor: Black Moss Press, 1990. 97.

D43 "The Heart Must from Its Breaking." *Best Canadian Stories 1990*. Eds David Helwig and Maggie Helwig. Ottawa: Oberon Press. 161-183.

D44 "The Blue Baby." *Fiction of the Eighties: A Decade of Stories from TriQuarterly*. Eds Reginald Gibbons and Susan Hahn. *TriQuarterly* 78 (Spring-Summer 1990): 400-408.

D45 "House of the Sleeping Drunkards." *The American Story: The Best of Story Quarterly*. Eds Anne Brashler, Melissa Pritchard and Diane Williams. New York: Cane Hill Press, 1990. 151-156.

D46 "A Bolt of White Cloth." *Elements of Fiction*. Rev Canadian ed. Eds Robert Scholes and Rosemary Sullivan. Toronto: Oxford Univ Press, 1990. 722-731.

D47 "A Bolt of White Cloth." *Reading Our World: The Guelph Anthology*. Eds Constance Rooke, Renee Hulan and Linda Warley. Needham Heights: Ginn Press, 1990. 189-195.

D48 "The Woman Who Talked to Horses." *Black Water 2, More Tales of the Fantastic*.

Ed Alberto Manguel. Toronto: Lester & Orpen Dennys, 1990. 460-468.

D49 "The Only Daughter." *From Ink Lake: Canadian Stories*. Ed Michael Ondaatje. Toronto: Lester & Orpen Dennys, 1990. 461-484. Pub in the United Kingdom as *Contemporary Canadian Short Stories*, Faber & Faber. In the United States as *Contemporary Canadian Short Stories*, Viking Penguin. Rpt Alfred A. Knopf, Canada, Vintage ed., 1992.

D50 "Biography." *The Possibilities of Story*, Vol. One. Ed J.R. (Tim) Struthers. Toronto: McGraw-Hill, Ryerson, 1991. 201-204.

D51 "Regeneration." *Canadian Storytellers*, Vol. One. *New Directions from Old*. Ed J.R. (Tim) Struthers. Guelph: Red Kite Press, 1991. 156-157.

D52 "The Heart Must from Its Breaking." *15 Years in Exile*. Vol 2. Ed Barry Callaghan. Toronto: Exile Editions, 1992. 5-16.

D53 "Biographical Notes." *The Art of Short Fiction: An International Anthology*. Ed Gary Geddes. Toronto: Harper Collins, 1992. 619-641.

D54 "Art." *Likely Stories: A Postmodern Sampler*. Eds George Bowering and Linda Hutcheon. Toronto: Coach House Press, 1992. 211-217. (see *NAS* 155-180, Z 191-196).

D55 "The Deacon's Tale." *Canadian Classics*. Eds John Metcalf and J. R. (Tim) Struthers. Toronto: McGraw-Hill, Ryerson, 1992. 147-190. Incl author's commentary and selected bibliography.

D56 "The Birth Control King of the Upper Volta." *Canadian Classics*. Eds John Metcalf and J.R. (Tim) Struthers. Toronto: McGraw-Hill, Ryerson, 1992. 147-190. Incl author's commentary and selected bibliography.

D57 "First Day of the World." *An Ounce of Cure*. Ed Mark Jarman. Victoria: Porcepic Books, 1992. 34-53.

D58 "When Swimmers on the Beach Have All Gone Home." *The Possibilities of Story*, Vol. 2. Ed J.R. (Tim) Struthers, Toronto: McGraw-Hill, Ryerson, 1992. 125-136.

D59-62 "In Her Shoes," "Don't Cook a Pig," "Family Quarrels" and "Opening Night." *Snapshots: The New Canadian Fiction* Ed Kristina Russelo. Windsor: Black Moss Press, 1992. 107-110.

D63 "Unreliable Narrators." The Coach House Prospectus, nd.

D64 "The Heart Must from Its Breaking." *Myth and Voices: Contemporary Canadian Fiction*. Ed David Lampe. Fredonia: White Pine Press, 1993. 89-125.

D65 "The Heart Must from Its Breaking." Short vers. *Best Stories From the South*. Ed Shannon Ravenel. Chapel Hill: Algonquin Books of Chapel Hill. 1994. 215-221.

D66 "Fat Woman." *Opening Lines*. A supp to the Mar issue of *Quill & Quire*. Toronto: Harper Collins, 1994 n pag.

D67 "The Boy from Moogradi and the Woman With the Map to Kolooltopec." *Stag Line*. Ed Bonnie Burnard. Edmonton: Coteau Press, 1995. 99-113.

D68 "The Woman Who Talked to Horses." *The New Oxford Anthology of Canadian Fiction*. Eds Margaret Atwood and Robert Weaver. Toronto: Oxford Univ Press, 1995. 386-406.

D69　"Sweethearts." *Carnival: The Scream in High Park Anthology*. Ed Peter McFee. Toronto: Insomniac Press, 1996. 104-106.

D70　"Muffins." *The Porcupine's Quill Reader*. Eds Tim Inkster and John Metcalf. Erin: Porcupine's Quill, 1996. 171-178. Extracts and photographs.

D71　"A Bolt of White Cloth." *The Writers' Path*. Ed with Constance Rooke. Toronto: Nelson, 1997. 688-697

D72　"Wintering in Victoria." *Silver Anniversary Anthology: The Best of Canadian Fiction Magazine*. Ed Geoff Hancock. Kingston: Quarry Press, 1997. 30-42.

D73　"There Are Bodies Out There." *98: Best Canadian Stories*. Ed Douglas Glover. Ottawa: Oberon Press, 1998. 113-134.

D74　"Sweethearts." *The Bedford Introduction to Literature*. 5th ed. Ed Michael Meyer. Boston: Bedford-St. Martin's, 1998. 2150.

D75　"Dust." *Moosemilk: The Best of The Moosehead From 1977-1999*. Eds Patti Sonnta and Grout Loewen. Montreal: DC Books, 1999. 43-53.

D76　"Art." *And Other Stories*. Ed George Bowering. Vancouver: Talonbooks, 2001. 243-250.

D77　"The Yellow House." *Best Canadian Stories: 01*. Ed Douglas Glover. Ottawa: Oberon Press, 2001. 9-14.

D78　"The Line of Fire." *Editions: The Best from Five Decades*. Eds Saul Bellow and Keith Botsford. London and Connecticut: Toby, 2001. 811-874.

D89　"A Bolt of White Cloth." *Literature and Media 11*. Eds Neil Anderson and James Barry. Toronto: Nelson Thompson Learning, 2001 n pag.

D80　"The Winds of Change, The Winds of Hope, The Winds of Disaster." *Best Canadian Stories: 03*. Ed Douglas Glover. Ottawa: Oberon Press, 2003. 81-93.

D81　"A Bolt of White Cloth." *Short Fiction*. Eds Rosemary Sullivan and Mark Levine. Toronto: Oxford Univ Press, 2003. 528-537.

D82　"A New Relationship with Yoghurt," *When I Was a Child: Stories for Grownups and Children*. Eds Eric Henderson and Madeline Sonik. Ottawa: Oberon Press, 2003. 114-126.

D83　"A Bolt of White Cloth." *Inside Story III*. Sec ed. Ed Richard Davies and Jerry Wowk. Toronto: Harcourt Canada nd. 436-447.

D84　"Le Who's who de Balduchi." *Toronto, accidents de parcours*. Trans Marrianne Audourad. Ed Linda Spalding. Paris: Editions Autrement, 2004. 113-156.

D85　"A Bolt of White Cloth." *The Nelson Introduction to Literature*. 2nd ed. Eds Al Lalleau and Jack Finnbogason. Toronto: Thomson Nelson, 2004. 436-444.

E

TRANSLATIONS

E1　*El perro de Shakespeare*. (Shakespeare's Dog). Barcelona: Laia Literatura 1985 n pag.

E2　*Shakespeare's hond*. (Shakespeare's Dog). Trans Annelies Hazenberg. Utrecht/

Antwerpen: Spectrum 1985. 137

E3   "l. Malereien/II.Wasserfarben/III. Handgematte blumen, so viel sie tragen können, 25c." ("I. Paintings II. Water Colours III. Hand-painted Flowers, All You Can Carry, 25C"). *Die Horen* # 41, 31, Jahrgang, Band I/86, (Ausgabe, 1986): 61-64. Subsequently renamed "Art."

E4   "Razgovori sa Rut: farmerova priča" ("Conversation with Ruth: Farmer's Tale"). Trans Velimir Kostov. *Antologija kratke priče Kanade*. Ed Vladislav A. Tomović. Kruševac: Bagdala, Serbia, l986. 120-124.

E5   "Zimovanje u Viktoriji" ("Wintering in Victoria"). Trans Branko Gorjup. *Antologija kanadske pripovijetke*. Ed and introd Branko Gorjup. Zagreb: Nakladni Zavod Matice Hrvatske, Croatia, 1991. 231-244.

E6   "Inverno a Victoria" ("Wintering in Victoria"). Trans Francesca Valente. *Musica silente, racconti canadesi contemporanei*. Ed and introd Branko Gorjup, pref Agostino Lombardo. Catanzaro: Abramo, Italy. 1992.

E7-20 *Narciso allo specchio* (*Narcissus in the Mirror*). Fourteen stories in Italian. Ed and introd Branko Gorjup, trans Carla Plevano and Francesca Valente. Como-Pavia: Ibis. 1995. 256. (See A 22).

E21   "La donna che parlava ai Cavalli" ("The Woman Who Talked to Horses"). Trans Francesca Valente. *Altre terre, racconti contemporanei del Canada anglofono*. Ed and introd Branko Gorjup. Venezia: Supernova, Italy, 1996. 79-86.

E22-35 *Narcis u zrcalu* (*Narcissus in the Mirror*). Fourteen stories in Croatian. Ed and introd Branko Gorjup, trans Biljana Romić and Branko Gorjup, interv Giga Gračan. Zagreb: Konzor, Croatia, 1997. 278. (See A22a).

E36-38 *Arte. Tre fantasie in prosa* (*Art. Three Fictions in Prose*). Bilingual Eng-It ed. Trans Francesca Valente, ed Marco Fazzini, pref Roberto Sanesi, introd Branko Gorjup, commentary Giorgio Pressburger. Lugi: Edizioni del Bradipo, Italy, 1997. 72. (See A24).

E39   "Umjetnost" ("Art"). Trans Biljana Romić. *Godine nove* (1997): 61-62.

E40   "La fille unique" ("The Only Daughter"). *Nouvelles du Canada anglais*. Ed and trans Nicole Côté. Quebec City: L'Instant Meme, 1999. 181-222.

E41   "El Juez: arte de llanuras altas." ("The Judge: High Plains Art"). Trans Fernando Napoles Tapia. *Casa de las Americas* No. 220 (Julio-Septembre 2000): 76-79.

E42   "Zimovanie vo Victorii" ("Wintering in Victoria"). *Ticha hudbea, antologia anglo-kanadskych poviedok*. Trans Alojz Keniž and Marián Gazdik, ed and introd Branko Gorjup. Bratislava: Juga, Slovak Republic, 2000. 124-135.

E43   "Il Melone di Raffaello" ("Raphael's Cantalupo Melon"). *Oceano Canada*. Spec issue on English Canadian writing. Trans Francesca Valente, ed and introd Branko Gorjup. *Nuovi Argomenti* 14 (2001): 120-130.

E44   "La mujer que hablaba con los caballos" ("The Woman Who Talked to Horses"). *Los Universitarios*. Trans Mario Murgia. Universidad Nacional Autonoma de Mexico, nueva epoca num. 27 (Diciembre de 2002): 15-20.

E45   "La mujerque que hablaba con los caballos" ("The Woman Who Talked to Horses"). Ed and translated Claudia Lucotti. *Donde es Aqui? 25 Cuentos Canadienses*. Fondo de Cultura Economica, Mexico (2002): 150-163.

E46 *En chute libre. (The Fall of Gravity)*. Trans Richard Crevier, forwr Russell Banks. Paris: Phebus, 2002. 300.

E47 "La casa amarilla" ("The Yellow House"). Trans Francoise Roy and Letica Villagarcia. *Tragaluz, revista de entretenimiento cultural* Ano 1, num. 10 (Julio-Augusto 2003): 52-55.

E48 "Le Who's who de Balduchi." *Toronto, accidents de parcours*. Trans Marrianne Audourad. Ed Linda Spalding. Paris: Editions Autrement, 2004. 113-156.

F

REVIEWS

F1 Rev of *Entering Ephesus*, by Daphne Athas. *North Carolina Anvil* 20 Nov 1971: 8. (*North Carolina Anvil* contributions are incomplete. Rooke was a frequent book, movie, and theatre critic for this weekly newspaper "of politics and the arts," which he co-edited. He also reviewed freelance for other newspapers.)

F2 Rev of *The Hero's Great Great Great Great Great Grandson*, by George Cuomo. *Malahat Review* 20 (Oct 1971): 140-41.

F3 Rev of *The Journey of August King*, by John Ehle, *Malahat Review* 21 (Jan 1972): 119-20.

F4 Rev of *St. Urbain's Horseman*, by Mordecai Richler. *Malahat Review* 21 (Jan 1972): 118-119.

F5 Rev of *Best Little Magazine Fiction*, by Curt Johnson and Alvin Greenberg. *Malahat Review* 22 (Apr 1972): 133-34.

F6 Rev of *We Never Make Mistakes*, by Aleksandr Solzhenitsyn. *Malahat Review* 23 (July 1972): 145-46.

F7 Rev of *The Streets of Summer*, by David Helwig. *Malahat Review* 20 (Oct 1971): 140-41.

F8 Rev of *Walking Across Egypt*, by Clyde Edgerton. *News and Observer* 15 Mar 1987: 4D.

F9 "Bowles Is Spellbinding, Dazzling, Agile, Unique." Rev of *Collected Stories 1939-1976*, by Paul Bowles. *Gazette*, Montreal, 28 June 1980: 1, 17.

F10 Rev of *Man Descending* and *My Present Age*, by Guy Vanderhaeghe. *Philadelphia Inquirer* Nov 24, 1985: 1, 8.

F11 "Celebration and Determination in Stifling Surroundings." Rev of *The Elizabeth Stories*, by Isabel Huggan. *Philadelphia Inquirer* 6 Sept 1987: M5.

F12 "Anybody Ought to Have Their Choice in Things If They Can." Rev of *Rock Springs*, by Richard Ford. *St. Petersburg Times* 29 Nov 1987: 6D.

F13 "Tales from the Caboose." Rev of *Solomon Gursky Was Here*, by Mordecai Richler. *Books in Canada* Nov 1989: 11-13.

F14 "100 days in the creation of a great novel." Rev of *Working Days: The Journals of The Grapes of the Wrath* and the new ed of *Grapes of Wrath*, by John

Steinbeck, *Globe and Mail* [Toronto] Apr 22, 1989: C16.

F15 Rev of *Joe*, by Larry Brown. *New York Times Book Review* Nov 10, 1991: 25.

F16 "Do the Job, She Said, an Did It." Rev of *I Been In Sorrow's Kitchen and Licked Out All the Pots*, by Susan Straight. *New York Times Book Review* 16 Aug 1992: 15.

F17 "Sergeant Muldrow Finds Transcendence." Rev of *To the White Sea*, by James Dickey. *New York Times Book Review* 19 Sept 1993: 14.

F18 "Mississippi Burning." Rev of *Wolf Whistle*, by Lewis Nordan. *Book World* [*Washington Post*] 3 Oct 1993: 4.

F19 "Whistling Past the Graveyard." Rev of *High Lonesome*, by Barry Hannah, *New York Times Book Review* 27 Sept 1996: 14.

F20 "His Old Kentucky Home." Rev of *Out of the Woods*, by Chris Orcutt, *New York Times Book Review* 7 Mar 1999. 16.

G

INTERVIEWS

By Leon Rooke

G1 "New Black Playwrights: An Interview with William Couch." *North Carolina Anvil* 4 Jan 1969: 5, 11.

G2 "Interview with Richard Ford." With Constance Rooke. *The Writers' Path: An Introduction to Short Fiction*. Eds Constance Rooke and Leon Rooke. Toronto: Nelson Canada, 1998. 896-899.

G3 "Interview with Russell Banks." With Constance Rooke. *The Writers' Path: An Introduction to Short Fiction*. Eds Constance Rooke and Leon Rooke. Toronto: Nelson Canada, 1998. 892-895.

G4 "Interview with Diane Schoemperlen." With Constance Rooke. *The Writers' Path: An Introduction to Short Fiction*. Eds Constance Rooke and Leon Rooke. Toronto: Nelson Canada, 1998. 905-908.

G5 "Interview with Thomas King." With Constance Rooke. *The Writers' Path: An Introduction to Short Fiction*. Eds Constance Rooke and Leon Rooke. Toronto: Nelson Canada, 1998. 900-904.

With Leon Rooke

G6 Interview. By Geoff Hancock. *Canadian Fiction Magazine* 38 (1981): 107-34. Spec issue on Leon Rooke. Rpt in *Canadian Writers at Work* as "Interviews with Geoff Hancock." Toronto: Oxford Univ Press, 1987. 164-186.

G7 Interview. By Philippe Desquieu. *Books in Canada* Mar 1983: 24-26.

G8 "An Interview with Leon Rooke." By Peter O'Brien. *Rubicon* 2 (Winter 1983-84): 36-60.

G9   Interview. By Harry Vanderlist. *Ars Victoriana*, Victoria College, Univ of Toronto 169.1 (Fall 1984): 38-46.

G10   "WQ Interview with Leon Rooke." By Bruce Meyer and Brian O'Riordan. *Cross-Canada Writers' Quarterly* 7.3-4 (1985): 32-35. Photograph by Bruce Meyer.

G11   Interview. By Clint Burnham. *Random Thought* 1.2 (1985): 1-3. Cover story-photographs.

G12   "Reading Foreign Writers: An Interview with Leon Rooke." By Clint Burnham. *Waves* 14.3 (1986): 5-7.

G13   Interview. *Gabereau Tonight*. CBC radio, 1986.

G14   "Leon Rooke Interview." By Peter O'Brien. *So To Speak: Interviews with Contemporary Canadian Writers*. Ed. Peter O'Brien, Montreal: Véhicule Press, 1987. 284-309.

G15   Interview. By Geoff Hancock. *Canadian Writers at Work: Interviews with Geoff Hancock*. Ed Geoff Hancock. Toronto: Oxford Books. 1987. 145-186.

G16   Interview with reading. Host Paul William Roberts. TVO *Imprint*. Sept 1989.

G17   Interview. "The Thin Man Makes the Fat Woman, Shakespeare's Dog and a Good Baby." *Off the Shelf*. The Bookshelf Cafe, Guelph, Nov-Dec 1989: l. Cover-story photograph.

G18   Interview. "Getting There by Degrees." By Bruce Meyer and Brian O'Riordan. *Lives & Works*. Eds Bruce Meyer and Brian O'Riordan. Windsor: Black Moss, 1992. 90-99.

G19   "Leon Rooke: A Conversation." By Hilda Kirkwood. *Between the Lines: The Oberon Interviews*. Ottawa: Oberon Press, 1994. 55-66. Rpt in *Brick* 49 (Summer 1994): 28-33. With author's 1962 and 1994 photographs.

G20   Interview. "Il caleidoscopio di Narciso." By Marco Fazzini. *Il Giornale di Vicenza*, Vizenza 3 Dec 1995: 6. Rprt as "Narcissus's Kaleidoscope: An Interview with Leon Rooke" in *Il Tolomeo* 1 (1995): 77-78.

G21   Interview. "Leon Rooke/Hit Single." By Nancy Wigston. *Books in Canada* Oct 1995: 6-10. Cover and inside photographs.

G22   Interview. By Gabriella Skubincan. *Blood and Aphorisms* 17 (Winter 1995): 33-37.

G23   "Austin Clarke Interviews Leon Rooke." *Literati* (television series). Harbourfront Nov 1997.

G24   Interview. "Blues s kanadskog sjevera." ("Blues from the Canadian North"). By Ivan Salečić Jr. *Godine nove* 1 (Summer 1997): 58-61.

G25   Interview. By Giga Gračan. *Narcis u zrcalu* (*Narcissus in the Mirror*). Ed Branko Gorjup. Zagreb: Konzor, Croatia, 1997. 269-276.

G26   "TDR Interview: Leon Rooke." By Michael Bryson and Natham Whitlock. *Danforth Review*. http://www.danforthreview.com/features/interviews/leon_rooke_interview.htm

G27   Interview. "Rooke's Rise." By Jake MacDonald. *Globe and Mail* [Toronto] 9 Sept 2000: D6-7. Author's photograph by Robert Tinker.

G28   "Tina Srebotnjak Interviews Leon Rooke re *The Fall of Gravity* and Margaret Atwood re *The Blind Assassin*." Show # 1, TVO *Imprint* 27 Sept 2000.

G29 Interview. "Would-be Opera Star, Writing from a Sea of Fluff." Questionnaire Leon Rooke. *National Post* [Toronto] 21 Oct 2000: B12.

G30 Interview. By Olivier Burrot. Radio France 3, 18 Oct 2002.

G31 "Lingering on Posted Land: An Interview with Leon Rooke." By Branko Gorjup. *WLT Magazine* (*World Literature Today*) 3.1 (Apr-June 2003): 49-56.

H

STAGE PRODUCTIONS

H1 *The Black and the Black.* Mars Hill College prod First Prize winner, State Drama Festival, April, 1957.

H2 *The Thief and the Hunchback.* The Carolina Playmakers, 1958. Samuel Selwyn Prize.

H3 *Gone for Broke* by Jake Phelps. Dir by Leon Rooke. Tri Angel Professional Theatre, Durham, NC. Sept 1960.

H4 *Lady Psyche's Cafe.* The Arts in Louisville Players. Louisville Art Centre, Louisville Ky. 1960.

H5 *Of Mice & Men* by John Steinbeck. Dir by Leon Rooke. Unto These Hills Theatre Company, Cherokee, NC. July 1960.

H6 *Evening Meeting of the Suicide Club.* The Gallery Players. Victoria Art Gallery, Victoria, BC 1972.

H7 *Sword/Play.* Dir by Jon Bankson. Perf Peter Jaenicke, Yvonne Adalian, Marti Maraden and Rob Michael Graham. The New Play Centre, Vancouver, 1973. One-act vers.

H8 *Ms. America.* Dir by Timothy Bond. Perf Nuala Fitzgerald and David Brown. Factory Lab Theatre. New Theatre, Toronto, 1974.

H9 *Sword/Play.* Dir by Neil Flanagan. Perf Amanda Davies, James Doerr, Elaine Sulka and Sturgis Warner. The Cubiculo National Shakespeare Company, New York, May 1975. Full-length vers.

H10 *Krokodile.* Harbourfront Theatre. Prod by Orillia Native Stage Group. nd (c1976).

H11 *Cakewalk.* Dir by Perry Leuders. Canby Community Players, Southwest State Univ Marshall, MN. 1976.

H12 *Swim/Suit.* As above.

H13 *Ice and Men.* A Collaborative with Paul Thompson and the Company. Theatre Passe Muraille, Toronto, Dec-Feb 1984-85.

H14 *A Bolt of White Cloth.* Adpt by the author. National Book Week Festival Players, Open Space, Victoria, BC. Apr 1986.

H15 *The Good Baby.* Play in two acts. Dir by Paul Thompson. Caravan Stage Company. British Columbia tour June-Aug 1987. Final perf Detroit Mich. Sept 1987.

H16   *Shakespeare's Dog*. Adpt by Blair Haynes. Workshop West Theatre, Edmonton, Sept-Oct 1989.

H17   *The Good Baby*. Rev script. Touring production US-Canada. Caravan Stage Co. Closed Key West, Florida, Dec 1990.

H18   *The Coming*. A collaborative with Paul Kirby, Leon Rooke, Robert Priest and Deborah Porter. Music by Grier Coppins. Caravan Stage Co. Prod. Wolfe Island ON, Summer 1991. Rev script Du Maurier World Stage Festival, 19-28 May 1992.

H19   "The Woman's Guide to Home Companionship." Staged reading. Perf by Nancy Beatty and Ann Anglin, 11 Sept 1994, Eden Mills Writers' Festival.

H20   *Hooker, el gos de Shakespeare*. Catalan adpt by Pere Sagrista. Artenbrut Theatre, Barcelona, Spain, Nov 1995.

H21   "Want to Play House?" Staged reading. Dir by David Bogoslaw. Lincoln Centre Theatre Directors Lab July 1996. Monologue for Clairmont High School BC student placed first in International Recitation Competition, Prague, 1990.

H22   "King Billy Blue" and "Oopsie-Doopsie." Benefit perf by Leon Rooke. Kaleidoscope (Children's) Theatre Magic Carpet Series, Victoria, BC Mar 1992

H23   "Dirty Heels of the Fine Young Children." Staged reading. Adpt and dir by David Bogoslaw. Lincoln Centre Theatre Directors Lab July 1996.

H24   "Dirty Heels of the Fine Young Children" Adpt and perf Mia Anderson. *Writ Large*. Canadian tour, 1996.

H25   *Shakespeare's Dog*. Adpt by students/faculty, George Washington Univ Drama Dept Washington, DC, 1998.

H26   *Shakespeare's Dog*. Adpt by Jeff Pitcher. Lyrics by Leon Rooke. Caravan Barge Theatre. Opened Mar 2000, St. Petersburg, Fla. for two-year nine-month runs along Eastern Seaboard and inland water routes. 2000 season closed at Coconut Grove (Miami), Fla. 2001 season closed at Navy Pier, Chicago.

H27   *Shakespeare's Dog*. DiDo Productions. Hill Street Theatre. Edinborough Fringe Festival, Aug 2001.

I

FILMS, TELEVISION DOCUMENTARIES, RADIO PLAYS, SOUND RECORDINGS, VIDEOTAPES

I1   "D Day at the Gung Ho." Univ of N Carolina Radio Workshop, 1961. Half-hour show.

I2   "Daddy, Take Me Home." Univ of N Carolina Radio Workshop, 1961. Half-hour show.

I3   *The Bennett Place*. Script by Leon Rooke. Prod by the Univ of North Carolina Educational Network, 1965.

I4   "Stalled." *The Hornby Collection*. CBC radio, Vancouver prod 1979.

I5   "Susan March" *The Hornby Collection*. CBC radio, Vancouver prod 16 Jan 1982.

I6   "Shoe Fly Pie." *CBC Radio Anthology*. CBC radio, Toronto prod 16 Mar 1984.

I7   "Leon Rooke on Cormac McCarthy." *State of the Arts*. CBC FM radio. Toronto prod 8 Dec 1985. CBC AM 9 Dec 1985.

I8   "How We Founded Our Great City and Conquered the Dreaded Gnomes." Radio play. *State of the Arts*. CBC FM radio. Toronto prod 22 Dec CBC AM 23 Dec 1985. Best Radio Play nom. Carousel Theatre, Victoria, BC. Perf by Leon Rooke. 1992.

I9   "The Situation at Henny Penny Nursery Is Intolerable." *State of the Arts*. CBC FM radio, Toronto prod. nd.

I10   "Child's Play." *State of the Arts*. CBC FM radio, Toronto prod 21 Dec 1986. CBC AM 22 Dec 1986.

I11   *Love Clinic*. Film script by Michael Ondaatje. Directed by Richard Rose, The role of "The Reverend" perf by Leon Rooke. Film Institute for Advanced Film Development, Toronto, 1990.

I12   "Zimovanje u Viktoriji" ("Wintering in Victoria"). Prod Giga Gračan. *3 Program*, Croatian National Radio, Zagreb 13 Oct 1990.

I13   "The Heart Must from Its Breaking." *Cloud 9*. Perf by Leon Rooke. CBC AM 25 Oct 1992. Re-broadcast 15 Nov 1992.

I14   "The Woman Who Talked to Horses." CBC AM, FM, 1992.

I15   "Who Do You Love?" *Harbourfront Reading*, May 19 1992 CBC broadcast, June 1992.

I16   *The Heart Must from Its Breaking*. Sleeping Giant Productions, Bravo TV. Toronto, Jan 1998.

I17   *A Good Baby*. Dir Katherine Dieckman. Perf by David Straithern, Henry Thomas and Cara Seymour. New York, 2000.

I18   "Canadian authors getting praise they deserve..." *The Last Word*. Op-ed delivered at conclusion of Global-TV's national evening news. Global TV, Sept. 30, 2002.

I19   The CBC Literary Awards/Prix Litteraires. *The Arts Tonight*, CBC/Radio Canada live broadcast from Ottawa. 25 Mar 2003. Author reading. Subsequent multiple story broadcast on Radio One.

I20   Allcock, Michael. Doc film. "Leon Rooke in Eden Mills." TV Ontario broadcast, 25 and 29 Sept 2003.

I21   "Le dernière fois" ("The Last Shot"). Trans Denis Leblond. Radio Canada 2 Feb 2004. Read by actor. Available on line, CBC Radio Arts.

J

MISCELLANEOUS: INTRODUCTIONS, PREFACES, FOREWORDS, NEWSPAPER ARTICLES, CONFERENCE PAPERS.

J1   "We Are Not Surprised." *Reflections* 2.1 (Fall 1962): 7-8.

J2   "Response." *Red Clay Reader* 1 (1964): 88.

J3   "The Writer and His World." *Rhetor* 4 (1965): 5-6.

J4   "Speaking of Socks." *Red Clay Reader* 3 (1966): 116-17.

J5   "Jessie Rehder." *Durham Morning Herald* 26 Feb 1967: 5D.

J6   "Anvil?" *North Carolina Anvil* 15 April 1967: 8.

J7   "The Streets of Edgemont." *North Carolina Anvil* 15 Apr 1967: 1-3.

J8   "Economic Development in North Carolina, Part One." *North Carolina Anvil* 22 Apr 1967: 1-2.

J9   "Economic Development in North Carolina, Part Two." *North Carolina Anvil* 2 May 1967: 1-2.

J10   "Soc(IE)ty (that is)." A society (or gossip) column written periodically by Leon Rooke. *North Carolina Anvil* 2 May 1967: 8.

J11   "Workers in the Mills." *North Carolina Anvil* 2 May 1967: 2.

J12   "On the Path of Father Parker." "On the Path" column written by Leon Rooke. *North Carolina Anvil* 25 Aug 1967: 7-8.

J13   "On the Path of Aaron Hartman." *North Carolina Anvil* 15 Sept 1967: 7.

J14   "On the Path of De Anna, Belly Dancer." *North Carolina Anvil* 18 Nov 1967: 6.

J15   "A Short Happy Talk with the Editor of *Red Clay Reader*, An Unhappy Appraisal of the New Baby, and This Sample Illustrating Why the Reviewer Swings." *North Carolina Anvil* 25 Nov 1967: 3, 10.

J16   "Obituary for Resurrection City, U.S.A." *North Carolina Anvil* 29 June 1968: 5.

J17   "Unmasking Strangers: The Face of the Poor at Resurrection City, U.S.A." *North Carolina Anvil* 29 June 1968: 1, 2, 3, 8.

J18   "Red Clay Reader 5 a Hot Item for the Money." *North Carolina Anvil* 9 Nov 1968: 5, 11.

J19   "Daphne Athas: An Appreciation." *North Carolina Anvil* 10 Sept 1969: 8.

J20   "The Novels of John Ehle." *North Carolina Anvil* Aug, 1970 n pag.

J21   "Leon Rooke." *Canada Writes!: The Members' Book of the Writers' Union of Canada.* Ed K. A. Hamilton. Toronto: The Writers Union of Canada, 1977. 295.

J22   "Tragedy or Comedy: The Flute Dance of Dr. Prince." *Canadian Drama* 3 Spring 1977: 75-76.

J23   "On 'When Swimmers on the Beach Have All Gone Home.'" *Transitions II: Short Fiction; A Source Book of Canadian Literature.* Ed Edward Peck. Vancouver: CommCept, 1978. 273-74. Photograph of the author, 272.

J24   "Biographical Notes and Author's Statements." *New West Coast Fiction.* A note on the making of "Art." 134. (See C71, D14, D53).

J25   "'If Lost Return to the Swiss Arms.'" *Stories Plus: Canadian Stories with Authors' Commentaries.* Ed John Metcalf. Toronto: McGraw-Hill Ryerson, 1979. 181-84. (See D6)

J26   "Voices." *Making It New.* Ed John Metcalf, Toronto: Methuen, 1982. 257-261. The author discusses "Winter Has a Lovely Face" and "The Problem Shop." (See D20)

J27   "...What's in a Tale." Introduction. With John Metcalf. *82: Best Canadian Stories,* Ottawa: Oberon Press, 1982. 5-11.

J28   Introduction. With John Metcalf. *The New Press Anthology: Best Canadian Short Fiction # 1*. Toronto: General Publishing, 1984. 7-8.

J29   "Rash Undertakings: The Fiction of Cormac McCarthy." *Brick* 1984: 37-40. Rpt in *The Brick Reader*. Eds Michael Ondaatje and Linda Spalding. Toronto: Coach House Press, 1991. 304-308.

J30   Introduction. With John Metcalf. *The New Press Anthology: Best Canadian Short Fiction # 2*. Toronto: General Publishing, 1985. 8-11.

J31   "Best First Novel." Judge's Comment. *Books in Canada* Apr 1985: 8-9.

J32   "Is You Is or Is You Aint My Baby: Canadian Fiction Against the Headwinds." *Brick* 33, Spring 1988: 24-30. *How Stories Mean*. Eds John Metcalf and J.R. (Tim) Struthers. Erin: Porcupine's Quill Press, 1993. 230-243. A paper delivered at the Seventh International Conference on Canadian Literature, Catania, Italy, May 1988.

J33   Introduction. With John Metcalf. *The Macmillan Anthology No 1*. Toronto: Macmillan of Canada, 1988. 2.

J34   "Position Paper." Introduction. "Statements On Their Craft by 37 Writers." Signed L.R. *The Second Macmillan Anthology*. Ed with John Metcalf. Toronto: Macmillan of Canada, 1989. 190-92.

J35   "Wanted." Under pseudonym T.L. Duff. *The Second Macmillan Anthology*. Ed with John Metcalf. Toronto: Macmillan of Canada, 1989. 225-26.

J36   Photograph with Russell Banks, *Brick* 37 (1989): 30.

J37   "Statement." *Singularities*. Ed Geoff Hancock. Windsor: Black Moss Press, 1990. 97 (See D42).

J38   Foreword. *The Happiness of Others*. Erin: The Porcupine's Quill, 1991. 7-12.

J39   "A Coherent Fictional *Oeuvre*." Three stories with attached criticism. *Canadian Storytellers: New Directions from Old*. Vol. 1. Ed J.R. (Tim) Struthers, Guelph: Red Kite Press, 1991. 151-160. (See C203a, D51).

J40   "Southern Writing, Coming Home." North Carolina Writers' Conference, Raleigh, NC, July 1991.

J41   "Looking Back: Southern Literature in Exile." North Carolina Writers' Conference, Raleigh, NC, 1992.

J42   "Canadian Fiction." Intersection for the Arts, San Francisco, Oct 1992.

J43   "Author's Commentary on 'If Lost Return to the Swiss Arms.'" *How Stories Mean*, Ed John Metcalf. 1993. 154-157.

J44   "Talking Carolina Talk." *North Carolina Literary Review* 1.2 (Spring 1993): 212-214.

J45   "John Ehle—Tributes by his Peers." *Pembroke Magazine* 26 (1994): 160-173. Proc of the 1993 North Carolina Writers' Conference. Raleigh, NC. 1993.

J46   "What I Would Be If I Were Not a Writer." *Brick* 50 (Fall 1994): 13.

J47   "Metcalf's Shoes." *New Quarterly* 16.3 (Fall 1996): 88-90.

J48   "Fat Woman." *The Bookshelf Sampler of Canadian Writing*. Ed B. Minett. Guelph: The Bookshelf, 1996. 22.

J49   "Letter." *North Carolina Literary Review* 5 (1996): 206.

J50   Photograph and drawing. *Incontro: Where Canada and Italy Meet—*

Photrographs, John Reeves. Ed Francesca Valente. Toronto: Istituto Italiano di Cultura-Exile Editions, 1996. 54-55.

J51 Photo-text. *Exile* 16.2-3 (1996): 10-11.

J52 "Last Post." Guest column-photo. *Sympatico Netlife*, Ontario and Quebec eds. (Sept-Oct 1997): 48.

J53 "Introduction." *Young Canadian Voices* 2 (1997): 1-2.

J54 "From the Author: Leon Rooke." *Canadian Bookseller* 22.7 (Sept 2000): 31.

J55 "What I Might Have Said to the Young Me Starting Out." *First Chapter, the Canadian Writers Photography Project*. Don Denton. Banff: Banff Centre Press, 2001. 87.

J56 Photograph. *First Chapter, The Canadian Writers' Photography Project*. Ed and photographed by Don Denton. Banff: Banff Centre Press, 2001. 86.

J57 "Leon Rooke's History of the Eden Mills Festival." 2002 programme of the Eden Mills Writers' Festival. 1. http://www.edenmillswritersfestival.ca/leonhistory.htm

J58 Panel Discussion. "The Nature of Influence." *New Quarterly* XXI.2-3 (Winter 2002): 275-295.

J59 "Welcome to this Spring Miscellany." Introd to *Bad Men Who Love Jesus!* Ed by Leon Rooke. *New Quarterly* 86 (Spring 2003): 14-17.

J60 "Welcome to this Spring Miscellany." *New Quarterly* 86 (Spring 2003): 18-20. Rept in 2003 programme of the Eden Mills Writers' Festival. 1.

J61 "Dolcezza e amaritudine" ("Bittersweet"). Introd to *Niente è solo l'eco di sempre (Never Is Only an Echo of Forever)*. By Barry Callaghan. Roma: Cosmo Iannone Editore, 2003. 7-10

J62 *"Geraldine Bradshaw—*Calder Willinghom" and *"The Tenants of Moonbloom—*Edward Lewis Wallant." Essays. *Lost Classics*. Eds Michael Ondaatje, Michael Redhill, Linda Spalding and Esta Spalding. Toronto: Knopf Canada, 2000. 227-232. New ed London: Bloomsbury, 2003. 185-189.

PART TWO

K

Essays, Critical Articles, Introductions, Prefaces

K1   Scobie, Steven. "The Inner Voice." *Books in Canada* Nov 1981: 8-10.

K2   Garebian, Keith. *Leon Rooke and His Works*, Toronto: ECW Press. 1989. pp 61.

K3   Hancock, Geoff. Ed spec issue on Leon Rooke. *Canadian Fiction Magazine* 38. (1981): pp 174. Eight stories, photographs, interview, essays and bibliography.

K4   ——. "The Hi-Tech World of Leon Rooke." *Canadian Fiction Magazine* 38 (1981): 135-145.

K5   Struthers, J.R. (Tim), Lesley Hogan and John Orange. "A Preliminary Bibliography of Works by Leon Rooke." *Canadian Fiction Magazine* 38 (1981): 148-64.

K6   "Leon Rooke." *Contemporary Literary Criticism.* Vol 25. Ed by Jean C. Stein. Detroit: Gale Research Company. 1983. 390-395.

K7   Brown, Russell. "Rooke's Move." *Essays on Canadian Writing* 30 (Winter 1984-85): 287-303.

K8   Body, Marjorie. "A Curved Mirror." *Writers' Quarterly* 7.3-4 (1985): 30-31. Photograph by Bruce Meyer.

K9   Vauthier, Simone. "'Entering Other Skins'—or, Leon Rooke's 'The End of the Revolution.'" *Literary Review* 28.3 (Spring 1985): 456-479. Also in *Writers in Aspic*, 222-249. (See D34.)

K10   Moss, John. Essay on *Fat Woman. A Reaader's Guide to the Canadian Novel.* 2nd ed. Toronto: McClelland and Stewart, 1987. 317-319.

K11   Pitavy-Souques, Danièle. "Tissu de rêve/Tissé de rêves: *A Bolt of White Cloth.*" *RANAM Espaces de la nouvelle canadienne Anglophone* [Paris] XX (1987): 127-13.

K12   Spriet, Pierre. "La Construction de l'indécidable dans une nouvelle de Leon Rooke." *RANAM Recherches Anglaises et Nord-Américaines* [Paris] XX (1987): 137-146.

K13   Henderson, Bill. "Shakespeare's Dog." *Rotton Reviews II: A Literary Companion.* Ed Bill Henderson. Pushcart Press, 1987. 63. Penguin ed 1988.

K14   Gotter, Cheryl. "Leon Rooke." *Contemporary Authors: New Revision Series* Vol. 23. Ed Deborah A. Straub. Detroit: Gale Research Company. 1988. 349-352.

K15   Matthews, Lawrence. "'A Bolt of White Cloth': Leon Rooke as Parabolist." *RANAM Recherches Anglaises et Nord-Américaines* [Paris] XXII (1989): 105-11.

K16 Kaltembach, Michèle. "A Man Locked Up in a Freezer: A Reading of Leon Rooke's Story "The Blue Baby."" *Commonwealth Essays and Studies* 12.1 (Autumn 1989): 54-59.

K17 David, Jackel. "Short Fiction." *Literary History of Canada* Vol. IV. Ed W.H. New. Toronto: Univ of Toronto Press. 1990. 59-60.

K18 Kaltembach, Michèle "Leon Rooke's Distinctive Mode of Writing in *A Good Baby.*" *Commonwealth Essays and Studies* 14.1 (Autumn 1991): 41-46.

K19 ——. "Leon Rooke and the Destructuring of Reality." *La nouvelle de langue anglaise: The Short Story.* Paris: Presses de la Sorbonne Nouvelle, 1991. 33-42.

K20 MacKendrick, Louis K. "Reordering the Real: Metcalf and Rooke's *81 Best Canadian Stories.*" *Canadian Storytellers: New Directions From Old.* Ed J.R. (Tim) Struthers. Guelph: Red Kite Press, 1991. 129-50.

K21 De Luca, Anna Pia. "Leon Rooke's *Shakespeare's Dog*: A Postmodern Historiographic Parody." *Atti del Convegno dell' Associazione Italiana di Anglistica* [Parma]: 1992. 291-300.

K22 Kaltembach, Michèle. "Un fondu enchaîné, de l'image au texte, du texte à l'image: une nouvelle de Leon Rooke." *Image et Récit* [Paris]: Presses de la Sorbonne Nouvelle, 1993. 133-141.

K23 Garebian, Keith. "Leon Rooke." *ECW's Biographical Guide to Canadian Novelists.* Eds Robert Lecker, Jack David and Ellen Quigley, 1993. 252.

K24 Vauthier, Simone. "Dangerous Crossing: A Reading of Leon Rooke's 'The Birth Control King of the Upper Volta.'" *Les Cahiers de la nouvelle/Journal of the Short Story in English* 4 (Spring 1985): 109-139. Rpt in *Reverberations: Explorations in the Canadian Short Story.* Toronto: Anansi Press, 1993. 10-42.

K25 Thompson, Kent. "The Performing Artist." *Essays on Canadian Writing* (Spring, 1995): 147-153.

K26 Gorjup, Branko. "I mondi imaginari di Leon Rooke." Introd *Narciso allo specchio (Narcissus in the Mirror).* Fourteen selected stories. Ed Branko Gorjup, Como-Pavia: Ibis Editore, 1995. 7-19. Rpt as "Imaginarni svijetovi Leona Rookea" in *Narcis u zrcalu,* the Croatian ed of *Narcissus in the Mirror,* Konzor, Zagreb, 1997. 5-21, and as "Perseus and the Mirror: Leon Rooke's Imaginary Worlds" in *World Literature Today* (Spring 1999): 269-274.

K27 Skubincam, Gabriella. "Leon Rooke." *BandA: New Fiction (B&A)* 17 (Winter 1995): 33-37.

K28 Cumming, Peter. "When Men Have Babies: The Good Father in *A Good Baby.*" Spec issue on "Masculinities in Canadian Literature." Eds D. Coleman and C. Bullock. *Textual Studies in Canada* 8 (1996): 96-108.

K29 Gorjup, Branko. "L'interspazio favoloso di Leon Rooke." Introd *Arte. Tre fantasie in prosa (Art. Three Fictions in Prose).* Bilingual Eng-It ed. Ed Marco Fazzini. Lugi: Edizioni del Bradipo, Italy, 1997. XI-XVI.

K30 Davey, Frank. "Leon Rooke." *The Oxford Companion to Canadian Literature.* 2nd ed. Eds Eugene Benson and William Toy. Toronto: Oxford Univ Press, 1997. 1014-1015.

K31 Solecki, Sam. "Novels in English: 1960-1982." *The Oxford Companion to Canadian*

Literature. 2nd ed. Eds Eugene Benson and William Toy. Toronto: Oxford Univ Press, 1997. 830.

K32   Sanesi, Roberto. "Dato che non puoi smettere mai di guardare." Pref *Arte. Tre fantasie in prosa* (*Art. Three Fictions in Prose*). Bilingual Eng/It ed. Ed Marco Fazzini. Lugi: Edizioni del Bradipo, Italy, 1997. VII-X.

K33   Bruni, Valerio. "Una imperfezione perfetta: Narciso allo specchio di Leon Rooke" Atti del Covegnio Internazionale di Studi (Udine, 20-22 maggio 1998). *Palinsesti culturali: Gli apporti della immigrazione alla letteratura del Canada.* Eds Anna Pia De Luca, Jean Paul Dufiet and Alessandra Ferraro, Udine: Forum, 1999. 83-102.

K34   Wright, M. Charlotte. *Plain and Ugly Janes: The Rise of the Ugly Woman in Contemporary American Fiction (Literary Criticism and Cultural Theory: The Interaction of Text and Society).* New York: Garland, 2000. 17, 61-63, 99.

K35   Banks, Russell. Forwr *En chute libre.* (*The Fall of Gravity*). Paris: Edition Phebus, 2002. 9-12.

K36   Rogers, Shelagh. Introd *Shakespeare's Dog.* 20th anniv issue. Toronto: Thomas Allen Publishers 2003. IX-XII.

K37   Jeringan, Kim. "Bad Men Who Love Jesus—The Contest." *New Quarterly* 86 (2003): 10-14.

K38   Sabatini, Sandra. "The Wider Truth: Infants in the 1980s and 1990s." *Making Babies: Infants in Canadian Fiction.* Waterloo, ON: Wilfrid Laurier Univ Press. 2004. 137-166

L

REVIEWS

L17   *Nariso allo specchio*
L18   *Narcis u zrcalu*
L19   *Oh!: Twenty-seven Stories*
L20   *Who Goes There*
L21   *The Fall of Gravity*
L22   *Painting the Dog*

• L1 *Last One Home Sleeps in the Yellow Bed* (YB) [A1]

L1.1   Anonymous. *Choice: A Publication of the Assoc of Colleges and Research Libraries, A Division of the American Library Association* 6.11 (Jan 1970): 577-78.

L1.2   Beauman, Sally. "A Past Like Fragments of a Movie." *New York Times Book Review* 2 Mar 1969: 42-3.

L1.3   Garebian, Keith. "Short Stories: The New Anthologies of Rooke and Hodgins." Rev with *The Barcley Family Theatre*, by Jack Hodgins. *Montreal Calendar Magazine* Nov 1981: 35.

L1.4   Green, L. James. *Studies in Short Fiction* IX.1 (Winter 1972): 285-87.

L1.5   Lennox, John. "Rooke's Stories." *Canadian Literature* 95 (Winter 1982): 123-125.

• L2 *The Broad Back of the Angel* (BBA) [A5]

L2.1   Anonymous. *Kirkus Review* 45 (1 Aug 1977): 801.

L2.2   Baker, Kenneth. "Fancy Fiction: *The Broad Back of the Angel*." *New York Times Book Review* 1 Jan 1978: 6.

L2.3   Blaise, Clark. Rev with *Love Parlour*. *Canadian Literature* 81 (Summer 1979): 118-19.

L2.4   Brown, Rosellen. *American Book Review* 1.2 Apr-May 1978: 12

L2.5   Garrett, George. "Coming Out of Left Field: The Short Story Today." *Sewanee Review* LXXXVI (Summer 1978): 468.

L2.6   Hogan, Leslie. Rev with *Love Parlour*. *Canadian Fiction Magazine*. 30-31 (1979): 222-25.

L2.7   Mills, John. "Book Reviews & Review Articles: *The Broad Back of the Angel*." *Fiddlehead* 117 (Spring 1978): 127.

• L3 *The Love Parlour* (LP) [A6]

L3.1   Blaise, Clark. Rev with *The Broad Back of the Angel*. *Canadian Literature* 81 (Summer 1979): 118-19.

L3.2   French, William. "Crumbling Relationships Fill *The Love Parlour*." *Globe and Mail* [Toronto] 2 Feb 1978: RY 2.

L3.3   Mills, John. Rev with *It's Easy to Fall on Ice* by Elizabeth Brewster. *Canadian Forum* 58 (Apr 1978): 41.

L3.4   Hogan, Leslie. Rev with *The Broad Back of the Angel*. *Canadian Fiction Magazine*. 30-31 (1979): 222-25.

L3.5   Struthers, J.R. (Tim). "Cadence, Texture and Shapeliness." Rev with *It's Easy to Fall on the Ice*, by Elizabeth Brewster. *Journal of Canadian Fiction*. 31-32 (1981): 245.

L3.6   Taylor, Michael. "Old Soldiers Never Die: Some Canadian Short Stories." *Fiddlehead* 120 (Winter 1979):

• L4 *Cry Evil (CE)* [A7]

L4.1   Anonymous. *Cry Evil. Quill & Quire* 46 (Aug 1980): 27.
L4.2   Brown, Russell M. "Experiment and Compulsion." *Canadian Forum* Aug 1980: 36.
L4.3   Pell, Barbara. *Canadian Book Review Annual*, 1979. 139-40.
L4.4   Wasserman, Jerry. "Fantasy Lives." Rev with *Shoeless Joe Jackson Comes to Iowa*, by W. P. Kinsella. *Canadian Literature* 91 (Winter 1981): 106-109.

• L5 *Fat Woman (FW)* [A8]

L5.1   Anonymous. *Kirkus Review* 49 (15 Feb 1981): 244.
L5.2   ——. *Library Journal* 106 (Apr 1981): 904.
L5.3   ——. *Choice: A Publication of the Assoc of Colleges and Research Libraries, A Division of the American Library* (Apr 1981): 1079.
L5.4   ——. *Quill & Quire* 47 (Apr 1981): 32.
L5.5   ——. *Publisher's Weekly* 219 (Mar 1981): 90.
L5.6   ——. *Saturday Review* 8 (July 1981): 76.
L5.7   Adams, Timothy Dow. *American Book Review* 4.3 (Mar-Apr 1982): 8.
L5.8   Bemrose, John. "You Won't Look at a Fat Woman in Same Way Again." *Toronto Star* 3 Jan 1981: B9.
L5.9   Body, M(arjorie). *Canadian Book Review Annual*, 1979. 89-90.
L5.10   Collins, Anne. "On the Rocks." *Books in Canada* June 1982: 29.
L5.11   E., J. M. *Booklist* 77 (Apr 1981): 904.
L5.12   Fagan, Carry. "God's Ugly People." *Canadian Forum* 60 (Mar 1981): 34.
L5.13   Hoskin, Cathleen and John Bemrose. *Maclean's* 94.8 (23 Feb 1981): 55.
L5.14   Johnson, Derek. "Obesity Breeding Philosophy: A Day in the Life of Ella Mae, Not As Fat As a Circus Freak, Whose Gluttonous Mind Is Thick with Folds of Guilt, Fear and Self-Loathing." *Globe and Mail* [Toronto] 17 Jan 1981: 13.
L5.15   Malone, Michael. *Nation.* 219 (20 June 1981): 766.
L5.16   Marshall, Tom. *Canadian Literature* 89 (Summer 1981): 120-21.
L5.17   Quammen, David. *New York Times Book Review* 17 May 1981: 15.
L5.18   Schemering, Christopher. *Book World.* [*Washington Post*] 7 June 1981: 6-7.
L5.19   Sherrill, Bob. "Magic—That's What You Need for Great Writing." *Durham Morning Herald* 13 July, 1981: Sec. B.
L5.20   Steinberg, Sybil. *Publisher's Weekly* 230 (29 Aug 1986): 393.

• L6 *Death Suite (DS)* [A9]

L6.1   Anonymous. Rev with *The Magician in Love. Choice: A Publication of the Assoc of Colleges and Research Libraries, A Division of the American Library Association.* 19 (Apr 1982): 1075.
L6.2   ——. *Books in Canada* Nov 1981: 8.
L6.3   E., J. M. Rev with *The Magician in Love. Booklist* 78 (15 Feb 1982): 745.

L6.4 Fagan, Carry. *Quarry Magazine* 31.2 (1982): 79-82.

L6.5 Hennig, Sharon. "Madness, Mayhem from Leon Rooke." *Calgary Herald* 17 Dec 1981: F15.

L6.6 Hoskin, Cathleen. "Laughter Trimmed in Basic Black." *Maclean's* 11 (Jan 1982): 58-59.

L6.7 Johnson, Derek B. "Magic and Death." *Globe and Mail* [Toronto] 24 Oct 1981: E16.

L6.8 Leighton, Betty. "His Subtleties Set Our Heads Spinning." *Winston-Salem Journal-Sentinel* 1982: 32.

L6.9 Martens, Debra. *Quill & Quire* 47 (Nov 1981): 24.

L6.10 Perrone, Fernanda. *Scrivener* 4.1 (Winter 1983): 42.

L6.11 Scobie, Stephen. "The Inner Voice." Rev with *The Magician in Love*. *Books in Canada* 10 Nov 1981: 8-10.

L6.12 Wade, Barbara. "Recourses of the Troubled Mind." *Waves* 10.3 (1982): 75-78.

L6.13 Wertheimer, Leonard. *Canadian Book Review Annual*. 1981: 187.

• L7 *The Magician in Love* (ML) [A10]

L7.1 Anonymous. Rev with *Death Suite*. *Choice: A Publication of the Assoc of Colleges and Research Libraries, A Division of the American Library Association*. 19 (Apr 1982): 1075.

L7.2 Gray, C. S. *Canadian Book Review Annual*, 1984. 274.

L7.3 Scobie, Stephen. "The Inner Voice." Rev with *Death Suite*. *Books in Canada* 10 Nov 1981: 8-10

• L8 *Shakespeare's Dog* (SD) [A11]

L8.1 Adachi, Ken. "Leon Rooke's Dog Tale a Triumph of Invention." *Toronto Star* 28 May 1983: H12.

L8.2 ——. *Kirkus Review* 51 (1 Mar 1983): 267.

L8.3 ——. *Library Journal* 108 (1 May 1983): 921.

L8.4 ——. *New York Times Book Review* 29 May 1983: 11.

L8.5 ——. *Canadian Literature* 104 (Spring 1985): 109-11.

L8.6 ——. *Los Angeles Times Book Review* 10 July 1983: 4.

L8.7 ——. *People Weekly* 20 (July 1983): 12.

L8.8 ——. *Virginia Quarterly* 59 (Aug 1983): 126.

L8.9 ——. *Atlantic Provinces Book Review* 10 (Nov 1983): 27.

L8.10 ——. *Antioch Review* 41 (Fall 1983): 509.

L8.11 Collins, Anne. "A Canine Search for Poetic Justice." *Maclean's* 96 (16 May 1983): 44.

L8.12 E., J. M. *Book List* 79 (June 1983): 1263.

L8.13 French, William. "A Bard's Doggerel." *Globe and Mail* [Toronto] 14 May 1983: E16.

L8.14 Galt, George. "Nothing Like the Bard." *Books in Canada* May 1983: 18.

L8.15 Keith, W. J. "Consolidating Reputation." *Fiddlehead* 138 (1984): 88-90.

L8.16 McGrath, Joan. *Canadian Book Review Annual*, 1983. 182.

L8.17 Mimmi, Dino C. "Something's Afoot with Play-spinning Young Will." *Sun*

[Vancouver] 17 July 1983: L31.

L8.18 Oakley, Barry. "The Bard Gives His Dog a Few Hints on the Canine Condition." *Sidney Morning Herald* 30 July 1983: 36.

L8.19 Schaire, Jeffrey. *Harper's Magazine* 266.1596 (May 1983): 92.

L8.20 Schoenbaum. S. "To Woof or Not to Woof." *Book World. [Washington Post]* 22 May 1983: 5.

L8.21 Dubois, Diana. Rev of DiDo Production of *Shakespeare's Dog. Scotsman Festival Guide* 10 Aug 2001: 10.

• **L9** *The Birth Control King of the Upper Volta (BCK)* **[A12]**

L9.1 Adachi, Ken. "Quirky, Witty Books That Deal with Failures." *Toronto Star* 18 Dec 1982: F12.

L9.2 Conklin, Jamie. *Quill & Quire* 49 (Mar 1983): 63.

L9.3 Currie, Rod. "The Birth Control King and His Valliant Band." *Vancouver Sun* 21 Jan 1983: The same review appeared under different titles in the following newspapers: *Daily Townsman* [Cranbrook, BC] 14 Jan 1983; *Guelph Mercury* [ON] 15 Jan 1983; *Stratford Beacon Herald* [ON] 19 Jan 1983; *Gazette* [Montreal] 22 Jan 1983; *Victoria Times* [BC] 22 Jan 1983.

L9.4 E., J. M. *Book List* 79 (Mar 1983): 946

L.9.5 Halladay, Barbara J. "A Rooke's Gallery." *Whig Standard Magazine* [London, ON] 19 Mar 1983; 19.

L9.6 Hill, Douglas. "Letters in Canada." *University of Toronto Quarterly* (1982): 323-24.

L9.7 Johnson, Derek. "Fairy Tales for Adults Who Don't Believe in Magic." *Globe and Mail* [Toronto] 8 Jan 1983: 12.

L9.8 Matyas, Cathy. *Canadian Book Review Annual*, 1982. 212-13.

L9.9 Mirolla, Michael. "Rooke's Vision Lights Up City." *Calgary Herald* 30 Apr 1983: G3.

L9.10 O., T. P. *Rubicon.* 1 (Spring 1983): 131-32.

L9.11 Rankin, William. "Rooke's Imagination Is Undeniably Clever." *Edmonton Journal* 11 June 1983: D2.

L9.12 Reaney, James Stewart. "Rooke's Prose a Bit Too Mannered and Maillard's Work Turns Sloppy." Rev with *Cutting Through*, by Keith Maillard. *London Free Press* 25 June 1983: E 10.

L9.13 Sharman, Vincent. *University of Windsor Review* XVII.2 (Spring-Summer 1983): 95-96.

L9.14 Stevens Peter. "Short, Sweet and the Same." *Windsor Star* [ON] 5 Mar 1983: C9.

L9.15 Taylor, Michael. "Courting Indifference." Rev with *I Don't Want to Know Anyone Too Well*, by Norman Levine. *Canadian Forum* 63 (Apr 1983): 29.

L9.16 Wasserman, Jerry. *The Reader* II.2 (1983): 12-13.

• **L10** *Sing Me No Love Songs I'll Say You No Prayers (SMNLS)* **[A13]**

L10.1 Anonymous. *Kirkus Review* 52 (1 Feb 1984): 108.

L10.2 ——. *Los Angeles Times Book Review* 5 Aug 1984: 8.

L10.3 ——. *Quill & Quire* 50 (Aug 1984): 31.

L10.4 ——. *Virginia Quarterly* 60 (Autumn 1984): 130.

L10.5 French, William. "All That He Writes Is an Aberration." *Globe and Mail* [Toronto] 23 June 1984: E17

L10.6 Glover, Douglas. "Paradise Upended." *Books in Canada* Nov 1984: 12-13.

L10.7 H., K. S. *Booklist* 80 (15 Apr 1984): 1153.

L10.8 Howells, Coral Ann. *Canadian Literature* 105 (Summer 1985): 165-66.

L10.9 Leclair, Tom. "Overheard Stories." *Book World*. [*Washington Post*] 5 Aug 1984: 8-9.

L10.10 Manguel, Alberto. "Protean and Surreal." *New York Times Book Review* 1 Apr 1984: 20.

L10.11 Steinberg, Sybil. *Publisher's Weekly* 225 (17 Feb 1984): 71.

L10.12 Williamson, Michael. *Library Journal* 109 (15 Apr 1984): 821.

• L11 *A Bolt of White Cloth* (BWC) [A14]

L11.1 Adachi, Ken. "These Little Chats Have Nine Tales." *Toronto Star* 17 Nov 1984: M 14.

L11.2 Dawson, Anthony. *Canadian Literature* 106 (Fall 1985): 155-57.

L11.3 Dempster, Barry. *Canadian Forum* Apr 1985: 31-32.

L11.4 French, William. "Good Questions." *Globe and Mail* [Toronto] 5 Jan 1985: 12-13.

L11.5 Lynch, William. *Monday Magazine*, [Victoria, BC] nd n pag (c1985).

L11.6 Sherbaniuk, Richard. "Style as King." *Writer's Quarterly* 7.3-4 (1985): 35, 46.

L11.7 Stuewe, Paul. "More Than Meets the Eye." *Books in Canada* May, 1985: 20-21.

• L12 *How I Saved the Province* (P) [A15]

L12.1 Bell, Doug. *Quill & Quire* 56 (Jan 1990): 25.

L12.2 French, William. "Writer Revealed as Talented Satirist." *Globe and Mail* [Toronto] 27 July, 1989: C5.

L12.3 Hartman, Matt. *Canadian Book Review Annual*, 1989. 205-206.

L12.4 Stuewe, Paul. "High-Wire Act." Rev with *A Good Baby*. *Books in Canada* Dec 1989: 25-26.

• L13 *A Good Baby* (GB) [A16]

L13.1 Anonymous. *Kirkus Review* 58 (15 July 1990): 959.

L13.2 ——. *Chronicler-Herald* [Halifax] 10 Aug 1990: B6.

L13.3 ——. *Booklist* 87 Sept 1990: 141.

L13.4 ——. *Gazette* [Montreal] 7 Sept 1993: J1.

L13.5 ——. *Village Voice Literary Supplement* Nov 1991: 32.

L13.6 ——. *New Yorker* 19 Nov 1990: 55-56.

L13.7 ——. *Publisher's Weekly* 238 (2 Aug 1991): 69.

L13.8 ——. *Tribune Books: Weekly* [*Chicago Tribune*] 6 Oct 1991: 32.

L13.9 Bartlett, Brian. "Leon Rooke: An Obsessive Drama in a Feast of Language." *Gazette* [Montreal] 3 Feb 1990: J2.

L13.10 Bauer, Douglas. *New York Times Book Review* 30 Sept 1990: 12.

L13.11 Bell, Douglas. *Quill & Quire* Nov 1989: 22.

L13.12 Bisson, Terry. "Two Men and Another Baby." *Book World*. [*Washington Post*] 4 Nov 1990: WBK7.

L13.13 ———. "*Good Baby* a Right 'Witchified' Search for Love Amid Loneliness." *Houston Post* 11 Nov 1990: C11.

L13.14 Donnell, David. "Written to Read New Book *A Good Baby*." *Alliston Herald Courier* [ON] 7 July 1990: 7.

L13.15 Eder, Richard, "A Backwoods Valhalla Hosts Battle between Good and Evil." *Los Angeles Times* 30 Aug 1990: E11.

L13.16 Fost, Michelle. *Philadelphia Inquirer* 13 Jan 1991. n pag.

L13.17 Gilchrist, Mary. "Real People Part of Horror Story." Rev of *A Good Baby*. *Star Phoenix* [Saskatoon] 9 Dec 1989. n pag.

L13.18 Glover, Douglas. "Tent Preacher from Hell." *American Book Review* 13.4 (Oct-Nov 1991): 27.

L13.19 Goffin, Jeffrey. "Rooke's Work Rousing." *Calgary Herald* 27 Jan 1990: C14.

L13.20 Gowdy, Barbara. "The World's Most Desirable Baby." *Globe and Mail* [Toronto] 25 Nov 1989: C19. Caricature of the author by Anthony Jenkins.

L13.21 Heward, Burt. "Sharing Crazy Thoughts in Haunting Gothic Novel." *Ottawa Citizen* 9 Dec 1989: H5BOO.

L13.22 Idema, James. "An Innocent Baby Eludes Wickedness." *Chicago Tribune* 11 Oct 1990: 53.

L13.23 Lehman, Steve. *Canadian Book Review Annual*, 1990. 179.

L13.24 Mackendrick, Louis K. "Distinctive Fiction Separates Rooke from Rest." *Windsor Star* 20 Jan 1990: E5.

L13.25 Malyon, Carol. *Cross-Canada Writers' Magazine* 12.2 (1990): 27.

L13.26 Marchand, Philip. *Toronto Star* 25 Nov 1989: M3.

L13.27 Margoshes, Dave. *Leader Post* [Regina] 17 Feb 1990: D5.

L13.28 Mirolla, Michael. *Event* 19.3 (1990): 19.

L13.29 ———. "Rooke Has It in Him, But Has Yet to Write a Masterpiece: A Nice Try." *Daily News Sunday Magazine* 1 Apr 1990: 8.

L13.30 Peters, Joanne. *CM: A Reviewing Journal of Canadian Materials for Schools And Libraries for Young People* 18 (Mar 1990): 81.

L13.31 Steinberg, Sybil. *Publishers Weekly* 237 (3 Aug 1990): 61.

L13.32 Sullivan, Rosemary. "A Good Baby." *Brick* 40 (Winter 1991): 54-56.

L13.33 Summers, Cathy. *Metropolis* 2.35 (18 Jan 1990): 20.

L13.34 Taylor, Maurice. *Library Journal* 115 (16 Sept 1990): 102.

L13.35 Thomas, Joan. "Leon Rooke Works Wonders." *Winnipeg Free Press* 25 Nov 1989: 25.

L13.36 Toller, Carol. "Method in the Madness." *Whig Standard Magazine* [London, ON] 17 Feb 1990: 21.

L13.37 Van Luven, Lynne. "A *Good Baby* Just Cries Out to Be Picked Up and Read." *Edmonton Journal* 11 Nov 1989: G4.

- **L14 *The Happiness of Others* (HO) [A18]**

L14.1 Drobot, Eve. "Sterling Reputation Tarnished." *Globe and Mail* [Toronto] 11

Sept 1991: D2.

L14.2 Geddes, Gary. "Literary Houdini's Trick Is to Be Entertaining." *Ottawa Citizen* 2 Nov 1991: 17BOO.

L14.3 Glover, Douglas. "Golden Oldies." *Books in Canada* Mar 1992: 38.

L14.4 Kirkwood, Hilda. "A Wizard's Tale." *Canadian Forum* Sept 1992: 30-31.

L14.5 Precosky, Don. *Canadian Book Review Annual*, 1991. 185.

L14.6 Smith, Stephen. "The Rude Plenty of Leon Rooke." Rev with *Who Do You Love? Quill & Quire* 58 (May 1992): 19.

• **L15 *Who Do You Love?* (WDYL) [A19]**

L15.1 Anonymous. *Financial Post* [Toronto] 6-8 May 1992: S14.

L15.2 ——. *Canadian Literature* (Spring 1992): 115.

L15.3 ——. "Storyteller in Top Form with New Collection." *Calgary Herald* 30 April, 1993: 3.

L15.4 Auerbach, Elaine. "Black Holes in Fiction." Rev with *July Nights and Other Stories*, by J. A. Hamilton. *Canadian Literature* 140 (Spring 1994): 115.

L15.5 Boothroyd, Jim. "Lovers of Fiction, Listen to the Voices of Leon Rooke." *Gazette* [Montreal] July 4 1992: I4.

L15.6 Britt, Robin. *Books in Canada* 21 (Oct 1992): 48.

L15.7 Darling, Michael. "Distinct, Appropriate Voices." *Globe and Mail* [Toronto] 23 May 1992: C17.

L15.8 Geddes, John. "Rooke Tales Told in Myriad Voices." *Financial Post* 8 June 1992: S14.

L15.9 Heward, Burt. "Rooke Fans Should Enjoy Author's Tales." *Ottawa Citizen* 1 Aug 1992: B8.

L15.10 Marchand, Philip. "Leon Rooke Mixes Comedy with Horror." *Toronto Star* 23 May 1992: H13.

L15.11 McGoogan, Kenneth. "Short-Fiction Binge Reveals Treasure Trove." *Calgary Herald* 27 June 1992: B11.

L15.12 Mirolla, Michael. "Making the Old New Again." *Halifax Daily News* 18 Oct 1992. n pag.

L15.13 Oliver, Hugh. *Canadian Book Review Annual*, 1992. 3124.

L15.14 Robinson, Jill. "Rooke Teeters on the Brink Like a Walker on a Tightrope." *Edmonton Journal* 7 June 1992: C6.

L15.15 Smith, Stephen. "The Rude Plenty of Leon Rooke." Rev with *The Happiness of Others. Quill & Quire* 58 (May 1992): 19.

L15.16 Tefs, Wayne. *Border Crossings* 12 (Winter 1993): 53.

L15.17 Thomas, Joan. "The Power of a True Voice." *Winnipeg Free Press* 18 July 1992: F6.

L15.18 Vaudry-Carey, Janice. *CM: A Reviewing Journal of Canadian Materials for Young People* 20 (Oct 1992): 276.

• **L16 *Muffins* (M) [A21]**

L16.1 Anonymous. *Paragraph* 18 (Summer 1996): 26.

L16.2 Carlson, Tim. "New Voices Speak to a Literary Cabaret." *Vancouver Sun* 28

Oct 1996: C3.

L16.3 Malin, Irving. "Performing, Deforming, Informing." *American Book Review* 17.5 (June-July 1996): 26.

L16.4 Pitt, Steve. *Canadian Book Review Annual*, 1995. 184.

• **L17 *Narciso allo specchio* (NAS) [A22]**

L17.1 Crivelli, Renzo S. "Aiuto, ho rovesciato il drink." *Il Sole-24 Ore* [Milano] 11 Feb 1996: 30.

L17.2 Paci, Francesca. *Il Tolomeo* [Univ of Venice Literary Review] 1 (1995): 56-57.

L17.3 Veltri, Clotilde. "Rooke, il 'Narciso' canadese." *La Provincia Pavese*, [Pavia] 14 Nov 1995. n pag.

• **L18 *Narcis u zrcalu* (Z) [A22a]**

L18.1 Dragojević, Dunja. "Glavno da se dobro završi." *Obzor* [Zagreb] 12 June 1997: 52.

L18.2 Dragojević, Rade. "14 Izabranih pripovjedaka." *Novi List* [Rijeka] 5 June 1977: 14.

L18.3 Dragojević, Rade. "Americanac u Kanadi." *Novi List* [Rijeka] 27 Aug 1997: 14.

L18.4 Džebić, Branka. "Začudni Rookeovi svijetovi." *Vijesnik* [Zagreb] 5 June 1997: 16.

L18.5 Gračan, Giga. "Kako su to posredovali." *Vijenac* [Zagreb] 90.V (June 1997): 29.

L18.6 Lasić, Igor. "Evo pisca!" *Slobodna Dalmacija* [Split] 29 June 1997: 7.

L18.7 Lokotar, Kruno. "Poigravanje s dosadom." *Vjesnik* [Zagreb] 11 Sept 1997: 16.

L18.8 Romić, Biljana. "Krajolik triju naraštaja." *Vijenac* [Zagreb] 90.V (June 1997): 29.

L18.9 Vučemil, K. "Rooke daje dignitet malom čovjeku." *Primorsko-goranski dnevnik* [Rijeka] 7 June 1997: 9.

• **L19 *Oh!: Twenty-seven Stories* (OH) [A25]**

L19.1 Anonymous. *Prairie Fire* 19.2 (Summer 1998): 158-160.

L19.2 Daniels, Wayne. "The Stories of Oh." *Books in Canada* June 1998: 9.

L19.3 Fitzgerald, Judith. "Rooke Delights, Infuriates." *Toronto Star* 3 Jan 1998: M13.

L19.4 Glover, Douglas. "Rooke a Kissin' Cousin to Southern Gothic Writers." *Globe and Mail* [Toronto] 13 Dec 1997: D22.

• **L20 *Who Goes There* (WG) [A26]**

L20.1 Daniels, Wayne. "Rooke's Country Revels." *Globe and Mail* [Toronto] 28 Nov 1998: E7.

L20.2 Garebian, Keith. "Straining for the Voices of Morality." *Toronto Star* 21 Feb 1999: D31.

L20.3 Halpern, Daniel Noah. "Inter Affairs." *National Post* [Toronto] 19 Dec 1998: 21.

• **L21 *The Fall of Gravity* (F) [A27]**

L21.1 Anonymous. *Danforth Review* II.I Sept 2000. http://collectionNnlc-bnc.ca/ 100/201/300/danforth/1999-000/02n01/danforth2 1/reviews/

rooke_turner.html

L21.2 ——. *Malahat Review* 133 (Dec 2000): 113-15.

L21.3 ——. "Carnival Atmosphere." *Calgary Herald* 12 June 2002: A2.

L21.4 ——. "Tous sur la route." *Sud Quest Dimanche* [Bordeaux] 12 Jan 2003. n pag.

L21.5 Aubert, Marie-Caroline. "La revelation Rooke." *Marie Claire* [Paris] Nov 2002. n pag.

L21.6 Binet, Violaine. "Maman est en cavale, la famile, en Morceaux. Au Terme d'un road-movie tendre et hypnotique, surgit la résurrection Leon Rooke, superbe écrivain Canadien, enfin publié en Francais." Photograph by Edouard. *Vogue* [Paris] Dec/Jan 2003. Text/interview. n pag.

L21.7 Chalet, Marie-Antoinette. "Il court, il court, le rêve américain." *Haute-Marne Dimanche* [Chaumont] 1 Dec 2002. n pag.

L21.8 Crom, Natalie. "En Vedette." *La Croix* [Paris] 17 Oct 2002: 19.

L21.9 Garebian, Keith. "Goin' Down the Road." *Toronto Star* 10 Sept 2000: E15.

L21.10 Glover, Dan. "A Postmodern Chase Novel, With Detours." *National Post* 9 Sept 2000: B11. The same review appeared under different titles in *Gazette* [Montreal] 9 Sept 2000: J4; *Calgary Herald* 14 Oct 2000: G10; *Halifax Daily News* 12 Nov 2000: 40.

L21.11 Harvey, Caroline. "Everywhere but Here." *Vancouver Sun* 16 Sept 2000: H11.

L21.12 Haubruge, Pascale. "Sur la route avec Leon Rooke." *Le Soir* [Bruxelles] 30 Oct 2002: 3.

L21.13 Hild, Pierre. "Leon Rooke." *Page Des Libraires* 78 [Paris] (Nov 2002): 36.

L21.14 Homel, David. "L'homme au masque de chien." *La Presse* [Montreal] 19 Jan 2003. n pag.

L21.15 Jackson, Lorna. *Quill & Quire* 66 (July 2000): 33.

L21.16 Jordis, Christine. "Appels d'air." *Page Des Libraires* [Paris] Sept 2000: 58.

L21.17 Julliard, Claire. "En chute libre." *Le Nouvel Observateur* [Paris] 6 Mar 2003: 110.

L21.18 Kattan, Naim. "Sul la route du continent" *Le Devoir* [Montreal] April 5-6, 2003: F5

L21.19 Kertzer, John. *Border Crossings* 19.4 (Nov 2000): 89-90.

L21.20 Laval, Martine. "Complètemenet à l'Ouest." *Télérama* [Paris] No. 2755. 30 Oct 2002: 67.

L21.21 Martin, Daniel. "Fugue amoureuse." *Centre-France/La Montagne* 13 Oct 2000. n pag.

L21.22 Mason, Julia. "Snookered by Rooke." *Ottawa Citizen* 15 Oct 2000: C17.

L21.23 Perrier, Jean-Claude. "L'énigmatique Mr. Rooke." *Livres Hebdo* [Paris] 28 June 2002. n pag.

L21.24 Rousseau, Christine. "La magie Rooke." *Le Monde* [Paris] 18 Oct 2002. n pag.

L21.25 Pitteloud, Anne. "Laussez tomber la gravité et les penseés mauves." *Le Courrier* [Geneva] 30 Nov 2002. n pag.

L21.26 Sergent, Julie. "En chute libre de Leon Rooke." *Voir* [Montreal] 17. 3 (23 Jan 2003): 28. http://www.voir.ca/livres/livres.aspx?ildarticle = 24461-83k-

L21.27 Smith, Ray. "Rooke's *Fall of Gravity* Celebrates Life, The Open Road." *Halifax Daily News* 12 Nov 2000: 40.

L21.28 Thomas, Joan. "O Come All Ye Faithless." *Globe and Mail* [Toronto] 9, Sept 2000: D7.

L21.29 Walther, Daniel. "Voyages orphiques." *Dernièrs Nouvelle d'Alsace* 25 Oct 2002. n pag.

• **L22** *Painting the Dog: The Best Stories By Leon Rooke* **(PD) [A28]**

L22.1 Bryson, Michael. *Danforth Review* Sept 2001. http://www.danforthreview.com/reviews/fiction/rooke_bestof.htm

L22.2 Homel, David. "A Wound At the Heart: Rooke's Monsters Draw Compassion." *Gazette* [Montreal] 19 May 2001: 13.

L22.3 Lyon, Annabel. "Leon Rooke: One Rare Bird: Gaudy as a Parrot, Predatory as a Vulture, Sweet as a Dove—This Short Fiction Wings Its Way to Glory." *Vancouver Sun* 30 June 2001: H15.

L22.4 Moher, Frank. "Don't Ask Me Why, But These Stories Make Me Laugh." *National Post* [Toronto] 23 June 2001: B11.

L22.5 Robertson, Ray. "Upsetting the Apple Cart." *Toronto Star* 20 May 2001: D15.

L22.6 Stewart, Ian. "Rooke Master of Short Story." *Winnipeg Free Press* 29 May 2001: D4.

L22.7 Whitlock, Nathan. *Quill & Quire* 67 (June 2001): 43-44.

L22.8 Pitt, Steve. *Canadian Book Review Annual.* 2002: 199.

L22.9 Paci, Francesca. "Le Voci nel collo della clessidra: Rooke's *Painting the Dog.* Il Tolomeo* 8, (2004), n pag.

M

MISCELLANEOUS WRITING ON LEON ROOKE

M1 "Leon Rooke." *Canada Writes!: The Members Book of the Writers Union of Canada.* Ed K. A. Hamilton. Toronto: Writers Union of Canada, 1977. 294-95.

M2 "Canadian-Australian Award." *Canada Weekly* 10.22 (June 1982): 7.

M3 "Leon Rooke." Bennett, Donna and Russell Brown. *An Anthology of Canadian Literature.* Eds Donna Bennett and Russell Brown. Toronto: Oxford Press. 1983. 344-45.

M4 Taylor, Michael. "Courting Indifference." *Canadian Forum* Apr 1983: 29-30.

M5 Collins, Anne. "A Canine Search for Poetic Justice." *MacLean's* 16 May 1983: 44, 46.

M6 Peterson, Leslie. The Peterson Leslie Column. *Sun* [Vancouver] 17 July 1983: L31.

M7 Adachi, Ken. "Toronto Writer Wins Governor-General's Award for Fiction" *Toronto Star* 20 June 1984: B1.

M8 French, William. "CanLit Fiction's Leading Award Goes to the Dog." *Globe and Mail* [Toronto] 21 June 1984: E1.

M9 ——. "Calgarian Wins." *Toronto Star* 21 June 1984: G3.

M10   Carey, Elaine. "This Southerner Walked Away with Our Top Award for Fiction" *Toronto Star* 8 July, 1984: D1. Photo of the author by Michael Stuparyk.

M11   Fuller, Peter. "Canadian and Australian Writers More Confident." *Literatore-Bookcase* 19 Aug 1983: np.

M12   Zutt, Jerome. "Rooke's Cast of Characters." *Varsity* [Univ of Toronto] 25 Oct 1984: 9.

M13   Slopen, Beverly. "Look North for Writers." *Publisher's Weekly* 229 (28 Feb 1986): 59.

M14   Moyes, Robert. "Canada's Voice of New Fiction: As Writer and Editor Leon Rooke Has a Typewriter That Spans the Globe." *Monday Magazine* [Victoria, BC] 12.24 (June 4-10, 1986): cover, 8-10, 12. Cover story photographs by Robert Moyes.

M15   Naumoff, Lawrence. "In the Carolina Writing Tradition: Leon Rooke." *Carolina Alumni Review* (Summer 1986): 10-12.

M16   Norbury, Keith. "Horse Drawn Drama: Circle the Wagons! Short Story Writer Leon Rooke Is Taking on the Evangelists." *Monday Magazine* [Victoria, BC] 13.29 (July 1987): 14-16. Cover photograph.

M17   Vincent, Isabel. "Cultivating Literary Grassroots." *Globe and Mail* [Toronto] 17 Oct 1989: A10.

M18   Smith, Stephen. "Uncommon Elements." *Kingston Whig Standard Magazine* 17 Feb 1990: 23.

M19   Vandermoer, Jamie "Leon Rooke Profile." *Symposium* [Univ College, Toronto] 3.1 (1990): 4. Cover page photograph.

M20   Ibsen, Joy. "Famed Author Helps London's Would-be Writers." *Today's Seniors* July 1991: 18, 32.

M21   Jung, Daryl. "Wild Man of the Podium Promises Rowdy Reading at the Univ of Toronto Workshop." *Now* July 18-24, 1991: 56.

M22   Marchand, Philip. "Free Fall into Creative Writing." *Toronto Star* 10 Aug 1991: J3.

M23   Ross, Val. "Rooke Ponders Parallels between Writing and Sculpting." *Globe and Mail* [Toronto] 9 Sept 1991: C13.

M24   Marchand, Philip. "Audience Loved Vintage Leon." *Toronto Star* 10 Sept 1991: F8.

M25   ——. "In a State Close to Rapture." *Toronto Star* 6 June 1992: G14.

M26   Thomas, Joan. "Characters Take Over When Rooke Writes." *Winnipeg Free Press* 18 July 1992: F62.

M27   Redhill, Michael. "Eden's Idyllic Mill." *Books in Canada* Dec 1992: 7-8.

M28   Hodges, Betty. "North Carolina Writer's Conference." *North Carolina Literary Review* 1.2 (Spring 1993): 210-211.

M29   Marchand, Philip. "Big Little Eden Mills Fest Shows Writers Learning How to Read." *Toronto Star* 18 Sept 1983: J 4.

M30   "Vancouver Writer Tops Eden Festival." *Globe and Mail* [Toronto] 13 Sept 1994: D5.

M31   Mamoli Zorzi, Rosella. "Rooke, *Narciso allo specchio* tra paesaggi esterni e mondi interiori." *Il Gazettino* [Venezia] 17 Nov 1995: 12

M32   Pressburger, Giorgio. Commentary, cover flap. *Arte. Tre fantasie in prosa (Art. Three Fictions in Prose)*. Bilingual Eng/It ed. Trans Francesca Valente. Ed Marco Fazzini. Lugi: Edizioni del Bradipo, Italy, 1997. 72.

M33   Punter, Jennie. "Small Respite from the War of the Words." *Toronto Star* 4 Sept 1997: G7.

M34   Taubin, Amy. "Landscape with Alienated Figures." Rev of the film *A Good Baby*. Dir by Catherine Dieckmann, 2000. *The Village Voice*. http://www.village voice.com/issues/0048/taubin.php

M35   Garrett, Stephen. "Slow Thriller with a Tender Heart." Rev of the film *A Good Baby*. Dir by Catherine Dieckmann, 2000. IndieWIRE. Festival Review. www.http://indiewire.com/onthescene/fs_99LAIFF_990421_g_2A4EE.html

M36   Murakami, Tamoeh. "The Bard Sails Up the River." *Philadelphia Inquirer* 4 June 2000: BR01.

M37   MacDonald, Jake. "Rooke's Rise." *Globe and Mail* [Toronto] 9 Sept 2000: D6-D7. Photograph by Robert Tinker.

M38   *The Fall of Gravity* selected as one of "100 Best Books of the Year." Citation Joan Thomas. *Globe and Mail* [Toronto] 25 Nov 2000: D24.

M39   Holden, Stephen. "'A Good Baby': A Traveling Salesman, an Adorable Foundling." Rev of the film *A Good Baby*. Dir by Catherine Dieckmann, 2000. *The New York Times* on the web 1 Dec 2000. http://www.nytimes.com/2000/12/01/arts/01BABY.html?ex=1079672400&en=d599ccb82e31ce67&ei=5070

M40   LaSalle, Mick. Rev of the film *A Good Baby*. Dir by Catherine Dieckmann, 2000. *San Francisco Chronicle* 2 Mar 2001: C3. http://www.sfgate.com/cgi-bin/article.cgi?file=/chronicle/archive/2001/03/02/DD207134.DTL#ba

M41   Mistry, Rohinton. "How Leon Rescued Me from the Bank." *Globe and Mail* [Toronto] 31 May, 2001. R1.

M42   Martin, Sandra. "A Pair of Mighty Rookes." *Globe and Mail*, [Toronto] 31 May 2001. R1, R9.

M43   Besner, Neil. "Fiction." Letters in Canada. Part 2, *University of Toronto Quarterly* 71.1 (Winter 2001): 20.

M44   Mandel, Charles. "Rooke Wins Mitchell Prize." *Calgary Herald* 12 June 2002: D13/Front.

M45   Martin, Sandra. "Mentor Earns Rooke the W. O. Mitchell Prize: Author Leon Rooke Gets the Credit He Deserves for His Encouragement of Other Writers." *Globe and Mail* [Toronto] 13 June 2002: 1.

M46   Vanderlist, Harry. "Lionizing Leon Rooke." *Calgary's News & Entertainment Weekly* 20 June 2002. On line: http://www.ffwdweekly.com/Issue/2002/0620/bookend.htm

M47   Martin, Sandra. "Country Culture: A Writer's Retreat." *Globe and Mail* [Toronto] 18 Sept 2002: R1-2.

M48 "Rooke Takes CBC's Award for Short Fiction." *Globe and Mail* [Toronto] 26 Feb 2003: N3.

M49 "Veteran Leon Rooke Wins CBC Literary Prize." *Ottawa Citizen* 26 Feb 2003: E3.

M50 D'Entrement, James. "Putting Shakespeare's Dog to Sleep," A lengthy online explication of the Boston banning of the play *Shakespeare's Dog* 4 Aug 2004. http://users.cn.com/kyp/dog.htm/

N

TEACHING AND RESIDENCES (Partial listing)

N1 Writer-in-residence, University of North Carolina, 1968-69.

N2 Lecturer, University of Victoria, 1973-74, 1980-8, 1986.

N3 Artist-in-residence, University of Southwest Minnesota, 1975-76.

N4 Saskatchewan Art Guild Advanced Fiction Workshops at Fort San, 1984, 1985, 1986.

N5 Writer-in-residence, University of Toronto, 1984-85.

N6 Fiction Workshop, Northwest Writers' Conference, Bemidji, Mn. 1985.

N7 Writer-in-residence, University of Lethbridge, 1985.

N8 Writer-in-residence, University of Winnipeg, 1986.

N9 Upper Canada Writers' Workshop, Queen's University, 1987.

N10 Resource Artist, Artists' Centre, Banff, Alberta 1988.

N11 Writer-in-residence, University of Western Ontario, 1988.

N12 Ganaraska Writers' Workshop, Ganaraska, ON 1989.

N13 Centre for Writers, University of Southern Mississippi, 1989.

N14 Kingston School of Writing, Queen's University, Fiction Workshop, 1989.

N15 Fiction Workshop, University of Toronto, 1990.

N16 Writer-in-residence, University of Western Ontario, 1990-91.

N17 Writer-in-residence, University of Toronto, Scarborough Campus, 1991.

N18 Master Class Fiction Workshop, University of Toronto, 1991.

N19 Writer-in-residence, Writers' Workshop, University of Toronto, 1991.

N20 Writers-in-Electronic Residence, Writers' Development Trust, 1992.

N21 Writer-in-residence, Intersection for the Arts, San Francisco, California, 1993.

N22 Fiction Workshop, University of Guelph, 1993, 1999.

N23 Reed College Workshop, Portland, Oregon, 1994.

N24 Instructor, Victoria School of Writing, 1996.

N25 Workshop, Teachers' Assoc. of BC, Victoria, 1997.

N26 Writers in Electronic Residence, a program of the Writers' Trust, Toronto. Workshop available to high school students throughout Canada, Spring 1998, and to the students in Wyoming, Fall 1998.

N27 Approximately 800 readings in Canada, U.S., and Europe.

O

FUNCTIONS

O1   Judge, Canada/Australia Literary Prize, 1983, 1984.
O2   Director, Eden Mills Writers' Festival, 1988-2000.
O3   Judge, Prism International Fiction Awards, 1989.
O4   Judge, Ontario Arts Council, 1989 and various years thereafter.
O5   Judge, BC Federation of Writers Fiction Awards, 1989.
O6   Co-founder Artistic Director, Eden Mills Writers' Festival, 1989-2002.
O7   Judge, Best (State of) Georgia Fiction Award, 1990.
O8   Editorial Board, Coach House Press, 1990-1996. Seen through the press the following: *The Brick Anthology*, eds Michael Ondaatje and Linda Spalding; *A Marriageable Daughter* and *Divine Diva*, by Daniel Gagnon; *Miss You Like Crazy*, by Eliza Clark and *Kay Darling* by Laura MacDonald and Alex Pugsley.
O9   Selection Committee, Ontario Arts Council Literary Officer, 1990.
O10   Judge, Governor General's Fiction Award, 1990, 1993.
O11   Out-of-press Editor, 3rd *Journey Prize Anthology* and James Michener Award. 1991.
O12   Judge, Manitoba Book Awards, 1994.
O13   Judge, Saskatchewan Book Awards, 1996.
O14   Writers' Representative, Ontario Arts Council review, 1997.
O15   Judge, Short Fiction Prize, *Prairie Fire*, 1998, 2003.
O16   Judge, Manitoba Arts Council, 1999, 2002.
O17   Judge, Sunburst Award, 2001.
O18   Advisory Board, Winnipeg International Writers' Festival, 2000.
O19   Chair, Artistic Committee, Winnipeg Writers' Festival, 2001-2002.
O20   Judge, Upper Canada Short Fiction Award, 2002.
O21   Artistic Director, Eden Mills Writers' Festival, 2000-2003.
O22   Judge, ReLit Short Fiction Award, 2003.
O23   Judge, Marion Engel Prize, 2003.
O24   Judge, Neustadt International Prize, 2003.
O25   Judge, Canada Council, various years.

P

AWARDS, FELLOWSHIPS, GRANTS (Partial Listing)

P1   MacDowell Fellowship, 1974.
P2   Canada Council theatre and fiction grants, 1974, 1975, 1976, 1979, 1983, and 1985.
P3   Yaddo Fellowship, 1976.

P4 National Endowment for the Arts Fellowship, 1979.
P5 Best Paperback Novel of the Year Award, 1981, for *Fat Woman*. Short-listed for Governor General's Award and Books in Canada First Novel Award, 1981.
P6 Canada/Australia Literary Prize, 1981, for overall body of work.
P7 Short-listed for Stephen Leacock Award, 1983.
P8 Governor General's Literary Award for *Shakespeare's Dog*, 1984.
P9 Author's Award for short fiction, Foundation for the Advancement of Canadian Letters, 1986.
P10 North Carolina Award for Literature, 1990.
P11 Canada Council Senior Writing Grants 1999 (3 others).
P12 W.O. Mitchell Literary Prize, 2002.
P13 ReLit Short Fiction Award, 2002.
P14 CBC Literary Prize, 2003.
P15 Canada Council Fellowships, national and regional awards, short listings, short story awards, citations, etc.

NAME INDEX

This index lists the names of authors and editors, and it includes selected subjects.

J

Jackel, David, K17
Jackson, Lorna, L21.15
Jarman, Mark, D57
Jeringan, Kim, K38
Jerome, Judson, C2
Jewinski, Ed, C147, D28
Johnson, Derek, L5.14, L6.7, L9.7
Jones, Donald, L13.23
Jordis, Christine, L21.16
Julliard, Claire, L21.17
Jung, Daryl, M21

K

Kaltemback, Michèle, K16, K18, K19, K22
Kattan, Naim, L21.18
Keith, W. J., L8.15
Kerr, Don, C39, D11
Kertzer, John, 21.19
Kinsella, W. P., L4.4
Kirby, Paul, H18
Kirkwood, Hilda, G19, L14.4
Kostov, Velimir, E4

L

Lalleau, Al, D85
Lampe, David, D64
LaSalle, Mick., M40
Lasić, Igor, L18.6
Laval, Martine, L21.20
Leacock, Stephen, P7
Leblond, Denis, I21
Leclair, Tom, L10.9
Lecker, Robert, D35, K24
Lehman, Steve, L13.23
Leighton, Betty, L6.8, L6.8
Lennox, John, L1.5
Levine, Mark, D81
Levine, Norman, L9.15
Lokotar, Kruno, L18.7
Lombardo, Agostino, E6
Luccotti, Claudia, E47
Lynch, William, L11.5

TITLE INDEX

The index includes the titles of both primary and secondary sources, titles reviewed by Rooke, and titles referred in the entries. The name in the paranthesis is that of the author, editor or translator. If the title is not followed by the name, Rooke is the author or editor. Interviews and recordings have been treated as primary sources.

D

E

G

'Getting There By Degrees,' (Meyer, O'Riordan) G18
'Gin and Tonic,' A12, C119, D29
'A Girl and a Dummy and the Dummy's Best Friend,' C57
'The Girl Who Collected Husbands,' C63
'The Girl Who Made Time,' C39, D11
'Glavno da se dobro završi,' (Dragojević, D) L18.1
'God's Ugly People,' L5.12
'Going for Broke.' C110
'Golden Oldies,' L14.3
Gone for Broke, H3
'Good Questions,' L11.4
A Good Baby A16, C192, K18, K29, L13, L13.14, L13.17, L13.32, L13.39
The Good Baby (play), H15, H17
A Good Baby (film), I17, M34, M35, M36, M39, M40
'"Good Baby" a Right 'Witchified' Search for Love Amid Loneliness,' (Bisson) L13.13
'A Good Radio Voice,' C250
'Grace Troup,' C171
'The Guacamole Game,' A25, C232
'Gypsy Art,' A25, C240

H

'Hanging Out With the Magi,' A9, C97, D12
The Happiness of Others, A18, J38, L14, L15.15
'Harry the Tiger Enters His Fiftieth Year,' C43
'Hat Pandowdy,' A12, C101
'The Heart Must from Its Breaking,' A18, A22, A22a, A28, C193, C207, C215, D43, D52, D64, D65, D66
'The Heart Must from Its Breaking,' (author's perf) I12,
The Heart Must from Its Breaking (play) I16
'The Hatted Mannequins of 54th Street,' C28
'Hello, I'm Jane Doe,' C72
The Hero's Great Great Great Great Great Grandson,' F2
'The Hi-Tech World of Leon Rooke,' (Hancock) K3
'High-Wire Act,' (Stuewe) L12.4
'His Old Ketucky Home,' F20
'His Subtleties Set Our Heads Spinning,' (Leighton) L6.8
'The History of England, Part Four,' A13, C114
'Hitting the Charts,' A12, C90
'Hoćeš li da se igramo kuće?' (trans Romić) A22a, C209, E22-35
'L'homme au masque de chien,' (Homel) L21.14
Hooker, el gos de Shakespeare,' H20

'Leon Rooke on Cormac McCarthy,' I7
'Leon Rooke Works Wonders,' (Thomas) L13.35
'Leon Rooke's Distinctive Mode of Writing in *A Good Baby*,' (Kaltemback) K18
'Leon Rooke's Dog Tale a Triumph of Invention,' (Keith) L8.1
'Leon Rooke's *Shakespeare's Dog*: A Postmodern Historiographic Parody,' (De Luca)
    K21
'Let Me Not to My True Mind Disdain Euphoria,' C129
'Licking Up Honey,' C109
'Life of a Progressive Party Civil Servant Called Out of Retirement in Benefit of a
    Busy Nation,' C278
'Light Bulbs,' A19, C164
'The Line of Fire,' C3, D78
'Lingering on Posted Land: An Interview with Leon Rooke,' (Gorjup) G31
'Literary Houdini's Trick Is to Be Entertaining,' (Geddes) L14.2
'The Lithuanian Wife,' A25, C224
'Lost Kafka Manuscript,' C26
'Love Child,' C151
Love Clinic, (film) I11
The Love Parlour, A6, C65, L3, L3.2
'Lovers of Fiction, Listen to the Voices of Leon Rooke,' (Boothroyd) L15.5
'LR Loves GL,' A19, C166
'Lunch Detail,' (A19)

M

'*The Macmillan Anthology No. 1*,' (with Metcalf) B5
'*The Macmillan Anthology No. 2*,' (with Metcalf) B6
'Madness, Mayhem from Leon Rooke,' (Hennig) L6.5
'The Madwoman of Cherry Vale,' A14, C137
'Magi Dogs,' C267
'Magic and Death,' L6.7
'Magic—That's What You Need for Great Writing,' (Sherrill) L5,19
The Magician in Love, A5, A10, C46, L6.1, L6.3, L6.11, L7, L17.1,
'The Magician in Love,' C46, C60, C62, C92
'The Magician in Love: Love and Ethics,' A5, C46
'The Magician in Love: Love and Trouble,' A5, C54
'The Magician in Love: Love and War,' A5, C62
'The Making of Saints,' C252
'1. Malereien/II.Wasserfarben/III. Handgematte blumen, so viel sie tragen können,
    25c,' E3
'Mama Tuddi,' C168
'Mama Tuddi Done Over,' A9, A13, C16, C74, D9
Man Descending, F10
'"A Man Locked Up in a Freezer": A Reading of Leon Rooke's Story "The Blue

T

NOTES ON THE CONTRIBUTORS

Russell Banks is the author of over a dozen works of fiction, including *The Sweet Hereafter*, *Affliction*, *Continental Drift*, and *Rules of the Bone*. He has been the recipient of such prestigious literary prizes and awards as the O. Henry and Best American Short Story Awards, the John Dos Passos Prize, and the Literature Award from the American Academy of Arts and Letters. He is the Howard G.B. Clark University Professor at Princeton.

Dubravko Barač graduated from the Zagreb Academy of Music and played double bass in the Zagreb Radio-Television Orchestra for four years. He emigrated to Canada in 1989 and is presently working in the field of information technology. He is a frequent contributor to magazines in Croatia on issues related to Croatian diaspora.

Russell Brown is the editor of *The Collected Poems of Al Purdy* (McClelland & Stewart) and co-editor (with Donna Bennett) of the recently published *New Anthology of Canadian Literature* (Oxford University Press). His short monograph, "Borderlines and Borderlands in English Canada," discusses the way the symbolism of the border has structured Canadian consciousness. He has published essays on such writers as Mordecai Richler, Margaret Atwood, Robert Kroetsch, Saul Bellow, George Bowering, Morley Callaghan, and Marshall McLuhan; and on topics such as Canadian criticism, Canadian postmodernism, and the differences between American and Canadian literary traditions. His recent articles include "Oedipus and Telemachus: Images of Tradition and Authority in Canadian and American Fiction," "The Practice and Theory of Canadian Thematic Criticism: A Reconsideration," and "'The Seriousness of Things beyond Your Understanding'" (on the visionary tradition in English-Canadian writing).

Neil Besner is Dean of Humanities at the University of Winnipeg, where he has taught since 1987, and currently President of ACCUTE. He writes mainly on Canadian literature, with monographs on Mavis Gallant and Alice Munro. He has co-edited anthologies of poetry and short fiction with Oxford UP Canada; his most recent books are a translation of a Brazilian biography of Elizabeth Bishop (2002), a special co-edition of a Brazilian journal, *Desterros*, on Postcolonialism in Canada and Brazil (2003), and an edited collection of essays, *Carol Shields: The Arts of a Writing Life* (2003).

Barry Callaghan is the award-winning author of poetry, novels, and collections of short stories. He was the winner of W.O. Mitchell Award and has been recognized with seven National magazine Awards for Journalism, as well as the Toronto Arts Award. Callaghan is the publisher of Exile and Exile Editions. His most recent books were *Barrelhouse Kings: A Memoir* and *Hogg and The Seven Last Words*.

Nicole Côté is associate professor at University of Regina, Canada. She has translated a number of Canadian stories into French, including Leon Rooke's "The Only Daughter," collected in *Nouvelles du Canada anglais* (L'instant même 1999), edited by

Nicole Côté. Her other translations include stories by Mavis Gallant, *Vers le ravage* (L'instant même, 2002), and Jane Urquhart, *Verre de Tempête* (L'instant même,1997) and *Les petites fleurs de Madame de Montespan* (Tryptique, 2000). She co-edited with Peter Sabor *Varieties of Exile: New Essays on Mavis Gallant* (Peter Lang, 2002), and has contributed to numerous journals. She is a member of the advisory board of *Tessera*, a bilingual feminist journal.

Peter Cumming is Assistant Professor of Children's Literature and Culture in the Division of Humanities at York University. His PhD dissertation at The University of Western Ontario was entitled "Some 'Male' from Canada: 'Post' Heterosexual Masculinities in Contemporary Canadian Writing." At the universities of Guelph and Western Ontario, Cumming has taught Children's Literature, Canadian Literature, Native Literatures, Theatre and Drama, and Expository, Electronic, and Creative Writing. He is a children's author and playwright . . . and a father.

Eva Darias-Beautell teaches American and Canadian literatures at the University of La Laguna, Spain. She has been a Visiting Scholar at the University of Toronto on several occasions, was a Government of Canada Award holder from 1992 to 1993, received a Faculty Enrichment Program Grant (Government of Canada) in 1997 and in 2002, and has also enjoyed post-doctoral fellowships at the University of Berkeley in 1998 and the Universities of Ottawa and Toronto in 2000. She is the author of *Division Language and Doubleness in the Writings of Joy Kogawa* (University of La Laguna, 1998), *Shifting Sands: Literary Theory and Contemporary Canadian Fiction* (Mellen, 2000), and *Graphies and Grafts: (Con)texts and (Inter)texts in the Fiction of Four Contemporary Canadian Women* (Peter Lang, 2001). She is currently directing a research team on canon revision, gender and genre in the North American literature of the turn of the 20th century. Her present fields of research also include literary theory, criticism and contemporary Canadian fiction.

Anna Pia De Luca received degrees from the University of Toronto and Trieste and now teaches courses in English language and literature at the University of Udine (Italy). Her main fields of interest are in contemporary Canadian literature in which she has published numerous articles on M. Atwood, M. Laurence, A. Munro, L. Rooke and T. Findley. Recently her interests also include Italian-Canadian female writing, especially writers whose origins are in the Friuli Venezia Giulia Region such as Caterina Edwards, Doré Michelut, Genni Gunn and Marisa De Franceschi. She is co-editor of two volumes, "Palinsesti Culturali: gli apporti delle immigrazioni alla letteratura del Canada" (Forum 1999) and "Italy and Canadian Culture: Nationalisms in the New Millennium" (Forum 200) while a third volume, "Oltre la storia/ Beyond History/ Au-delà de l'histoir: l'identità italo-canadese contemporanea," is currently being published.

M.A.C. Farrant is the author of seven collections of satirical and humorous short fiction, most recently *Darwin Alone in the Universe* (Talonbooks, 2003) and a novel-length memoir, *The Turquoise Years*, (Annick Press, 2003, Toronto). Her work has been dramatized for television and appears frequently on CBC Radio 1, Between the Covers and Richardson's Roundup. Her many anthology contributions include *And Other Stories* (Ed. George Bowering, Talonbooks, 2001). She is the West Coast organizer and Host of the annual Canadian small press ReLit Awards.

Keath Fraser, novelist and story-writer, published *The Voice Gallery: Travels with a Glass Throat* in 2002.

Michèle Kaltemback teaches Canadian studies in the department of English at the University of Toulouse, France. Her field of study is Canadian writers from the West and the short story. She has recently co-edited a collection of essays, *Decoding and Telling the Canadian Landscape*.

Douglas Glover is the author of four novels, four story collections, and a book of essays. His novel *Elle* won the Governor-General's Award for Fiction in 2003.

Branko Gorjup has edited, for Longo's Peter Paul Series of Contemporary Canadian Poetry, bilingual selections by Irving Layton, Gwendolyn MacEwen, P.K. Page, Al Purdy, Margaret Atwood, Michael Ondaatje, Margaret Avison and Dennis Lee. His other editorial work includes several anthologies of short fiction, selection of essays by Northrop Frye and a special issue on English Canadian contemporary writing for Mondadori's *Nuovi Argomenti*, entitled "Oceano Canada." Branko Gorjup teaches Canadian literature at the University of Toronto at Scarborough.

Michael H. Keefer teaches Renaissance studies and literary theory at the University of Guelph. He did his doctoral work on Renaissance hermeticism and the Faustus legend under the direction of Tony Nuttall at the University of Sussex. The author of *Lunar Perspectives, Field Notes from the Culture Wars*, he has also published essays on a wide range of Renaissance subjects, as well as an edition of Marlowe's *Dr Faustus* for Broadview Press, and is completing an edition of Thomas Nashe's the *Unfortunate Traveller*. He is a former president of ACCUTE and a co-winner of the Nelson prize of the Renaissance Society of America.

Janice Kulyk Keefer is Professor of English at the University of Guelph. The author of numerous works of poetry and fiction, she has also published literary criticism on Canadian maritime fiction and on the *oeuvre* of Mavis Gallant. She has lectured on Canadian literature and given readings from her own work across Canada and Europe, as well as in New Zealand and Australia, Japan and the United States. Her most recent novel, *Thieves*, was published by Harper Collins in the spring of 2004. A winner of the Marian Engel prize, and of many national magazine and CBC Radio literary competitions, she has twice been nominated for a Governor General's award.

Paola Marino graduated in cinema from the Universita' degli Studi di Bologna, Italy. She has produced and directed documentary videos on Italian artists, such as Sandro Chia, Mimmo Paladino and Marino Marini and several short films set in Canada, including *Sun Day, Identities* and *Grains of Rice*. She is currently employed with the Italian Cultural Section of the Consulate General of Italy, Toronto.

Mike Matthews teaches at Malaspina University-College. He has written articles and reviews on Canadian fiction for a variety of journals, and is a co-author of a novel, *Piccolo Mondo*.

Thomas McHaney is Kenneth M. England Professor of Southern Literature at Georgia State University in Atlanta. Most of his scholarly publications concern the texts and life of William Faulkner, including co-editorship of the 44-volume *William Faulkner Manuscripts* (Garland, 1987-89) and three recent volumes for Gale: a biography of Faulkner, a critical work on *The Sound and the Fury*, and a history of the 'Southern Renaissance' with which Faulkner is associated.

John Metcalf is a writer and editor who lives in Ottawa. His latest books are *An Aesthetic Underground: A Literary Memoir* and *Standing Stones: The Best Stories of John Metcalf*. Both are published by Thomas Allen Publishers.

Anne Michaels published three collections of poetry: *The Weight of Oranges, Miner's Pond* and *Skin Divers*. Her celebrated debut novel, *Fugitive Pieces*, won numerous literary prizes, including the Trillium Award, Orange Prize and the Chapter/Books in Canada First Novel Award, and was translate into more than twenty languages. Anne Michaels lives in Toronto.

Karen Mulhallen is the award-winning editor of *Descant*, and former Arts Feature Editor of *The Canadian Forum* magazine. She is the author of seven volumes of poetry including *Modern Love, In the Era of Acid Rain, War Surgery*, and the long poem *Sheba and Solomon*.

Lawrence Naumoff is the author of 5 novels: *The Night of the Weeping Women; Rootie Kazootie; Taller Women; Silk Hope; A Plan for Women*, and a new one just finished but not yet out currently titled *A Southern Tragedy*. His books are published in the U.S. and throughout Europe and Great Britain. He has published the usual short stories and essays, won prizes (the Whiting in 1990), and spent many years living away from the literary and urban worlds. He earned his living building houses, starting as a helper and working up to chief carpenter and contractor. He did this for 25 years. He's been married, has a son, and recently broke his lifelong vow never to teach. For 3 years now, he has been having thrilling adventures with the writing students at the University of North Carolina at Chapel Hill, where he, himself, began as a student of Leon Rooke's.

Francesca Romana Paci, for ten years Professor of English at Ca' Foscari University in Venice, is now Professor of English and Postcolonial Literatures at 'Amedeo Avogadro,' University of Piemonte Orientale, in northern Italy. Her main areas of interest are Romanticism, Neo-Romanticism and Contemporary Studies, particularly Irish and Canadian Literatures. Besides working on many English authors, such as Smart, Coleridge, Shelley and Byron, she has written on Moore, Mangan, Joyce, MacNeice as well as Heaney, whom she has edited and translated into Italian. Among her recent publications is the Italian prefated editions of Anne Michaels' poetry, *Quello che la luce insegna*, 2001, Alistair Mac Leod's short stories, *Il dono di sangue del sale perduto*, 1999 and 2003, and Yvonne Vera's novels *Il fuoco e la farfalla*, 2002 and *Le vergini delle rocce* (forthcoming). She is co-editor of the academic review *Tolomeo*.

Danièle Pitavy-Souques, Director of the Center for Canadian Studies, is professor emeritus at the University of Burgundy. Among her many publications on Canadian and Southern Literature, she edited two volumes of essays on Canadian Literature, *L'Homme et la Steppe*, with Maryvonne Perrot, Dijon, EUD, 1999, and *Femmes et écriture au Canada*, Dijon, EUD, 2002. She is currently preparing an edition of essays on Canadian Shores.

Rosemary Sullivan is a poet and biographer. She has published ten books, including *Shadow Maker: The Life of Gwendolyn MacEwen* for which she won the Governor General's Award; *Labyrinth of Desire: Women, Passion and Romantic Obsession*; and *Cuba: Grace Under Pressure*. She teaches at the University of Toronto where she is Canada Research Chair in Literature, Culture and Discourse. She is a fellow of the Royal Society of Canada.

Joan Thomas is a contributing book reviewer for *The Globe and Mail*, and a teacher and curriculum writer for Manitoba high schools. She has co-edited *Turn of the Story*, a collection of Canadian short fiction at the end of millennium.

Ken Thompson is a fiction writer, radio playwright, broadcaster, sometime actor, theatre director, teacher, editor and frequent commentator on the arts. He has published five novels, three collections of short stories and the usual slim chapbooks of poetry. Thompson is also frequently heard on CBC's radio program, *Talking Books*, and has served as reviewer for *The Fiddlehead* and *The Globe and Mail*.

Simone Vauthier founded at the University of Strasbourg a Canadian Research Center for the study of Canadian Literature with a specific emphasis on the genre of the short story. She organized numerous conferences and published widely on canonical authors, including Margaret Atwood, Margaret Laurence, Mavis Gallant, Carol Shields, Michael Ondaatje and Timothy Findley, as well as on such authors of the promising new generation as Isabel Huggan and Edna Alford. Her other scholarly contributions to the study of the story are dedicated to the works of such distinguished practitioners in the field as Jack Hodgins, David Arnason, Leon Rooke, Clark Blaise, Norman Levine, John Metcalf and Alistair McLeod, which are in part collected in the volume entitled *Reverberations: Explorations in the Canadian Short Story*, published by the House of Anansi in 1993. Simone Vauthier was professor emeritus until her death in 2004.

INDEX